Praise for *Power, Legitimacy, and World Order: Changing Contours of Preconditions and Perspectives*

'The current fragility of institutional legitimacy at every level of social organization is no secret. This important volume addresses the growing crisis of legitimacy in international politics and emphasizes the need to focus on (re)building legitimacy if humanity is going to successfully face current threats such as global climate change and rising authoritarianism.'

Jayne Seminare Docherty, *Professor Emeritus, Center for Justice and Peacebuilding, Eastern Mennonite University*

'A most valuable compilation of thought-provoking and richly resourced essays examining the state of disorder and inequality in the world today. Very often there is a disconnect between power and legitimacy, both domestic and international. The emphasis on the concept of legitimacy brought out in the volume is timely and needs to be recognised by those in power.'

Chinmaya R Gharekhan, *former Indian ambassador and United Nations Under-Secretary-General*

'Recent developments reinforce the pitfalls of approaching international politics and international economics in silos. The blatant and increasing deployment of crude political power is undermining the legitimacy of many global institutional and trade frameworks. This volume unpacks the challenges of legitimacy that confront global governance frameworks. The excellent essays demonstrate that legitimacy and credibility of global economic architecture can be strengthened by fortifying principles such as transparency, reciprocity, fairness and equity.'

Rajat Kathuria, *Dean, School of Humanities & Social Sciences, and Professor of Economics, Shiv Nadar University*

'In this timely, valuable collection a formidable team of analysts examine, in all of their complexity, two concepts – power and legitimacy – that are crucial in world affairs. Diverse regions are assessed from a refreshing diversity of perspectives which take the analysis beyond conventional western perceptions.'

James Manor, *Emeka Anyaoku Professor, School of Advanced Study, University of London*

'This excellent, insightful and occasionally provocative volume on *Power, Legitimacy, and the World Order* merits careful study among policymakers and within global institutions. Its strength lies in its capacity to capture the contested nature of the concept and application of legitimacy. It should inspire serious debate on the legitimacy of a world order which is undergoing seismic changes.'

Rehman Sobhan, *Chairman, Centre for Policy Dialogue, Dhaka*

'This volume views today's world order – or, more accurately, crisis, disorder and fragmentation – through the prism of "power" and "legitimacy" and their interaction. The book's core strength is that it unpacks "legitimacy" from a diverse range of intellectual and geographical perspectives. The Western vision of world order, based on liberal democracy at home, and US power and Western-shaped multilateral institutions abroad, is contested more than at any time since the end of the Second World War – and not only by China. The COVID-19 pandemic and the Russia-Ukraine war have widened this legitimacy divide and further fragmented the world order. This volume helps us to understand these megatrends and navigate our way through an ever more uncertain future.'

Razeen Sally, *Former Professor of International Political Economy at the London School of Economics and the National University of Singapore*

POWER, LEGITIMACY, AND WORLD ORDER

This book reflects on the reasons for the decline of international cooperation in world politics and studies ways to restore legitimacy in the international order. It engages with the concept of legitimacy in international relations theories and practices to examine the discussions around power shifts, the decline of liberalism, demands for inclusive international architectures, and challenges to multilateralism, as well as established norms by leaders and nationalisms. It studies the impact of the post-COVID-19 world order on the nature of power in the international system and changes in normative concerns of security. The volume also interrogates political legitimacy through an area studies lens by examining the concept of legitimacy separately in the USA, Europe, South Asia, Southeast Asia, Latin America, and Africa.

An important and timely text featuring contributions from eminent scholars, this book will be of use to students and researchers of modern history, political science, and international relations. It will also be of interest to think tanks and policy-making bodies concerned with international affairs and foreign policy.

Sanjay Pulipaka is the Chairperson of the Politeia Research Foundation. He was previously a Senior Fellow for Research Programmes and Strategic Neighbourhood at the Delhi Policy Group; Senior Fellow at the Nehru Memorial Museum and Library; and Senior Consultant at the Indian Council for Research on International Economic Relations (ICRIER). He was also a Pavate Visiting Fellow at Cambridge University and a former Fulbright Fellow in the Conflict Transformation Programme.

Krishnan Srinivasan is a former Indian Foreign Secretary and Commonwealth Deputy Secretary-General. He has been a visiting fellow at Cambridge, Leiden, and Uppsala and has published or edited eight works on international relations.

James Mayall is Emeritus Professor of International Relations and Fellow of Sidney Sussex College, Cambridge, and Emeritus Professor of International Relations at the LSE. He is a Fellow of the British Academy. He has published widely on the international relations of African states, North–South relations, international theory, and the impact of nationalism on international relations.

POWER, LEGITIMACY, AND WORLD ORDER

Changing Contours of Preconditions and Perspectives

Edited by Sanjay Pulipaka, Krishnan Srinivasan, and James Mayall

LONDON AND NEW YORK

Cover image by FrankRamspott / Getty Images

First published 2023
by Routledge
4 Park Square, Milton Park, Abingdon, Oxon OX14 4RN

and by Routledge
605 Third Avenue, New York, NY 10158

Routledge is an imprint of the Taylor & Francis Group, an informa business

© 2023 selection and editorial matter, Sanjay Pulipaka, Krishnan Srinivasan, and James Mayall; individual chapters, the contributors

The right of Sanjay Pulipaka, Krishnan Srinivasan, and James Mayall to be identified as the authors of the editorial material, and of the authors for their individual chapters, has been asserted in accordance with sections 77 and 78 of the Copyright, Designs and Patents Act 1988.

All rights reserved. No part of this book may be reprinted or reproduced or utilised in any form or by any electronic, mechanical, or other means, now known or hereafter invented, including photocopying and recording, or in any information storage or retrieval system, without permission in writing from the publishers.

Trademark notice: Product or corporate names may be trademarks or registered trademarks, and are used only for identification and explanation without intent to infringe.

British Library Cataloguing-in-Publication Data
A catalogue record for this book is available from the British Library

Library of Congress Cataloging-in-Publication Data
Names: Pulipaka, Sanjay, editor. | Srinivasan, Krishnan, 1937- editor. | Mayall, James, editor.
Title: Power, legitimacy and world order : changing contours of preconditions and perspectives / edited by Sanjay Pulipaka, Krishnan Srinivasan and James Mayall.
Description: First Edition. | New York : Routledge is an imprint of the Taylor & Francis Group, 2023. | Includes bibliographical references and index. | Identifiers: LCCN 2022054274 (print) | LCCN 2022054275 (ebook) | ISBN 9781032268507 (Hardback) | ISBN 9781032472409 (Paperback) | ISBN 9781003385233 (eBook)
Subjects: LCSH: Legitimacy of governments--Case studies. | Power (Social sciences)--Case studies. | Security, International. | COVID-19 Pandemic, 2020---Political aspects. | World politics--21st century.
Classification: LCC JC497 .P69 2023 (print) | LCC JC497 (ebook) | DDC 320.01/1--dc23/eng/20230106
LC record available at https://lccn.loc.gov/2022054274
LC ebook record available at https://lccn.loc.gov/2022054275

ISBN: 978-1-032-26850-7 (hbk)
ISBN: 978-1-032-47240-9 (pbk)
ISBN: 978-1-003-38523-3 (ebk)

DOI: 10.4324/9781003385233

Typeset in Bembo
by Deanta Global Publishing Services, Chennai, India

CONTENTS

List of Contributors	*ix*
Preface	*xiii*
Acknowledgements	*xvi*
Abbreviations	*xvii*

1 Introduction: Power, Legitimacy, and World Order   1
   Krishnan Srinivasan

2 Power, Authority, and Shifting Sands of the Legitimacy   20
   Sanjay Pulipaka

3 The View from the United Nations   38
   Mats Berdal and James Mayall

4 From Taboo to Legality: Human Rights and the United Nations   51
   Radhika Coomaraswamy

5 Domestic Politics, External Engagement, and Legitimacy: A Perspective from the US   63
   A. Peter Burleigh

6 The Shifting Grounds of Power and Legitimacy in the European Union   74
   Fredrik Erixon

7	Is the Putin System Partially Legitimate? *Julius George Stephen Fein*	86
8	Power and Legitimacy in the People's Republic of China *Michael Puett*	99
9	Legitimacy and "A Global Community of Shared Future" *Wang Yiwei*	109
10	Tribalism and the Limits of Liberalism: A (Conservative) Japanese Perspective on Legitimacy in World Politics *Tadashi Anno*	118
11	Autocracy, Institutional Weakness, and Latin American Concept of Legitimacy *Deepak Bhojwani*	131
12	Power and Legitimacy: A 21st-Century Perspective on Africa *Rajiv Bhatia*	141
13	Authoritarianism, Resistance, and Legitimacy in the West Asian Political Order *Talmiz Ahmad*	152
14	Power and Legitimacy in Pakistan and Bangladesh: To Be Muslim or Islamic? *Kingshuk Chatterjee and Devadeep Purohit*	171
15	Interrogating Power and Legitimacy in the Information Age from an Indian Perspective *Pranay Kotasthane and Nitin Pai*	189
16	Legitimacy, Political Power, and Tibetan Buddhism *Jigme Yeshe Lama*	198
17	In Search of Legitimacy: The ASEAN Way *Preeti Saran*	209

Index 221

CONTRIBUTORS

Talmiz Ahmad has been India's ambassador to Saudi Arabia, Oman, and the UAE. After retirement, he holds the Ram Sathe Chair in International Studies, Symbiosis International University, Pune, India. He writes regularly in Indian and West Asian journals on West Asian, Eurasian, and Indian Ocean issues, political Islam, and energy security. His latest book, *West Asia at War: Repression, Resistance and Great Power Games*, was published in April 2022.

Tadashi Anno is Professor of Political Science at Sophia University and Director of the Sophia Institute of International Relations. He is the author of *National Identity and Great-Power Status in Russia and Japan: Non-Western Challengers to the Liberal International Order* (2018) and a co-editor of *Dynamics of the Global Society* ([in Japanese] 2007). His research focuses on questions of nationalism, national identity, and their impact on international order.

Mats Berdal is Professor of Security and Development in the Department of War Studies, King's College London, where he is also Director of the Conflict, Security and Development Research Programme (CSDRG). From 2015 to 2016, Berdal served on the Commission of Inquiry set up by the Norwegian Government to examine Norway's military, humanitarian, and development contributions to allied operations in Afghanistan between 2001 and 2014. Mats Berdal is a member of the Academia Europaea and an associate of LSE Ideas.

Rajiv Bhatia is a Distinguished Fellow, Gateway House, and a former Ambassador of India. As Director General of the Indian Council of World Affairs (ICWA), he played a key role in strengthening India's Track-II activities. While in the Indian Foreign Service, he served as Ambassador to Myanmar and Mexico and High Commissioner to Kenya and South Africa. A prolific columnist, he is also a regular speaker on foreign policy and diplomacy in India and abroad. He holds a Master's degree in political science from Allahabad University. His recent books *India-Myanmar Relations: Changing Contours* (Routledge 2016) and *India-Africa Relations: Changing Horizons* (2022) have received critical acclaim.

Deepak Bhojwani joined the Indian Foreign Service in 1978 and served in Asia and Europe. From 2000 to 2012 he served in Latin America as Consul General Sao Paulo and Ambassador resident in Colombia, Venezuela, and Cuba, concurrently in Ecuador, Costa Rica, Dominican Republic, and Haiti. His consultancy LATINDIA promotes relations between India and Latin America. His book *Latin America, the Caribbean and India: Promise and Challenge* was published in 2015. His writings and speeches, mainly on Latin America, can be seen on his blog – www.latindia.in.

Peter Burleigh is a retired US diplomat who served in the Department of State for 33 years. He was US Ambassador to the United Nations (1997–99); to Sri Lanka and the Maldives (1995–97); and for Counter-Terrorism (1990–92). In between foreign assignments, he was in senior positions in the Department of State multiple times. After retiring, he was called back to temporary service in India (2009 and 2011–12) in charge of the US Embassy.

Kingshuk Chatterjee is Professor in the Department of History, Calcutta University, and is associated with the Institute of Foreign Policy Studies, Kolkata. He has previously served as a Founding Professor in the Department of History, School of Humanities and Social Sciences at Shiv Nadar University and as a Fulbright Scholar-in-Residence at the United States Naval Academy in Annapolis, Maryland. Chatterjee's area of expertise is in Middle Eastern politics, and he specialises in political Islam in the modern world. He is the author of *Ali Shari'ati and the Shaping of Political Islam in Iran* and *A Split in the Middle: the Making of the Political Centre in Iran (1987–2004)*.

Radhika Coomaraswamy received her BA from Yale University, her JD from Columbia University, and her LLM from Harvard University. In Sri Lanka, she was the Chairperson of the Sri Lankan Human Rights Commission (2003–06). From 2015 to 2018, she was a member of the Constitutional Council. She served as UN Under-Secretary-General and as Special Representative of the Secretary-General on Children and Armed Conflict (2006–12) and the UN Special Rapporteur on Violence against Women (1994–2003). In 2014, the UN Secretary-General asked Radhika Coomaraswamy to lead the Global Study to review the 15-year implementation of Security Council Resolution 1325 on Women, Peace, and Security. In 2017 she was appointed to the UN Fact Finding Mission in Myanmar and also appointed as a member of the Secretary-General's Board of Advisors on Mediation.

Fredrik Erixon is the founding Director and Chief Executive of the European Centre for International Political Economy (ECIPE), Europe's leading think tank on trade and global commercial policy. He is the author of several books and papers on European policy and global affairs, especially in the fields of international economics, technology, and economic diplomacy. Erixon started his career as an economist in the Prime Minister's Office in Sweden and has later worked for the World Bank, JP Morgan, and the UK government. Erixon was educated at the Oxford, London School of Economics, and Uppsala University.

Julius George Stephen Fein studied at the London School of Economics and then spent 50 years in international trade. He returned to London University for his MSc and PhD, which were the basis for his book *Hitler's Refugees and the French Response, 1933–38*. In addition to essays for the French journal *Revue d'Histoire Diplomatique*, he has published several articles in Indian newspapers and magazines.

Pranay Kotasthane is Chairperson of the High-Tech Geopolitics Programme at the Takshashila Institution, an independent centre for public policy research and education. He teaches public policy, international relations, and public finance at Takshashila's graduate programmes.

Jigme Yeshe Lama is Assistant Professor in the Department of Political Science at the University of Calcutta. His doctoral dissertation was on "Challenges to China's Legitimacy in Tibet: Issues of Hegemony and Contestation, 1995–2013," and he participated in numerous international conferences and workshops. He was awarded the 2014 MSB Award instituted by the Institute of Chinese Studies for the best paper titled "Economic Liberalization in China's Tibet and Its Impact on State-Society Relationship."

David M. Malone is the Rector of the United Nations University (UNU). Prior to joining the United Nations University on 1 March 2013, Malone served (2008–13) as President of Canada's International Development Research Centre, a funding agency supporting policy-relevant research in the developing world. Malone had earlier served as Canada's Representative to the UN Economic and Social Council and as Ambassador to the United Nations (1990–94).

Nitin Pai is co-founder and director of the Takshashila Institution, an independent centre for research and education in public policy.

Michael Puett is the Walter C. Klein Professor of Chinese History and Anthropology at Harvard University. His interests are focused on the inter-relations between religion, philosophy, anthropology, and history, with the hope of bringing the study of China into larger historical and comparative frameworks. He is the author of *The Ambivalence of Creation: Debates Concerning Innovation and Artifice in Early China* and *To Become a God: Cosmology, Sacrifice, and Self-Divinization in Early China*, as well as the co-author, with Adam Seligman, Robert Weller, and Bennett Simon, of *Ritual and Its Consequences: An Essay on the Limits of Sincerity*.

Devadeep Purohit is a senior journalist with *The Telegraph*, the highest circulated English daily in eastern India. A management graduate from IIM Calcutta and a postgraduate in economics from Delhi School of Economics, Devadeep has tried to weave in an analytical perspective in his reportage. He specialises in political economy and writes extensively on the state of the Indian economy, and the policy issues that affect the lives of common people. He also takes a keen interest in India's relationship with its eastern neighbours like Bangladesh, Bhutan, Nepal, and Myanmar. Bangladesh is his area of special interest, and he has been writing about Bangladesh since 2011.

Preeti Saran joined the Indian Foreign Service (IFS) in 1982 and superannuated as Secretary (East) in the Ministry of External Affairs (MEA) in 2018, after serving as Ambassador in Vietnam from 2013 to 2016. Her other overseas assignments include Toronto, Geneva, Cairo, Dhaka, and Moscow. She has experience in India's neighbourhood, the Indo-Pacific region, the Americas, multilateral work, and cultural diplomacy. She was re-elected for a second term as a member of the UN Committee on Economic, Social, and Cultural Rights from 2023 to 2026. She is a member of the Governing Council and the Governing Board of the Indian Council for World Affairs.

WANG Yiwei is Jean Monnet Chair Professor, Vice President of Academy of Xi Jinping Thought on Socialism with Chinese Characteristics for a New Era, Director of the Institute of International Affairs, and Director of the Center for European Studies at Renmin University of China. He is expert adviser of CCPIT Advisory Committee and Turkish TRT World Forum. The Council Member of China Center for International Economic Exchanges, CCIEE) and Chinese People's Institute of Foreign Affairs (CPIFA). He was formerly a diplomat at Chinese Mission to the European Union (2008–11) and distinguished professor at Tongji University (2011–13), professor of Center for American Studies at Fudan University (2001–08), visiting professor of Yonsei University (2005), and Fox Fellow of Yale University (2000–01).

PREFACE

As I write these lines, the happier world we expected in the second half of 2022, as we learned to manage the economically and socially devastating COVID-19 epidemic, has not materialised.

Developing countries are wrestling with global economic inequalities that are exacerbated by the crisis, with their own currencies losing value while those of the wealthiest countries appreciate in relative terms, with wretched consequences for global trade and dangerous ones for developing continents, particularly Africa and Latin America. At the worst possible time, the president of the Russian Federation unleashed a war on Ukraine, with which its history has been intertwined, resulting in a near-deadlock. The United States seems an ever more divided country unable to agree on core values and policies. Meanwhile, although China's international profile improved continually since Deng Xiaoping's economic reforms more than 40 years ago, the country, over recent decades, developed prickly relations with a number of its neighbours and is seen more as a potential threat in Asia than as a global saviour.

Issues of legitimacy and power have rarely been more relevant than they are today. Hence, not just the relevance but also the urgency of this volume.

Emerging from the Second World War, the victorious powers for too many decades assumed that their views were self-evidently right, while those of opponents (mainly the Soviet Union and its allies) were simply wrong. Little account was taken of more nuanced views, and even less the interests, of newly independent countries.

Western powers, haughtily at times, worked to disabuse them of their delusions, while the United States as of the early 1960s, plunged into a series of disastrous conflicts in Southeast Asia and the Middle East, greatly corroding the country's credibility, and by association, that of other industrialised countries. However, signal fiascos in Vietnam, Iraq, and most recently Afghanistan have induced a degree of introspection within the USA and wider Western world, much of which was opposed to these military interventions except for the brief and successful UN-mandated expulsion of Iraqi invading forces from Kuwait in 1990–91.

It is unprofitable to think of Asia as a whole except in terms of its vast land mass, economic dynamism, and potential. Indeed, Asia today, while rising impressively as a whole, exhibits pockets of deep distress, such as Myanmar, and, as a result of spectacularly incompetent leadership, Sri Lanka. But overall, it has been performing impressively, benefiting from two powerful continental locomotives, China and India, from entrepreneurial countries such as Vietnam, and from impressive economic actors such as Indonesia. Southeast Asia's preference for "talk talk" rather than "war war," to paraphrase Churchill, while at times disappointing in terms of outcomes, has worked well for Southeast Asia. And Bangladesh's sustained high economic growth rates over several decades have been one of the impressive success stories, although environmental factors threaten its future as a flat country in a world of rising sea levels.

While Asia continues to grow economically, it also faces intractable political challenges. Border disputes and other sources of internal and regional friction also continue to proliferate. Yet, Asia is rightly held up as an example of a continent in which talk-talk is not always vacuous, in which regional and sub-regional bodies can at times play important roles as ASEAN has done fitfully with respect to Myanmar, and whose economic agreements and organisations, sometimes including non-Asian partners as APEC and CPTPP, can be globally relevant. However, internationally, Asia has distinctly punched under its potential weight.

Its profile at the UN, for example, hardly corresponds to the continent's potential in global affairs. This is not an accident: it flows from choice. But as global power relations become more fractious, this choice is to be regretted, but only the Asian themselves can address the dilemma. Meanwhile, there can be little doubt that the UN and other key international organisations will increasingly come to rely on a range of Asian governments to guide and support its work. The era during which the Western countries at the UN determined the running either by proposing strategies or resisting those of others is fast drawing to a close. With the Ukraine conflict largely paralysing the Security Council, the UN General Assembly will become more relevant.

The United Nations, whose humanitarian and technical programmes have generally worked well, is riven by political discord among its member states on many issues of global importance, making the job of the Secretary-General, infinitely more challenging than it would normally be.

The UN was able to signal clearly, through two votes of the UN General Assembly, its membership's rejection of Russia's attack on Ukraine; to sponsor effectively for developing countries and their specific needs during the

COVID-19 crisis; to persevere in its criticism of human rights violations the world over; to advocate for and cater to the rising tide of refugees and internationally – as well as, in some cases internally – displaced people; and to bring together most countries on key global, regional, and national priorities. So, against the odds, the UN is still with us, 67 years after it was founded. And there is no prospect at present of replacing it with something better that a majority of countries could agree to, and resolve to fund as they most often, however reluctantly and incompletely, do the UN.

The volume's focus, mainly through chapters offered by a number of excellent writers from the sub-continent, abetted by those of other regions, is apposite: Asia is the only clearly rising continent and is rising fast relative to others, either in decline, as Latin America sometimes seems, beset by stagnation, as Africa often teeters on the verge of being after a very promising 15 years from 2000 to 2015, or muddling along much of the time rather aimlessly as the industrialised world has come to do.

I learned a good deal from each of the chapters of the book, which, beyond Asia, range to the USA, Europe, Latin America, the Middle East, and Africa, take a deep dive into Bangladesh and Pakistan, and extend to the influence of Buddhism on public policy. My own happy years in India, Nepal, Bhutan, and Japan confirm many of its insights. My hope is that this volume will receive the attention it deserves and that its authors and editors have earned. I am very grateful to each of them.

David M. Malone
Rector of the United Nations University
Under-Secretary-General of the United Nations

ACKNOWLEDGEMENTS

The editors would like to thank Ms Shoma Choudhury, Commissioning Editor of Routledge India, for her help and guidance.

ABBREVIATIONS

ACC	ASEAN Cultural Council
AEC	ASEAN Economic Council
AI	Artificial Intelligence
AMM	ASEAN Ministerial Meeting
AOIP	ASEAN Outlook for the Indo-Pacific
APRM	African Peer Review Mechanism
APSC	ASEAN Politico-Security Council
ARF	ASEAN Regional Forum
ASEAN	Association of Southeast Asian Nations
AU	African Union
AUKUS	Australia, United Kingdom, and the United States
BCE	Before Common Era
BNP	Bangladesh National Party
BRI	Belt and Road Initiative
BRICS	Brazil, Russia, India, China, and South Africa
CAI	Comprehensive Agreement on Investment
CCP	Chinese Communist Party (CCP)
CICIG	The International Commission against Impunity in Guatemala (Comisión Internacional contra la Impunidad en Guatemala)
CIS	Commonwealth of Independent States
CLMV	Cambodia-Laos-Myanmar-Vietnam
CPC	Chinese Communist Party
CSTO	Collective Security Treaty Organization
DRC	Democratic Republic of Congo

ECOWAS	Economic Community of West African States
EPG	Eminent Persons Group
EU	European Union
FARC	The Revolutionary Armed Forces of Colombia
FATA	Federally Administered Tribal Area
FTA	Free Trade Area
GATT	General Agreement on Tariffs and Trade
GCC	Gulf Cooperation Council
GCSF	Global Community of Shared Future
GDP	Gross Domestic Product
GNH	Gross National Happiness
IAI	Initiative for ASEAN Integration
ICC	International Criminal Court
ICRC	International Committee of the Red Cross
ICT	Information Communication Technologies
IMF	International Monetary Fund
IR	International Relations
IRA	Irish Republican Army
IRGC	Islamic Revolution Guard Corps
IS	Islamic State
ISIS	Islamic State of Iraq and Syria
ISS	Institute for Security Studies
KGB	Komitet Gosudarstvennoy Bezopasnosti
LDC	Least Developed Countries
LGBTQ	Lesbian, Gay, Bisexual, Transgender, and Queer
MBS	Mohammed bin Salman Al Saud
NATO	North Atlantic Treaty Organisation
NEPAD	New Partnership for Africa's Development
NGO	Non-governmental Organisation
OAS	Organisation of American States
OAU	Organisation of African Unity
ODA	Official Development Assistance
OECD	Organisation for Economic Co-operation and Development
ONUC	United Nations Operation in the Congo
PCA	Permanent Court of Arbitration
PKK	Kurdistan Workers' Party
PLA	People's Liberation Army
PRC	People's Republic of China
PRI	Institutional Revolutionary Party
PSC	Peace and Security Council
PSUV	United Socialist Party of Venezuela
R&D	Research & Development
R2P	Responsibility to Protect
RAB	Rapid Action Battalion

RCEP	Regional Cooperation for Economic Partnership
ROC	Russian Orthodox Church
ROs	Regional Organisations
SAARC	South Asian Association for Regional Cooperation
SCO	Shanghai Cooperation Organisation
SCS	South China Sea
SG	Secretary General
TAC	Treaty of Amity and Cooperation
UAE	United Arab Emirates
UK	United Kingdom
UN	United Nations
UNCLOS	United Nations Convention on the Law of the Sea
UNCTAD	United Nations Conference on Trade and Development
UNHCR	United Nations High Commissioner for Refugees
UNICEF	United Nations Children's Fund
US	United States
USSR	Union of Soviet Socialist Republics
WHO	World Health Organization
WTO	World Trade Organization
WWI	World War I
WWII	World War II

1
INTRODUCTION

Power, Legitimacy, and World Order

Krishnan Srinivasan

1.1 Introduction

There is a widespread belief that the political world – and particularly the world order within which it is located – is in crisis. Many will be inclined to argue that the world is better characterised by disorder than order, but few will dispute that all is not well. The chapters in this book attempt to diagnose the nature of this crisis. They do this by interrogating the ways in which two foundational concepts of political thought and practice – power and legitimacy – are understood in relation to the current world from a range of geographical and intellectual perspectives. The title sounds definitive and the three notions are connected, though their scope and worth change over time. This makes it necessary to deal with a nexus of constantly changing concepts and relationships rather than fixed notions viewed over a narrowly defined period. Could the power and legitimacy of 1918 or 1945 be viewed in the same light as that of 2022?

A part of the problem may lie in the values assigned to these two terms. The first may cover military power – both nuclear and conventional – economic, moral like that exerted by Gandhi and Mandela – or soft power, shading into influences like culture and language, or a combination of all of these, ranging in exemplars from the USA to East Timor. As for legitimacy, much will depend on the background and convictions of its interpreters. This is not an argument for moral relativism, but rather the recognition that standards vary, even among liberal democratic societies. Is the USA, for example, less legitimate when a president secures a majority in the electoral college of states but has only a minority of the popular vote? Is the Netherlands considered less legitimate because ministers may not be members of the Lower House? Does the Indian practice of offering financial inducements to elected representatives to defect to other parties violate electoral legitimacy?[1] What also is meant by world order? Does this imply, uniquely, the present state of affairs despite the constant disturbance to its equilibrium originating from climate change, pressure on and dispute over resources, war/terrorism/adventurism, both national or international? The international order as posited by the big powers normally signifies the rules and standards laid down by themselves, and they feel no compunction to flout the same international order, with impunity, when it suits their priorities and perceptions of national interest. This volume attempts to deal with some of these aspects in an admittedly ever-shifting scenario.

There have been three axial moments in the modern era when an attempt was made by the West to find a new model for international society. In 1918, American President Woodrow Wilson launched the idea of a multilateral institutional order based on three concepts – a world made safe for democracy, the principle of national self-determination as the basis of the state, and a system of collective security. After 1945, these ideas were revived with a clarification, an interpretation, and an addition. The clarification concerned the relationship between law and power. All sovereign states are equal under international law, but they are obviously not equally powerful. The tension between an egalitarian order of law and the hierarchical order of power was to be resolved pragmatically through division of labour between the United Nations General Assembly and the Security Council. The interpretation concerned the principle of national self-determination, by which communities were to have a right to form a state and participate in international affairs as legitimate actors. The situation that emerged was that former colonies of European imperial powers gained independence without recognition of any further domestic claims of secessionist self-determination. The addition was the creation of parallel institutions at Bretton Woods to manage the world economy to promote full employment in the industrial world and development in the former colonial world. After 1989 the hope was that freed from constraints imposed during the Cold War, a new world order could be constructed that would be based on democratic government at all levels, local, national, and international, the rule of law, respect for human rights, and an open economy.[2]

The three watershed moments had two things in common. First, while the architecture was intended to be both inclusive and supportive of multilateral diplomacy, and while non-Western states were generally more enthusiastic in their support than the great powers of the day, the underlying ideas and values were Western in origin. Second, on each occasion, while the results of institution-building and reform were not without positive impact on world politics, they never achieved the transformation that the internationalists had envisaged. The main reason for the disillusion that rapidly ensued on each occasion was the persistence of old patterns of behaviour, notably national rivalries and power politics.

Would states, particularly a few Asian states that are now more powerful than at any time since the 17th century, take the initiative to refashion international society, not merely to protect their own interests, but in the aftermath of the recent COVID-19 pandemic? The pandemic was a crisis which shut down the whole globe to an unprecedented degree and is likely to have long-term political consequences. COVID-19 began in Asia, and many Asian countries have been more effective than Western ones in dealing with it. The disruption caused to global trade, investment, and welfare has been massive, and the post-pandemic period should lead to reflection on the nature of power in the world order. The vulnerabilities of even major powers which were on view during this pandemic could herald changes in normative concerns about global and national security.

1.2 Power

From earliest times, with the propensity for irreconcilable interests and confrontation as an unavoidable feature of human existence, power has been synonymous with authority. Machiavelli opined that it was better to be feared than loved if one cannot be both. Mao Zedong famously said, "political power grows out of the barrel of a gun";[3] Karl Popper, "there is no history of mankind, only many histories of all kinds of aspects of human life. And one of these is the history of political power. This is elevated into the history of the world";[4] and Charles James Fox said that "all political power is a trust."[5] While those who wield power enjoy the trust of their subjects, then power is exercised legitimately. The only legitimate right to govern, in other words, is the grant of power from the governed.

Power is the capacity to direct the decisions and actions of others. It derives from strength and will and comes from the transformation of resources into capabilities. The use of power need not necessarily involve the use of force, the threat of force, or other means of coercion. Early writings on the subject tended to judge states by the realist criterion, as expressed by A. J. P. Taylor when he noted that "The test of a great power is the test of strength for war."[6] Later writers expanded this test, attempting to define power in terms of overall military, economic, and political capacity. Kenneth Waltz uses a set of five criteria to determine great power: "population and territory, resource endowment, economic capability, political stability and competence, and military strength."[7] These expanded criteria can be divided into three heads: power capabilities, spatial aspects, and status.[8] The world is moving to multi-polarity with power as an important variable in international politics, and economic, political, cultural, and military capabilities that define national power have witnessed significant shifts. With the growth and consolidation of communication technologies, there are new challenges to international cooperation, and acquiring/maintaining legitimacy in international politics has assumed greater salience.

1.2.1 Soft Power

Power, throughout history, has been defined as the strength of the mighty and hegemonic. Hard power is the default bedrock from which soft power draws effectiveness, durability, and reach. Without it, soft power has little strength or viability. Soft power is "the ability to obtain preferred outcomes through attraction rather than coercion." Its major characteristics are "culture (when pleasing to others), values (when attractive and consistently practiced) and policies (when inclusive and legitimate)," where rather than generating fear, the priority is to inspire optimism and hope.[9] Soft power must be tied to the strength of governance, constitutional values, openness, sensitivity in dealing with minorities, the dynamism of an economy, the cleanliness and "smartness" of cities, protection of human rights, the attraction of entertainment, style and fashion, high standards of education, tourism, heritage conservation, and environmental protection. The capacity to adapt, innovate, and embrace change should be a constant.

South Korea, with few hard power attributes, and having been invaded countless times, is now an exemplar in soft power projection. "South Korea provides a new model of what a 21st-century Asian country can look like: an advanced economy mixed with an ancient civilisation that is at once irrevocably democratic, technologically innovative, and culturally vibrant."[10] Russia's problem, for example, is not only its relative military weakness compared to the United States; it is its weakness in all relevant forms of power, including the power of attraction. China, not lacking in hard power, has consciously sought to soften its image abroad and receive respect, using the appeal of Chinese art, architecture, cinema, literature, universities, and its gigantic economy.

What is the power of soft power? Despite cultural richness, it is multiplied with the image of a dynamic, progressive, democratic, equitable society that is a responsible stakeholder in world politics and a contributor to the global public good. As Australia's Lowy Institute defines it, resources like economic and military capability, resilience, and future potential, combined with measures of influence like cultural and diplomatic, defence networks, and economic relationships, together make up the power of a state.[11] Smart power, as defined by Joseph Nye, is the combination of *soft* and *hard power* in the right mix in the appropriate context.[12]

1.3 Legitimacy

Legitimacy is not something wholly distinct from power; it should be one of its essential foundations. If power shapes the nature and development of international orders, then the politics of legitimacy will feature prominently in the construction, continuation, and dissolution of such orders. Two sites in which the politics of legitimacy had a profound effect on the development of the modern international order are the globalisation of the system of sovereign states, a four-century-long process of imperial expansion, and crisis and fragmentation into successor states, a process in which struggles over legitimacy played a key role. The second was the definition and distribution of special responsibilities for managing functional challenges among states. In an international order characterised by formal sovereign equality on the one hand, and the imbalances caused by material capabilities on the other, a mechanism had to be found for containing and harnessing power to meet the problems faced by the international community. Historically, this has been achieved through the allocation of special responsibilities to particular states, usually the great powers. But if regimes of special responsibilities create patterns of more or less formal hierarchy among states, they are also sites of intense battles over legitimacy.[13]

The exercise of power is insufficient to be a dominant geopolitical player; legitimacy is also needed. The most powerful leaders crave legitimacy both at home and abroad. Leadership aspirations cannot be fulfilled without followers willing to support its rise. Domestically, religion can and is mobilised to support the leadership; so can patriotism and bread and circuses. Internationally, no amount of the exercise of power at home can make up for lack of accepted legitimacy abroad – hence the efforts of North Korea, Russia's Putin administration, and the Taliban Afghan regime seeking international recognition, and short of that, at least attention.

The liberal democratic world is weakening and the international system throws up uncertainties as a result. But what constitutes a world order? How can states aspire to world leadership, and how can any state shape the world order? If every person of the world's 7.8 billion people had a vote, the one billion mostly white, presently rich and powerful, would be outvoted to create a very different world order. A rules-based order therefore raises the question – who sets the standards, norms, and rules? And are the rules equitable to all and enforced justly and transparently? The idea of a global rules-based order to guarantee international governance and regulate state behaviour is based on certain assumptions, but rules conceived to ensure collective harmonisation of interests can be enforced only provided ingredients, such as overwhelming coercive power, a centre of uncontested and legitimate leadership, and an effective multilateral consensus, are present.

The phrase "world order" suggests just arrangements and rational distribution of power, and legitimacy and power are both components on which any order is based. But each nation will try to promote rules on which it believes its version of global order rests, and great powers are inclined to indulge in selective observance of international law. As Henry Kissinger wrote,

> None of the most important countries which must build a new world order have had any experience with the multi-state system that is emerging. Never before has a new world order had to be assembled from so many different perceptions, or on so global a scale.[14]

Any system of order is based on a set of commonly accepted rules that define the limits of permissible action, and a balance of power that enforces restraint when rules break down, preventing any one power from subjugating the others. A consensus on the legitimacy of existing arrangements does not foreclose competition or confrontation but helps to ensure they occur as adjustments within an existing order rather than as fundamental challenges to it. A balance of forces cannot secure peace by itself but, when invoked, can limit the scope and frequency of fundamental challenges and curtail their chance for success when they occur.

Power refers to the ability to impose one's will over others, irrespective of the other's will. Such power is obtained by a combination of many factors: a strong military, favourable geography, big growing economy, nuclear deterrence, and so on. But even the most powerful states need more essential factors to transform into world leaders, namely, an exercise of power deemed legitimate by the other actors. Great power status is the quest for authority, an exercise of power that is more than coercion, yet considered legitimate. To strike the balance between power and legitimacy becomes the essence of statesmanship because power without a moral dimension will turn all disagreements into a test of strength, and countries would have to resort to force and calculations about the shifting locus of power. Moral prescriptions without concern for balance, on other hand, will tend towards crusades or tempting challenges with risks of endangering the international order itself.

How states become powerful is well recognised; how leaders come to exercise power legitimately is less so. Legitimacy requires conformity to a set of rules. Because the international system is not governed by any single set of rules, leaders seek legitimacy by projecting their own rules as superior to others and then acting as upholders of those values. The distinction between power and legitimacy will shed light on the important world order shifts of the past and present. Take, for example, the emergence of the USA as a world leader. By the end of World War II, all the former European powers were exhausted. Power was a major step towards world status, but that power had to transform into authority. There were the values of democracy and liberty which the new international order was intended to encourage, and the creation of multilateral institutions to reassure others that the USA was willing to limit its authority. States accepting this order were provided with security cover, economic assistance, and technological transfer. This package made the USA not only the most powerful but also a legitimate nation in the modern world order. This is also the reason why the USA is now declining; it remains powerful, but its legitimacy is being questioned. Despite the strong American consensus among its elite that the USA must indefinitely remain "the indispensable nation," no longer do states linked to the USA feel they benefit from such linkage as the benefits of the US order have diminished, and the USA turned against the very multilateral institutions it had created, with a resulting loss of credibility. When the world is increasingly more digital and state-driven, and globalisation is under stress, the requirement is for multilateral cooperation. That USA was not seen as leading the international response, and when it equated diplomacy with weakness, this diminished its legitimacy.

How does this reflect on other nations' claim to leadership? No one yet approaches the USA in power capability and China's claim to legitimacy has problems. The theory asserts that authoritarian systems, centralisation, coercion, and personal, not institutional, power will lead to unrest and dissatisfaction, but there is no evidence that the Chinese Communist Party is losing legitimacy or popular support. Twenty million aspire to join the CCP each year while only 125 get in, and the bottom half of China's population has seen its greatest-ever improvement in living standards. China takes the Westphalian route – territorial sovereignty and integrity, with no external interference – which pre-dates the US ascent but provides no direction for the future, and the multilateral institutions China creates are alternate additionalities with no enunciated norms and a hierarchical worldview. This may make China more powerful but not the most authoritative, when access to legitimacy as commonly defined requires a cosmopolitan culture, diversity, plurality, and humanity, along with continental size and a multi-ethnic, multi-religious, liberal democratic polity.

1.3.1 Aspects of Legitimacy

Power in world politics implies hierarchy. Humans are not born equal and physical aggression is part of the human psyche. States are also not equal, are naturally aggressive some or most of the time, and require a hegemon with possession of force and the willingness to use it to maintain order. "All governments tell us they will never yield to force; all history tells us they never yield to anything else."[15] Hegemony is inherent in a strong nation that exercises influence and generates power beyond its borders. Cooperation cannot take place in the absence of more than one hegemony; it is not possible for peace and justice to prevail in a unipolar world. Nor are prospects bright for a world order based on the rule of law administered by a supra-national body like the UN. The presence of hegemonic states brings order, and equality leads to balance of power. "In a world of players of operationally more or less equal strength, there are only two roads to stability. One is hegemony, the other is equilibrium."[16]

What might be the definition of a great power in this century? A nation accorded the international status befitting a great power and receiving equal respect by existing great powers. This implies recognition not only by peers but by weaker countries willing to accept its legitimacy and authority. Regional preponderance would represent an important element of such status. Such a nation would demonstrate the will and ability to exercise power beyond its borders and to fulfil an order-producing and managerial role in its region and readiness to intervene to prevent chaos or destabilisation. It will participate responsibly in international consultations, boost its domestic image, and generate soft power in terms of characteristic, influential, civilisational, cultural, philosophical, and/or intellectual contributions.

Relative power is a combination of diverse factors but will include the ability of a government to extract resources from its citizens to advance national goals. The potential for power cannot be realised without political capacity. The size of population is important in terms of those able to work and fight, but it must be productive. The essentials for legitimate power projection will be physical size, a large working-age population with total factor productivity – meaning value added from all means of production including labour and capital – internal cohesion, strong national identity, size of the economy, modern technology, military prowess, a stable strong currency, knowledge-based and capital exports, access to resources including energy, food, and water, attractiveness to investible funds, a cultural endowment that radiates across its borders, and the ability to withstand environmental and climate change degradation.[17]

1.3.2 Democracy and Legitimacy

Legitimacy is both domestic and international in nature and found in various models of direct, semi-direct, participatory, and representative democracy. Some of these are experiencing a crisis of legitimacy because of the growing disconnect between elected representatives and the electorate with a risk that democracy itself may become collateral damage of the credibility crisis resulting from the phenomena of social media, fake news, fake history, and fake law. The need is to return to the true meaning of democracy as the rule of, by, and for the people. Nevertheless, the central problem of representative democracy, which has been evident at least since the French Revolution, remains valid,[18] namely, whether direct democracy is possible in modern conditions, when there is no means of avoiding representation. The related question arises, how then do people hold their representatives to account when under many democratic constitutions, it is possible to have an elected dictatorship?

The presumption still remains that Western liberal democracy can be universalised and will attract other countries, but Western nations have ceded ground as role models, and liberal values are now mainly political rhetoric as almost every nation seems set on an independent sovereign course to gain more political, economic, and ideological control domestically. With the pandemic, governments have tended to expand their authority and the security state, and atrophy the social state, which leads to inequality. With COVID-19's decline, there could be millions of workers losing jobs, with the resultant potential for anger, bigotry, neo-fascism, and hyper-populist political culture.

Elections were the first marker of procedural democracy, then accountability, civil liberties, a free press, an independent judiciary, and institutions to make these substantive. Modern democracies are crushed when people lose trust, do not believe in the legitimacy of the system, or when institutions are captured from within while retaining some democratic facade. Power grabs by financial political elites, and inequality and powerlessness of voters hasten the downward slide. The autocratic pattern is to make political appointments to the civil service and judiciary, limit academic freedom, curtail civil society, delegitimise the political opposition as enemies of state, and vitiate the electoral process through fraud. Populism disdains facts, embraces xenophobic narratives, corrodes self-sacrifice and discipline, and prefers ideological perceptions over expertise.

Dignity is a core value of democracy, enabling people to make meaningful choices. Lacking this, people take refuge in group identity, the power of the group or "tribe," the preference for a strong leader capable of protecting the group against others competing for scarce resources and establishing order. In these circumstances, authoritarianism is a cherished leadership quality. Psychologists believe that people are drawn to leaders who represent the same group. Such leaders elevated into authority are not typical but prototypical members of the group, exemplifying its ideals and acting in its best interests. Such leaders are those who take a stand to protect that which is core and distinctive of the group.[19]

The UN General Assembly in 2005 unanimously adopted Resolution 60/1 "that democracy is a universal value based on the freely expressed will of people to determine their own political, economic, social and cultural systems and their full participation in all aspects of their lives." In other words, democracy is another term for the right to self-determination. Participation in governance means a system that guarantees equality, pluralism, transparency, accountability, rotation of power, an independent judiciary, robust civil society, and free media, all essentials to maintain human dignity. And the General Assembly reaffirmed that "while democracies share common features, there is no single model of democracy, that it does not belong to any country or region."

A democratic system is not limited to the ballot box but a comprehensive paradigm based on institutions, not individuals. It requires a civil society to raise awareness of the culture of democracy and consolidate its practices and primarily needs a genuine consensus on a social contract which guarantees freedom, equality, and dignity for all. Democracy will always be a work in progress that should be adjusted to experience on the ground. There are different models for its application, but there are, nonetheless, minimum criteria for what can be called a democratic system, most notably freedom of expression and belief, and guarantees to exercise civil and political rights including establishing parties and independent unions and associations.

People everywhere share the same aspiration to enjoy peace and prosperity in freedom, and several questions arise: how to bridge the disconnect between nominally democratic governments and their electorates, how to give the electorate genuine policy choices and not merely the opportunity of voting for a candidate, how to ensure that the public has access to information and pluralistic views to enable them to make choices, how to block media conglomerates that disseminate fake news in order to manufacture consent, how to construct realistic transparency and accountability by governments, how to ensure the freedom of the press, and how to give visibility to disenfranchised indigenous peoples in the conduct of public affairs.

Elections are not the sole or sufficient indicator of public trust. Electoral democracy can appear to coexist with a lack of other liberal elements like absence of the rule of law, separation of powers, and basic freedoms. Freedom House 2021 states, "Democracy [is] under Siege" since 2001, and democracy declined for 15 years in a row. V-Dem the same year claims "Autocratisation turns Viral" with 68 per cent of the world population under autocracy, including India as an "electoral autocracy." According to the Economist Intelligence Unit's

Democracy Index 2020, 75 out of 167 nations live in some type of democracy, but only 8.4 per cent of the world population live in a complete democracy. The real threat is the inability of governments to tackle problems that complex globalised societies face daily, including corruption, climate change, technological disruption, power concentration, pandemics, social inequalities, and income loss by the middle class. In this crisis of leadership, the public may choose outside the establishment and prefer the strong man.[20] This has led to an increase in the number of authoritarians democratically elected through reasonably free and fair elections, a strong leader who could address the root cause and a clear identifiable enemy, whose appeal lies in performance, something that engages an audience. Even in Germany which has recent historical good reason to distrust populism, this is "a time in which authoritarianism populist views and right wing slogans are gaining ground."[21]

One needs to assess democracy with greater nuance; countries have different histories, cultures, systems, and development models. Prior to the Ukraine invasion by Russia, during the Beijing winter Olympics, Presidents Putin of Russia and Xi of China signed a document that heralded the start of a "New Era of International Affairs," cementing their "friendship without limits." Important in terms of contemporary political theory, China and Russia rejected the Western definition of democracy and proffered their own based on historic heritage and long-standing traditions, relying on "thousand years of experience of development, popular support and consideration of the needs and interests of citizens." This brand of democracy is primarily outcome and results driven, often without granting comparable weight or consideration to questions of procedural legitimacy – how inclusive, open, or contested are the procedures employed? The new "whole-process people's democracy" replaces the more typical criteria for measuring democracy (enfranchisement and suffrage) with a holistic measurement of whether people's lives are materially and substantively improved. The Chinese system works because it is allegedly adaptive, meritocratic, and frequently attains satisfaction and approval from its nationals. So, if China and Russia have their say, the new era would be shaped by values other than those the world had known to be universal, namely those emanating from the West.

Half the world's democracies appear to be guilty of liberal backsliding, but democracy has the capacity for self-correction. Its greatest challenge is that autocrats claim their systems were more efficient at tackling contemporary problems. Democracy is in trouble the world over and liberal democracy is fading – it now pertains only to 14 per cent of the world population according to V-Dem.[22] Democracies tend to decline in slow stages and individuals are oppressed not only by the state but by non-state actors and weak state ability to maintain the rule of law. The Asian Tigers were non-democratic in the process of becoming rich and in most cases democratic; can liberty, equality, and fraternity be achieved without first a concentration of power and state capacity?

No system of thought prevails indefinitely; we have authoritarianism across the world after decades of liberalism, though China's political system has yet no appeal beyond its border. An authoritarian leader appears to be a symbol of wisdom and strength, popular, independent of action, someone who shapes the narrative of his/her choice. Social media and the digital revolution have created conditions in which governments compete in the stories they tell. The stories are heavily coloured by propaganda and the advantage lies with the person in office. It is possible today to have total control over all key elements of official machinery without even being blatantly undemocratic. The media and courts can be oddly compliant and some institutions have almost ceased to function. There is also a limitless ability to keep the religious pot boiling, with the branding of trouble makers as anti-national.

Democracy needs the trust of the people. Loss of public trust occurs when governments fail to do what is perceived to be right, where they cannot be trusted to act as the protector of the public interest, the common weal. Trust is on what legitimacy, stability, and the effectiveness of the political system depend. Even if the executive loses trust, the system may yet be democratic if other branches, the agencies, electoral machinery, and judiciary, act fairly and remain unsubservient.

1.3.3 Inequality and Legitimacy

The happiest societies are the most equal societies,[23] and social democracies work because they benefit every tier of society. Inequality is hugely detrimental to legitimacy, causing structural injustice between the ruling class and the ordinary people and the establishment versus the governed, with the pain felt by the middle and lower levels and fostering incipient revolt against incumbent elites.[24]

Inequality is the product of a corrupt political class, a discredited authority, shoddy infrastructure, non-functioning bureaucrats, a polarised public, and an unequal economy, arousing bitterness towards the political class and asset-stripping politics. Some statistics can be cited for the largest democracy and the oldest one: in 2021, the bottom 50 per cent of the population in India held only 6 per cent of the national wealth and 98 of the richest persons owned the same wealth as 552 million compatriots.[25] A new survey of YouGov, Mint, and Centre for Policy Research suggests that 51 per cent of Indians are disillusioned with democracy and would prefer rule by a strong man, military general, or unelected technocrat, which is an indictment of the political system and political class in India. Pew Research Center in April 2019, covering 27 democracies including India, Indonesia, and Mexico, also showed a majority dissatisfied with democracy. Yet, paradoxically, these same people cherish the vote and value the right to participate in elections.[26]

The USA, the oldest democracy, is another case in point. It upholds the individual at the expense of community and family, and there is no compassion or safety net in society. By the 1960s, 40 per cent of marriages ended in divorce with the collapse of the working-class family. The lower and middle class have lost power. The three richest Americans have more money than 160 million of their country folk.²⁷ Twenty per cent of the population have zero or minus net worth; this becomes 37 per cent in the case of African Americans. With the COVID-19 pandemic, 41 per cent of African American-owned businesses were closed.²⁸ Fundamental rights like access to health, education, and a safety net for the weak and infirm are derided as "socialism." Extreme politics in America are couched in libertarian terms, the far right is more anarchic than anywhere else. Former President Trump was not a one-man aberration when his administration intensified rancour and exacerbated economic inequality and social divisions with "competing facts." Populism and the cult of the individual is a product of the US societal decline, which contributes to fostering hatred, validates anger, and targets enemies, in contrast with elements that reinforce social solidarity like religion, family, tradition, equality, and non-jingoistic patriotism. The USA emphasises freedom but not equality, individual rights but not an equal society.

Legitimacy in a political system can never be sustained when the vast majority is impoverished despite abundant natural and human resources, when hyper-nationalism is privileged over diversity and pluralism, with civil society dissent and disagreement suppressed as anti-national, and promiscuous filing of sedition charges. Populist leaders rail against the modern world, using social media to express hatred based on race, gender, religion, citizenship, education, and region. Administrations based on political nihilism are founded on amateurism, nepotism, and corruption, influenced by ideologues and sycophants, when the need is for empathy and solidarity.

1.4 World Order

The international order, and the principle of multilateralism on which it is based, is under greater threat than since the end of World War II and the era of de-colonisation though the need for cooperation in the age of globalisation is greater. Globalisation has made the world uneven, introducing protectionism and nationalism. In part, the crisis concerns power politics, of managing the co-existence of rising powers, mainly sited in the East, with the slow and relative decline of the West. In part, it is a crisis of legitimacy, of declining authority and credibility of institutions that were designed to facilitate international cooperation. These two aspects are linked, and it is unlikely that they can be resolved separately. The issues that need to be explored are the reasons for the decline of international cooperation, and what needs to be done to restore the legitimacy of the international order.

One of the major sources of the legitimacy crisis is the widening gap between the rich and others under neo-liberal economics, allowing in the process private interests to exercise disproportionate power over international institutions. An example is the World Health Organization to which today only 16 per cent of its finances are provided by governments through assessed membership dues without "strings." The rest is largely provided as voluntary contributions, often with tight and sometimes restrictive conditions, and usually across two-year cycles.

As well as making long-term planning impossible, this has resulted in the progressive weakening of the WHO's ability to perform the vast and ever-growing array of tasks that all governments, and therefore their populations, demand and need.[29]

Another aspect is the rise of populist leaders across the world, including many elected through acceptable democratic procedures, who prefer bilateral transactional processes to multilateral institutions in order to promote their policies. At the same time, people observed that some of the countries faring badly in the pandemic – such as the USA and Brazil – were led by charismatic populists of a similar hue. "These leaders – the UK's Johnson, USA's Trump, Brazil's Bolsonaro – came to power … pursuing culture wars within and beyond their countries."[30] Protection is on the rise, democracy and human rights are in retreat, hyper-nationalist regimes proliferate, and international law recedes.

Nations are less free, prosperous, equal, and more fragmented when democracy and human rights are contested in a battle of narratives. Added to this is the change wrought in economies, leaving the working class vulnerable to shocks. Globalisation has led to capital seeking cheaper labour, which affects nations that have not invested in intangibles, whose industry has not moved to robotics, artificial intelligence, and labour substitution. This new type of wealth creation does not need physical labour or capital; it will be capitalism without capital and production without workers, and the transition for nations mainly in the developing world will be especially painful with this qualification; historically the most suffering has not been born by the poorest, who continue to live largely in a subsistence economy, but by countries transitioning to a wage-led industrialising economy, in other words, with a proletariat that has largely lost contact with its rural roots.

Technological development is accelerating. Apart from an already well-globalised economy, digital technologies like artificial intelligence and climate change issues such as energy security have redefined the traditional landscape of conflicts. Countries are investing more in remote warfare capabilities and precision technologies, as opposed to having occupying forces. Future conflicts will probably stem from four basic archetypes, namely counterterrorism, grey-zone conflicts, asymmetric fights, and high-end combat.[31] They are likely to place a premium on being able to operate at a considerable range.

There are four main imbalances in the world today; pandemic injustice against poor countries with the mass of vaccines used only in a few developed nations; military spending contrasting with global poverty with the USA accounting for 39 per cent of the $2 trillion in 2020, when world GDP fell by nearly 5 per cent and ODA was only $168 billion; the rich have got richer while about 110 million fell into extreme poverty; and Global Climate Risk Indices of 2021 warned that warming and disaster costs may be more severe than anticipated, but only a handful of nations contributed to this. Only 100 companies account for 71 per cent of carbon emissions since 1988 and the USA accounts for 25 per cent of historical carbon emissions and Europe for 22 per cent.[32] The one area that demands global cooperation is climate change, but climate change concerns have provided fresh domains for geopolitical competition. The pursuit of non-fossil fuel energy sources has created demand for minerals like copper, nickel, cobalt, chromium, and platinum that are largely found in Africa, possibly making the latter the centre of new global extractive exploitation.[33]

There were varied early responses to the pandemic in Southeast Asia and the West. The former was proactive and responded as a disciplined community, but most European countries were dismissive of the threat. This divide was most apparent in actions taken by China and the Western democracies. While Europe became the epicentre of the pandemic, China vigorously enforced mass quarantine, widespread lockdowns, mass testing, and setting up of residential committees to monitor the health of residents, enforcing home isolation and arranging home deliveries of food and other necessities. The pandemic also sharpened geopolitical competition between the USA and China. From the outset, China saw the pandemic as a war that impinged on its global stature, a conflict that it had to win. China's economy survived most of the crisis: In 2020, its share of the global gross domestic product increased by 1.1 per cent, the largest in several decades. Its economy grew by 2.3 per cent in 2020, the only major country with positive growth that year. Its trade surplus reached $535 billion, the highest since 2015. The trade surplus with the USA was $316 billion, a record. By contrast Europe saw the pandemic as a disaster and the USA moved from denial to scapegoating to escapism, the last phase culminating in the arrival of the vaccine at the end of 2020. The pandemic highlighted deep inequalities within and between nations – US employment was about 57 per cent in November 2020, the lowest since 1983, while its 100 richest people added $600 billion to their wealth. Initial responses to the pandemic were shrill demands to go national and end globalisation, but both trade and technology remain central to Sino-US geopolitical competitions.[34]

Viruses being no respecters of national borders, the threat of a pandemic appeared genuinely global. In demonstrating the costs rather than the benefits of globalisation, it should set the stage for initiatives aimed at reframing the multilateral order in which the international collaboration that characterises scientific research could be extended to the political realm but in less intrusive ways than has been the case since 1989. What is required is the rebuilding of trust in the overall benefits of the multilateral system. The West would have to be co-opted, but the lead should this time perhaps come from the East.

Legitimacy may be a Western nostrum, but it is not identical to legality, even if it should be consistent with it most of the time. The chapters in this volume were intended to prompt reflection on the concept of legitimacy through diverse intellectual and geographical traditions. While the concept of power has received acceptance, there is a need to examine its relation to legitimacy both in theory and practice. There is also the tension between individual rights and the rights of supra-individual entities, the instrumental use of religion by political groups to gain legitimacy, and the role of states in according legitimacy to non-governmental political entities in fragmented polities which are often the site of intense contest for power. Added to these are the impact of the COVID-19 pandemic on the legitimacy of major powers in international society, the extent, and limits, of deployment of soft power tools to gain legitimacy, the role of democratically elected populist leaders in generating tension, including through disavowal of multilateral mechanisms, and the legitimacy of multilateral institutions in both political and functional areas. And there is the Ukraine conflict, which though directly confined to Eastern Europe in a limited sense has far wider ramifications with the heavy economic, monetary, and financial sanctions imposed on Russia by the West, and the resulting geo-economic contest will necessitate a broad reassessment of national security and realpolitik.

Violation of sovereignty and territorial integrity is something that Asia has seen and experienced in the past at the hands of major powers, even after the era of classical colonialism but novel to Europe in the current century. The Russian invasion of Ukraine seems likely to lead to greater fragmentation of the global order. Far from consolidating the democratic world, the war has underscored its basic incoherence because the varied responses to the war belie the vision of democracies pitted against autocracies. Several democracies such as India and South Africa abstained from the UN voting; others like Brazil and Mexico refused to participate in sanctions. Close to half of all Asian and African countries abstained or voted against anti-Russian UN resolutions. Only three Asian countries embraced US sanctions against Russia, Singapore, Japan, and South Korea.

The initial assessment is that the Ukraine conflict will heighten the possibility of the future use of nuclear weapons and their geographical proliferation, increase economic protection and roll back globalisation, create opposition to unilateral sanctions that have damaging collateral effects on third countries, and promote greater opposition to the use of the dollar as the dominant reserve currency. Nevertheless, the major geopolitical disputes and security dilemmas that affect the global order are concentrated in East and Northeast Asia as the world seeks an equilibrium to account for China's rise. China's economic dependence on the West will continue and the balance of power in Asia at the time of writing is unlikely to be significantly affected, only reinforcing Asia's focus on stability and trade, which has served Asian countries well in recent decades.

Sixteen authors recognised internationally for their expertise have contributed to this volume, and their varying perspectives will provoke further discussion on this subject. Sanjay Pulipaka traces the scholastic history of the concept of legitimacy and political power and concludes that despite growth in inter-government and non-state communications and institutions, nation-states alone are still considered legitimate in the international landscape. The appeal of, and desire for, domestic and international legitimacy is stressed by several authors, including Julius Fein, Deepak Bhojwani, Wang Yiwei, and Peter Burleigh, but they make the point that elections *per se* are insufficient to confer legitimacy. James Mayall and Mats Berdal believe that though there is a distinction between law and legitimacy, an equilibrium between power and legitimacy can be found at the UN, and along with Radhika Coomaraswamy, suggest that the UN can act as legitimiser, though many of its important agencies are starved of funding and the UN is criticised for double standards and impunity.

Many contributors like Talmiz Ahmad, Michael Puett, Kingshuk Chatterjee/Devadeep Purohit, Jigme Lama, and Fein also note the role of religion in bestowing legitimacy to a regime. So too does peace as a value in the case of ASEAN, according to Preeti Saran; meritocracy and invocation of early exemplars in China, according to Puett; and soft power as a legitimising contributor in Burleigh's chapter.

Ahmad observes that many Arab states inherited their legitimacy from erstwhile colonial empires and that the COVID pandemic has expedited moves towards nationalism and expansionism. Like other authors such as Rajiv Bhatia and Chatterjee/Purohit, he notes that the basis of legitimacy is a social contract between rulers and the ruled.

Popular support is essential for legitimacy according to Bhatia, Chatterjee/Purohit, and Wang. Conversely, the role of the military as a de-legitimising institution is marked by several contributors such as Chatterjee/Purohit, Bhojwani, and Bhatia, as well as the negative influence of weak or non-existing democratic institutions and legal frameworks leading to a strong-man syndrome, media control, and concentration of power at the top, as laid out by Burleigh, Saran, and Fein. Further, authors such as Bhojwani, Burleigh, and Puett point to the undermining of legitimacy by inequality and lack of social justice.

Saran and Puett consider technology to be a strength, whereas Pulipaka shows that Information Communication Technologies democratise the political landscape but also stimulate polarisation such as identity politics. Nitin Pai/Pranay Kotasthane point out that in our age of rapid digital globalisation, when weapon systems are digitised and information is weaponised, liberal democracies need to mobilise social harmony and popular will to combat digital opposition.

Kingshuk/Purohit sense that legitimacy can derive from a sense of insecurity, and Fredrik Erixon supplements this by noting that exogenous shocks like the pandemic and the Russian invasion of Ukraine have induced the European Union to rediscover the virtues of solidarity and integration that have introduced a positive approach to internal legitimacy. The EU, adds Erixon, whose previously perceived strength was in values and economic heft, will henceforward represent a strong trans-national community different from the post-modern concept of nation-states.

Tadashi Anno and Wang however remain sceptical of the Western concept of liberalism. Anno wonders whether liberalism was ever universalised, and its appeal might be drawing to a close with the weakness of the USA. He considers popular opinion to be based on "tribal" affiliation, and like Mayall and Berdal, argues that neither legitimacy nor power by themselves is adequate. Wang puts forward a new concept of Chinese legitimacy based on drawing from the past, present, and future and embracing the whole planet.

These diverse viewpoints present the basis for reflection and further discussion on how a conjuncture of power and legitimacy can best be contrived for the benefit of mankind in a new and better global order.

Notes

1. It should be noted that the Indian practice of offering financial inducements to elected representatives to defect to other parties is an unconstitutional practice.
2. Boutros Boutros-Ghali, 'An Agenda for Peace Preventive Diplomacy, Peacemaking and Peace-keeping', *Report of the Secretary-General Pursuant to the Statement Adopted by the Summit Meeting of the Security Council* (31 January 1992).
3. Edward A. McCord, 'Mao Zedong and the Issue of Military Power in the 1926 National Revolution', *American Journal of Chinese Studies 25*, no. 2 (2018): 123–31.
4. Karl R. Popper, *The Open Society and Its Enemies: The High Tide of Prophecy (Volume II)* (London: Routledge & K. Paul, 1962), 465.
5. cited in Otto Gierke, *Political Theories of the Middle Age* (New Jersey: The Lawbook Exchange Ltd, 2002), xxxvi.
6. See A.J. P. Taylor, *The Struggle for Mastery in Europe, 1848–1918* (Oxford: Clarendon Press, 1954), xxiv.
7. Kenneth N. Waltz, 'The Emerging Structure of International Politics', *International Security 18,* no. 2 (1993): 50.
8. Iver B. Neumann, 'Russia as a great power, 1815–2007', *Journal of International Relations and Development 11* (2008): 128–151.
9. Joseph S. Nye, 'Soft Power', *Foreign Policy 80* (1990): 153–71.
10. Nirupama Rao, 'The Case for Harnessing Soft Power, or Why India Cannot Be Insular', *The Wire* (06 January 2022).
11. Nirupama Rao, 'The Case for Harnessing Soft Power, or Why India Cannot Be Insular', *The Wire* (06 January 2022).
12. Maxime Gomichon, 'Joseph Nye on Soft Power', *E-International Relations* (08 March 2013).
13. Christian Reus-Smit, *The Chinese Journal of International Politics* 7, no. 3 (2014), 341–59.
14. Henry Kissinger, *Crisis : The Anatomy of Two Major Foreign Policy Crises* (New York : Simon & Schuster, 2003).
15. Albrecht Schnbel & Ramesh Thakur, 'Kosovo and the Challenge of Humanitarian Intervention', *UNU Press* (2000): 448.
16. Henry A Kissinger, 'We Live in an Age of Transition', *Daedalus 124*, no. 3 (1995): 102 (99–107). Also see Robert Cooper, *The Breaking of Nations* (London: Atlantic Books, 2003): 76.
17. James Mayall and Krishnan Srinivasan, *Towards the New Horizon* (New Delhi: Standard Publishers, 2009),140.
18. Benjamin Constant, 'The Liberty of Ancients Compared with that of Moderns (1819)', *The Online Library of Liberty.* https://oll-resources.s3.us-east-2.amazonaws.com/oll3/store/titles/2251/Constant_Liberty1521.html.
19. By Stephen D. Reicher, Michael J. Platow and S. Alexander Haslam, 'The New Psychology of Leadership', *Scientific American* (01 August 1 2007). https://www.scientificamerican.com/article/the-new-psychology-of-leadership-2007-08/
20. Andrew Sheng, 'Democracy on a Ventilator?', *The Statesman* (02 January 2022): 7.
21. John Kampfner, *Why the Germans Do It Better* (London: Atlantic Books, 2020), 35.
22. Stefan Kalberer, 'V-Dem report 2021: Global Wave of Autocratization Accelerates', *Democracy without Borders* (14 March 2021). https://www.democracywithoutborders.org/16165/v-dem-report-2021-global-wave-of-autocratization-accelerates/.

23 Tamás Hajdu and Gábor Hajdu, 'Are More Equal Societies Happier? Subjective Well-Being, Income Inequality, and Redistribution', *KTI/IE Discussion Papers* (2013).
24 Jan-Emmanuel De Neve and Nattavudh Powdthavee, 'Income Inequality Makes Whole Countries Less Happy', *Harvard Business Review* (12 January 2016).
25 'Top 98 Richest Indians Own Same Wealth as Bottom 552 Million', *Outlook* (17 January 2022). https://www.outlookindia.com/business/top-98-richest-indians-own-same-wealth-as-bottom-552-million-news-31912.
26 Swaminathan Aiyar, 'Do Indian Voters Really Prefer Rule by a Strongman?', *Times of India*, (23 January 2022): 14.
27 Noah Kirsch, 'The 3 Richest Americans Hold More Wealth than Bottom 50% of the Country, Study Finds', *Forbes* (09 November 2017). https://www.forbes.com/sites/noahkirsch/2017/11/09/the-3-richest-americans-hold-more-wealth-than-bottom-50-of-country-study-finds/?sh=498251953cf8 https://www.forbes.com/sites/noahkirsch/2017/11/09/
28 Rodney A. Brooks, 'More than Half of Black-Owned Businesses May Not Survive COVID-19', *National Geographic* (18 July 2020). https://www.nationalgeographic.com/history/article/black-owned-businesses-may-not-survive-covid-19.
29 Gordon Brown and Helen Clark, 'There Is an Urgent Need to Make WHO Financially Fit for Purpose', *Aljazeera* (24 January 2022). https://www.aljazeera.com/opinions/2022/1/24/there-is-an-urgent-need-to-make-who-financially-fit-for-purpose.
30 John Kampfner, *Why the Germans Do it Better: Notes from a Grown-Up Country* (London: Atlantic Books, 2020), 278.
31 In "high-end" combat, the best quality of power is deployed to achieve a specific objective. The achievement of the objective is demonstrative, and there is no intention by the protagonist, to escalate the situation.
32 Andrew Sheng, 'Obscene Imbalance in Worlds Balance Sheet', *The Statesman* (01 August 2021): 7.
33 Bruno Macaes, *Geopolitics for the End Time: From the Pandemic to the Climate Crisis* (London: Hurst, 2021).
34 Ibid.

Bibliography

Aiyar, Swaminathan. 'Do Indian Voters Really Prefer Rule by a Strongman?'. *Times of India* (23 January 2022).

Boutros-Ghali, Boutros. 'An Agenda for Peace Preventive Diplomacy, Peacemaking and Peace-keeping'. *Report of the Secretary-General Pursuant to the Statement Adopted by the Summit Meeting of the Security Council* (31 January 1992).

Brooks, Rodney. 'More Than Half of Black-Owned Businesses May Not Survive COVID-19'. *National Geographic* (18 July 2020). https://www.nationalgeographic.com/history/article/black-owned-businesses-may-not-survive-covid-19.

Brown, Gordon, and Helen Clark. 'There is an Urgent Need to Make WHO Financially Fit for Purpose'. *Aljazeera* (24 January 2022). https://www.aljazeera.com/opinions/2022/1/24/there-is-an-urgent-need-to-make-who-financially-fit-for-purpose.

Cooper, Robert. *The Breaking of Nations*. London: Atlantic Books, 2003.

Gierke, Otto. *Political Theories of the Middle Age*. New Jersey: The Lawbook Exchange Ltd, 2002.

Gomichon, Maxime. 'Joseph Nye on Soft Power'. *E-International Relations* (8 March 2013).

Hajdu, Tamás, and Gábor Hajdu. 'Are More Equal Societies Happier? Subjective Well-Being, Income Inequality, and Redistribution'. *KTI/IE Discussion Papers* (2013). https://hbr.org/2016/01/income-inequality-makes-whole-countries-less-happy.

Kalberer, Stefan. 'V-Dem Report 2021: Global Wave of Autocratization Accelerates'. *Democracy Without Borders* (14 March 2021). https://www.democracywithoutborders.org/16165/v-dem-report-2021-global-wave-of-autocratization-accelerates/.

Kampfner, John. *Why the Germans Do It Better: Notes From a Grown-Up Country.* London: Atlantic Books, 2020.

Kissinger, Henry. *Crisis: The Anatomy of Two Major Foreign Policy Crises.* New York : Simon & Schuster, 2003.

Kissinger, Henry. 'We Live in an Age of Transition'. *Daedalus* 124, no. 3 (1995): 102.

Macaes, Bruno. *Geopolitics for the End Time: From the Pandemic to the Climate Crisis.* London: Hurst, 2021.

Mayall, James, and Krishnan Srinivasan. *Towards the New Horizon.* New Delhi: Standard Publishers, 2009.

McCord, A. Edward. 'Mao Zedong and the Issue of Military Power in the 1926 National Revolution'. *American Journal of Chinese Studies* 25, no. 2 (2018): 123–131.

Neumann, B. Iver. 'Russia as a Great Power, 1815–2007'. *Journal of International Relations and Development* 11 (2008): 128–151.

Nye, Joseph S. 'Soft Power'. *Foreign Policy*, no. 80 (1990): 153–171.

Popper, R. Karl. *The Open Society and Its Enemies: The High Tide of Prophecy (Volume II).* London:Routledge & K. Paul, 1962.

Rao, Nirupama. 'The Case for Harnessing Soft Power, or Why India Cannot Be Insular'. *The Wire* (6 January 2022).

Reicher, D. Stephen, Michael J. Platow, and S. Alexander Haslam. 'The New Psychology of Leadership'. *Scientific American* (1 August 2007). https://www.scientificamerican.com/article/the-new-psychology-of-leadership-2007-08/.

Reus-Smit, Christian. *The Chinese Journal of International Politics* 7, no. 3. Oxford: Oxford University Press, 2014.

Schnbel, Albrecht, and Ramesh Thakur. *Kosovo and the Challenge of Humanitarian Intervention.* Tokyo: UNU Press, 2000.

Sheng, Andrew. 'Democracy on a Ventilator?'. *The Statesman* (2 January 2022).

Sheng, Andrew. 'Obscene Imbalance in Worlds Balance Sheet'. *The Statesman* (1 August 2021).

Taylor, A. J. P. *The Struggle for Mastery in Europe, 1848–1918.* Oxford: Clarendon Press, 1954.

Waltz, Kenneth N. 'The Emerging Structure of International Politics'. *International Security* 18, no. 2 (1993): 44–79.

2
POWER, AUTHORITY, AND SHIFTING SANDS OF THE LEGITIMACY

Sanjay Pulipaka

2.1 Introduction

In today's world politics, gaining and sustaining legitimacy in domestic and international realms is proving to be a challenging enterprise. States struggle to maintain political legitimacy due to rapid ongoing social changes, easy movement of people, quick shifts in employment patterns owing to globalisation, and new technologies enabling enhanced access to information. In the international realm, because of power shifts, particularly from West to East and the debates over international legitimacy generated by these shifts, the structure and decisions of various multilateral organisations are being constantly interrogated. As a result, international cooperation is becoming difficult as legitimacy has become increasingly fluid in domestic and world politics. If international cooperation is to be restored to its former level, let alone be improved, there is a need for a better understanding of how legitimacy interacts with power and authority in world politics. This chapter is divided into six sections. After the introduction, Section 2.2 deals with the theoretical foundations and conceptual frameworks pertaining to legitimacy. This is followed by the evolving dynamics between civil society, the market, and the state in Section 2.3. Section 2.4 maps the impact of social media on identity politics and democracy, and Section 2.5 provides reflections on war, peace, and legitimacy. Section 2.6 concludes the chapter.

2.2 The Argument

The concepts of power, authority, and legitimacy are sometimes used interchangeably when describing political developments. It is useful to note the difference between these concepts. For Robert Dahl, "the intuitive idea of power is something like this: A has power over B to the extent that he can get B to do something that B would not otherwise do."[1] A more complete statement on power, he noted, would include source, means, amount, and scope of power.[2] If A can deploy weapons to inflict pain on B, then power tends to be an arbitrary application of physical force. However, if B feels obliged to adhere to A's directives because of legal frameworks or a societal norm, then A has authority over B. On the other hand, if B perceives actions of A are aimed at the larger good and therefore decides to abide by such actions, then the concept of legitimacy comes into play.

Legitimacy is one of the important aspects of political philosophy. While the power of rulers varied over time and geography, they initially drew legitimacy from the notion of divine right, ordained by God: the source of legitimacy was located in the spiritual or religious realm. Muslims claimed descent from the Holy Prophet, Chinese from a Mandate of Heaven, and Hindus from association with religious discipleship. With societal changes caused, inter alia, by the advent of the printing press, there was greater engagement and increased access to new ideas, and the concept of divine right was steadily undermined, giving way to the idea of "contract" that validated political authority; a heuristic device to reflect political arrangements perceived as legitimate. According to Thomas Hobbes, in order to escape the state of nature in which human life would be untold misery, people should mobilise in order to establish a contract to form a sovereign authority. The failure to abide by the directives of this sovereign would result in the re-emergence of the state of nature. Therefore, the source of political legitimacy was located not only in the social contract but in the violent consequences of failing to recognise the authority of the ruler. For John Locke, the social contract placed supreme power in the hands of the sovereign, but the power needed to be operationalised under various constraints. He notes that power

> is not, nor can possibly be absolutely Arbitrary over the Lives and Fortunes of the People … It is a Power that hath no other end but preservation, and therefore can never have a right to destroy, enslave, or designedly to impoverish the Subjects.[3]

From Locke's perspective, the sovereign derived legitimacy from the social contract, but the continued recognition of legitimacy was contingent on protecting the rights of the subjects, such as the right to life and property. Rousseau had a more benign understanding of life under a state of nature and interpreted inequality as a consequence of alienation from nature; individuals could regain lost freedom only by recognising that "general will or general interest should prevail over their own individual one."[4] It is at the intersection of the general will and individual freedom, for Rousseau, that political legitimacy operated. For Jeremy Bentham, "it is the greatest happiness of the greatest number that has been under challenge for some time, not the measure of right and wrong,"[5] but John Stuart Mill located political legitimacy at the conjunction between liberty and authority; an important function of political authority was to protect liberty.

John Rawls advanced a sharp critique of utilitarianism and proceeded to "construct a workable and systematic moral philosophy."[6] For Rawls, public policy based on the utilitarian principle – greatest happiness of the greatest number – often results in unfair outcomes. Drawing upon the social contractual position, Rawls calls for a thought experiment that involves imagining an original position wherein people are located behind a veil of ignorance.[7] Conceptualising societal norms and rules from behind the veil of ignorance will satisfy the following two principles of justice:

> (1) Each person has to have an equal right to the most extensive scheme of equal basic liberties compatible with a similar scheme of liberties for others. (2) social and economic inequalities are to be arranged so that they are both: (a) reasonably expected to be to everyone's advantage, and (b) attached to positions and offices open to all.

Rawls's concerns were about the basic structure or institutional design that makes the least advantaged better off.[8] While the social contract theorists focused on identifying conditions under which a legitimate state is constituted, John Rawls focused on how state institutions "should behave once their legitimacy is established."[9]

For Marxists, political authority that represented the interest of, and constituted by, the working class was the only legitimate form of government and attempts to stimulate revolution to facilitate the emergence of state apparatus defined by the working class were considered legitimate political activity. For many neo-Marxists, the notion of legitimacy itself is problematic because, in liberal democracies, legitimacy could be a consequence of bourgeois hegemony.[10] Therefore, an understanding was required to unpack the institutions and processes through which consent was generated.[11]

Max Weber also went beyond the study of coercive methods to understand modes of securing compliance by political authorities. For Weber, the rulers drew their legitimacy from three types of authority: legal, traditional, and charismatic. Given its legal impersonalism, discipline, and specified functional roles, the rational-legal authority, according to Weber, constituted a distinctive achievement in the progression of history. David Easton rightly pointed out that Weber's analysis focuses substantially on sources of legitimacy and does not give sufficient focus to the "subjects of authority."[12] To fill this analytical lacuna, he propounded his behavioural approach to understanding the "legitimacy problem" wherein "the way the members of society view authority, their structure and mode of exercising power" became the focus of analytical constructs.[13]

The international order and associated legitimation frameworks are also defined by the interests of major powers. Therefore, despite widespread cultural and value diversity across the world, debates relating to power, authority, and legitimacy continue to be based almost exclusively on Western sources and intellectual traditions. However, with the rise of new powers, the established intellectual traditions of understanding legitimacy may get contested. This is because new powers may base their understanding of power, authority, and legitimacy on their respective intellectual traditions, cultural context, and interest. Therefore, power transitions in international politics may also be accompanied by shifts in intellectual traditions pertaining to power, authority, and legitimacy. It is also possible, given prolonged and intense historical engagement with the West, that new approaches to understanding international politics may not be qualitatively different.[14]

2.2.1 Authority and Legitimacy

It is important to recognise that an authority (an individual/organisation) because it is a legally constituted entity does not automatically acquire legitimacy. An ability to deploy expertise for the larger social good constitutes one criterion for an authority to gain legitimacy.[15] Commanding respect for expertise tends to be challenging. For instance, the financial crisis of 2008 raised a question as to whether the technocrats should be the only people making decisions in specialised domains such as financial markets and banking. Referring to the financial crisis, Britain's Queen Elizabeth II, during a visit to the London School of Economics, asked a group of economists: "Why did no one see it coming?"[16] The Queen's query hinted that unquestioned faith in expert opinion may have contributed to the financial crisis. The 2008 crisis demonstrated that fierce debate and rigorous questioning, which should be the hallmark of any democracy, may not have percolated down to all the institutions. The excessive reliance on technocratic advice and its impact on large political systems were also alluded to earlier by Jürgen Habermas.[17] Habermas stated that in many polities, while institutions and procedures could be democratic in form, often people "enjoy the status of passive citizens."[18] Such passivity is not conducive to the efficient functioning of democracies. Ha-Joon Chang notes that the "willingness to challenge professional economists and other experts is a foundation stone of democracy," and he adds, "if all we have to do is to listen to the experts, what is the point of having democracy?"[19] In essence, Ha-Joon Chang calls for deliberative practices to compel "authorities" to act more legitimately.

2.2.2 Actors and Legitimacy

Sovereign states, irrespective of domestic political frameworks, are seen as legitimate representatives of the people they claim to represent. There are a few states now with a monarch as head of state, but their representation on international platforms is premised as representatives of the people rather than alleged divine descendant status. There are non-state actors such as Boko Haram, Al Qaeda, or Islamic State (ISIS) which seek to draw legitimacy through religious rhetoric and symbolism. Such bodies may be perceived as legitimate political actors by small communities spread across various countries, but they are not regarded as such in international politics. In modern international institutions, sovereign states alone are regarded as legitimate.

This definition has been under challenge for some time, partly as a consequence of powerful international corporations and partly because some political NGOs have undermined the sovereignty of the states in which they operate. Taliban, until recently considered a terrorist organisation by the United Nations, has mutated into a recognised player in Afghanistan's politics. While its leadership is still under the UN Security Council sanctions, the US–Taliban agreement states, "Taliban will not provide visas, passports, travel permits, or other legal documents to those who pose a threat to the security of the United States and its allies to enter Afghanistan." After taking complete control of Afghanistan, Taliban is yet to receive formal international recognition from many leading powers. Taliban's instance suggests the need to map the access to power and territorial control whereby an "illegitimate" non-state actor becomes a semi-legitimate political player in the international realm.[20]

Civil war may result in rival factions controlling different spaces in a given country. The absence of a victor results in challenges for the international community in terms of recognising the legitimate government to represent the people of that country on global platforms. The support of powerful countries to rival factions assumes importance. For instance, while the Chinese Communist Party was able to establish control over large parts of the country, US support for Chiang Kai-shek ensured that the status of Taiwan remained ambiguous and a point of acrimony to this date.

Sometimes actors disappear, and new actors emerge in the international arena. The collapse of the Berlin Wall facilitated the reunification of Germany. The disintegration of the Soviet Union resulted in the emergence of new nation-states, and the re-emergence of others that had been conquered by the Romanov empire and then taken over by the Bolsheviks after the revolution. The disintegration of the Soviet Union heralded the end of the Cold War.

2.3 Civil Society, Market, State, and Legitimacy

The collapse of the Berlin Wall and the end of the Cold War constituted a watershed moment in the relationship between civil society, the market, and the state. With the collapse of the communist states, there was a critical evaluation of the legitimate role of the state in economic activity. The pursuit of liberal economic policies with an emphasis on the private sector acquired momentum in many countries. The withdrawal or reduced role of the state in economic activities happened with varying degrees of intensity and through deployment of diverse economic strategies.

Civil society[21] emerged as a democratising force as it enabled the participation of diverse stakeholders in the decision-making process. It should be noted that the civil society existed prior to the end of the Cold War. For instance, the Chipko movement (1973) and Amul cooperatives (1946) in India are examples of thriving civil society initiatives that existed prior to the end of the Cold War. However, the collapse of many (not all) communist countries prompted intense discussions on the need to give greater prominence to civil society organisations even in implementing government schemes. In addition to national planning processes,[22] various multilateral institutions such as the United Nations (UN) and national governments accorded formal consultative status to many non-profit organisations.[23]

However, civil society participation in the government's decision-making was sharply criticised and questions were raised as to "where does civil society derive its legitimacy" to participate in the decision-making process.[24] After all, it was argued that non-governmental organisations (NGOs) were not elected by the people. Moreover, the funding mechanisms of various NGOs dented their credibility. Many NGOs were dependent on funding under the corporate social responsibility mechanism. In fact, many successful business leaders/institutions today have massive development assistance programmes administered through NGOs not just in the industrialised world but also in developing countries. However, there is a concern that big corporations sometimes influence NGO activities in developing countries. Therefore, the policies pertaining to the social sector are not merely responding to the demands from the grassroots but are influenced by big global NGOs which are often supported by large multinational corporations.

On the other hand, the 2008 Financial Crisis buried the idea that an unfettered private sector would result in significant prosperity. The Financial Crisis Inquiry Commission pointed out that the "failures in government regulation, corporate mismanagement and heedless risk-taking by Wall Street," resulted in an avoidable disaster.[25] Many big banks and other financial institutions encountered a severe "crisis of legitimacy as even their right to exist was questioned."[26] Many governments adopted the Keynesian approach, implying that economic crises are not self-correcting and require active government intervention. The use of public funds to bail out the private banks/financial institutions elicited sharp criticism from ordinary people, and there were demands for a greater role of the state in the economy.

Over a decade later, the COVID-19 pandemic has fundamentally altered the discourse on the state and has reiterated its centrality in public welfare. The experiences since 2020 have again demonstrated the undiminished importance of the state apparatus. In the past two to three years, there has been little discussion on the role of civil society to contain the spread of the virus or let the market have a free run to contain the pandemic. Instead, the state apparatus has been constantly interrogated for its pandemic response, which points to its growing relevance. During the pandemic, there was a remarkable expansion of "state-power/government power." Many governments worldwide used diverse tools such as lockdowns, economic stimulus packages, the closing of educational institutions, curfews, and digital tracking of infected patients to combat the spread of COVID-19.[27] As the vaccines rolled out, the governments decided on the modalities for administering the doses. These measures have demonstrated the growing reach of the government during the pandemic and reiterated the legitimacy of the state as a principal institution to promote human welfare.

What role did the characteristics of sovereign states play in responding to the COVID-19 crisis? There is no clear evidence to pronounce judgements as to whether democratic systems or authoritarian systems fared better. While authoritarian regimes may have claimed victory in battling the virus, many others such as South Korea and Japan have also performed well. The COVID-19 pandemic has demonstrated the inherent inefficiencies and dangers associated with large authoritarian political systems which deliberately limit the exchange of information. It is increasingly becoming evident that it is probably easier to identify and report an epidemic outbreak in a country with open participatory political frameworks than in an autocracy. While China has claimed that it has successfully contained the virus in a relatively shorter period, there is a lack of transparency as to when the virus originated in China and the actual number of people affected by it. The rigorous lockdown of Shanghai, with 25 million residents, in March–April 2022 and the reports of food shortages in the city demonstrate that the prevalence of COVID-19 in China continues to be shrouded in mystery.[28] Around the same time, there was also an upsurge in other cities such as Shenzhen, Tianjin, and Jilin, which raised questions regarding the efficacy of Chinese vaccines and inoculation strategies.[29] On the other hand, across the world, there seems to be greater trust in vaccines developed in democratic countries. While one could argue about the relative efficiencies and inefficiencies of authoritarian and democratic states in combatting the pandemic, the debate points out the state's continued relevance in safeguarding human life and promoting welfare.

The importance of the state in economic activities was also reinforced by the growing scepticism that globalisation constituted a force for good. In the 1990s and 2000s, there were calls among the developed countries for speeding up the globalisation process, on the premise that opening up markets in the developing countries will serve as a prudent path to economic well-being.[30] However, three decades later, many developed countries remain hesitant about further opening their economies. Due to the low wage rates and absence of labour regulatory frameworks, many developing countries have become the destination for outsourced jobs. They are also able to export more to developed countries. In this regard, Branko Milanovic contends that the middle classes in emerging countries lost out because of the globalisation process.[31] This has led to a role reversal with developed countries hesitant to open their markets and emerging economies demanding more access to markets of the developed world. It is broadly in this context that the pandemic amplified concerns about an integrated global economy. Since many supply chains traversed through China, the pandemic-related lockdown had a deleterious impact on the global economy. Consequently, anti-globalisation sentiment is gaining ground with references to the need for reduced interdependence by delinking economies and greater emphasis on self-help strategies.[32] However, decoupling the existing supply chain networks is proving to be very difficult, which suggests the need for an inclusive international trading system that values not only efficiency but also resilience.

A robust globalisation process requires healthy international cooperation through multilateral frameworks. Unfortunately, the pandemic has not resulted in enhanced multilateral cooperation. Many sovereign states have focused on providing healthcare and necessary medical equipment to their citizens, which is indeed the primary function of any government. However, many regional organisations and multilateral frameworks have failed in fostering cooperation during the pandemic. For instance, the World Health Organization (WHO) took considerable time to declare COVID-19 a pandemic.[33] Subsequently, the WHO witnessed an intense power struggle to initiate a probe into the origins of the virus. More than 120 countries backed a UN motion to investigate the origins of the virus, despite objections from China.[34] However, only in July 2021, after more than 550,000 people had died globally, the WHO sent a two-member team to "organise an investigation into the origins of the novel coronavirus."[35] Moreover, there is criticism of the organisation that it has expanded the terms of reference of the probe by reiterating China's stance that "the source could well be outside Wuhan."[36] The experience of the WHO during the pandemic is a clear example of power play undermining the legitimacy of an international organisation. Simultaneously, the UN Secretary-General Antonio Guterres' statement that global vaccine distribution is "scandalously unequal" constitutes an admission that international organisations have not been able to generate consensus among major powers on the need for vaccine equity.[37] All through the pandemic, sovereign states placed a premium on self-help strategies, which was evident in the hoarding of vaccines and medical equipment.[38]

While globalisation may have had some pushback in segments such as multilateral cooperation, there continues to be an upward trend in the realm of global information flows. The emergence of digital technology on a global scale has had a significant impact on international politics and the domestic politics of various countries.

2.4 Identity and Democracy: Social Media the Arbitrator of Legitimacy?

Democracy is based on citizens exercising their political choice, which is contingent upon free flow of information. With the advent of social media, there was an explosion in the number of platforms available for accessing and sharing information. Today, anyone with a social media account can broadcast information to the world. Many marginalised groups used free social media platforms to advance their agendas. The relatively less expensive mode of communication and wide reach facilitated conversations on social inequities, LGBTQ rights, and climate change.[39] The information-sharing processes in many countries have been democratised, and diverse ideas getting articulated in a society with greater intensity and multiple narratives/agendas are jostling for public attention. However, on the downside, there is no editorial authority to decide and check the veracity of the information being circulated. Consequently, propaganda and fake news have become the norm. The emergence of social media has also resulted in a new wave of identity politics.

New modes of communication often result in the emergence of new identities or consolidation of the existing identities. In his work *Imagined Communities*, Benedict Anderson points out that the advent of new technology, the printing press, provided Protestantism with tools to contest the established authority of the papacy.[40] Anderson argues that national consciousness in Europe came about because of the "interaction between a system of production and productive relations (capitalism), a technology of communications (print), and the fatality of human linguistic diversity."[41] There have been other instances wherein technology ushered in new political dynamics. For example, the increased levels of literacy and the emergence of regional newspapers in India resulted in the strengthening of regional identities and the emergence of strong regional parties in the 1970s and 1980s.[42] In the past few years, with the emergence of digital media, there has been a simultaneous and vociferous articulation of many identities (national, regional, religious, and linguistic, among others). Consequently, there is now a more significant contestation on identity-related issues such as teaching history in many democracies. For example, there was considerable discussion on the curriculum and school uniforms in various countries such as India, France, Korea, Japan, and Canada.[43] In the US, over 1,000 books dealing with identity issues such as racism and gender were "banned from U.S. classrooms and school libraries" in 2021–2022.[44] The increased frequency and tactics associated with the book ban, to a large extent, are also being fuelled by social media.[45]

On the other hand, digital technologies have enabled people from marginalised backgrounds and non-establishment leaders (such as Barrack Obama) to make their mark in the political process.[46] In addition to the emergence of new political leaders, there was considerable enthusiasm that Information and Communication Technologies (ICT) will significantly expand democratic spaces worldwide in the first decade of this millennium. Larry Diamond referred to the ICT as liberation technology as it "enables citizens to report news, expose wrongdoing, express opinions, mobilise protest, monitor elections, scrutinise government, deepen participation, and expand the horizons of freedom."[47] The use of social media by protestors in Southeast Asia and the Middle East gave hope that increased internet penetration would catalyse democratic development.[48]

In the economic realm, Thomas L. Friedman argued that dramatic technological changes have made it possible to "connect all the knowledge pools in the world together."[49] The flattening of the world was supposed to result in a more egalitarian order as "anyone with smarts, access to Google and a cheap wireless laptop can join the innovation fray."[50] However, amid excitement regarding the positive political impact of the ICT, even liberation technology enthusiast Larry

Diamond expressed apprehensions, though subdued, as to whether the ICT will be able to liberate individuals in authoritarian countries.[51] Subsequently, Clay Shirky also noted that the ability of digital technologies to bring in significant changes in a country would be contingent on the overall political environment, including robust enforcement of fundamental freedoms.[52]

The hope that ICT would erode legitimacy of dictatorial regimes quickly evaporated. Instead, authoritarian regimes such as China use digital technologies to consolidate their hold on the governance process.[53] Further, reports indicate that China exported surveillance technologies to over 63 countries, including many countries with authoritarian regimes such as Myanmar, Iran, and Venezuela.[54] The ICT has shifted the domestic balance of power in favour of authoritarian regimes. With such countries creating robust firewalls to prevent the easy flow of information, there is now a fragmented global internet order in the international realm. There are also concerns that countries are seeking to influence domestic politics in other countries using ICT. For instance, there were reports that Russia hacked and released information and placed advertisements on social media, which damaged the candidature of Hillary Clinton in the 2016 US presidential elections.[55] Similarly, Iran reportedly conducted disinformation campaigns to undermine the image of then Prime Minister Benjamin Netanyahu.[56] There have been reports that Turkey and Pakistan are collaborating to create social media narratives "that suit their geo-political interests in South Asia."[57] The above examples demonstrate that external powers can modulate public opinion during elections in democracies by using social media platforms. The social media interventions can raise questions regarding the legitimacy of the electoral results.

More importantly, it is possible to vitiate social harmony in other countries by generating/encouraging divisive conversations on digital platforms. Sometimes, it is unclear whether the polarisation on social media is a consequence of domestic attitudes or of externally induced polarisation. There is now a concern that ICT may create conditions for increased intolerance in some societies.[58] Paradoxically, the core principle of keeping information flows open often makes many polities vulnerable to targeted communication/social media campaigns that seek to undermine the legitimacy of various governments.

Within sovereign states and on international platforms, social media/digital technologies have emerged as new nodes for seeking legitimacy. Despite many beneficial consequences, the ICT is having a corrosive impact on international politics. Many states and non-state actors are deploying social media to influence domestic politics and social harmony in other countries. Such activities are aimed at denting the legitimacy of governments in the domestic as well as international realms, and in the long run will contribute to a trust deficit in international politics. Further, as noted, the ICT has spawned a new wave of identity politics, which has engendered a parochial approach to public policy and fuelled scepticism about the increased delegation of functions to multilateral organisations. Attempts to delegate more functions to transnational frameworks have often generated accusations about national interests getting undermined. Therefore, there is a pushback against various frameworks of engagement such as the European Union and Trans-Pacific Partnership. So, overall, the rise of identity politics and the weaponisation of social media have added new impediments to international cooperation through multilateral frameworks.

The emergence of information warfare/cyberwarfare has not transformed physical confrontation or war into an anachronism. Deployment of coercive power has been a regular occurrence in different geographies. In 2020, there was a physical confrontation between soldiers of China and India, and an ongoing tense stand-off between the two most populous countries has continued since. The larger East Asian region is dotted with flashpoints such as the South China Sea and the Senkaku Islands. The Russian invasion of Ukraine is also a humanitarian disaster and has altered the security dynamic in Europe. Many continue to see the war as an important tool to protect and promote their national interests.

2.5 War, Peace, and Legitimacy

The primary function of a sovereign state in international politics is the promotion of its national interest. Many sovereign states indulge in continuous pursuit of economic and military power to advance their national interest. What and who represents national interests is open to question, but it is realistic to assume that states have something termed as national interest, and its pursuit on international platforms is considered a legitimate activity. Since the end of World War I, while the use of force was permitted for defensive purposes, it has been illegal to use war as an instrument of foreign policy. This does not mean its deployment has disappeared; after the Cold War, there has been a revival of the debate about the "Just War" theory. Just War theorists have sought to identify principles including *jus ad bellum* (the legality of beginning a war as just cause and right intention) and *jus in bello* (the legality of the means of fighting, such as discrimination, proportionality, and least harmful methods) to validate war as an instrument of state policy with some constraints.[59] The tension between individual rights and rights of supra-individual entities tends to animate Just War theorists such as Michael Walzer.[60] More important, various principles such as right intention, proportionality, and the time/location of war initiation are contentious. John Yoo argues that Walzer's frameworks not only fail to reject utilitarian approaches but also do not deal with questions such as "targeting of civilian property, but without causing civilian casualties" by using advanced technology.[61] There continues to be ambiguity on the legitimacy of even theoretically defensive war as an instrument of state policy.

2.5.1 Institutions and Legitimacy

Attempts were made to negate war initiation and deployment of power through the creation of supra-national institutions. The United Nations is a consequence of a contract among countries to ensure peaceful world order; the Preamble of the UN Charter states,

> we the peoples of the United Nations determined to save succeeding generations from the scourge of war ... agreed to the present Charter of the United Nations and do hereby establish an international organisation to be known as the United Nations.

When the UN acts, its authority is perceived to derive from the consent of sovereign states and its statements the opinion of the world community. Nevertheless, the actions of the UN do not always carry legitimacy for three reasons: first, since the contract did not create a supra-national government and the UN is not the final arbiter of disputes between sovereign states; second, the UN decision-making process has not been truly democratic and inclusive. The Security Council, with five permanent veto powers, fails to satisfy the inclusivity principle. Third, given its non-inclusive character, the UN often acts as a platform for power projection among major powers.

The UN struggles to protect both the sovereignty of the states and human rights, which are inherently contradictory. In order to overcome such challenges, the World Summit Outcome Resolution (2005) mandated that "each individual State has the responsibility to protect its populations from genocide, war crimes, ethnic cleansing and crimes against humanity."[62] The resolution added that if a state failed to perform its sovereign responsibilities, "the international community, through the United Nations, also has the responsibility to use appropriate diplomatic, humanitarian and other peaceful means ... to protect populations."[63] When the Security Council authorised military intervention in Libya in 2011 under the rubric of the Responsibility to Protect, UN legitimacy was compromised when the West interpreted the mandate to permit regime change rather than save civilian lives, which further damaged the UN in the eyes of all but Western powers.[64]

The UN Charter, adopted in 1945, did not use the word "community." In contrast, the UN's 2005 World Summit Outcome Resolution refers to "community" almost a dozen times. In the period 1945–2005, the notion of an international community or society gained greater prominence. While the international system continues to be anarchical, as Hedley Bull notes, a functional society of states came into play with common values/interests and a system of conventions which preserves order.[65] Given the emergence of international society, legitimate attempts to protect/promote national interests require the deployment of non-coercive techniques such as working to protect global public goods and public commons, developing cross-cultural interactions, provision of development aid, and building state capacities in other countries. With the growth of information technologies, inter-governmental institutions, and non-state global organisations, international leadership increasingly "becomes in part a competition for attractiveness, legitimacy, and credibility."[66] As the world witnesses a power shift from the West to East, countries such as China, Japan, and India have scaled up soft power tools including educational exchanges, development aid, development of connectivity networks, and engagement with their diaspora. Emerging non-Western states would like to accrue and deploy their legitimacy to reshape the international order according to their interests.

2.6 Conclusion

The above discussion demonstrated the increasing fluidity of legitimacy in international politics. In the past few decades, there have been dramatic changes in the structure of international politics. World politics shifted from bipolarity to unipolarity to multipolarity. There is now a clamour for a new international order. The attempts to shape international order by non-Western powers will be a prolonged affair. There are many divergences among non-Western powers regarding the trajectory of the proposed new international order. Consequently, the demands to reform the multilateral frameworks have not been concretised. Meanwhile, the UN and WHO's functioning was sharply criticised during the pandemic.

The pandemic may have ushered in shifts in the global balance of power but has reinforced the post-Westphalian world order. First, the legitimacy of the state, the principal unit in international politics, has been reiterated. Second, the anarchical nature of the international system was reinforced as there was a visible demonstration of the limitations of international organisations and multilateral frameworks. Third, there was a greater emphasis on self-help during the pandemic. Paradoxically, while states continue to be principal agents in international politics, the legitimacy of governments/leaders and social harmony have become fragile because of pernicious deployment of new digital technologies. More than ever, there is a need for a robust global order that fosters international cooperation. An international order is defined not only by hierarchical power relations but also by various multilateral institutions and normative frameworks. However, there is considerable diversity in the characteristics of sovereign states, and the recent attempts to promote liberal democratic values as foundational values that should define government-making received considerable backlash. Further, the legitimacy of some democratically elected countries came under the scanner as their conduct with reference to liberal values was less than satisfactory. The wide variety in political systems mandates that the international order is rooted, as James Mayall notes, "in a pluralist international society that must be able to accommodate non-democratic regimes – or those that call themselves democratic but don't meet the western liberal criteria for democratic government."[67]

In the realm of theoretical discussions, utilitarian ideas – the greatest happiness of the greatest number – are increasingly being contested. At their core, various social/political movements with diverse agendas are contesting utilitarian principles. Various sovereign states and multilateral organisations should be aware of the shift in dynamics to buttress their claims to legitimacy in a fast-changing world.

Notes

1 Robert A. Dahl, 'The Concept of Power', *Behavioral Science* 2 (3 July 1957).
2 Ibid.
3 John Locke, Second Treatise, 89–94, 134–42, 212, available at http://press-pubs.uchicago.edu/founders/documents/v1ch17s5.html#note4
4 Anne Deneys-Tunney, 'Rousseau Shows Us That There Is a Way to Break the Chains – from Within', *The Guardian* (15 July, 2012). https://www.theguardian.com/commentisfree/2012/jul/15/rousseau-shows-us-way-break-chain.
5 H. L. A. Hart, 'Bentham and the United States of America', *The Journal of Law & Economics* 19, no. 3 (1976): 547–67. www.jstor.org/stable/725081
6 John Rawls, *A Theory of Justice* (Harvard: Harvard University Press, 1999), xvii.
7 The veil of ignorance implies that "no one knows his place in society, his class position or social status ... his intelligence and strength, and the like" (p.118).
8 Introduction to Rawls: A Theory of Justice, Then and Now (3 July 2020). https://www.youtube.com/watch?v=n6k08C699zI
9 Grace Kiersznowski, 'Rousseau and Rawls on Legitimacy and Justice', *The Classical Journal*. https://theclassicjournal.uga.edu/index.php/2020/05/04/rousseau-and-rawls-on-legitimacy-and-justice/#:~:text=While%20Rousseau's%20theory%20of%20establishing,obtaining%20justice%20in%20contemporary%20states.
10 James Martin, 'Hegemony and the Crisis of Legitimacy in Gramsci', *History of Human Sciences* 10, no. 1 (1997): 37–56.
11 'Hegemony and the Legitimation of the State', in James Martin, *Gramsci's Political Analysis: A Critical Introduction* (London: Palgrave Macmillan, 1998).
12 R.W. Smith, 'The Concept of Legitimacy', *Theoria: A Journal of Social and Political Theory* 35 (October 1970): 17–29.
13 Ibid.
14 Amitav Acharya and Barry Buzan, 'Why is there no Non-Western International Relations Theory? Ten years on', *International Relations of the Asia-Pacific* 17, 3 (2017): 341–370.
15 An authority such as Planning Commission may be legally constituted, but its ability to gain legitimacy is contingent on the respect it commands for its expertise.
16 'The Economic Forecasters' Failing Vision', *Financial Times* (15 December 2008). https://www.ft.com/content/50007754-ca35-11dd-93e5-000077b07658
17 Jürgen Habermas, *Legitimation Crisis* (Cambridge, Polity Press, 1992).
18 Ibid.
19 Ha-Joon Chang, 'Economics Is Too Important to Leave to the Experts', *The Guardian* (30 November 2017). https://www.theguardian.com/commentisfree/2014/apr/30/economics-experts-economists
20 Shakti Sinha, 'US, Taliban and the Doha Agreement: Afghan Government Short-Shrifted', *South Asia Monitor* (10 March 2020). https://southasiamonitor.org/spotlight/us-taliban-and-doha-agreement-afghan-government-short-shrifted. There were instances of conversion from illegitimate to legitimate status during decolonisation, such as the Mozambique Liberation Front (Frelimo) in Mozambique and The People's Movement for the Liberation (MPLA) in Angola.
21 "Civil society ... refers to a wide array of organizations: community groups, non-governmental organizations [NGOs], labour unions, indigenous groups, charitable organizations, faith-based organizations, professional associations, and foundations." See https://www.weforum.org/agenda/2018/04/what-is-civil-society/

22 For instance, India's 8th Five-Year Plan (1992–1997) clearly states that the role of the NGOs should be expanded instead of state officials/inspectors in implementing minimum wage schemes.
23 'The UN and Civil Society', United Nations. https://www.un.org/en/get-involved/un-and-civil-society
24 Saskia Brechenmacher and Thomas Carothers, 'Five Ways to Build Civil Society's Legitimacy around the World', *Carnegie Endowment for International Peace* (9 May 2018). https://carnegieendowment.org/2018/05/09/five-ways-to-build-civil-society-s-legitimacy-around-world-pub-76294
25 Sewell Chan, 'Financial Crisis Was Unavoidable, Inquiry Fails', *The New York Times* (25 January 2011). https://www.nytimes.com/2011/01/26/business/economy/26inquiry.html
26 Blair Sheppard and Ceri Ann Droog, 'A Crisis of Legitimacy', *Strategy+Business* (5 June 2019). https://www.strategy-business.com/article/A-crisis-of-legitimacy
27 'Coronavirus: The World in Lockdown in Maps and Charts', *BBC* (7 April 2020).
28 'Shanghai: Residents "running out of food" in Covid lockdown', *BBC* (7 April 2022). https://www.bbc.com/news/world-asia-china-61019975
29 CK Tan and Grace Li, 'Shanghai's Extended COVID Lockdown Highlights China's Hazy Exit Path', *Nikkei Asia* (5 April 2022). https://asia.nikkei.com/Spotlight/Asia-Insight/Shanghai-s-extended-COVID-lockdown-highlights-China-s-hazy-exit-path
30 Joseph E. Stiglitz, *Globalization and Its Discontents* (New York: W.W. Norton, 2002).
31 Branko Milanovic, *Global Inequality: A New Approach for the Age of Globalization* (Cambridge: Harvard University Press, 2016).
32 'The Coronavirus Is Killing Globalization as We Know It', *Foreign Policy* (12 March 2020).
33 Donald G. McNeil Jr., 'Coronavirus Has Become a Pandemic, W.H.O. Says', *The New York Times* (11 March 2020).
34 Tom Porter, 'More than 120 Countries Are Backing a UN Motion to Investigate the Origins of the Coronavirus, Despite China's Objections', *Business Insider* (18 May 2020).
35 Stephanie Nebehay, 'WHO Advance Team Heads to China to Set Up Probe into Coronavirus Origin', *Reuters* (10 July 2020).
36 Christian Shepherd, 'Chinese Media Step Up Campaign to Muddy Probe into Covid Origins', *Financial Times* (26 November 2020).
37 Antonio Guterres, Twitter Post, March 11, 2022, 07:30 AM IST.
38 Stephanie Nebehay and Josephine Mason, 'WHO Warns against Vaccine Hoarding as Poorer Countries Go Without', *Reuters* (9 December 2021).
39 Bimo Andrio and Rika Safrina, 'The Power of Social Media to Fight Climate Change', *ASEAN Climate Change and energy project* (13 January 2021). https://accept.aseanenergy.org/the-power-of-social-media-to-fight-climate-change/
40 Benedict Anderson, *Imagined Communities* (London: Verso, 2006), 37–46.
41 Ibid., 42–43.
42 Robin Jeffrey, 'Telugu: Ingredients of Growth and Failure', *Economic and Political Weekly* 32, no. 5 (1997): 192–95.; also see K. C. Suri, 'Telugu Desam Party: Rise and Prospects for Future', *Economic and Political Weekly* 39, no. 14/15 (2004): 1481–90.
43 Julian Ryall, 'Japan's "Nationalist" School Books Teach a Different View of History', *DW.COM* (14 April 2022). https://www.dw.com/en/japans-nationalist-school-books-teach-a-different-view-of-history/a-40092325. Stephen Evans, 'Why South Korea is Rewriting Its History Books', *BBC News* (1 December 2015). https://www.bbc.com/news/world-asia-34960878.; Kadish Morris, 'EsiEdugyan: 'At School in Canada, Slavery Was Never Mentioned', *The Guardian* (19 February 2022). https://www.theguardian.com/books/2022/feb/19/esi-edugyan-at-school-in-canada-slavery-was-never-mentioned.
44 Sharon Bernstein, 'U.S. Schools Pull More than 1,000 Book Titles in "Unparalleled" Censorship Bid, Report Finds', *Reuters* (8 April 2022). https://www.reuters.com/

world/us/us-schools-pull-more-than-1000-book-titles-unparalleled-censorship-bid-report-2022-04-07/
45 Elizabeth A. Harris and Alexandra Alter, 'Book Ban Efforts Spread across the U.S.', *The New York Times* (30 January 2022). https://www.nytimes.com/2022/01/30/books/book-ban-us-schools.html
46 'Digital Political Fundraising: How Obama Mapped a Course for Future Candidates', *Digital Media Solutions* (19 April, 2019).https://insights.digitalmediasolutions.com/articles/digital-fundraising-political-campaigns
47 Larry Diamond, 'Liberation Technology', *Journal of Democracy* 21, 3(July 2010):70. https://www.journalofdemocracy.org/wp-content/uploads/2012/01/Diamond-21-3.pdf
48 Michael L. Best and Keegan W. Wade, 'The Internet and Democracy: Global Catalyst Or Democratic Dud?', *The Berkman Society for Internet and Society at Harvard Law School* (October 2005). https://cyber.harvard.edu/wg_home/uploads/503/12-InternetDemocracy.pdf
49 Thomas L. Friedman, 'It's a Flat World, After All', *The New York Times Magazine* (3 April 2005). https://www.nytimes.com/2005/04/03/magazine/its-a-flat-world-after-all.html
50 Ibid.
51 Larry Diamond, 'Liberation Technology', *Journal of Democracy* 21, no. 3 (July 2010): 70. https://www.journalofdemocracy.org/wp-content/uploads/2012/01/Diamond-21-3.pdf
52 Clay Shirky, 'The Political Power of Social Media: Technology, the Public Sphere, and Political Change', *Foreign Affairs* 90, no. 1 (2011): 28–41.
53 Ross Andersen, 'The Panopticon Is Already Here', *The Atlantic* (September 2020). https://www.theatlantic.com/magazine/archive/2020/09/china-ai-surveillance/614197/
54 'China exports AI surveillance tech to over 60 countries: report', Nikkei Asia (16 December, 2019). https://asia.nikkei.com/Business/China-tech/China-exports-AI-surveillance-tech-to-over-60-countries-report#:~:text=TOKYO%20(Kyodo)%20%2D%2D%20Chinese%20companies,by%20a%20U.S.%20think%20tank
55 Abigail Abrams, 'Here's What We Know So Far about Russia's 2016 Meddling', *Time* (18 April 2019). https://time.com/5565991/russia-influence-2016-election/
Also see Scott Shane, 'These Are the Ads That Russia Nought on Facebook in 2016', *The New York Times* (1 November 2017). https://www.nytimes.com/2017/11/01/us/politics/russia-2016-election-facebook.html; Deepa Seetharaman, 'Russian-Backed Facebook Accounts Staged Events Around Divisive Issues', *The Wall Street Journal* (30 October 2017). https://www.wsj.com/articles/russian-backed-facebook-accounts-organized-events-on-all-sides-of-polarizing-issues-1509355801
56 Tom Bateman, 'Iran Accused of Showing Israel Discontent with a Fake Jewish Facebook Group', *BBC* (3 February 2022). https://www.bbc.com/news/world-middle-east-60229146
57 'Turkey-Pakistan Creates Joint Media Strategy for Geopolitical Goals in South Asia Alleges Report', *The Economic Times* (14 April 2022). https://economictimes.indiatimes.com/news/defence/turkey-pakistan-creates-joint-media-strategy-for-geopolitical-goals-in-south-asia-alleges-report/printarticle/81226546.cms
58 Emmanuel Akinwotu, 'Facebook's Role in Myanmar and Ethiopia Under New Scrutiny', *The Guardian* (7 October 2021). https://www.theguardian.com/technology/2021/oct/07/facebooks-role-in-myanmar-and-ethiopia-under-new-scrutiny
59 Brian Orend, 'Just and Lawful Conduct in War: Reflections on Michael Walzer', *Law and Philosophy* 20, no. 1 (2001): 1–30. www.jstor.org/stable/3505049
60 Graham Parsons, 'The Incoherence of Walzer's Just War Theory', *Social Theory and Practice* 38, no. 4 (2012): 663–88. www.jstor.org/stable/23558766
61 John Yoo, 'Michael Walzer, Just and Unjust Wars (1977)', *Hoover Institution* (6 February 2019). https://www.hoover.org/research/michael-walzer-just-and-unjust-wars-1977

62 'Resolution adopted by the General Assembly on 16 September 2005', *General Assembly, United Nations* A/RES/60/1 (24 October 2005). https://www.un.org/en/development/desa/population/migration/generalassembly/docs/globalcompact/A_RES_60_1.pdf
63 Ibid.
64 'S/RES/1973 (2011)', *United Nations Security Council* (17 March 2011). https://www.undocs.org/S/RES/1973%20
65 Andrew Linklater, 'The English School', in Scott Burchill, Andrew Linklater, Richard Devetak (et al), *Theories of International Relations* (New York: Palgrave Macmillan, 2005).
66 Joseph S. Nye Jr., 'The Benefits of Soft Power', *Business Research for Business Leaders* (2 August 2004). https://hbswk.hbs.edu/archive/the-benefits-of-soft-power
67 Personal conversations. Also see James Mayall, *Nationalism and International Society* (Cambridge: Cambridge University Press, 2011).

Bibliography

Acharya, Amitav and Barry Buzan. 'Why Is There No Non-Western International Relations Theory? Ten Years On'. *International Relations of the Asia-Pacific* 17, no. 3 (2017): 341–370.

Anderson, Benedict. *Imagined Communities*. London: Verso, 2006.

Bernstein, Sharon. 'U.S. Schools Pull More Than 1,000 Book Titles in "unparalleled" Censorship Bid, Report Finds'. *Reuters* (8 April 2022).

Chang, Ha-Joon. 'Economics Is Too Important to Leave to the Experts'. *The Guardian* (30 November 2017).

Dahl, Robert A.. 'The Concept of Power'. *Behavioral Science* 2, 3 (July 1957).

Diamond, Larry. 'Liberation Technology'. *Journal of Democracy* 21, no. 3 (July 2010): 70.

Friedman, L. Thomas. 'It's a Flat World, After All'. *The New York Times Magazine* (3 April 2005).

Habermas, Jürgen. *Legitimation Crisis*. Cambridge: Polity Press, 1992.

Hart, H. L. A. 'Bentham and the United States of America'. *The Journal of Law & Economics* 19, no. 3 (1976): 547–67.

Jeffrey, Robin. 'Telugu: Ingredients of Growth and Failure'. *Economic and Political Weekly* 32, no. 5 (1997): 192–195.

Linklater, Andrew. 'The English School', in Scott Burchill, Andrew Linklater, Richard Devetak (et al). *Theories of International Relations*. New York: Palgrave Macmillan, 2005.

Mayall, James. *Nationalism and International Society*. Cambridge: Cambridge University Press, 2011.

Milanovic, Branko. *Global Inequality: A New Approach for the Age of Globalization*. Cambridge: Harvard University Press, 2016.

Nye, S. Joseph Jr. 'The Benefits of Soft Power'. *Business Research for Business Leaders* (2 August 2004).

Parsons, Graham. 'The Incoherence of Walzer's Just War Theory'. *Social Theory and Practice* 38, no. 4 (2012): 663–688.

Rawls, John. *A Theory of Justice*. Harvard: Harvard University Press, 1999.

Shirky, Clay. 'The Political Power of Social Media: Technology, the Public Sphere, and Political Change'. *Foreign Affairs* 90, no. 1 (2011): 28–41.

Smith, RW. 'The Concept of Legitimacy'. *Theoria: A Journal of Social and Political Theory* 35 (October 1970).

Stiglitz, E.Joseph. *Globalization and Its Discontents*. New York: W.W. Norton, 2002.

The Berkman Society for Internet and Society at Harvard Law School (October 2005).

'The Coronavirus Is Killing Globalization as We Know It'. *Foreign Policy* (12 March 2020).

Yoo, John. 'Michael Walzer, Just and Unjust Wars (1977)'. Hoover Institution (6 February 2019).

3
THE VIEW FROM THE UNITED NATIONS

Mats Berdal and James Mayall

The story of the political life of the United Nations has been, to a considerable extent, the story of a continuous effort to improvise around and to sidestep, the obstacle of fundamental great power differences, and to find substitutes for the great power unanimity which had originally been intended to be the main driving force of the new organization.

– *Sir Brian Urquhart,* A Life in Peace and War

3.1 Introduction

This chapter presents a view from the United Nations of the increasingly troubled relationship between the exercise of power in international politics and the legitimacy of the institutions – primarily the UN itself – that were set up after 1945 to provide a framework for international order. It does so by asking three further questions: first, was the organisation's legitimacy strengthened or weakened by the end of the Cold War; second, does the rise of new power centres, primarily in the East, reduce the power of the UN; third, does the general retreat from multilateralism consign the UN to political irrelevance in the future?

The goal of the United Nations and other organisations created after World War II was to promote transnational cooperation and promote peace among nations. There were debates about whether this kind of cooperation could be achieved while maintaining cultural and political diversity or it would require a high degree of value consensus and similarity across countries and their regimes. In other words, was the UN an attempt to impose cultural hegemony and Western concepts and practices on the world? Or was it an attempt to create an organisation that could help diverse nations build minimal standards of acceptable behaviour that would counteract the use of raw power by states?

DOI: 10.4324/9781003385233-3

Another issue was whether the UN could achieve legitimacy if it could not impose laws. To this, we argue that legitimacy and law are not synonyms. Legitimacy is about political acceptability and the expectation that attempts will be made to resolve political disputes through consensus and negotiation. As an organisation of sovereign states, the UN could not impose laws to achieve its goals, but it could establish and maintain its legitimacy. This was because its legitimacy historically depended on its ability to mitigate a large array of threats to humanity which are, themselves, understood differently by the member states.

Maintaining such legitimacy requires a continuous process of adjusting the activities of the organisation in relation to changing threats, and it involves the use of power and influence by member states and UN staff to shape the agenda for responding to those threats. We will look at the ways that power and legitimacy were negotiated over time in response to changes in the international order since 1945. We start with the questions as they were present during the establishment of the UN. Then we consider changes in the source of UN legitimacy as they were enacted at the end of the Cold War and changes that are happening in response to new centres of power, the resurgence of authoritarian governments, and a general retreat from multilateralism.

3.2 The 1945 Settlement

In 1945 the wartime alliance between the Western democracies and the USSR was already fraying but held together long enough to allow the creation of a successor organisation to the League of Nations and to secure agreement on the UN Charter. This story has been told many times, and there is no need to repeat it here. These days it is fashionable for critics of the UN system to represent it as a kind of "continuation of empire by other means," an instrument for the preservation of Western hegemonic interests. There is no doubt, as Mark Mazower has powerfully argued, that the basic architecture of the UN was a Western design.[1] Nonetheless, it will be useful to make three points about the 1945 settlement that have a direct bearing on the central issue with which this book is concerned. They also testify to the organisation's relevance and legitimacy beyond the West.

First, there was general agreement that if the grand alliance was to underpin a realistic system of collective security, the vital interests of its members had to be protected – hence the inclusion of the veto for the five permanent members of the Security Council (P5). Although the Western powers – and particularly the United States – saw the UN as a framework for a liberal world order, paradoxically the onset of the Cold War, which marginalised the organisation's role in the security field, helped to establish its political legitimacy in the world beyond the West and the Soviet Union.

Second, the political legitimacy of the UN essentially rested on the core value at the heart of the Charter, namely sovereignty and its twin implications that international cooperation had to depend on non-interference in domestic affairs of other states and respect for territorial integrity. It is true that the Preamble to the UN Charter also "reaffirmed faith in fundamental human rights, in the dignity and worth of the human person, in the equal rights of men and women and of nations large and small." Nonetheless, the emphasis placed on sovereignty made the organisation attractive to existing states that could not claim great power status, and more importantly, to anti-colonial nationalists everywhere. The fact that for entirely different reasons the two superpowers were initially strong supporters of "the right of all peoples" to self-determination no doubt hastened the dismemberment of the European overseas empires, but the new states themselves saw the UN as the guarantor of their independence, and as a platform on which they could advance and protect their interests.

Third, Cold War rivalry inevitably penetrated and constrained the work of the UN. In the early period Soviet vetoes were a frequent occurrence as in the last 15 years or so were American and Western ones. Perhaps this symmetry helped, as broadly speaking the balance between power and legitimacy held until its end. Only one state – Indonesia – ever left the organisation and that only very briefly.[2] The UN did much useful work finding a way to ease intractable problems left over from World War II such as the disposal of the Italian colonies, it developed the theory and practice of peacekeeping as a safety valve to prevent the escalation of great power conflict where it might otherwise have occurred, and under the influence of the non-Western majority, the General Assembly was on occasions able to outflank Western opposition to its priority concerns – as for example with the establishment of the United Nations Conference on Trade and Development (UNCTAD) in 1964.

The creation of UNCTAD is a particularly telling case of how the balance between power and legitimacy was maintained throughout the Cold War. The Bretton Woods institutions[3] which were set up in 1944 and the 1947 General Agreement on Tariffs and Trade (GATT) were affiliated with the UN but operated at arm's-length from it. The position of the Western powers, led by the United States, was that this framework was all that was needed to underwrite an open world economy. The majority of UN member states disagreed and believed that if they were to benefit from international trade and investment, a new international institution was needed "to level the playing field." Despite the fact that the North-South divide on this issue was in reality a South-West divide, the majority was strongly supported by the Eastern bloc and in the end the West gave way. The UNCTAD still exists, but since 1981 its impact on the world economy has been minimal. Indeed, it may be no exaggeration to say that the adoption of supply-side economic doctrines by the American and British administrations in the first instance, followed by the IMF, World Bank, and the Organisation for Economic Co-operation and Development (OECD), marked the point when legitimacy began to drain away from the UN system, at least so far as its economic role is concerned. This statement is open to challenge since several countries including China and India flourished in the era of economic deregulation, but their success had little to do with the UN. As we shall see, the story in the political and security fields is even more ambiguous.

3.3 The End of the Cold War and Its Impact on Multilateralism

The answer to the first question – whether the end of the Cold War strengthened or weakened the UN's legitimacy – is more ambiguous because despite a period of intense activity and enthusiasm at the outset, which was predictably followed by serious disenchantment in the wake of a succession of failures, including the responses to the Rwandan genocide of 1994, the massacre in the allegedly safe haven of Srebrenica in 1995, and the paralysis in the Security Council caused by the divisions amongst the P5 over the invasion of Iraq in 2003, the level of UN activity in the political and security sectors has continued to be high by historical standards as has participation in these activities by African, Asian, and Latin American countries.

Initially, the end of the Cold War was seen as a major vindication of the principles of international solidarity. Not only was the UN used by the Russians to signal their willingness to collaborate with the United States and the international community as a whole, but the Iraqi invasion of Kuwait, a blatant attempt by one member state to absorb another, was repulsed under a Chapter 7 resolution without serious argument. When the UNSC met for the first time in its history at the level of Heads of State and Government in January 1992, it commissioned the then Secretary-General, Boutros Boutros-Ghali, to produce his *Agenda for Peace*. The sense of promise generated by the end of the Cold War and the Kuwait war is reflected throughout this document. To take an example almost at random, the Secretary-General suggested that "The nations and peoples of the United Nations are fortunate in a way that those of the League of Nations were not. We have been granted a second chance to create the world of our Charter that they were denied."[4] Although the Agenda was overly optimistic and was later modified, in a Supplement designed to make its lofty objectives more realistic, it appeared to commit the UN to build a democratic order and to restore the organisation's central role in the architecture of global security. The Supplement – its publication fell between the Rwandan genocide and the Srebrenica massacre in Bosnia – was not to revise the Agenda for Peace but, in its own words, "to highlight selectively certain areas where unforeseen, or only partly foreseen, difficulties have arisen and where there is a need for the Member States to take the hard decisions."[5]

During the period between the end of the Cold War and the mid-1990s, both the number of peacekeeping missions and the number of personnel involved expanded exponentially, as did the roles that the peacekeepers were asked to perform and the mandates under which they operated. In January 1988, five peacekeeping operations were in existence, deploying 9,570 personnel. By the time the Supplement to the Agenda for Peace was published in January 1995, 21 new operations had been established with nearly 80,000 peacekeepers deployed in the field. At first sight the conclusion that can be drawn from all this activity would seem to be that both multilateralism and the legitimacy of the UN system had been strengthened by the end of the Cold War. This conclusion is reinforced by the observation that the number of participating countries also expanded significantly, many from the Global South but also from the membership of the UNSC itself, including the P5.

Unfortunately, the impact of liberal internationalism on the multilateral order and the legitimacy of the UN system itself is not as clear cut as this account suggests. From the start there were considerable misgivings in the General Assembly and amongst the non-permanent members of the Security Council about the possibility that the emphasis that the major Western powers and their allies increasingly placed on a raft of liberal internationalist values masked their real objective, namely to embed their continued domination of the international order.[6] For the most part they accepted the proposition that the UN should play a central role in providing security to the international community. Indeed, they still do. Participation also accords with the preferred security architecture of the Non-Aligned Movement, to which many of them belong, to the extent that it is still relevant, and to the priorities of most regional organisations which certainly are.

The tension between theoretical support and active participation in UN peacekeeping and continued suspicion of Western objectives can be illustrated from both ends of the post-Cold War period. First, the Western powers would not risk a return to the Security Council to seek a Chapter 7 resolution to protect the Kurds when they rebelled against Saddam Hussein after the first Gulf War. The reason was that they feared inviting Russian and Chinese vetoes and the predictable opposition of India and Zimbabwe amongst the non-permanent members; instead they relied on an earlier wide-ranging humanitarian resolution. With the help of Turkey, a NATO member state, which had its own agenda for containing the PKK, the Iraqi Kurdish opposition party, the Western powers were effectively able to partition Iraq from the air, using Turkish airfields, and so to protect the Iraqi Kurds. Practitioners would be likely to argue, with some justification, that it got the job done, although hardly in a way that was likely to reassure the majority of member states that UN decisions were grounded in multilateralism.

The second example is drawn from the Canadian-led effort to rescue the principle of humanitarian intervention after some of the peace-building failures of the 1990s.[7] The high drama of 9/11 followed closely by the American attack on Afghanistan and the second Gulf War drove public interest in the debate on humanitarian intervention underground, although it continued at the diplomatic level and within the UN. Eventually, at the Millennium Summit in 2005, the final "Outcome Document" adopting "the Responsibility to Protect" (R2P) was passed unanimously.[8] The negotiations that led to this outcome were highly contested. No details were provided as to how R2P might be operationalised, though the document did make it clear that any collective action under the R2P would have to be vested in the Council under Chapter 7. It seems safe to assume that the unanimous vote was at least partly reflective of the political possibilities of grandstanding – a kind of global photo opportunity – rather than any widespread conviction.

Admittedly, this judgement may be unduly harsh.⁹ It is difficult to know for certain the level of support that exists for R2P since within the UN itself and amongst professional experts on UN peace missions, it is widely held that the language surrounding the principle has seeped into the mind-set of those drafting peace-building resolutions and indeed into the operating assumptions of those charged with executing them on the ground. This is the normal process, so it is argued, by which the soft law of UN resolutions gradually hardens into customary law. There is some circumstantial evidence to support this claim. The Rwandan genocide and Srebrenica massacre created a "never again" moment, which sparked the Canadian-led commission and culminated in Kofi Annan's speech to the General Assembly in 1999, when he presented his Annual Report in the aftermath of the Kosovo intervention and stressed that sovereignty must never again be allowed to block or trump an effective response – if necessary involving the use of force – to mass atrocity crimes (welcoming what he called a "developing international norm in favour of intervention to protect civilians from wholesale slaughter").¹⁰

The long-term impact of this "normative turn" for UN legitimacy is obscure, if only as a consequence of the Libyan intervention in 2011, when a high-profile mission was mounted under the R2P principle, ostensibly to save civilian lives. The opposition of Russia and China, but also of two non-permanent members, India and Brazil, was overcome only after the Arab League had indicated their support, thus reversing the traditional interpretation of Chapter 8 of the Charter, which allows regional organisations a role in support of the UN rather than making it mandatory. In the event, the Western powers exceeded their mandate in supporting regime change, with predictable results. The Russians and Chinese, who had abstained in the resolution vote out of respect for the Arab League's support, now openly criticised the Western powers, accusing them of using the resolution as a cover for regime change, while South Africa, which had originally voted in favour of the resolution, joined them in criticising Western policies and intentions.

On the other hand, the governments of none of these countries objected when the UN sought to protect fleeing civilians from the civil war in South Sudan in 2013, nor when the UNSC increased the size of the mission; nor again did they object to the setting up of a mission in the Central African Republic in 2014 whose main purpose was concern about mass atrocities and the abuse of human rights. The United States and France have been urging the UN to leave the Democratic Republic of the Congo since 2015, but perhaps because they fear that the cure would be worse than the disease they have not pressed, their opposition to the point of vetoing the resolutions under which the operation continues to operate.

Despite what happened in Libya and continuing suspicion about Western motives, there are now more UN peacekeepers deployed across the world than there were in 1995 and their principal function is to "protect civilians." Nor have Russia, China, and the General Assembly non-Western majority fundamentally objected to the shift towards the Protection of Civilians (POC) as a core mandate for UN peacekeepers.[11]

Two final points may be relevant to assessing the long-term impact of R2P on UN legitimacy. First, despite the belief of many critics that Western policy in Libya killed the principle stone dead, it remains unclear whether regime change was pre-planned. Even Hardeep Singh Puri, the Indian Ambassador to the UN at the time, who was privy to Security Council internal discussions, and was one of the most ardent critics of the West, concluded that "the jury is still out on whether regime change was the original objective."[12] Nonetheless, the resolution allowed NATO to become a party to the Libyan civil war and clearly damaged it, as the former diplomat Lord David Hannay had warned the British government that it would.[13] Second, the assumption of global solidarity in relation to UN legitimacy may be becoming increasingly anachronistic. The main growth area for UN peace operations is in Africa, the one region where there is a formal partnership agreement between the regional organisation, the African Union, and the UN. The organisation's legitimacy in the West itself and in parts of Asia may be more open to question. Whatever else, therefore, the Libyan intervention can hardly be claimed as a major vindication of the multilateral order.

3.4 The UN in the 21st Century: Solidarist Imperative or a Global Dystopia?

At first sight the need for increased global cooperation would seem to be self-evident. Most of the world's major security, economic, and social problems such as the transmission of infectious diseases or climate change cannot be contained within the frontiers of a single state. The Specialised Agencies – in particular UNHCR, World Food Programme, UNICEF, WHO, and also the Intergovernmental Panel on Climate Change – have performed vital functions for international society in this context. The problems with which they deal are mostly also interlinked, e.g., both local civil wars and the global economic downturn caused by the ongoing pandemic have increased the flow of international refugees – the UN has, for example, looked after around 13 million refugees across the Middle East. By the same token, these problems have also fed the anti-multilateral backlash and the rise of new variants of exclusive nationalism.

One should not exaggerate the formal international order's loss of legitimacy. When the General Assembly debated the Russian invasion of Ukraine on 2 March 2022, only four countries (North Korea, Syria, Belarus, and Eritrea) supported Russia in opposing the resolution.[14] On the security front, as we have seen, the UN continues to deploy more troops on international peacekeeping and building missions than at any time in its history. And while there has been often well-deserved criticism of the assumption that liberal internationalist values are universal, few states are prepared to challenge openly the proposition that international society should be based on a respect for human rights and dignity. Although Russia's invasion of Ukraine in February 2022 has brought relations among permanent members of the Council to a new post-Cold War low, it has not led to a complete paralysis, with members still finding areas of common interest in a "split world." Thus, in mid-March 2022 the Council extended the mandate for the UN missions in both South Sudan and Afghanistan for another year, notwithstanding the tensions generated by Russia's unambiguous violation of the Charter's order-related principles.

The problem is that the UN system is increasingly viewed, particularly perhaps in the West, in institutional terms as just another set of professional experts, who are more answerable to political elites and their interests than to the needs and welfare of ordinary people. Indeed, the greatest danger to the UN system may be that it is increasingly running on borrowed time, that is on the institutional capital built up over the past 70 years rather than political vision or commitment. International institutions seldom collapse altogether, and in the case of the UN its networks of expertise over a vast range of human activities should be sufficient to ensure that it remains an influential force in world politics over the foreseeable future. But will it be sufficient to regenerate deep political support for predominantly Western values that have dominated the UN since the beginning, and in an even more extreme form since the end of the Cold War? Even within Western Europe, the most integrated confederation of states in the modern world, the retreat from multilateralism is palpable. After all *realpolitik* has as deep, if not deeper, roots in the West than in any other region of the world.

The answer to this question depends in part on leadership, which needs to be more proactive and visionary than it has been in the recent past and is at the moment. This in turn requires both the great powers to be more imaginative in who they are prepared to accept as Secretary-General and member states in general to renew their political commitment to exploring and developing, what the second Secretary-General, Dag Hammarskjold called "the possibilities of substantive action by the United Nations in a split world."[15]

The split may be along different lines now, but the world remains as divided as ever. If the Western powers were serious about revitalising the UN and restoring faith in the multilateral order, they would also need to engage in much more sensitive economic diplomacy with China and other Asian states than they have done up to now. The issue of funding has a crucial bearing on the perception of how power is exercised within the UN and its affiliated organisations and therefore of the system's overall legitimacy. Historically, the bulk of the peacekeeping budget has been met by the United States, supported by a few other major countries,[16] as it has for the regular assessed contributions for the organisation as a whole.[17]

At the Millennium Summit, the reform of the UN finances was widely debated. One proposal for example was that no country should pay more than 4 per cent of the budget and that this would reflect a more accurate representation of the distribution of world income and so demonstrate the international community's genuine commitment to the multilateral system. Like the reform of the UNSC it did not happen: not only were the majority of countries that presently pay only a fraction of the budget reluctant to increase their contributions, but the United States in particular was not interested in reducing its influence over the organisation which is an inevitable by-product of its financial power.

What remains unclear is what impact the rapidly increasing gap between the super-rich and everybody else both within countries and between them since the 2008 financial crisis has had on the legitimacy of the organisation. Perhaps given the importance of its work around the world, the fact that a private organisation, the Bill and Melinda Gates Foundation, is now the second largest funder of the WHO after the United States, whose former President Donald Trump, initiated proceedings to withdraw the United States from the organisation, will not adversely damage its international standing and reputation. But since the Foundation is also the major funder of the Vaccine Alliance, at the very least it will provide ammunition to the strong, although largely censored, anti-authoritarian opposition movements that exist across the Western world although less obviously elsewhere. Paradoxically, much of the Western criticism of China's alleged design for a new Sino-centric world order[18] revolves around the belief that China wishes to close down open societies in favour of an intrusive and domineering state-based world order, precisely the charge that Western "anti-vax" and libertarian dissidents level against their own governments.

Whatever may be the People's Republic of China's (PRC) long-term objectives for the international order, for the time being the PRC has continued to work within the UN system. Indeed, Beijing has gradually become more assertive in the UN and its affiliated agencies. For example, although China, which has a seat on the IMF Executive Board, made no public criticism of the surprising decision announced in August 2021 not to include Afghanistan in the distribution of Special Drawing Rights to offset the costs of the COVID-19 pandemic,[19] it did criticise the freezing of Afghan assets in the explanation of its abstention in the voting on UN Security Council Resolution 2395. A further example is cited in a Brookings article published in 2020 in which the author acknowledged that China had been both active and largely compliant in the IMF, World Bank, and World Trade Organization (WTO). He also argued, sensibly enough, that China should be offered a more prominent role – commensurate with its relative economic power – in the governance of these institutions. Unhappily, he also linked this proposal to a demand that China should give up claiming the exemptions from great power responsibility due to a developing country, which hardly seems the most subtle way of sending a diplomatic signal.[20]

What are the implications of these observations for the UN itself and its affiliated agencies? An optimist might argue that it provides evidence of the continued relevance of the world body, in that China has continued to engage with it, and has even apparently used the back channels that it provides to hold bilateral discussions with the United States, for example, over the potential threat of Taliban inspired international terrorism in Afghanistan. It is even tempting to consider the possibility that the rise of China has restored the balance between power and legitimacy that prevailed during the Cold War. As then, international cooperation will depend on a pluralist interpretation of the international community as defined at the beginning of this chapter. As during the Cold War also, this will not prevent all sides trumpeting the superiority of their own ideological positions; it merely means that behind the rhetorical posturing, when desirable – or perhaps more accurately when unavoidable – serious diplomacy will continue within the United Nations.

This optimistic view needs to be tempered with a measure of historical realism. UN legitimacy during the Cold War was not achieved as the result of a process of rational debate and consensus. It emerged from the confrontation of the superpowers and their respective allies in international crises in which the United Nations was either directly or indirectly involved. The most dramatic example occurred during the United Nations Operation in the Congo (ONUC) between 1960 and 1964, when African politics and superpower rivalry became intertwined and the Cold War was effectively imported into the UN system. On that occasion the Soviet Premier, Nikita Khrushchev, accused the Secretary-General of siding with the colonial powers and demanded he be replaced by a troika representing the Western and Eastern blocs and the Non-Aligned. This proposal failed to attract significant support and the balance between power and legitimacy within the organisation eventually consolidated after the bilateral Cuban Missile crisis between the two superpowers in October 1962.

Pessimists will maintain that this analogy is false. They are likely to argue that not only has the political landscape changed beyond recognition, but the analogy ignores fundamental differences between the political culture and strategic vision of the Soviet Union and China. For thinkers such as Francis Fukuyama,[21] the Cold War was essentially a European civil war over the legacy of the Enlightenment. Both liberal democrats and Marxists accepted the concept of universal values that transcended cultural and national variations and experiences. The essential difference was that the Marxists were wedded to a historical teleology and the liberals were not. The contrast is illustrated by the clarion call of the 1848 Communist Manifesto, "Workers of the world unite you have nothing to lose but your chains," measured against the timeless idea of universal human rights as spelled out in the 1948 Universal Declaration. The original Soviet position at the United Nations was to oppose the Declaration on the grounds that human rights were an example of "bourgeois morality" and would only be possible under communism. Faced with the opposition of the majority of member states, the Soviet Union and its allies abandoned this position and quietly signed the two 1966 Conventions,[22] a further example of the way the UN system balanced between the demands of power politics and institutional legitimacy.

Historically, China had not been deeply involved in this Western debate about the nature of universal enlightenment. Its traditional view of the world was both Sino-centric and hierarchical. Its experience of engagement with the

West was one of humiliation during the 19th and 20th centuries. It is perhaps not surprising, therefore, that at the end of the civil war in 1949, Mao Tse-tung made no mention of international cooperation on a socialist or any other basis. Instead he announced that "the Chinese People have stood up," a legacy that China's critics maintain Xi Jinping is now using to craft a new international order "with Chinese characteristics" that is fundamentally opposed to the values on which the UN is based. On this view, the range of regional and wider economic institutions that act as an irresistible pole of attraction for countries in the Global South, together with China's ambitious programme of port construction within the Asia Pacific region, and increasingly also further afield, is a modern version of the tributary system that harks back to the golden age of the middle kingdom. Similarly, pessimists will point out that China's participation in the existing international order is always on its own terms and strictly tactical. Thus its signature and ratification of the UN Law of the Sea Convention has not prevented it from asserting its sovereignty over the East and South China seas and – at least in theory – denying the principle of the right of free navigation to other states. China, we are frequently told, is good at playing a long game. On this view we can expect that Beijing will continue to work within the existing system so long as it is in its interests to do so. By the same token, once its economic position is unassailable, it will be content to see the UN wither on the vine and to sink into political irrelevance.

3.5 Conclusion

We must hope that this dystopic vision of the UN's future can be avoided. The reason for spelling it out in some detail refers back to one of the operating assumptions on which this chapter is based, namely that in any international order it is the great powers that will shape the system more than they are shaped by it, and that this will hold regardless of whether the underlying values of the system are solidarist or pluralist. It would seem to follow that the idea of a neo-Kantian order of like-minded states of the kind favoured by many liberal internationalists since the end of the Cold War must be ruled out if the UN is to survive.

This does not mean that the UN, or even the values on which it was originally founded, either will or should be consigned to long-term irrelevance. Hypocrisy, it has been said, is the price that vice pays to virtue. All politicians are prone to exaggerate their own virtues and the vices of their opponents. In the past international crises have frequently occurred, which have required the UN to contain, if not often to resolve them. It is implausible to think that this will not happen again in the future. It is worth ending therefore by pondering the wisdom of the famous verdict on the UN offered more than 35 years ago by the veteran Irish diplomat, the late Connor Cruise O'Brien:

> The United Nations cannot do anything, and never could; it is not an animate entity or agent. It is a place, a stage, a forum and a shrine … a place to

which powerful people can repair when they are fearful about the course on which their own rhetoric seems to be propelling them.[23]

Notes

1. Mark M. Mazower, *No Enchanted Palace: The End of Empire and the Ideological Origins of the United Nations* (Princeton, NJ: Princeton University Press, 2009).
2. Indonesia left in 1965 during its confrontation with Malaysia and in protest with Malaysia assuming a non-permanent seat on the Security Council. After the coup later that year, Indonesia rejoined and was deemed merely to have suspended full cooperation with the UN for a few months.
3. The International Monetary Fund and the International Bank for Reconstruction and Development, familiarly known as the World Bank.
4. *An Agenda for Peace*, A/47/277-S/24111 (17 June 1992), paragraph 20.
5. *Supplement to An Agenda for Peace*, A/50/60-S/1995/1 (25 January 1995), paragraph 6.
6. See, for example, Chinmaya R. Gharekhan, *The Horseshoe Table* (New Delhi: Pearson Education, 2021).
7. ICIISS (International Commission on Intervention and State Sovereignty), *The Responsibility to Protect: Report of the International Commission on Intervention and State Sovereignty* (Ottawa: International Development Research Centre, 2001).
8. '2005 World Summit Outcome', UNGA A/RES/60/1, 25 October 2005.
9. For a full and measured assessment of the origins and impact of R2P, see Mats Berdal, 'Revisiting the "Responsibility to Protect" and the Use of Force', *Asian Journal of Peacebuilding* 7, No. 2 (2019): 239–264.
10. Kofi Annan, 'Two Concepts of Sovereignty', *United Nations* (18 September 1999) https://www.un.org/sg/en/content/sg/articles/1999-09-18/two-concepts-sovereignty
11. Mats Berdal, 'Revisiting the "Responsibility to Protect" and the Use of Force', 246–247.
12. Harddep Singh Puri, *Perilous Interventions: The Security Council and the Politics of Chaos* (New Delhi: Harper Collins, 2016), 103.
13. Mats Berdal, 'Revisiting the "Responsibility to Protect" and the Use of Force', 252.
14. General Assembly Res. ES-11/1, 2 March 2022. There were also 35 abstentions including by India, China, Pakistan, and South Africa.
15. 'Introduction to the Annual Report of the Secretary-General on the Work of the Organisation, 1959–1960', GA, A/4390/Add.1 (1960): 4.
16. In 2021, the top ten contributors to the UN peace-keeping budget were: United States (27.89 per cent); China (15.21 per cent); Japan (8.56 per cent); Germany (6.09 per cent); United Kingdom (5.79 per cent); France (5.61 per cent); Italy (3.30 per cent); Russian Federation (3.04 per cent); Canada (2.73 per cent); Republic of Korea (2.26 per cent). United Nations Peacekeeping. A4P, accessed 5 January 2022.
17. It is worth emphasising that it is the *"perception"* of how power is exercised that is critical, not the actual sums involved. These are in comparative terms, small. To take a domestic analogy from the United States, no doubt dubious on that account but telling – the UN peacekeeping budget for 2021 was $6.3bn; the UN's regular budget around $3bn, allegedly less than the annual budget for the New York Police Department.
18. See, for example, Elizabeth Economy, 'Xi Jinping's New World Order, Can China remake the International System?', *Foreign Affairs* 101, No. 1 (January/February 2022): 52–67.
19. BBC News, *IMF Suspends Access to Funds* (18 August 2021). The decision appears to run counter to the IMF's Articles of Agreement which forbid it from taking political positions. www.bbc.com>business 38263525, accessed (5 January 2022).

20 David Dollar, 'Reluctant Player: China's Approach to International Economic Relations', *Brookings* (14 September 2020). https://brookings.edu.
21 Francis Fukuyama, *The End of History and the Last Man* (New York: The Free Press, 1992).
22 The Convention on Civil and Political Rights and the Convention on Economic and Social Rights.
23 *New Republic* (4 November 1985).

Bibliography

BBC News. *IMF suspends access to Funds.* 18 August 2021.

Berdal, Mats. 'Revisiting the 'Responsibility to Protect' and the Use of Force'. *Asian Journal of Peacebuilding* 7, No. 2 (2019): 239–264.

Dollar, David. 'Reluctant Player: China's Approach to International Economic Relations'. *Brookings* (14 September 2020). https://brookings.edu.

Economy, Elizabeth. 'Xi Jinping's New World Order, Can China remake the International System?'. *Foreign Affairs* 101, No. 1 (January/February 2022): 52–67.

Fukuyama, Francis. *The End of History and the Last Man.* New York: The Free Press, 1992.

Gharekhan, Chinmaya R. *The Horseshoe Table.* New Delhi: Pearson Education, 2021.

ICISS (International Commission on Intervention and State Sovereignty). *The Responsibility to Protect: Report of the International Commission on Intervention and State Sovereignty.* Ottawa: International Development Research Centre, 2001.

Mazower, Mark M. *No Enchanted Palace: The End of Empire and the Ideological Origins of the United Nations.* Princeton, NJ: Princeton University Press, 2009.

Singh Puri, Hardeep. *Perilous Interventions: The Security Council and the Politics of Chaos.* New Delhi: Harper Collins, 2016.

Urquhart, Brian. *A Life in Peace and War.* New York: Harper & Row Publishers, 1987.

4
FROM TABOO TO LEGALITY

Human Rights and the United Nations

Radhika Coomaraswamy

4.1 Introduction

This chapter will examine the evolution of international human rights within the United Nations system. While national bills of rights were present since the 18th century, international human rights only came into existence at the end of World War II. Horrific wars bring seismic shifts in international law and relations. After the absolute violence of the holocaust, especially the concentration camps and other forms of Nazi terror, there was a belief that "never again"[1] should this be allowed to happen.

When the UN Charter was discussed, it was the representative from Panama, Ricardo Alfaro, who brought forward this idea of international human rights, a matter that had been under discussion since the Treaty of Versailles.[2] As a result, a Commission on Human Rights was created – a sub-body of the Economic and Social Rights Council. The drafters of the UN Charter wanted it to be a low-key, subordinate body since there was a lot of uncertainty and debate about its inclusion, and the legitimacy of the Charter was always suspect. For many it was a challenge to sovereignty; the basis of the structure of the United Nations through the Charter begins with the words, "We, the peoples." Eleanor Roosevelt was made the Chairperson of the first Human Rights Commission and its first task was to draft the Universal Declaration of Human Rights.

It was only in 2005 – almost 60 years later – that the UN Human Rights Commission was elevated in status and became the Human Rights Council – the third pillar of the United Nations System with equal status to the Security Council and the Economic and Social Council. It is this new, elevated Human Rights Council, elected by the General Assembly, which is now entrusted with implementing human rights within the United Nations system. This chapter,

DOI: 10.4324/9781003385233-4

therefore, discusses the transformation of human rights as a taboo subject into a legitimate arena of international action in five phases.

4.2 Phase One: Era of Standard Setting

The first phase was from 1947 to 1966 and may be called the era of standard setting. The Human Rights Commission at that time engaged in efforts to draft international conventions on human rights. The Commission worked hard: they produced the Genocide Convention, the International Covenant on Civil and Political Rights, and the International Covenant on Economic and Social Rights. Later, they would go on to create the Convention on the Elimination of Racial Discrimination, and the Torture Convention.

This standard setting phase paralleled the period of decolonisation, and many of the provisions from these Conventions were directly incorporated into the national constitutions of the newly formed nation-states. Many European countries also amended their constitutions. If one goes to the Sri Lankan Constitution of 1978 and the Fundamental Rights Chapter, one will notice that some of the provisions are exact words from the International Covenant on Civil and Political Rights.

The important thing to notice about this first phase is that it dealt with developing standards, norms, and themes. There was no mention of individual countries. There was no naming and shaming of governments and it was considered heresy to interfere in the internal affairs of countries. The concept of national sovereignty remained supreme.

Many governments would like the UN human rights system to remain in this phase without naming and shaming individual governments. They feel the Council should only deal with general thematic issues. They act as if the next four phases of international human rights have not happened – however, as we will see the system has moved on.

4.3 Second Phase: Piercing the Veil of Sovereignty

The second phase of development with regard to international human rights may be called the era of piercing the veil of sovereignty and the beginning of naming and shaming governments. The issue that brought the belief that the international system must respond to unconscionable things happening within countries and that it must interfere in the internal affairs of a country was the issue of apartheid. It was Africa then that was initially determined to pierce the veil of sovereignty. Resolution 1235 was passed in 1967[3] allowing the Human Rights Commission to intervene in situations of grave violations against human rights. A Working Group on Apartheid[4] was also set up. The reports from this group along with concerted international action led to the suspension of South Africa from the United Nations in 1974.[5] From then on the Human Rights Commission has never looked back and continuously comments on the internal issues of countries. In this way it testifies to one aspect of the illegitimacy of such usurping regimes.

The first real test for the UN system after apartheid were the disappearances that were taking place in Latin American countries in the 1970s and 1980s. To avoid state liability, military dictatorships were sending personnel dressed in civvies and unmarked vans to kidnap and transport subjects to unknown destinations for torture and extrajudicial killing. The state would then feign ignorance and say it must have been the act of private parties. No one of course was arrested. Thousands died during this process. This practice perfected by the Latin American military juntas is now all too familiar in other parts of the world as well.

In response, the UN Human Rights Commission created the Working Group on Disappearances, and later a Special Rapporteur on Torture, a Special Rapporteur on Extra Judicial Killings, and a Working Group on Arbitrary Detention. These mechanisms not only filed reports but also were given the power to visit countries and to name and shame governments. These actions along with agitation by activists in Latin America and their supporters abroad led to a famous international legal principle articulated in the Velasquez case of the Inter-American Court[6] – not a European or a US Court – where primarily Latin American judges held that states have a positive, due diligence duty to prevent, prosecute, and punish those who commit criminal acts against others. Allowing impunity for such crimes was itself now seen as a clear violation of international human rights.

4.4 Third Phase: Golden Era of UN Human Rights Activity

The third phase of human rights development may be called the golden era of UN human rights activity in which there was near universal consensus and activism on human rights matters. This took place at the end of the 1980s and through the 1990s.

With the end of the Cold War, again, there was a whole bloc of countries taking their place at the UN having used international human rights to fight off dictatorships and regimes that lacked legitimacy. The countries of Eastern Europe and the countries of North Asia such as South Korea became strong supporters of international human rights.

The 1990s was indeed the golden era of UN human rights activity. There was a committed, universal spirit in the corridors of the United Nations. I was fortunate to be the Special Rapporteur on Violence Against Women during that period. Women's and Children's rights came to the fore during this era and the concept of sovereignty completely receded to the background and was rarely mentioned. The Women's and Children's Conventions dramatically pierced the veil of sovereignty, going so far as to claim the right to transform national societies and change individual and state behaviour. Phrases like "eliminating traditional practices" and "modifying social behavior" were used throughout these documents.[7]

In addition, by the end of the decade, there were around 40 special rapporteurs or working groups of the Commission each tasked with reporting and naming and shaming governments with regard to their own particular issue – whether it be freedom from torture, the right to education, or violence against women.

These special rapporteurs and working groups have developed well-established procedures, and regardless of the political currents of the day, they continue to fact-find, document, collect evidence, and file reports on a regular and consistent basis. No country is immune from this process. Not even the United States. The Special Rapporteur on extrajudicial killings, the Special Rapporteur on Torture, and the Working Group on Arbitrary Detention have all written very strong reports on the United States. I visited US prisons, as there were allegations of sexual abuse of female prisoners.

Behind the bluster and Machiavellian deals made by member states at international arenas, there is the quiet, constant, and consistent collection of human rights information by UN human rights mechanisms, departments, and agencies. In that sense the United Nations Office of the High Commissioner for Human Rights is an international archive where violations against human rights globally are collected, collated, and preserved for future use.

4.5 Fourth Phase: Accountability and the Responsibility to Protect

The fourth phase of human rights – what may be called the era of accountability – came about after the terrible wars in Bosnia and Rwanda – wars we have now forgotten. Like the holocaust they were so horrific that they brought about a major philosophical shift in the international system. The Security Council in 2000 for the first time recognised that violations of human rights and humanitarian law are a threat to international peace and security and therefore under its purview. In addition, till then international processes had only been concerned with naming and shaming governments. Now we move into the phase where there is a call for individual accountability of perpetrators and for sending individuals to jail. International humanitarian law was now augmenting and supplementing international human rights.

International humanitarian law – the law of armed conflict – is based on two principles.[8] The first is the principle of distinction between combatants and civilians – combatants may be killed during combat, but if they are taken prisoner, there are certain very important safeguards.

Civilians, on the other hand, must be protected as much as possible except in situations of military necessity. If there is uncertainty, the International Committee of the Red Cross (ICRC), the assigned custodian of the Geneva Conventions,[9] has repeatedly said that the additional protocols point to the fact that the benefit of doubt must go to protecting the civilian.

The second principle of international humanitarian law is the principle of proportionality – if a state is using force that force must be reasonable and proportionate. In ascertaining proportionality, the ICRC has also set out guidelines and procedures to minimise civilian casualty.

In addition, international humanitarian law means that a perpetrator can theoretically be tried anywhere in the world under what is termed universal jurisdiction.[10] The individual actors can now face personal accountability. This type of invocation of universal jurisdiction will depend on the legal system and judges of each country.

The other very important aspect of international humanitarian law is that it also applies to non-state actors. Government soldiers as well as individual members of armed rebel groups can be held criminally liable.

I cannot even begin to describe the horrors of the two wars in Bosnia and Rwanda. I went to Rwanda a month after the genocide. I was taken to a church. I was initially struck by a beautiful image of the Virgin Mary, but when I looked down there was layer upon layer of skeletons, thousands of them, their limbs torn apart by machete blows and physical abuse – and all this in a house of worship where Hutu nuns had called in the Interhamwe militia to kill off the Tutus who had found refuge with them.

I have also interviewed countless Bosnian and Croatian women who spoke about how they were repeatedly gang raped until they were pregnant with the perpetrators continually saying, "you will now bear a Serb baby."

As a result of all these atrocities, there was a seismic shift in the international system forcing it to move beyond naming and shaming governments to the criminal accountability of individuals. The Security Council set up the International Tribunal on the Former Yugoslavia and the International Tribunal on Rwanda. It is important to note that none of the P5 cast a veto. In 1997, a Permanent International Criminal Court, the ICC, was created under the Rome statute. Individuals could now be brought to an international criminal trial though the jurisdiction is still based on the consent of the nation-state.[11]

In the next two decades, witnesses have come before these courts and people have been prosecuted and convicted. I was involved in the case of Thomas Lubanga, a man who had recruited thousands of child soldiers. In this context, I had the interesting experience of submitting an amicus curiae or an expert opinion and giving evidence before the International Criminal Court or the ICC.[12]

This trajectory of criminal accountability by the international human rights movement has met with a great deal of criticism, especially by academics.[13] Allegations of double standards, the African focus of the Courts, and some of its procedures and judgments have led to a substantive body of criticism. Recently, Samuel Moyn's book *Humane*[14] which argues that this flowering of international humanitarian law may actually lead to endless wars that no one wants to bring to a close has received widespread attention.

Because of these wars in Bosnia and Rwanda another major development took place. The old hazy concept of humanitarian intervention that had been in disuse was reborn as the Doctrine of the Responsibility to Protect or R2P. It is a doctrine really born out of the efforts of three people, General Dallaire, a Canadian, who was the head of UN Peacekeeping forces in Rwanda during the genocide, Kofi Annan who was head of the UN Department of Peacekeeping at that time, and Bill Clinton, then President of the United States.

Just before the Rwandan genocide was about to break, General Dallaire pleaded with his superiors to allow him to be more active and to go and collect the weapons of the militias since he knew where they were stored. The United States after a disastrous intervention in Somalia was very reluctant to have an international response, so Kofi Annan, head of Peacekeeping, did not give the necessary instructions. As a result, nearly a million people are estimated to have been killed. General Dallaire[15] resigned from the United Nations, suffered a breakdown, and after he recovered, made it his mission to campaign for this doctrine.

With growing international interest, a Commission was set up in Canada with Gareth Evans, the former foreign minister of Australia, as Chair to formulate the doctrine of R2P. What the Commission came up with was very broad: it allowed for humanitarian intervention in the event of widespread war crimes as well as in the case of natural disasters. It also endorsed multilateral as well as unilateral use of force by nation-states to prevent a humanitarian disaster – a recommendation that was very controversial – the unilateral part gave many countries real anxiety.

Kofi Annan took up the report and introduced some elements into the Heads of State Summit held in 2005. It had been cut down to include humanitarian intervention only in the case of war crimes, crimes against humanity, and genocide – not natural disasters – and only allowed the use of military force through endorsement by the Security Council under Chapter 7 where Russia and China would also be present with their vetoes. This placated the heads of state gathered there at that time and they all signed the Summit document.[16]

The final paper presented by the Secretary-General made it clear that R2P had three pillars: the first pillar recognised that the primary responsibility for the protection of citizens lay with the nation-state and that a fundamental duty of sovereignty was to protect one's citizens.

The second pillar was diplomacy. If it looks like a country is failing to protect all its citizens or part of its citizens, there should be intensive multilateral and regional diplomacy. As we know from the recent past, a country will be inundated with dozens of international visitors. If all that fails and there is still an imminent danger to the population, then there could be a use of military force pursuant to a Security Council resolution.[17]

It must be recognised that during the Cold War humanitarian military intervention was also conducted by many non-Western states. Vietnam went into Cambodia to get rid of Pol Pot, Tanzania went into Uganda to get rid of Idi Amin, and India helped create Bangladesh.

What R2P within the UN system tries to do is to systematically develop the concept that countries have in the past used unilaterally to evolve a consensus on the meaning and content of humanitarian intervention and also to create a recognisable process without leaving it to the arbitrary whims of individual nation-states. Nevertheless, it has become the cause celebre, used by nations as well as progressive and right-wing groups against interventionist multilateral action. Academic critics of R2P in the 2000s view R2P as a cover for Western imperialistic ambitions and developments in Libya and Syria.

4.6 Fifth Phase: The War on Terror

The final and fifth phase of human rights at the international level has developed in reaction to the War on Terror. This War on Terror was launched by the United States under the administration of President George Bush, Dick Cheney, and Donald Rumsfeld. Terrorism in the past was seen as a police operation operating within a human rights framework; for example, that is how the British dealt with the IRA or Spain with the Basque nationalists. The Bush administration made it into a "war" both domestic and international – a major conceptual leap that sent human rights activists spinning.

In response to 11 September 2001, the Bush administration basically wiped out many of the safeguards in the law, especially with regard to the settled area of human rights law – civil and political right, including freedom from torture – the first generation of rights and especially as it applied to the Muslim population. The United States adopted the Patriot Act[18] which had draconian powers and enabled extensive surveillance of the population.

In addition, after 11 September, we have had to deal with the dark areas of international law known as Guantanamo, which at best could be described as beyond the law where military commissions are meting out rough justice. I was involved in one of the cases – the case of Omar Khadr – a child soldier.

Guantanamo will not go away because the US Congress refuses to let any of the inmates into the United States to face a fair trial and home countries refuse to take their nationals who are kept in Guantanamo but have not been charged. The American Civil Liberties Union and the Center for Constitutional Rights, brave and persistent lawyers, many of them from the Jewish faith, pointing again to the universalist vision of human rights, keep struggling against many odds, including threats to their own security and hate from their neighbours, to protect the rights of their Muslim clients. Yet Guantanamo lingers like cancer on the body politic.

Finally, the Bush administration's aggressive pursuit of counter-terrorism later strengthened by President Trump has raised a whole host of technological and legal issues. For example, the widespread use of the strategy of targeted assassinations, invented by the Israelis, has created major problems for those of us interested in the protection of civilians. Under what regime do we look at targeted assassinations? Are they "armed conflict" under an international humanitarian law regime where one can kill combatants including what is now termed "continuous combatants"[19] even while they are sleeping? This is the argument that was used by the United States with regard to the killing of Osama Bin Laden.

"Armed conflict" is also the framework used to justify targeted assassinations by bombing an alleged terrorist from the air in a public location or a building regardless of the collateral damage. Under this line of argument wherever an alleged terrorist is present, that place becomes a justifiable military target. In that case no one is safe anywhere as the children in the UN school in Gaza found out.[20] Though certain national courts have written about this, the ICRC has not endorsed this line of thinking.[21]

The alternative is apprehending and assassinating terrorists to be approached as a "police style operation" – after all there is no armed battle of any sort taking place. Then the use of force would operate under a human rights regime where one can kill only in self-defence or if such killing is absolutely necessary. For example, when pursuing the Boston marathon bombers, a pursuit that is technically a part of the War on Terror, no one was bombing buildings from the air and killing Americans and calling it collateral damage. It would not even have crossed their minds and instead a police operation was conducted.

There are other areas too that remain problematic. In situations of armed conflict whenever I hear the words "human shield"[22] or "grey area between combatants and civilians," or "old women forced into building bunkers" are really combatants, my antennas go up. It only means that someone is saying that someone else's life is not worth the extra effort in saving – usually a member of another ethnic or religious group. Luckily the ICRC so far has not given in to the pressure from the so-called counter-terrorism lobby to change the substance of international humanitarian law.

Nevertheless, there is another area where new international action is necessary with regard to international humanitarian law and that is in the area of drones and other similar technological innovations used for armed attack. What are the procedures that must be taken prior to a drone attack to avoid civilian casualties? How do we measure the humanitarian doctrines of collateral damage and military necessity in the eventuality of drone attacks? Can drones cross national boundaries using the "hot pursuit" legal argument?

In drone attacks the claim is that collateral damage is far less and the strikes more precise than with the usual type of aerial bombardment, but this is deeply contested even by the ICRC which says drones create unreachable military expectations of precision. There is still collateral damage and the surveillance and intimidation of the population are constant and total. According to reports children are terribly traumatised by the persistent droning sound above their head throughout the day and night.[23] There is now a growing international movement for developing an international convention on drones and similar technology. It is time that we move the international system to start responding and regulating the new technologies of warfare.

The actions of terrorists around the world; the ghastly bombings of civilian places; beheadings of dissenters, journalists, and westerners; and the absolutely outlandish use of child soldiers are also horrific. Perhaps even more troubling is when we see children training to be suicide bombers. Nothing can condone this kind of behaviour. However, the deathly nature of modern weapons and warfare compels us to ensure the strict, effective, and proper implementation of the rule of law, especially the laws of war, or we are asking for widespread destruction and impunity. We cannot expect civilised behaviour from the terrorists, but we can definitely expect it from the member states of the United Nations.

This fifth stage of international human rights evolution described above has therefore been a pushback on civil and political rights internationally, especially by the counter-terrorism lobby led by previous administrations of the United States. In addition the polarising nature of the Trump administration policies and increasing discourse on sovereignty and non-interference by Russia and China destroyed the consensus and universalism that had emerged on human rights in the 1990s leading to fraught discussions both at the Security Council and the Human Rights Council.

At the same time the institutions and processes set up earlier in the 1980s and the 1990s are now working in an even more systematic manner, constantly fact-finding, gathering evidence, and filing reports. As I said earlier, information on human rights abuses is gathered and processed on a constant basis. As a result, violators of human rights today have really no place to hide. We then have this strange paradox of intensive human rights activity from the grassroots upward existing alongside major human rights challenges at the international level.

4.7 Conclusion: Double Standards

As a global community we have inherited this edifice of human rights that has been created over decades. We cannot escape it, and our best diplomats have understood that and have engaged it successfully at different stages of our history. Nevertheless, the one question on everyone's mind is of course the question of double standards. I hear this constantly. If the United States is not in the dock for Iraq, why anyone else?

There is no question that international power and politics insulate some countries over the others. And yet, the truth is that double standards do exist even in national legal systems. The rich, the powerful, and the influential in most systems of law get better treatment or enjoy impunity. So we must ask ourselves, is the answer to these double standards at the national and international level to do nothing, dismantle the entire criminal justice system, let everyone go free, and allow for widespread impunity? Surely not – the answer is to keep putting the pressure so that impunity will eventually disappear and everyone will finally be held accountable.

The humanitarian approach to all these developments has always been very patient – one step at a time. Justice for one person is better than justice for none. There may be double standards, but with one conviction there will also be a measure of deterrence. Convictions always send a very strong signal. After the case against Thomas Lubanga was filed by the ICC with regard to child soldiers, whenever I met rebel groups in Sudan or even the Philippines, the first question was "what about the ICC?" That to me is the beginning of deterrence.

As one can see from what I have written, the theory and practice of human rights at the United Nations has been long in the making. It is not the plot of an individual country or groups of countries, it is a discourse used by everyone and is precious to many blocs around the world. It is a concept that has grown and evolved because of situations on the ground whether it is World War II, apartheid in South Africa, disappearances in Latin America, genocide in Rwanda, or the new technologies of war.

Just before I left the UN, I met an Asian diplomat who said that the days of human rights and Western dominance were over and that it may be the best time to leave. As he said this with a cynical smile, I thought of the countless women and children whom I have met around the world, victims of the worst kind of brutality for whom human rights was devoid of politics and a real whisper of hope. I remember one woman in Rwanda, who had been brutally raped and who was forced to kill her own child by burying him in the sand, say to me, "Take my story, take it to Geneva – this must never happen to another woman."

Notes

1 Richard J. Evans, 'From Nazism to Never Again: How Germany Came to Terms With Its Past', *Foreign Affairs* (February 2018). https://www.foreignaffairs.com/articles/western-europe/2017-12-12/nazism-never-again
2 Michael Buchanan, 'These Voices Identified Our Universal Human Rights', *ShareAmerica* (8 December 2015). https://share.america.gov/these-voices-identified-our-human-rights/
3 'Question of the violation of human rights and fundamental freedoms, including policies of racial discrimination and segregation and of apartheid, in all countries, with particular reference to colonial and other dependent countries and territories', *UN. Economic and Social Council* (42nd sess., New York, 1967). https://digitallibrary.un.org/record/214657?ln=en
4 'The Struggle against Apartheid: Lessons for Today's World', *UN Chronicle*. https://www.un.org/en/chronicle/article/struggle-against-apartheid-lessons-todays-world
5 Kathleen Teltsch, 'South Africa Is Suspended By U.N. Assembly, 91-22', *New York Times* (13 November 1974). https://www.nytimes.com/1974/11/13/archives/south-africa-is-suspended-by-un-assembly-9122-un-session-barssouth.html
6 'Case of Velásquez-Rodríguez v. Honduras', *Inter-American Court of Human Rights Judgment* (29 July 1988). https://www.corteidh.or.cr/docs/casos/articulos/seriec_04_ing.pdf
7 'Convention on the Elimination of All Forms of Discrimination against Women New York, 18 December 1979', *The Office of the High Commissioner for Human Rights* (18 December 1979); also see 'Guiding documents', *UN Women*. https://www.unwomen.org/en/about-us/guiding-documents

8 Clapham Andrew & Gaeta Paola (eds.), *The Oxford Handbook of International Law in Armed Conflict* (Oxford: OUP, 2014).
9 'Geneva Conventions and their Additional Protocols', *Legal Information Institute*. https://www.law.cornell.edu/wex/geneva_conventions_and_their_additional_protocols#:~:text=The%20Geneva%20Conventions%20are%20a,)%2C%20or%20incapable%20of%20fighting.
10 'How "grave breaches" are defined in the Geneva Conventions and Additional Protocols', *ICRC* (4 June 2004). https://www.icrc.org/en/doc/resources/documents/faq/5zmgf9.htm
11 Some of the major powers such as United States, Russia, and China are not parties to the Rome Statute. For details see 'The States Parties to the Rome Statute,' ICC, https://asp.icc-cpi.int/en_menus/asp/states%20parties/pages/the%20states%20parties%20to%20the%20rome%20statute.aspx
12 'Submission by the Registrar of correspondence received from the United Nations in relation to the expert testimony of Mrs. Radhika Coomaraswamy,' International Criminal Court, 7 July 2009, available at https://www.icc-cpi.int/pages/record.aspx?uri=707208
13 See Chapter 2 titled, 'Individual and Collective Responsibility' in Carsten Stahn. *A Critical Introduction to International Criminal Law* (Cambridge: Cambridge University Press, 2019).
14 Samuel Moyn, *Humane: How the United States Abandoned Peace and Reinvented War* (New York: Farrar, Straus and Giroux, 2021).
15 Roméo A. Dallaire, *Shake Hands with the Devil: The Failure of Humanity in Rwanda* (Toronto: Vintage Canada, 2004).
16 'Resolution adopted by the General Assembly on 16 September 2005', *United Nations* (24 October 2005). https://www.un.org/en/development/desa/population/migration/generalassembly/docs/globalcompact/A_RES_60_1.pdf
17 Ibid.
18 'USA PATRIOT Act', *US Government Publishing Office* (26 October 2001). https://www.congress.gov/107/plaws/publ56/PLAW-107publ56.pdf
19 Sabrina Henry, 'Exploring the "continuous combat function" Concept in Armed Conflicts: Time for an Extended Application?', *International Review of the Red Cross* (2018). https://international-review.icrc.org/sites/default/files/reviews-pdf/2019-10/100_14.pdf
20 '"Appalled" by Attack on UN-Run School in Gaza, Ban Urges Halt to All Fighting', *UN News* (24 July 2014) https://news.un.org/en/story/2014/07/473752-appalled-attack-un-run-school-gaza-ban-urges-halt-all-fighting
21 'ICRC, International Humanitarian Law and the Challenges of Contemporary Armed Conflicts in 2015', *International Conference of the Red Cross and Red Crescent* (8–10 December 2015) https://casebook.icrc.org/case-study/icrc-international-humanitarian-law-and-challenges-contemporary-armed-conflicts-2015
22 'Practice Relating to Rule 97. Human Shields', *IHL Database*. https://ihl-databases.icrc.org/customary-ihl/eng/docs/v2_rul_rule97
23 'Living under Drones: Death, Injury, and Trauma to Civilians from US Drone Practices in Pakistan' *International Human Rights and Conflict Resolution Clinic at Stanford Law School and Global Justice Clinic at NYU School of Law* (2012). https://www-cdn.law.stanford.edu/wp-content/uploads/2015/07/Stanford-NYU-Living-Under-Drones.pdf

Bibliography

Andrew Clapham and Gaeta Paola (eds.). *The Oxford Handbook of International Law in Armed Conflict*. Oxford: Oxford University Press, 2014.

Buchanan Michael. 'These Voices Identified Our Universal Human Rights'. *ShareAmerica* (December 8, 2015). https://share.america.gov/these-voices-identified-our-human-rights/.

Carsten Stahn. *A Critical Introduction to International Criminal Law*. Cambridge: Cambridge University Press, 2019.

'Case of Velásquez-Rodríguez v. Honduras'. *Inter-American Court of Human Rights Judgment* (July 29, 1988). https://www.corteidh.or.cr/docs/casos/articulos/seriec_04_ing.pdf.

'Convention on the Elimination of All Forms of Discrimination Against Women New York, 18 December 1979'. The Office of the High Commissioner for Human Rights (18 December 1979); Also See 'Guiding Documents', UN Women. https://www.unwomen.org/en/about-us/guiding-documents.

Dallaire A. Roméo. *Shake Hands with the Devil: The Failure of Humanity in Rwanda*. Toronto: Vintage Canada, 2004.

Evans J. Richard. 'From Nazism to Never Again: How Germany Came to Terms With Its Past'. *Foreign Affairs* (February, 2018). https://www.foreignaffairs.com/articles/western-europe/2017-12-12/nazism-never-again.

Henry Sabrina. 'Exploring the 'Continuous Combat Function' Concept in Armed Conflicts: Time for an Extended Application?' *International Review of the Red Cross* (2018). https://international-review.icrc.org/sites/default/files/reviews-pdf/2019-10/100_14.pdf.

'How 'Grave Breaches' Are Defined in the Geneva Conventions and Additional Protocols'. *ICRC* (June 4, 2004). https://www.icrc.org/en/doc/resources/documents/faq/5zmgf9.htm.

'Living Under Drones: Death, Injury, and Trauma to Civilians From US Drone Practices in Pakistan'. *International Human Rights and Conflict Resolution Clinic at Stanford Law School and Global Justice Clinic at NYU School of Law* (2012). https://www-cdn.law.stanford.edu/wp-content/uploads/2015/07/Stanford-NYU-Living-Under-Drones.pdf.

Moyn Samuel. *Humane: How the United States Abandoned Peace and Reinvented War*. New York: Farrar, Straus and Giroux, 2021.

'Practice Relating to Rule 97. Human Shields'. *IHL Database*. https://ihl-databases.icrc.org/customary-ihl/eng/docs/v2_rul_rule97.

'Question of the Violation of Human Rights and Fundamental Freedoms, Including Policies of Racial Discrimination and Segregation and of Apartheid, in All Countries, With Particular Reference to Colonial and Other Dependent Countries and Territories'. *UN Economic and Social Council* (42nd sess., New York, 1967). https://digitallibrary.un.org/record/214657?ln=en.

'Resolution Adopted by the General Assembly on 16 September 2005'. *United Nations* (October 24, 2005). https://www.un.org/en/development/desa/population/migration/generalassembly/docs/globalcompact/A_RES_60_1.pdf.

Teltsch Kathleen. 'South Africa is Suspended By U.N. Assembly, 91–22'. *New York Times* (November 13, 1974). https://www.nytimes.com/1974/11/13/archives/south-africa-is-suspended-by-un-assembly-9122-un-session-barssouth.html.

'The Struggle Against Apartheid: Lessons for Today's World'. *UN Chronicle*. https://www.un.org/en/chronicle/article/struggle-against-apartheid-lessons-todays-world.

'USA PATRIOT Act'. *US Government Publishing Office* (October 26, 2001). https://www.congress.gov/107/plaws/publ56/PLAW-107publ56.pdf.

5
DOMESTIC POLITICS, EXTERNAL ENGAGEMENT, AND LEGITIMACY

A Perspective from the US

A. Peter Burleigh

5.1 Introduction

Analysts agree that the American role in the world is highly dependent on domestic politics. The deep divide among Americans, which has its base in demography, race, economic inequality, and cultural orientations, shows no signs of closing in the foreseeable future. Most polls of Americans' attitudes to their government as well as of their perceptions of and preferences towards the US global role reflect the divide personified by Donald J. Trump and Joseph R. Biden. The traditional US domestic consensus regarding foreign policy has long since atrophied. The only shared view among political leaders, and their parties, reflects antipathy towards, and concern about, China. Even that shared threat perception hides a deep divide over what to do about it.

The United States is facing a historic challenge: whether its people and their representatives can essentially agree to disagree but, in the process, protect inherited institutions and regain confidence in the processes of democracy, especially regarding elections. As of now, there is a fundamental chasm which has got worse since the November 2020 presidential election and the unprecedented attack on the US Capitol on 6 January 2021. There no longer is a widely held consensus regarding even voting rights and how to ensure that all qualified Americans both are able to vote and their votes will be counted fairly. The issue of elections and voting are core to any functioning democracy, and it is not clear how the challenge to both will play out over the coming few years.

While such core domestic issues are being clarified, the ability of the US, under any president, to pursue long-term, expensive, and controversial foreign policy goals will be limited. While foreign governments and observers will not doubt American power, they will be cautious in assessing whether they can depend on current US initiatives to endure beyond the four-year presidential term. The US

DOI: 10.4324/9781003385233-5

is facing twin challenges. The legitimacy of the domestic electoral processes and political norms are being critically evaluated. Simultaneously, there is considerable discussion on the legitimate role of the US in international politics.

5.2 Overview: Foreign Policy and Domestic Politics

It is not possible to understand, let alone predict, US foreign policy without a keen understanding of US domestic politics. Despite the unusually broad foreign policy powers given to the American president by the Constitution, such powers are circumscribed both by congressional authorities and public opinion. In short, it has not been possible for modern US presidents to sustain foreign initiatives without substantial public support.

The necessity of public support is most apparent when a president decides to initiate armed conflict. Recent examples would include both the wars in Afghanistan and Iraq. While initially supportive of the resort to arms, popular support can be and often is fickle. When a president can convey a compelling rationale for the initiation of hostilities, when majorities of the Congress agree or are passively accepting, and when other friendly governments decide to participate alongside the US, there is usually a period of at least a few years when public support can be sustained. However, as both these conflicts demonstrate, even in response to the Al-Qaeda attacks on the US on 11 September 2001, the US public can tire of such commitments if they do not appear to show progress and success. Lengthy conflicts, often with shifting justifications, and the obvious sacrifice of troops as well as financial drain, are particular anathema to the modern American public. In both the cases of Afghanistan and Iraq, broad segments of the US population had grown negative about sustaining what seemed to many to be "endless" wars.

Another aspect of the impact of US domestic politics on US foreign policy decisions is a general expectation that the US will not unilaterally head into potentially lengthy and challenging initiatives without the support of traditional allies. In that regard, the decisions taken by members of the NATO alliance, as well as other key countries such as Japan and Australia, have an impact on public opinion, both at the launching of complex foreign initiatives and in sustaining them once launched. Even this general orientation has limits, however, as the NATO commitment to the US effort in Afghanistan was not enough to impact substantially on public perceptions that the US was in a war it could not win decisively and quickly. Twenty years into that war, there was scarcely any popular support for its continuation and the general public had questioned what "winning" would look like. Thus, when the decision was made by President Biden to withdraw US forces from Afghanistan, there was public distress about the modalities of the withdrawals and the human costs involved, but there was no substantial criticism of the withdrawal itself.

A dimension of the "America First" orientation which has gained substantial ground among parts of the US population is an ingrained suspicion of international involvement and a generalised opposition to multilateral organisations and their efforts. Even coordination with traditional allies and partners is questioned, and there is an assumption that such coalition efforts will work to constrain US options. References to the rules-based international order are anathema to those with this orientation. It's a distinctive aspect of this orientation that simultaneously seeks to avoid foreign adventures with a predisposition to go alone when deemed necessary.

5.3 America Is Experiencing Dramatic Changes

For the past three decades, the US has been going through a fundamental change in its demographics and its economy, which have impacted the traditions/processes of accruing legitimacy. This change, particularly apparent since the election of Barack Obama, an African-American, as president in 2008, has been simultaneously welcomed and rejected by large numbers of Americans. The demographic transformation underway has been linked with another dramatic change in American life: an economy moving from its traditional base in manufacturing to one of a service economy. Neither of these trends has caused the other, but they have moved in parallel to such an extent that many Americans are convinced that they are linked. That perception of linkage is one of the core causes of the deep resentments felt by a substantial number of Americans who have simultaneously experienced challenges in sustaining a standard of living and job security commensurate with their middle-class aspirations at the same time that they perceive that the demographic changes the country has and is experiencing have worked to their disadvantage.

Without getting into the complexities of the US Census, and the changes in its questions over the decades, suffice it to point out that in 1950, 88 per cent of the Americans enumerated were White while 12 per cent were Black. Compare those numbers with the results of the 2020 Census: 62 per cent White; 12 per cent Black; 19 per cent Hispanic/Latino; 6 per cent Asian. (American Indians/Alaska natives were about 1 per cent in both.) And while racial intermarriage is increasing substantially, most demographers now estimate that White Americans will be a minority by 2045. For the purposes of this chapter, it is important to point out that many Americans welcome and celebrate these changes; however, it is also key to note that many do not, and among that many, are often those who see themselves and people like them also losing competitive employment opportunity as the economy continues to move away from manufacturing and towards a quickly expanding service/knowledge sector.

During the past decade, there has also been a dramatic increase in the financial and educational inequality in American society. The gap is now among the most dramatic in the developed democratic world. While the very rich have become richer, the well-educated, urban residents in the service economy have also been doing well. Other large chunks of the US population have not only not prospered but perceive that their social status and economic health are in decline. While there are many exceptions to the following, it is the case that these trends have political implications, both in terms of issues, like immigration, which motivate voters, and reflect a general suspicion of the world, as well as providing a basis for American Nativism and an "America First" foreign policy.

That "America First" orientation tends to lead to deep suspicions of the wisdom of involvement in the complexities of international relations, the compromises which often characterise such engagement, even among friendly countries and allies, and the attendant circumscription of America's ability to do what it wants, when it wants, in world affairs. This orientation, in short, leads simultaneously to preferred isolationism coupled, when necessary, with support for an assertive foreign policy which is characterised by unilateral actions.

Often linked with such inclinations is the view that a "Strong Man" leader is needed to carry them out. While the definition of such a leader is imprecise, in the American context, it often assumes that such a leader is impervious to, or dismissive of, inherited norms and procedures and is self-assured and prepared to use "muscle" (whether literal or figurative). Established multilateral institutions are perceived as impediments to be ignored and/or otherwise undermined on the grounds that they tend to inhibit the freedom of action needed to project and/or protect American interests. There is often also an unstated delight in challenging, either by ignoring or destroying, inherited traditions and procedures.

Since the Al-Qaeda attacks of 9/11, the US has gone through periods of international actions, especially with regard to the long wars in Afghanistan and Iraq that have been characterised by muddled and changing goals and objectives. When coupled with over-reach and the pursuit of impossible ends, it is no surprise that we have witnessed the humiliating withdrawal from Afghanistan and the dramatic reduction of US forces in Iraq. Such ill-starred and unsuccessful military campaigns are unusual in American history, and one of the lessons many Americans take from the experience is a renewal of support for an isolationism coupled with the America First outlook. However, even a Strong Man with an isolationist/unilateralist outlook needs public and Congressional support. In the US version of democracy, leaders are dependent on public support, not universal, but necessarily substantial. With the US public currently split approximately 50/50 over the two competing orientations (Traditionalist vs. Strong Man), sustaining adequate public support is challenging for both.

5.4 American Strengths: Hard and Soft Power

It is of fundamental importance in any discussion of Legitimacy and Power in relation to the United States, to remember that the country continues to have unmatched strengths which underlie both its hard and soft powers. Among these are the world's largest economy; the world's most important currency; and, by far, the strongest military. These are all comparative to other powers, but despite the slow decline in US dominance in these and other measures of relative clout, including the astonishing rise of China over the past three decades, there is still no overall competitor to the US in these – and other – areas.

Another important dimension of the US status and power in the world is its network of allied and friendly countries with which, when the US commits the requisite amount of time and high-level energy to consultation and coordination, it can magnify and compound the impact of its policy initiatives. The recent activism of the Quad grouping in Asia (Japan, Australia, India, and the US) is a case in point. Each member of the group brings different, and unique, strengths and capacities to the collaboration. Assuming it can be sustained, and further developed, it could have a determinative impact on the evolution of the region. It is a coalition of democracies which, together, can create serious competition with China for influence and leadership in East, Southeast, and South Asia. However, as the Quad evolves, it is clear that it has more potential for impact in the region than any one of the constituent members would have on its own.

Another contemporary example of the unique US capacity at coalition building is the current challenge regarding Ukraine and its future. In negotiations with the Russians, the US position is measurably strengthened by the full support of its NATO allies, especially including those like Germany with highly important economic and trade relations with Russia. Despite its overwhelming military capacity to dominate Ukraine, Russia must take very seriously the challenge to its own basic interests should it decide to move substantial numbers of troops across the international border. If western European powers and the US were not taking coordinated action, the risks to Russia would be much diminished, though not eliminated.

The case of Ukraine and Russia is illustrative of the real-world impact of the strength of the US and European economies, their potential financial clout vis-à-vis Russia, as well as the vulnerability of Russia to enhanced trade and financial sanctions when the western powers act in a coordinated and unified manner. There still is no country other than the US that can initiate and bring to fruition such coordination and this is despite the fact that the overall relationship between Europe and the US had been allowed to deteriorate and, in many ways, atrophy during the 2017–20 period.

With regard to the US military, and even in light of the perception and reality of its defeat in Afghanistan and Iraq, there is still no other world power with the capacity and potential to conduct challenging and complex military operations around the world. Its innate strength, coupled with its alliances, foreign bases, multilateral and bilateral training operations, and the inter-operability of much of its basic and advanced equipment, makes the US military a serious threat to any other power which might be inclined to challenge it. Because of its dominant status among other major military forces, it also undergirds and makes US diplomacy more credible since it suggests that the potential use of force is real. US adversaries have to calculate the risks involved in challenging the full force of the US capacities in the financial, trade, diplomatic, and military realms.

Another source of US power is often described as "soft." At its most basic level, soft power reflects the freedoms of American society which form the bedrock of the open press, the independent judiciary, the world-class universities and research centres, and the continuing prominence of the arts (music, movies, theatre, streaming services). The US role in creating, and still dominating, information technology is well-known. So is the entrepreneurial spirit and capacity which enables small, innovative businesses to prosper. All of these, and other, aspects of American society have made and continue to make the US attractive to others. Aspirational migrants want to come to the US; so do students who seek out American universities and colleges as do innovative thinkers and investors. Despite the challenges facing the US, the attraction of its soft power will continue to influence international perceptions of America and its role in the world.

5.5 Trump: A Sideshow or the Future?

America's role in the world has been severely impacted by the presidency of Donald J. Trump from early 2017 to early 2021. In summary, Trump's tenure in office represented a dramatic departure from conventional expectations and past US history, both in domestic and foreign policies. On the domestic front, the Trump administration will be remembered for its ability to take advantage of the public reactions to the demographic changes in the country described above. For those Americans who felt ignored and left out of the dramatic changes in the economy as well as the decline in the relative dominance of the White population, Donald Trump appeared to be the answer to their search for a political leader who understood their attitudes and grievances and was prepared to defend their interests.

Despite having been defeated in the November 2020 presidential elections, Trump continues to hold substantial political power and influence and has essentially taken over the leadership of the Republican Party. As of the time of this writing in late 2021, it appears highly likely that he will continue to play an impactful role in upcoming elections, both state and congressional (in 2022) and presidential (in 2024). And it cannot be ruled out that he may well attempt another run for the presidency. And, despite myriad serious legal problems, it must be assumed that he could prevail in that election.

Whether or not Mr Trump himself does pursue the presidency again, it is the case that the economic and demographic changes which fuelled his original electoral victory in 2016 are still realities which confront all US politicians (and citizens). Economic inequality, transformative changes in the manufacturing and service sectors, racial tensions, immigration controversies, weakening national and local institutions (including those combatting the COVID-19 pandemic), law and order questions, climate change impacts, and quality of life issues, all these and more still confront the US in 2021–22 and will do for the foreseeable future.

Another aspect of President Trump's legacy is his impact on the informal norms and conventions which have governed the US in past decades. In short, he has chosen to ignore and/or deliberately violate such norms and has aggressively contested them when they have worked to his political detriment. The US is still coping with, and trying to manage, Trump's unwillingness to accept his defeat in the 2020 elections. He has vigorously pursued a campaign to undercut the legitimacy of his successor, President Joe Biden. Most dramatically, the violent attack on the US Capitol on 6 January 2021 is representative of the extremes to which Trump and at least some of his public supporters are prepared to go in pursuit of his insistence that the election was "stolen" from him and that he is, in fact, the legitimate president.

Even the organisation and management of local, state, and national elections has come under challenge and many efforts are ongoing to alter the traditional independence of election administrators and bring them under hyper-politicised and partisan legislators. Another aspect of the US federal setup has erupted over the 2020–21 period: local control of School Boards and educational standards and policies.

While acknowledging these issues, it is also important to recognise that the free press, the independent judiciary, and the freedom to protest (and vote) are all core foundations of American democracy and that they have prevailed. So has the undiminished reach of US soft power as reflected in music, movies, books, as well as universities, foundations, and an innovative private sector.

Former President Trump's willingness to ignore and/or consciously violate domestic norms and conventions has also had a direct impact on the perception of the US in foreign countries. Both friendly and adversarial countries have been surprised, if not mesmerised, by the internal instability common during Trump's tenure. And that he continues to enjoy substantial domestic political support causes governments to calculate how their own interests and priorities would be impacted by a Trump return to office in 2024.

Trump's willingness, even apparent delight, in ignoring and/or denigrating many traditional US allies, especially in Europe, has caused consternation but also a deep re-consideration of relations with America. Assumptions about US dedication and commitment to core geo-strategic interests, such as the NATO alliance, as well as Treaty commitments in East Asia, have had to be re-evaluated by the countries concerned. The same can be said for the Trump administration's attitude to foundational multilateral institutions, most of which had American policy origins and continue to have substantial US financial support.

US adversaries and competitors have also had to reassess their assumptions, especially calculating whether the Trump era signalled a continuing generalised US pullback that would give them more scope to actively pursue their interests, often at the expense of US friends and allies. The US public's apparent desire to withdraw from many international commitments, coupled with Trump's parallel instincts, has confronted President Biden's Administration with dramatic challenges with which it is currently struggling.

5.6 Biden: Back to Normalcy?

Taking over the presidency in January 2021, Joe Biden was confronted with the challenge of convincing both friendly and unfriendly governments that the four-year Trump interregnum was an anomaly and that he and his Administration were focused clearly on re-establishing America's credibility and legitimacy as a constructive and reliable player in the world. He has set about doing that and has had some successes. Conclusions about whether he will ultimately be successful in this effort are premature, but he has worked at reaching out to allies and friends as well as adversaries, both through personal initiatives and through the efforts of his Administration's senior officials.

Biden faces the challenge not only of convincingly conveying his views of the US role in the world but also dealing with the fact that US domestic politics are volatile and unpredictable, with elections for Congress scheduled in November 2022 and for the presidency in November 2024. Friendly governments, in particular, are looking for reassurance that Biden's policies and general orientation, which they generally find appealing and reassuring, will continue past 2024. They all know enough about the US to understand that that cannot be guaranteed and may be impacted dramatically by the results of both elections. If the Democratic Party loses control of the House of Representatives and/or Senate in 2022, it will become very difficult for Biden to fully implement his preferred policies. And if he or another Democrat loses the presidential election in 2024 to Donald Trump or another Trump-like Republican, it is more than likely that there will be a relapse in the American role in the world which strongly resembles the 2017–20 period. Thus, given the realities of the complexities and uncertainties of the US domestic political scene, it is highly unlikely that other governments will opt to depend on what they are hearing from US representatives now, much as they might be inclined to. For competitors like China, they may well hope for the return to a more erratic and less dependable US which they may assess suits their immediate as well as long-term interests. Such a political regression in the US would also tend to confirm the Chinese view that America is in decline and that that decline opens substantial possibilities for China's assertions of its perceived interests.

Despite these daunting realities, the Biden Administration has been working assiduously to re-engage with the world as an active, reliable force which seeks to convince both friend and foe that American leadership is again fully engaged. Despite such assertions, however, the US has to deal with its recent reputation for unpredictable policy-making. The negative impact of the government's reputation for unpredictability on its legitimacy both at home and abroad is almost palpable. Domestically, the division between the two major parties is now so toxic that it is virtually impossible to achieve an operating consensus on almost any major policy issue; internationally, it is difficult to believe that the trust that underpinned much of the Western intelligence cooperation – primarily within the "five-eyes" agreement – or the belief that Article 5 of the North Atlantic Treaty would be honoured in an emergency, have survived undamaged. In East Asia, Japan and Taiwan plus a string of other countries in the Asia Pacific region have little alternative than to reinvest in their respective American alliances, and/or less formal cooperative arrangements, but they also view the future with understandable anxiety.

Biden has come to be defined by his favourite theme: that current world politics and future trends are reflections of a basic competition between Democracies and Authoritarians. In December 2021, he convened a virtual Summit for Democracies where he underscored this theme in his opening remarks, while also noting that democratic countries, including the US, need to be "renewed," in order to regain the confidence necessary to more effectively compete with and, if need be, confront various challenges from authoritarian governments. In reference to the domestic challenges the US faces, Biden said, "American democracy is an ongoing struggle to live up to our highest ideals and to heal our divisions; to recommit ourselves to the founding idea of our nation captured in our Declaration of Independence."

Simultaneous with the Summit, the US was challenged with real-world crises which directly tested both America's power but also its legitimacy in leading regional efforts to confront a possible invasion of Ukraine by Russia and, in East Asia, the Chinese attempt to intimidate Taiwan and possibly pursue military action to reintegrate Taiwan into mainland China. In both these and other real or potential crises, Biden's instinct has been to reach out to traditional allies and other friendly governments to attempt to create coalitions of governments which, when acting together, will enhance the credibility and impact of US efforts to defuse tensions and discourage the use of force. Whether these multilateral efforts can be sustained and will be successful remains to be seen.

Separate from, but linked to, the US role in the world, as well as its internal coherence and stability, is the ongoing challenge of the COVID-19 virus. As of the end of 2021, the credibility of the Biden Administration is directly linked to the US public's assessment of its competence and managerial skills in coping with the pandemic. So far, that assessment is decidedly mixed.

5.7 Conclusion

That the US is experiencing deep internal conflict is one of the core reasons that American legitimacy in the world remains in question. As the leading international advocate for democracy, and against authoritarianism, the US has to put its own house in order before being perceived as serious and dependable. As the noted American scholar Francis Fukuyama has written:

> What it (the U.S.) can hope for is to sustain, with like-minded countries, a world order friendly to democratic values. Whether it can do this will depend on recovering a sense of national identity and purpose at home.[1]

Speculating sensibly on the likelihood of this outcome is difficult. None of the major themes reviewed in this chapter – the destruction of the tradition of political compromise between the political parties, the implications of demographic change for a resurgence of minority and identity politics, and the perception of many ordinary Americans, some of them middle class and others aspiring to join them – that they have been betrayed by a self-serving political class, provides much room for optimism. The first has greatly widened the traditional debate over what it means to be an American; the second has introduced the bane of political correctness and the abandonment of common sense into American political culture; and the third has opened the door to a populism that draws on a tradition of nativist isolationism combined with the appeal of strong leadership and when necessary unilateral action. On the other hand, the United States has been here before and has always previously recovered. Oswald Spengler's *Decline of the West* was first published in 1918 and ever since a long line of writers have predicted the disintegration of American society and with it that of western and democratic societies everywhere.[2] That it hasn't happened has much to do with American resilience and perhaps even with the parochialism that pervades American, like most other, societies. The appeal of leading the world into the sunlit uplands of a liberal international order and away from the tyranny of authoritarian government has deep roots on both sides of the political divide – although the two visions of these uplands are very different – but so fortunately does the recognition that future survival, let alone prosperity, is dependent on coexistence in a diverse and complex world.

Notes

1 'The World Ahead 2022', *The Economist* (13 December 2021).
2 Oswald Spengler and Charles Francis Atkinson, *The Decline of the West* (New York: A.A. Knopf, 1928).

Bibliography

'Americans' Views of Government: Low Trust, But Some Positive Performance Ratings'. *Pew Research Center* (14 September 2020). https://www.pewresearch.org/politics/2020/09/14/americans-views-of-government-low-trust-but-some-positive-performance-ratings/.
Ben-Ghiat, Ruth. *Strongmen: Mussolini to the Present*. New York: W. W. Norton & Company, 2021.
Brands, Hal. 'The Emerging Biden Doctrine'. *The Foreign Affairs* (29 June 2021).
Frey, William H. *Diversity Explosion: How New Racial Demographics are Remaking America*. Washington, DC: Brookings Institution Press, 2018.
Fukuyama, Francis. 'The End of American Hegemony'. *The Economist* (18 August 2021).
Kupchan, Charles. *Isolationism: A History of America's Efforts to Shield Itself From the World*. New York: Oxford University Press, 2020.
Levitsky, Steven, and Daniel Ziblatt. *How Democracies Die*. London: Penguin Books, 2019.
Levitsky, Steven, and Lucan Way. 'America's Coming Age of Instability'. *Foreign Affairs* 101, no. 1 (20 January 2022). https://www.foreignaffairs.com/articles/united-states/2022-01-20/americas-coming-age-instability.

Poston, Dudley L., Jr. '3 Big Ways That the US Will Change Over the Next Decade'. *The Conversation* (2 January 2020).

Snyder, Timothy. *On Tyranny: Twenty Lessons From the Twentieth Century.* New York: Tim Duggan Books, 2017.

Spengler, Oswald, and Charles Francis Atkinson. *The Decline of the West.* New York: A.A. Knopf, 1928.

Tocqueville, Alexis de. *Democracy in America.* New York: Vintage Books, 1954.

Weatherford, M. Stephen. 'Measuring Political Legitimacy'. *The American Political Science Review* 86, no. 1 (1992): 149–166.

Whineray, David. 'Trump Has Irrevocably Changed American Relations With Europe—And Biden Probably Can't Fix It'. *Carnegie Endowment for International Peace* (6 May 2020).

6
THE SHIFTING GROUNDS OF POWER AND LEGITIMACY IN THE EUROPEAN UNION

Fredrik Erixon

6.1 Introduction

For almost two decades, the European Union (EU) has been characterised by drift and malaise. It has been unable to reform its institutions to gain better democratic legitimacy and make the EU more powerful in world politics. The Eurozone and the migration crises caused many frictions between member states and distanced the periphery from the centre.[1] With the departure of the United Kingdom (UK), the EU gave the image of being ungovernable and on the inevitable path of decline. Subsequent efforts by European leaders to create strategic autonomy and delink the EU from US technology and the global economy added new scepticism about Europe's ability to use its economic statecraft and shape outcomes globally.

COVID-19 and Russia's war on Ukraine have changed the EU – at least the conditions for institutional change. In response to external threats, the EU has started to act more like a classic state, with a new notion of itself and the sanctity of borders. It has also started to use its economic power. The EU has now a new opportunity to motivate itself and its power, and it is likely that European leaders will use that opportunity.

6.2 Optimism and Pessimism about Europe

Europe entered the new millennium with a spirit of optimism. The end of the Cold War had released Europe – and others – from a civilisational struggle. During the Cold War, Europe had been the junior partner in the Transatlantic firm, and once the threat of nuclear conflict in Europe had ended, it was free to pursue a strategy of multipolarity and could reduce its dependence on the United States. Moreover, there was more space to deepen the EU and make it a powerful

DOI: 10.4324/9781003385233-6

actor in world politics with its own distinct voice. It could position itself as a global actor that favoured human rights, a multilateral order, and diplomatic solutions to conflicts. Its own model of regional integration was an example to be exported to the rest of the world.

It was not just rhetoric. In the beginning of 1999, the continent had launched its own currency – the euro – and made real on decades-long pledges to end the hegemony of the US dollar – or the "exorbitant privilege" of the United States in having the international reserve currency. On the back of the Maastricht Treaty in 1992, the EU was planning for a new treaty that would empower federal institutions in Brussels (the Nice Treaty) and lead the way to a constitutional convention a few years later. Germany had been unified again a decade earlier and created a stronger central power in the EU. Several countries in the Baltics and Eastern Europe were already on track to become members of the EU, and Europe's new mission was to bring peace and help establish democratic institutions in its own neighbourhood.

In the new millennium, Europe was going to increase its power and better anchor its democratic legitimacy. Tony Blair, the then prime minister of the United Kingdom, wanted to make the EU a "superpower but not a superstate."[2] He later returned to the theme and said that the modern purpose of Europe was "not peace but power."[3] The sentiment was widely shared in many European capitals. Much of this power would be projected through values, institutions, and international economic policy – not through the point of a gun.[4] The EU was a normative power.[5] And the EU with this model of power, as suggested by a famous book at the time, was going to "run the 21st century."[6]

Two decades into the new millennium, pessimism had substituted for optimism as the guiding spirit of Europe. After the financial crisis in 2008, the European Union soon entered a Eurozone crisis that was both economic and political – and that had ramifications for both power and legitimacy. The crisis concerned the sustainability of sovereign debt in especially Greece, but it spilled over to Italy and other countries with high levels of public debt. It took a long while for the EU and Eurozone institutions to respond with effective measures. The fiscal and financial support that was given to crisis countries came with strong conditionality, effectively demanding long periods of structural fiscal surpluses and "internal devaluations" – what is popularly called "austerity policy."

These policies provoked political reactions in Greece and Italy. Established parties in Greece fell sharply and a new government with a strong and radical off-centre agenda took power in 2015. Three years later, after chaos in both economic policy and migration policy, Italy elected a new government based on the populist Five Star Movement and the far-right League. But there was political turbulence in creditor countries, too. Scepticism or hostility to seemingly never-ending packages of fiscal support to crisis countries had started to wear some electorates thin. Together with a big inflow of refugees and chaos in Europe's migration policy after the war in Syria, far-right parties gained traction – even in countries like Germany. At the time, many established parties at the centre of politics collapsed in the polls, including the social democratic parties in Austria, France, and Germany.

The twin crises of the euro and migration fed the perception that Europe had neither power nor legitimacy. The EU was in a state of constant crisis and did not have the financial capability and the instruments needed to respond effectively to new circumstances. It experimented with new policies along the way, but these policies could not change the material conditions much and rather stoked the feeling that Europe was becoming ungovernable. Ever since the founding of the European Project after World War II, it had been based on a compact of centre-right and centre-left political parties. Now these parties were badly bruised by electorates that were frustrated with leadership and its lack of legitimacy. The EU was not a model for how to run the 21st century, but how to ruin it.

Two other internal factors reinforced the shift from optimism to pessimism. In 2016, the UK voted in a referendum to leave the European Union. The UK had gradually been phasing itself out from European policy for some time. It was not a member of the Eurozone group, and the crisis of this club left many in the UK with a feeling that it should never become part of it. Nor was the UK a party to the Schengen agreement, which allows for passport-free travel and is a component part of the vision to make Europe a continent free of borders. This agreement had been suspended during the refugee crisis from 2015, and many EU countries reinstated border controls in the EU to stop flows of refugees arriving to their countries. However, it solidified an opinion in the UK that it was better to keep a distance from the EU than to be part of its central zones of policy.

Britain's departure added to the EU's existential crisis. It injured the notion that EU membership was infinite. Again, it forced the EU to spend a lot of time dealing with internal problems – and not to be focused on its power and global role. It also caused problems for several member states – smaller, non-euro, and/or free trade-leaning countries – that had seen its interest being protected in the EU by the UK. The UK had balanced the "federalist" or centralist instincts of some member states and been a buffer against the power of the big and core countries to dismiss the positions of smaller nations.

The second internal factor that caused introspection and friction in the EU was the growing distance between member states on the EU's eastern rim and the centre. These frictions have several sources, and all of them are not shared by all member states in Eastern and Central Europe. They are partly an issue of values: governments in countries like Hungary and Poland have been expressing traditionalist and social-conservative values – for instance, on gender and sexuality – and called for Christianity to remain the central religion and source of values in Europe. These governments have taken hard positions against Muslim migrants and refused to accept EU ambitions to share refugees between member states. Nationalism is a powerful idea in many countries in Central Europe.

The frictions also manifest different geopolitical and economic interests. Poland, for instance, has been appalled at Germany's "Ostpolitik," which it considers a product of strategic frivolity, and unwillingness to reorient its energy supply away from Russia. A country that is close to Ukraine – culturally, geographically, and historically – Poland reacted with fury against Chancellor Angela Merkel's weak reaction to Russia's invasion of Crimea in 2014 and nationalist forces in Poland felt vindicated: the EU is not capable of mustering a defence against Russia, and Poland will have to go it alone. By contrast, Hungary has gone in the opposite direction and the government of Victor Orban has over time tied itself closer to Russia – partly because of a perceived alliance with Russia in traditionalist values and partly because of opportunities for individuals to enrich themselves with the help of Moscow. Other countries in Europe's south-east have also moved closer to Russia and distanced themselves from Brussels and Washington, DC.

Brexit and the frictions between Europe's centre of eastern periphery reduced the power and legitimacy of the EU. Power is linear. Economic power and military capacity are not just matters of size and volumes. To be effective, they need to build on institutions and organisations that have legitimacy and the capability to act confidently in new circumstances. The European Union may be one of the biggest economies in the world, but the years of crisis and malaise showed that it lacked the institutions and legitimacy to use this economic size for the purpose of power. The EU that entered the 2020s had none of the optimism that characterised Europe at the start of the millennium. It was occupied by its internal woes and anxiety over its diminishing role in the world. It was not on the brink of collapse, but many feared it would follow the example of the Holy Roman Empire – too complex to change, too irrelevant to care about.

6.3 The Quest for Strategic Autonomy

A central response from EU institutions and notable member states to the European malaise has been to call for "strategic autonomy."[7] A central task for the EU, said Commission President Ursula von der Leyen when she launched her new European Commission in 2019, is to develop "strategic autonomy." Von der Leyen, she said, was going to lead a "geopolitical Commission."[8] Before that, the concept had featured in European security-policy circles and been picked up by French President Emmanuel Macron, whose vision of Europe's future has centred on strategic autonomy.[9] While it was initially a concept to strengthen Europe's defence capacity, it soon expanded into the field of industrial, trade, and technology policy. For the past two years, the pursuit of strategic autonomy in Brussels has mostly been about economic policy.

The ambition is understandable considering the problems that confronted the EU in the past 20 years. Right or wrong, the argument has been that strategic autonomy could revive the European project and give it a purpose that could glue together a membership that has been increasingly fractious. There are also other motivations. International challenges abound, and Europe's influence on their management has been weakening – partly because of the region's declining economic power. Europe's share of the global economy has been spiralling downwards for quite some time, with the result that Europe's voice in the world counts for less. In 2050, the EU will represent less than 10 per cent of the global gross domestic product (GDP). The effect is already being felt: 85 per cent of forecasted global GDP growth in the next couple of years will happen outside of the EU, leading many businesses and governments – also in Europe – to neglect Europe.[10] Europe's poor growth outlook has exacerbated the relative economic decline. An economy that grows at around 1 per cent per year will not command much attention in the world.

In the past, many observers used to think of Europe as an "economic giant but a political pygmy," meaning that Europe did not have the political and military leadership to equal the United States but that was powerful because of the size of its economy and its strong support for global institutions. Soon, however, Europe will not be an economic giant anymore – at least not one that can use its economy as the basis for consequential economic statecraft. Inevitably, this will have consequences for Europe's autonomy, and even more so for the autonomy of individual European nations. Therefore, if the EU wants to have a strong global role in the future, it needs to find new strategies that could help it punch above its weight.

Thus, the quest for strategic autonomy also goes to the heart of European prosperity. Relative economic decline is not just manifested in the falling share of global GDP. This development also entails that a greater part of all new technological breakthroughs and innovations in the world will emerge outside of Europe. In the past half-century, rising global prosperity has meant that new knowledge and new talents increasingly come from regions that are not mature economies like Europe and the United States. In this age of human capital and knowledge, a rapidly falling share of all new spending on higher education and Research & Development (R&D) in the world will be made in Europe. Obviously, this will reshape current patterns of competitiveness between countries and regions.

This development is a natural reflection of growing economic equality between nations. It also provides new opportunities: if Europe keeps its economic borders open, the region can increasingly raise its prosperity by using knowledge, technologies, and innovations from a growing number of talents, patents, and entrepreneurs in the world. However, the trend of relative economic decline also makes it more urgent to address Europe's structural economic weaknesses, because it will not be as easy as in the past for European firms and countries to make their way in the world as competitive enterprises and nations.

The competition for human capital can serve to illustrate this point. At present, there is a global race for talent reinforced by structural economic change and demographic shifts in countries like Germany, Italy, Japan, and China, which leads to growing demand for new human capital. The EU could certainly improve its position in this race. In Europe, there is already a big shortage of computer and artificial intelligence (AI) engineers, which is draining European firms of competitiveness. Moreover, an estimate by the European Investment Bank suggests that Europe has a big investment gap in AI and only accounts for 7 per cent of global equity investments in AI (the United States and China account for 80 per cent of the total).[11] Investments in R&D facilities have already moved out of European countries because of poor access to talent. Human capital shortages, especially for advanced labour, are about to become a fundamental economic problem that could dull much of the productivity gains from new technology in Europe.[12] For some countries, there is now a net outflow of engineering talent. For instance, in 2019 the outflow of computer engineers in Sweden was twice the size of its inflow.[13]

Human capital is central to any realistic notion of strategic autonomy. If Europe wants to maintain its autonomous capacity to understand, access, use, and develop new technologies and be at the frontier of innovation – which has been suggested to be the core economic meaning of "strategic autonomy" – it will have to invest far more resources in creating world-class education and research institutions. In a ranking of the 25 best universities in the world, eight are European – but none are located in the EU.[14] Among the top 50 universities in the world, there are seven times more universities in Asia than in the EU. This is just one of many examples of how Europe needs to improve its attractiveness to foreign talent and capital. However, without world-class universities that are close to or at the frontier of new knowledge and technological development, Europe will not be able to maintain and improve its autonomous capacity to understand and keep up with the pace of change at the frontiers of innovation. Hence, strengthening Europe's autonomous capacity to generate prosperity – and to make countries interested in following Europe's example – is most likely to happen by making the region far more dynamic, innovative, and attractive to the enterprises and individuals who are shaping future technology and markets.

However, few initiatives in the EU to increase its strategic autonomy have taken aim of raising its economic attractiveness to the world. In fact, it is difficult to find many traces of such an orientation in EU initiatives on commercial and regulatory policy. Expenditures on R&D are an example. In Europe, R&D spending has been stagnating for decades.[15] When the EU budget was released in 2020, it included real cuts to R&D spending. The EU's new long-term budget and the recovery plan from 2021 do not change much materially: boosting R&D spending isn't a priority. With a 13-plus trillion euro economy, the EU as a whole still misses almost 110 billion euros in R&D spending to reach the 2000 Lisbon Strategy's target to spend 3 per cent of GDP on R&D – a target that is far too unambitious in the 21st century.

There are some smaller initiatives that aim at improving Europe's position to shape norms and outcomes for global economic development. But domestic or intra-EU initiatives that aim to improve economic dynamism and performance are conspicuously absent from the European Union's programme. Interestingly, there is no special agenda anymore for deepening the single market or raising the EU's competitiveness.

In practice, there is no international trade agenda anymore either. Trade politics in Europe are becoming increasingly charged. Currently, there is only one major Free Trade Agreement up for ratification – with Mercosur. It has been kicked into the long grass because of member state opposition, chiefly by countries like Austria and France. The EU-China Comprehensive Agreement on Investment (CAI), which was politically blessed by major leaders by the end of 2020, also has an uncertain future. In fact, many observers think it was dead on arrival. And in 2021, political frictions in EU-China relations increased, not least after China put sanctions on some members of the European Parliament. While there are also trade negotiations with Australia and New Zealand – both countries could potentially sign agreements with the EU in the foreseeable future – there is little energy in these talks. There are existing mandates for negotiating with other countries, including high-growth countries in Southeast Asia. The old FTA with Chile is up for modernisation, and there are talks about talks with other countries such as India. But this is about it.

The absence of an agenda to negotiate better market access is surprising. Obviously, growth in the world economy has moved from the Atlantic towards the Pacific. Already, a policy for the European economy to grow will have to look at improving trade opportunities with growing economies. In a few decades, the global economy's centre of gravity will be located between China and India.[16] If Europe's choice is to avoid deeper engagement with the new growth regions, it will have a negative impact on its prosperity. Making sure that Europe's economy gets a better connection with the economic dynamism in Asia is probably the most important market-access objective for the EU. Moreover, if it really is Europe's intention to have the ability to "make its own choices and shape the world around it through leadership and engagement" – to quote the definition of open strategic autonomy in the EU's Trade Policy Review – there will have to be a lot more trade policy engagement from the EU with growth economies.[17] If the current strategy of little integration with new growth regions holds, Europe certainly will not be able to "shape the world around it." Key choices about norms and standards in the world economy will be made elsewhere.

The EU's international economic policy has moved in the direction of detachment. While it has still common to hear arguments for the EU to export its regulations to other parts of the world, that agenda has run out of steam. Neither market liberalisation nor the internationalisation of the EU's regulations is high up on the EU's agenda anymore. In areas of digital trade – and, more broadly, the digital transformation – the approach is still oriented towards getting others to comply with the EU regulatory model. But all too often this approach disregards the fact that Europe is a successful trade power in digital-enabled services with great interests in avoiding a regulatory development that chokes services trade and the "servicification" of industrial trade. Indeed, in matters of innovative technology, the industrial Internet and services (e.g. transport, telecom, and financial services), Europe has strong interests in an outward-oriented approach that also takes down non-standard forms of services market barriers, such as regulatory protectionism. However, there are very few such offensive interests in the EU's thinking. The EU has called for an agenda at the World Trade Organization (WTO) where digital standards and regulatory approaches should be agreed – knowing, of course, that this is not on the cards. There can, at best, be some smaller accords with a smaller group of WTO members.

It is far more common that the concept of "strategic autonomy" is charging policies that are protectionist or aim for strong regulatory interventions. Moreover, the ideas and rhetoric that accompany such initiatives are often nodding in the direction of reducing Europe's dependence on the world and developing "technological sovereignty."[18] For some, the model of self-sufficiency or import substitution is now beginning to look attractive. Others think there are transactional opportunities for a Europe that is less open to the world – or a world that is less open to Europe. "We must have mastery and ownership of key technologies in Europe" argued Ursula von der Leyen in a speech to the European Parliament.[19] Thierry Breton, the Commissioner for the Internal Market, argues that "globalization has gone too far" and launched in 2020 a proposal for a new industrial policy with the ambition "to make the most of localization as an opportunity to bring more manufacturing back to the EU in some sectors."[20] The former German Chancellor Angela Merkel and French President Emmanuel Macron have taken a step further and called for economic sovereignty in Europe.[21]

Expectedly, calls for strategic autonomy have also trickled down to EU member states who increasingly want their own economic sovereignty – sometimes in conflict with the single market and other EU countries. For instance, several countries now run their own industrial policies with the aim to repatriate value chains. Big EU countries now plan to take a larger share of tax revenues from smaller EU countries. For example, the French government has repeatedly been criticising carmakers Renault and Peugeot for having production in other EU countries like Slovenia.[22] Some governments want stronger regulatory oversight of big (US) platforms but resist the idea of outsourcing supervision to the Commission because they want to preserve the right to be more restrictive against firms that are established in another EU country.

Hitherto, calls and policies for strategic autonomy have not been able to defuse internal frictions in the EU, give it a new purpose, and improve its economic strengths. While strategic autonomy could be a useful concept for understanding influence, power, and dependence, its application in Europe has been fused with an illiberal economic attitude that is more about protecting Europe than to use its potential economic power. It is invariably used to motivate policies that support greater discretionary power for either Brussels or member state governments. By and large, it stands in opposition to a rules-based economic order – in the EU or globally – because rules are firm, and EU leaders now want flexibility. As in the past, such flexibility is used to favour some companies and member states in the EU at the expense of other firms and member states. Thus, the pursuit of strategic autonomy has created political frictions that undermine the legitimacy of the EU in several European nations – especially the smaller ones.

6.4 COVID-19 and the War in Ukraine

The European Union that exits the 2020s is likely going to be different from the EU that entered the same decade. The sources of changes will have been less about the EU's own strategies and efforts to make its voice in the world to be heard. They will rather have been exogenous shocks that gave the EU few chances to dither, delay, and dodge its responsibility for peace and stability in its own continent. These factors are of course Russia's war on Ukraine and the COVID-19 pandemic.

The history of the European Union has rarely moved as fast as in the winter of 2022. Just a week after Russia's 2022 invasion, Germany had ditched its Ostpolitik and committed the country to a programme of rearmament that will make Germany a bigger spender on the military than Russia by 2025. The new Nord Stream II pipeline was cancelled. Europe, not the United States, took the lead in developing an unprecedented programme of sanctions. Austria and Italy – two countries that previously have been calling for defrosting the relations to Moscow – supported financial sanctions that would severely hurt the biggest banks in these countries. Most EU countries have committed themselves to rapid increases in defence spending. The EU as an institution committed itself to spending on military equipment. Finland and Sweden started what seems to be a process to eventually join the North Atlantic Treaty Organization (NATO).

Many of these changes are significant in their own right. But they are principally of interest here because they indicate a more fundamental change in how Europe perceives power and itself, and how it will create more legitimacy for the continuing process of institutional change in the EU. In short, confronted with a direct threat to peace and stability in Europe, the relevance of internal problems and older frictions has been drastically reduced. It would be an exaggeration to say that previous frictions were manifestations of the narcissism of small differences – to use a Freudian concept. But there is some truth in it. The war has provided Europe with a better sense of what constitutes its core "national interest." Russia has reminded Europe about the purpose with the EU.

One likely institutional consequence is that the EU will get a far bigger central budget that will include spending on energy and defence. The energy transition is likely to accelerate, and Europe is going to make itself independent of others for its consumption of electricity. The defence industry is going to grow substantially and become a central part of European industrial policy. Other classic properties of a state are likely to follow, with a clearer concept about borders and the protection of them. It is likely that the EU will reduce its exposure to the global economy and rely more intensively on trade and technology cooperation with allies and partners. Transatlantic cooperation is likely to be rejuvenated.

The EU's relationship to China – guided by the belief that open trade with China would make it more prosperous and peaceful – will become turbulent.

Many of these developments had started already with the COVID-19 pandemic. Confronted with an external threat – and not with problems caused by the EU and its flailing institutions – the EU took strong measures of new policy integration. Its initial response to the pandemic, including export bans of medical equipment to other EU countries, was a source of embarrassment to many EU leaders. Soon, however, institutions reacted with surprising determination. The European Central Bank went further than most other central banks in supporting money supply and market liquidity. The EU agreed on a new Recovery and Resilience Facility – an off-budget vehicle for fiscal support that has been likened to the "Hamilton moment" in the history of the United States when federal institutions monetised the debt of the states. The efforts by the EU institutions to secure their own supply of COVID-19 vaccines added to the feeling that Europe needed more cooperation to manage the pandemic and a competitive world. While many of these policies are open to criticism, they created new foundations for the EU to build internal legitimacy for itself and exercise a form of power that is different from the post-modern concepts of states and power that guided Europe around the millennium. These foundations also helped Europe to move fast once Russia had invaded Ukraine.

6.5 Conclusion

Other crises may cause drift and malaise in Europe again. At the time of writing, the war in Ukraine is just a few weeks old and we do not know how and when it will end. EU countries may be dragged into it. The war may include the use of nuclear weapons. But Russia's invasion of Ukraine – and, before it, the COVID-19 pandemic – has fundamentally changed the context for European power and legitimacy. The problems and frictions that have dominated the EU for the past two decades have become less important, and there is a greater sense that EU members stand or fall together. There is now a new opportunity for European leaders to reform EU institutions and make them better equipped to perform duties of the state. If the EU seizes that opportunity, it will be able to pursue power and goals with greater determination.

Notes

1 For more information on Centre-Periphery in EU please see, José Magone, Brigid Laffan, and Christian Schweiger, *Core-periphery Relations in the European Union* (London: Routledge, 2016).
2 Tony Blair, 'A Superpower But Not a Superstate', *Guardian* (7 October 2000).
3 Tony Blair, 'Speech to the European Policy Centre', *Tony Blair Institute for Global Change* (1 March 2018).
4 Fredrik Erixon, 'How Trade and Security Became Europe's Unhappy Couple', *Carnegie Europe* (24 March 2015).

5 Richard G. Whitman (eds.), *Normative Power Europe: Empirical and Theoretical Perspectives* (Palgrave: Macmillan, 2018).
6 Mark Leonard, *Why Europe Will Run the 21st Century* (New York: PublicAffairs, 7 August, 2006).
7 Mario Damen, 'EU Strategic Autonomy 2013-2023: From Concept to Capacity', *European Parliamentary Research Service* (July 2022).
8 Georg Riekeles, 'The von der Leyen Commission: Time for Reset, Regroup and Get Things Done', *EPC Discussion Paper* (13 September 2021).
9 Ulrike Franke and Tara Varma, *Independence play: Europe's Pursuit of Strategic Autonomy* (European Council on Foreign Relations, 2018).
10 European Commission, 'Trade Policy Review – An Open, Sustainable and Assertive Trade Policy', *EU Monitor COM* 66 (2021).
11 European Investment Bank Innovation Financing Advisory, 'Artificial Intelligence, Blockchain and the Future of Europe: How Disruptive Technologies Create Opportunities for a Green and Digital Economy', *The EU Bank* (2021).
12 For some indicators of vacancy gaps of human capital shortages, see Philipp Lamprecht, 'What Is Wrong with the German Economy? The Case for Openness to Technology and Human Capital', *ECIPE Policy Brief* 4 (2021).
13 Stefan Fölster et al., 'Invandrade ingenjörer stängs ute från arbetsmarknaden', *Göteborgs-Posten* (12 October 2021).
14 QS World University Ranking 2022. The best-placed EU university is at rank 44. Other rankings – for instance the ranking by The Times Higher Education – differs slightly but not in any significant way from the QS ranking.
15 For an analysis of European R&D spending over decades, see Fredrik Erixon and Björn Weigel, *The Innovation Illusion: How so Little Is Created by so Many Working so Hard* (Yale: Yale University Press, 2016).
16 A study from 2011 suggested that this point will be reached by 2050. Since then, growth in Asia has been surprising positively while growth in Europe has been weaker than expected. See Danny Quah, 'The Global Economy's Shifting Centre of Gravity', *Global Policy Journal* 2, no. 1 (2011): 3–9.
17 European Commission, 'Trade Policy Review – An Open, Sustainable and Assertive Trade Policy', *EU Monitor COM* 66 (2021): 5.
18 Matthias Bauer and Fredrik Erixon, 'Europe's Quest for Technology Sovereignty: Opportunities and Pitfalls, ECIPE Occasional Papers', *ECIPE Occasional Papers* 2 (2020).
19 Ursula von der Leyen, 'Speech by President-elect von der Leyen in the European Parliament Plenary on the occasion of the presentation of her College of Commissioners and their programme', *European Commission* (2019).
20 European Commission, 'A New Industrial Strategy for Europe', *EU Monitor COM* 102 (2020).
21 Fredrik Erixon, '*Work for Others, not Yourself: Globalization, Protectionism and Europe's Quest for Strategic Autonomy*', ECIPE Policy Brief 7 (2020). See also Élysée, 'Initiative franco-allemande pour la relance européenne face à la crise du coronavirus' (18 May 2020).
22 See, for instance, Pauline Ducamp, 'Bruno Le Maire tacle PSA et Renault qui produisent au Maroc, en Slovénie et un Turquie', *BFM Business* (2 December 2019).

Bibliography

Bauer, Matthias, and Fredrik Erixon. 'Europe's Quest for Technology Sovereignty: Opportunities and Pitfalls, ECIPE Occasional Papers'. *ECIPE Occasional Papers* 2 (2020).
Blair, Tony. 'A Superpower But Not a Superstate'. *Guardian* (October 2000).

Blair, Tony. 'Speech to the European Policy Centre'. *Tony Blair Institute for Global Change* (March 2018).

Ducamp, Pauline. 'Bruno Le Maire tacle PSA et Renault qui produisent au Maroc, en Slovénie et un Turquie'. *BFM Business* (2 December 2019).

Élysée. 'Initiative franco-allemande pour la relance européenne face à la crise du coronavirus' (18 May 2020).

Erixon, Fredrik. 'How Trade and Security Became Europe's Unhappy Couple'. *Carnegie Europe* (March 2015).

Erixon, Fredrik. 'Work for Others, Not Yourself: Globalization, Protectionism and Europe's Quest for Strategic Autonomy'. *ECIPE Policy Brief* 7 (2020).

Erixon, Fredrik, and Björn Weigel. *The Innovation Illusion: How So Little is Created by So Many Working So Hard*. New Haven, CT: Yale University Press, 2016.

European Commission. 'A New Industrial Strategy for Europe'. *EU Monitor COM* 102 (2020).

European Commission. 'Trade Policy Review – An Open, Sustainable and Assertive Trade Policy'. *EU Monitor COM* 66 (2021).

European Investment Bank Innovation Financing Advisory. 'Artificial Intelligence, Blockchain and the Future of Europe: How Disruptive Technologies Create Opportunities for a Green and Digital Economy'. *The EU Bank* (2021).

Franke, Ulrike, and Tara Varma. 'Independence play: Europe's Pursuit of Strategic Autonomy'. *European Council on Foreign Relations* (2018).

Lamprecht, Philipp. 'What is Wrong With the German Economy? The Case for Openness to Technology and Human Capital'. *ECIPE Policy Brief* 4 (2021).

Leonard, Mark. *Why Europe Will Run the 21st Century*. New York: PublicAffairs, 2006.

Leyen, von der Ursula. 'Speech by President-Elect von der Leyen in the European Parliament Plenary on the Occasion of the Presentation of Her College of Commissioners and Their Programme'. *European Commission* (2019).

Quah, Danny. 'The Global Economy's Shifting Centre of Gravity'. *Global Policy Journal* 2, no. 1 (2011): 3–9.

Riekeles, Georg. 'The von der Leyen Commission: Time for Reset, Regroup and Get Things Done'. *EPC Discussion Paper* (September 2021).

Stefan, Fölster, Bo Jangenäs, and Berndt Molin. 'Invandrade ingenjörer stängs ute från arbetsmarknaden'. *Göteborgs-Posten* (12 October 2021).

Whitman, G. Richard (eds.). *Normative Power Europe: Empirical and Theoretical Perspectives*. Basingstoke: Palgrave Macmillan, 2018.

7
IS THE PUTIN SYSTEM PARTIALLY LEGITIMATE?[1]

Julius George Stephen Fein

7.1 Introduction

One hundred and five years ago, in 1917, Russia embarked on establishing the Communist Party as the sole authority of the State and the Soviet Union, one of history's most significant political transformations. In 1991, after 74 years, that system collapsed, and Russia re-emerged to embark on another significant transformation. What type of polity has emerged and how does that polity seek to gain legitimacy? This chapter is divided into two sections to address the above two questions. Section 7.2 maps the main characteristics of exercise of power in contemporary Russian polity, and Section 7.3 will deal with the main nodes around which the political leadership seeks legitimacy.

7.2 Power

7.2.1 The Type of System

In 1991 the collapse of the Communist Party left the Russian government without direction, the economy in tatters, and Russia without the countries that had made up the Soviet Union. Boris Yeltsin's effort to introduce a hybrid regime – an amalgam of some democracy and authoritarianism – opposed by the old guard, especially the Komitet Gosudarstvennoy Bezopasnosti (KGB), plus the State's weakness, the public's indifference, and Yeltsin's character flaws, resulted in unsuccessful reforms. The chaos that ensued over the following eight years led to Putin's Presidency.[2] Russia moved from a hybrid regime under Yeltsin to Putin's autocracy.[3] Timothy Fry describes Putin as a "personalist autocrat."[4]

There are several descriptions of the current Russian political system. The mainstream uses "hegemonic electoral authoritarianism," in which the democratic institution functions formally but in practice plays a decorative role.[5] Russia holds elections, but there is little doubt about their outcome. Other Russian experts give different descriptions. Marlene Laruelle, an expert on Russia and Eurasia, in her book entitled *Is Russia Fascist?* argues that it is not: instead, it is "illiberal." She posits that

> illiberalism is the only ideology in power in today's Russia that the presidential administration and the government support. It is a political paradigm that reasserts the rights of a supposed silent majority by insisting on political, economic and cultural sovereignty.[6]

Steven Fish calls the system "a conservative populist autocracy": Putin's goal is to re-establish Russia as a great power as a bulwark against the West and liberal values.[7] It is conservative because it has co-opted the Russian Orthodox Church and practises state capitalism, and populist because it is anti-liberal and anti-intellectual. It is nationalist and autocratic because it focuses on a single leader, is highly centralised, and concentrated in the executive. Kathryn Stoner sums up the descriptions by saying that Russia "is not a democracy after the two-decade-long rule of Vladimir Putin, but it is not precisely a dictatorship either."[8] The system is immature. After centuries of rule by autocratic Tsars and 74 years by one party, the political system is only now beginning to grow roots. Moreover, it has not yet found an ideology to replace the Communist one. This immaturity might explain Putin's apparent difficulty finding a successor and, consequently, the regime's increased authoritarianism.

Putin would like domestic and international legitimacy. As in most states the two are seen as being inextricably intertwined. Sovereignty, which faces both inwards and outwards, is the key concept. In Russia's case, international legitimacy is guaranteed by its permanent seat at the United Nations Security Council, which is essential for Russian domestic legitimacy, as well as by its leading role in a series of new regional and wider international institutions established since the end of the Cold War. However, this chapter will not deal with international legitimacy other than Russia's sovereignty, guaranteed by its permanent seat at the United Nations Security Council, which is essential for Russian domestic legitimacy.

7.2.2 Putin's Power

The eight years of Yeltsin rule immediately following the Soviet Union's collapse were years of turmoil and political, economic, and social instability. As a result of the collapse, Russia lost territory, population, superpower status, and its Western security barrier; hyperinflation undermined life savings and the withdrawal of social benefits, such as health and education. In contrast, Putin offered stability. Nevertheless, Putin brought about stability by centralising power in the hands of the federal executive and appointing members of his circle to head and staff state offices. Moreover, he ensured that foreign owners and foreign majority investors in sensitive Russian industries divested their holdings. Putin achieved economic success during his first years in office due mainly to world oil prices. This success included the stabilisation of the Ruble and the end of hyperinflation. In 2014, he had another success in annexing Crimea. Putin appealed to Russian nationalism, which is patriotic and, at times, xenophobic.

7.2.3 Russia Is Politically Autocratic and Authoritarian

The regime has become increasingly autocratic. It has become focused on a single leader, Vladimir Putin, who presents himself as capable and cunning. Putin lays great store by the legality of his measures for which he needs parliamentary approval, which is one crucial reason his regime continues to hold elections. Another reason is legitimacy.[9] There is no official censorship, but opposition to the regime, seen as a national security threat, is branded as foreign influence under the law on foreign agents and is closed down accordingly.[10] Thus, the regime has silenced the large independent media, rights groups, independent journalists, and activists. Exile or silence are threats to critics, with imprisonment (and sometimes alleged attempted murder, denied by the State) ensuring the threats' seriousness. Fear of the police and the army has become a routine weapon of coercion.[11] The primary concern of the opposition that remains is corruption.

7.2.4 State Capitalism

Putin and his circle ensured their grip on the Russian State and its riches.[12] As Putin's friends increased their hold on the levers of power, he has allowed corruption to bind them to the regime. However, increased authoritarianism comes at a cost. Income inequality persists because of a lack of diversification for which the Putin circle, which accumulates capital assets like oil and gas, is blamed. Allied with the average Russian's apathy and the increasing state sector, they make for a stagnant economy. According to the Carnegie Moscow Center report of November 2021:

> The only changes allowed are technocratic improvements from within with short time horizons and rapid political effects; no other policy or strategy recommendations are acceptable. Moreover, such an authoritarian system must not lose the loyalty of the masses or its veneer of legality
> *(its formal conformity with legislation, even if that legislation is repressive).*[13]

Thus, at the level of everyday life, Putin has ensured the liberalisation of the banking system and the tax regime. However, the economic stagnation has resulted in a loss of public support for the administration. In 2021, the recovery in raw material prices meant that federal revenues rose by more than 30 per cent, but apart from the construction industry, the government was reluctant to invest the additional revenue into Russia's economy. Moreover, the rate of inflation felt by ordinary people reached 17.7 per cent.[14]

7.2.5 Public Opinion

Like ordinary people in many, if not most, countries, the vast majority of Russians have little or no interest in politics providing they are left in peace to get on with their lives. As long as public opinion is apathetic and Russians are willing to trade individual liberty for political stability, preferring pragmatism to an ideology, Putin's regime can rely on the loyalty of the police and the army. However, should public opinion turn against the regime, this support is likely to defect.

Public opinion shapes the system, which at the same time uses its control of the media to influence the public. For example, the regime rallies public support by claiming that enemies in the West besiege Russia, and increased state authority means less chaos and unrest, whereas democracy means the opposite. Although the Carnegie Institute maintains that the appetite for war has changed,[15] and that "State propaganda has overused its powers of mobilisation. Instead of mobilisation, it has created a fear of world war," the Russian fear of war has deep roots in the devastation suffered by the population during World War II. At the end of 2018, 56 per cent of respondents to a Levada Center survey said there was a significant military threat from other countries.[16] Since Levada is the only poll organisation of any repute in Russia, Putin is likely to take notice. This year, the fear of war has increased dramatically, reaching a solid second place in a Levada Center list of the top issues causing Russians to worry. The other fears that have risen in parallel with that of war are those of an increasingly harsh political regime, mass repression, and arbitrary rule: the authoritarianisation of the Russian political regime has not gone unnoticed. It is symptomatic that the worsening of the public mood has gone hand in hand with a fall or stagnation in the president's approval ratings and overall authorities.

A pivotal year was 2018. The move to raise the retirement age destroyed the Putin social contract, which amounted to providing for them and leaving their Soviet-style social handouts alone, in return for their votes and take and lack of interest in the Kremlin's stealing and bribe-taking. The authorities interpreted Putin's high level of support in the 2018 presidential elections as real political credit rather than indifference and symbolic trust. The pandemic has confirmed this bifurcation in attitudes towards the authorities: we support the symbols – the flag, the national anthem, and Putin as a representation of our geopolitical might – but we do not trust specific initiatives and the actions of government at various political levels.[17] This sort of mute dissatisfaction was visible during the 2021 parliamentary elections when people voted for the Communist Party as an abstract alternative to the current authorities.

Frye says that Putin has increased repression and coercion to quell public disquiet. Facing term limits in 2024, he pushed amendments to the Constitution through the Russian parliament (the Duma) to allow him to stay in office should he win the elections in 2024 and 2028.[18] However, rather than rally around Putin, many Russians met the extension of his term with indifference. A survey carried out in January 2020 by the Levada Center that gave respondents several possible options for Putin after 2024 found that one-third of Russians wanted him to remain as president, one-third wanted him to remain in government in a different capacity, one-third wanted him to retire.[19]

7.2.6 Federal Election 2021

Evidence of the West's (and the Russian opposition's) criticism of the regime's behaviour was the September 2021 Federal election. The result was a victory for United Russia, the party in power, giving it 300 of the 450 seats in the lower house of the Duma. While the Kremlin maintained that the election was competitive and conducted with transparency and probity, the United States of America (USA) accused the Putin regime of not allowing the Russian people to exercise their civic rights. The United Kingdom said that the election witnessed a severe regression of plurality by marginalising civil society, reducing the independent media to silence, and forbidding the real opposition candidates from participating. It further added that it regretted that international observers were not permitted to attend. The European Union denounced a climate of intimidation. The Russian opposition accused the government of massive fraud.[20]

7.3 Legitimacy

7.3.1 Definitions

Bruce Gilley writes: "legitimacy is a topic that raises the most basic and enduring questions in political life: who has the right to rule, and from where does this right arise? States win and lose legitimacy."[21] He notes that legitimacy arises from "an ongoing and historically rooted process of state action and citizen response in which performance and legitimacy respond to each other." Furthermore, Bruce Gilley adds that "democracy, rights, governance, and development are the most universally valued sources of legitimacy."[22] However, his reference to democracy is biased to the West's ideals. A significant part of the world population, including China and Russia, does not accept democracy as a valued source of legitimacy. Indeed, Gilley's definition of legitimacy discards this idea: "a state, meaning the institutions and ideologies of a political system, is more legitimate the more it holds and exercises political power with legality, justification, and consent from the standpoint of all its citizens."[23] "Only a state whose institutions and ideologies are legitimate is a state at all" extends his definition to its logical conclusion.[24] Nevertheless, the bias towards democracy is fundamental to legitimacy being a Western concept and questions whether it should apply to autocracies like Russia. That said if it does not, the possibility of a legitimate world order becomes highly questionable.[25]

Gilley disagrees that legitimacy depends on having power, that if an autocrat has power, he is legitimate. For Gilley, legitimacy is self-standing; even if the State has the power, it does not have legitimacy. States desire legitimacy, which they must earn. The vicious circle is that autocrats and dictators who rule without legitimacy, in so doing, need to become increasingly despotic to maintain their power over the people – until there is a popular or a palace revolution or a coup d'état.

7.3.2 Measures of Legitimacy

Gilley's measures of legitimacy are legality, justification, and consent, weighting them as 25 per cent each for legality and consent and 50 per cent for justification.[26] Gilley analyses 72 states on a 0–10 scale (although he does not give a date for the table presumably, it refers to the years 1998–2000). Because this covers the Yeltsin years, unsurprisingly, Russia is bottom with 2.27 points: Denmark is top with 7.62 points.[27]

In Russia's case, among other matters, legality concerns the acceptance of electoral mandates without interference. Also, it regards media commentary and public demonstrations about corruption as off limits. Justification concerns the state's ability to persuade its citizens that political violence, the number of political prisoners, and the size and actions of internal secret services are necessary for stability as is the curbing of commentary on the political system, the government, and its leaders. Later analysts have included the concept of moral validity or rightful rule. For example, the political philosopher John Rawls talks about legitimacy following given norms that are entirely proper and appropriately exercised.[28] Gilley puts this into his category of justification.

Finally, consent regards the extent of citizens' engagement with state institutions, popular mobilisation for the regime, and voter registration and turnout for elections. Russia under Yeltsin was unable to achieve legitimacy. Supporters of the system say Putin is interested in approval, and if this coincides with legitimacy, so much the better. Nevertheless, assuming he also wants to be legitimate, Putin has only partly achieved it.

According to Max Weber, the foremost social theorist of the 20th century, the three sources of legitimacy are charismatic authority, legal authority, and traditional authority.[29] Putin has been in power for 20 years, thereby achieving charismatic authority. However, by presenting himself as the macho leader who defends traditional morality, he has gained legitimacy but at the expense of alienating minority sections of Russian society, such as feminists and homosexuals.

The unfulfilled requirement is the legal authority. The criminal courts tend to be subject to the executive's demands, and the bureaucracy tends to be corrupt. Both mean that the general public does not grant the regime legitimacy.[30] Moreover, the number of yes votes does not confer legitimacy. Many do not trust that 77.92 per cent voted in favour of the 2020 amendments to the Constitution. Nevertheless, the Russian Constitution signalled some legitimacy despite the Duma changing it to allow Putin two further terms as president.[31]

Traditional authority is the use the regime makes of Russian history. Foremost is its insistence on restoring the former Soviet Union's spheres of influence as set out in the official document: the Foreign Policy Concept of the Russian Federation, approved by the president of the Federation of Russia Vladimir Putin on 30 November 2016.[32] In Europe, it means fighting against what the regime sees the North Atlantic Treaty Organization (NATO) and the European Union (EU) as encirclement of Russia particularly, under the USA's leadership. As a result, the Baltic States, Poland, Czechoslovakia, Hungary, Romania, and Bulgaria, formerly in the Soviet Union's Warsaw Pact, have joined the EU, and the German Federal Republic has absorbed the Democratic Republic.

A delicate point is Ukraine. In Soviet times it was integrated as part of the Union, and although it became independent when the Soviet Union collapsed, it did not join NATO because Russia views it as its sphere of influence. However, a majority of the population in the West of Ukraine wants independence from Russian influence. The other country that did not join NATO and has remained firmly within Russia's sphere is Belarus.

Russia dominates the Collective Security Treaty Organization (CSTO) in Central Asia, whose members include Kazakhstan, Kyrgyzstan, and Tajikistan, which serves as a residual for Russia's military presence. The Shanghai Cooperation Organisation, founded by China, Russia, Kazakhstan, Kyrgyzstan, Tajikistan, and Uzbekistan in 2001, which now also includes India and Pakistan—is the regional organisation that can be considered influential. It is described in the Russian Foreign Policy Concept as consolidating "mutual trust and partnership with its members." There are two other relevant organisations. First, the Eurasian Economic Union is Russia's vehicle for economic integration, which has only two Central Asian members (Kazakhstan and Kyrgyzstan) and has an international influence that Russia can exercise on its own. Second, the Commonwealth of Independent States (CIS), the oldest body covering Central Asia, is a channel for Russian influence. It includes all five Central Asian states, with Turkmenistan as an observer. The Foreign Policy Concept is clear that while Russia respects the rights of its partners within the CIS to establish relations with other states, Russia expects CIS member states fully to implement their integration obligations within the CIS.[33]

Russian relations with China take the central stage. As Russia seeks an alternative to the West, China has become an essential strategic and economic partner in Moscow's geopolitical worldview. Sergey Karaganov, former foreign policy advisor to Russia's presidential administration from 2001 to 2013, says that the West is weakening politically, morally, and economically. Russia has the advantage of the experience of defeat in the Cold War and the absence of illusions and ideological blunders. Russia has used them as a part of the reasons to change its geopolitical position to transform China from an enemy into a friendly state. He adds that a new Cold War is unfolding from which Russia can emerge the victor.[34] Karaganov also pointed out that

> the country's fundamental weakness is that it has no future-oriented ideology that would replace the bygone ones. Great nations collapse without such ideologies or after their loss. The ruling circles' decision to avoid the long overdue 'new Russian idea' that would unite the majority is quite puzzling.[35]

The celebration and glorification of Russia's victory in the Great Patriotic War (World War II) is another aspect of reviving the former Soviet Union's influence. Indeed, Russia's Supreme Court's recent decision to close the Memorial International is seen by some as replacing Stalin, the creator of the Gulag, with Stalin the victor in the war.[36]

Also, Russian engagement in Syria, as is its use of soft power with cyberattacks, is part of the aim to revive Russia to great power status.

It is not clear how widespread the popularity of the reestablishment of the influence of the former Soviet Union is. It was popular in the case of the annexation of Crimea in 2014. However, if it leads to a military war with Ukraine, the public's backing may be less certain.[37] In addition to a foreign policy that aims to restore the Soviet Union's sphere of influence, domestically, Putin has continued the restoration of the Russian Orthodox Church (ROC) and the aura of the Tsars. Both policies have rejected the Communist doctrine. Orthodoxy's revival started in the 1990s. Although it is primarily a non-church phenomenon, a symbol has been the reconstruction of the great Cathedral in Moscow, Christ the Saviour. The main debate concerns the extent of the ROC involvement in Russian politics. Whereas the ROC holds a broad spectrum of beliefs, from ultra-conservative to ultra-liberal, under the Russian Patriarch, Kirill seeks to act in the name of *raison d'église*, not *raison d'état*. Nevertheless, this dichotomy led to criticism from both the conservatives and the liberals.[38] The ROC, therefore, decided in 2000 after three years of debate to set out its fundamental principles in the document *The Foundations of the Social Conceptions of the Russian Orthodox Church*. The document states that "the Church must refrain from intervening in political campaigns or supporting a political party or social leader but does have an obligation to express its views on secular issues." For example, it condemns homosexuality and abortion.[39] The ROC is independent of the State, and apart from the restitution of church property confiscated by the communists, the State does not fund the ROC. Nevertheless, Putin, a religious ultra-conservative, uses the ROC. He appears with the Patriarch on television and in photoshoots. In tandem with Putin, Kirill censured some priests who objected to the closure of opposition media. Furthermore, in 2018, Putin encouraged the ROC to sever its ties with the Patriarchate of Constantinople, the honorary primacy of Eastern Orthodoxy, after the latter approved the independence of the Orthodox Church of Ukraine from the ROC.

In 2000, the ROC announced the canonisation of Russia's last Tsar, Nicholas II, and his immediate family for their "humbleness, patience and meekness" when they were imprisoned and executed by the Bolsheviks. In 2008, 90 years after their execution, the Romanovs were legally "rehabilitated" or recognised as victims of "unfounded repression" rather than enemies of the State. At the same time, Putin's portrayal in the Western press is of a Tsar, although he has never admitted he has imperial ambition.[40]

7.4 Conclusion

Russia's political system is partially legitimate. However, the system depends on Putin and his regime. Opinion polls and surveys suggest that Putin's traditional power base is shrinking. Historically, it had consisted of civil servants and pensioners, to which had been added entrepreneurs, and young people following the annexation of Crimea. However, many pensioners have been dissatisfied since 2018, entrepreneurs are moving away, and young people are turning away from Putinism. As a result, the regime has lost their support. If the leaders who make up the country's political elite conclude that Putin can no longer guarantee stability and protect their interests, they will seek another option. However, perhaps in part due to the system's immaturity, there is no real prospect of a change in the Putin regime for the time being.[41]

The Russian experience is unique as the modalities of seeking legitimacy are defined by the memories of disintegration and political instability. There is always a spectre of a sudden collapse of the governance apparatus, as the political legitimacy is not locked into robust institutional frameworks. Given the institutional weakness, a strong personalist leadership finds some legitimacy and is able to invoke the legacy of a political culture based on authoritarian leadership both before and after 1917. The extraordinary size of the country's dimensions with 11 time zones and multiple ethnic groups also appear to, and are used to, justify the presence of a strong leader and centralised authority. However, the emergence of strong leaders undermines the emergence of robust institutions. The Russian political system will have to break free from the cycle of institutional weakness and strong leaders to resolve the challenges that emanate from a partial legitimate political order.

Post Scriptum

On 23 February, Kremlin spokesman Dmitry Peskov announced that the separatist leaders in Donetsk and Luhansk had sent a letter to Putin stating that Ukrainian shelling had caused civilian deaths and appealing for military support from Russia. Putin described the necessity to conduct a "special military operation" to demilitarise and "denazify" Ukraine. As a result, Russia invaded Ukraine on 24 February. Putin instructed the press to use "special military operation" to describe the invasion and continued the crackdown on dissent. Official television broadcast sanitised versions of the war (the independent channels were banned). Some 200,000–250,000 Russians left the country in the first week of hostilities, primarily urban and middle class. The Russian demands are within the context of its efforts to re-establish the Soviet Union and are seen by the West as colonialist and out of touch with the ethos of 2022.

Nevertheless, Putin's domestic legitimacy (as opposed to his international) seems not to have suffered. His regime may have become more authoritarian, but it continues to rule in the same pattern. Eager to reclaim its Soviet sphere of influence, the government's appeal to the nationalist, patriotic, and long-suffering bulk of the Russian population, despite the fall in per capita income from $16,000 to an estimated $10,000 now and to drop further once the economic sanctions have bitten, is successful according to the latest Levada poll.[42] In March 2022, Putin's approval rating was 83 per cent, and in April, Levada reported that:

> March 2022 was marked by significant shocks in the economic sphere and a change in consumer attitudes of the population. At the same time, emotional mobilisation forms rather positive expectations of Russians. This situation repeats the path followed in 2014: the growth of optimism is directed to the future, and the existing difficulties are perceived as temporary.[43]

Notes

1 This chapter was written before the Russian demands on Ukraine.
2 See Catherine Belton, *Putin's People: How the KGB Took Back Russia and Then Took on the West* (London: William Collins, 2020).
3 Luke March, 'Managing Opposition in a Hybrid Regime', *Slavic Review* 68, no. 3 (Fall 2009): 504–527.
4 Timothy Frye, 'Russia's Weak Strongman', *Foreign Affairs* 100, no. 3 (May-June 2021): 116–127.
5 Olga Nadskakula-Kaczmarkczyk, 'Sources of the Legitimacy of Vladimir Putin's Power in Today's Russia', *Politeja* 4, no. 49 (2017): 1–17.
6 Marlene Laruelle, *Is Russia Fascist? Unravelling Propaganda East and West* (Cornell: Cornell University Press, 2021), 26.
7 Kathryn Stoner, 'Wither Russia? Twenty-Five Years after the Collapse of Communism', *Comparative Politics* 50, no. 3 (April 2018): 295–303.
8 Ibid.
9 See page 8 and following.
10 Federal Law No. 481-FZ of 30 December 2020 (in Russian). State Duma.
11 The FSB, the Ministry of Defence, the National Guard, and the Interior Ministry.
12 See Belton, *Putin's People*.
13 Andrei Kolesnikov and Denis Volkov, 'The Coming Deluge: Russia's Looming Lost Decade of Unpaid Bills and Economic Stagnation', *Carnegie Center Moscow* (24 November 2021): 1–15.
14 *Memri Daily Brief*, No 350, 6 January 2022.
15 Andrei Kolesnikov, 'How do Ordinary Russians Feel about War with Ukraine?', *Carnegie This Week Moscow* (16 December 2021).
16 The Levada Center is one of the few non-governmental medial organisations to survive. Apparently, the government needs its unbiased reports.

17 See Matthew Blackburn, 'Political Legitimacy in Contemporary Russia 'from Below': 'Pro-Putin' Stances, the Normative Split and Imagining Two Russias', *Russian Politics* 5, no. 1 (2020): 52–80.
18 Decree of the President of the Russian Federation of 03.07.2020 No. 445 "On the official publication of the Constitution of the Russian Federation as amended".
19 Timothy Frye, *Weak Strongman: The Limits of Power in Putin's Russia* (Princeton: Princeton University Press, 2021), 17.
20 'Elections in Russia: The Kremlin Hails a Large Victory, London Denounces "a Decline in Freedoms"', *L'Obs* (20 September 2021).
21 Bruce Gilley, *The Right to Rule, How States Win and Lose Legitimacy* (New York: Columbia University Press, 2009), xiv and 222.
22 Ibid.
23 Ibid., 11.
24 Ibid., 8.
25 Please see the chapter by Berdal/Mayall chapter on 'The View from the United Nations' in this volume.
26 Ibid., 14–18.
27 Ibid., 13.
28 John Rawls, *Political Liberalism* (New York: Columbia University Press, 1996), 137, 225.
29 'Plato', *Stanford Encyclopedia of Philosophy* (2017) Preussicher Jahrbucher 187 January 1922.
30 See Oksana Antonenko, 'Winning the Referendum and Losing Legitimacy in Putin's Russia', *Kennan Cable No. 55 The Woodrow Wilson International Center for Scholars Washington D.C* (1 July 2020).
31 The Constitution of the Russian Federation – adopted by a popular vote on 12 December 1993, with amendments approved during a nationwide vote on 1 July 2020. See www.pravo.gov.ru. The United States Congress passing a motion considering Putin's Presidency illegal if it continued past 2024.
32 'Foreign Policy Concept of the Russian Federation (approved by President of the Russian Federation Vladimir Putin on November 30, 2016)', *Russian Ministry of Foreign Affairs* (1 December 2016). http://www.mid.ru/en/foreign_policy/official_documents/-/asset_publisher/CptICkB6BZ29/content/id/2542248.
33 See Craig Oliphant, 'Russia's Role and Interests in Central Asia', *Saferworld* (October 2013): 1–13; and Arkady Dubnov, 'Reflecting on a Quarter Century of Russia's Relations with Central Asia', *Carnegie Endowment for International Peace* (April 2018): 1–12.
34 *MEMRI 04/01/2022*, Special Dispatch no. 9706.
35 *Kommersant.ru*, 29 December 2021.
36 Ibid.
37 Andrei Kolesnikov, 'How do Russians Feel about War with Ukraine?', *Carnegie Moscow Center* (16 December 2021).
38 Marc Bennets, 'Why Orthodox Christians are Losing Faith in Putin', *Politico* (24 December 2019).
39 See Gregory L. Freeze, 'Russian Orthodoxy and Politics in the Putin Era Task Force White Paper', *Carnegie Endowment for International Peace* (9 April 2017).
40 See Michel Duclos, 'Russia – the Virus and the Tsar', *Institute Montaigne* (20 June 2020).
41 Ibid.
42 Ruchir Sharma, 'How Putin Aged into a Classic Oil State Autocrat', *The Financial Times* (11 April 2022).
43 'Press Release', *Levada Center* (12 April 2022). The AN Levada Center has been included in the registry of non-commercial organisations acting as foreign agents. Officials allow Levada, solely, to operate as a non-governmental organisation because they need an objective barometer of public opinion, whereas other NGO public-opinion

organisations are banned. Nevertheless, although Levada is fighting it in the courts, the Ministry of Justice branded Levada as belonging to agencies under foreign influence.

References

Antonenko, Oksana. 'Winning the Referendum and Losing Legitimacy in Putin's Russia'. *Kennan Cable No. 55 The Woodrow Wilson International Center for Scholars Washington D.C.* (1 July 2020). https://afghanistan.wilsoncenter.org/publication/kennan-cable-no-55-winning-referendum-and-losing-legitimacy-putins-russia.

Belton, Catherine. *Putin's People: How the KGB Took Back Russia and Then Took on the West*. London: William Collins, 2020.

Bennetts, Marc. 'Why Orthodox Christians Are Losing Faith in Putin'. *Politico* (19 October 2021). https://www.politico.eu/article/russian-orthodox-christians-lose-faith-in-vladimir-putin/.

Blackburn, Matthew. 'Political Legitimacy in Contemporary Russia 'From Below': 'Pro-Putin' Stances, the Normative Split and Imagining Two Russias'. *Russian Politics* 5, no. 1 (2020): 52–80.

'Chinas-role-and-interests-in-central-asia;hr'. *Human Rights Documents Online.* DOI: 10.1163/2210-7975_hrd-9830-3004.

Clark, Ian. *International Legitimacy and World Society*. Oxford: Oxford University Press, 2007.

Dubnov, Arkady. 'Reflecting on a Quarter Century of Russia's Relations With Central Asia'. *Carnegie Endowment for International Peace* (April 2018): 1–12. https://carnegieendowment.org/2018/04/19/reflecting-on-quarter-century-of-russia-s-relations-with-central-asia-pub-76117.

"Duclos." *Institut Montaigne.* Accessed 30 December 2021. https://www.institutmontaigne.org/en/experts/michel-duclos.

Freeze, Gregory L. 'Russian Orthodoxy and Politics in the Putin Era Task Force White Paper', *Carnegie Endowment for International Peace* (9 April 2017).

Frye, Timothy. *Weak Strongman: The Limits of Power in Putin's Russia*. Princeton, NJ: Princeton University Press, 2021.

Gilley, Bruce. *The Right to Rule: How States Win and Lose Legitimacy*. New York: Columbia University Press, 2009.

Hosking, Geoffrey. 'Kindler, Robert Stalins Nomaden. Herrschaft und Hunger in Kasachstan'. *The Slavonic and East European Review* 95, no. 3 (2017): 575–577.

'Index'. *God, Tsar, and People* 10 (2020): 389–398. DOI: 10.1515/9781501752117-007.

Kolesnikov, Andrei. 'How Do Russians Feel About a War With Ukraine?' *The Moscow Times* (30 December 2021). https://www.themoscowtimes.com/2021/12/17/how-do-russians-feel-about-a-war-with-ukraine-a75847.

Kolesnikov, Andrei, and Denis Volkov. 'The Coming Deluge: Russia's Looming Lost Decade of Unpaid Bills and Economic Stagnation'. *Carnegie Moscow Center* (24 November 2021). https://carnegiemoscow.org/2021/11/24/coming-deluge-russia-s-looming-lost-decade-of-unpaid-bills-and-economic-stagnation-pub-85852.

Laruelle, Marlene. *Is Russia Fascist?: Unravelling Propaganda East and West*. Ithaca, NY: Cornell University Press, 2021.

Memri. 'The Middle East Media Research Institute. Special Dispatch No. 9706. 4-1-2022. Daily Brief No. 350. 6-1-2022'.

Morozov, Yury. 'Central Asia as an Area of Collision of Strategic Interests of the USA, China and Russia'. *Problemy Dalnego Vostoka*, no. 5 (2020): 6–19.

Oliphant, Craig. 'Russia's Role and Interests in Central Asia'. *Saferworld* (October 2013).
Perry, John. *The State of Russia Under the Present Czar*. London: Routledge, 1967.
Rapkin, David P., and Dan Braaten. 'Conceptualising Hegemonic Legitimacy'. *Review of International Studies* 35, no. 1 (January 2009): 113–149.
Reisinger, William M., and Bryon J. Moraski. 'Regional Voting in Russia's Federal Elections and Changing Regional Deference to the Kremlin'. 67th Annual National Conference of the Midwest Political Science Association, (May 2021). DOI: 10.17077/g02k-n8zq.
Remler, Philip. 'Russia at the United Nations: Law, Sovereignty, and Legitimacy'. *Carnegie Endowment for International Peace* (22 January 2020). shttps://carnegieendowment.org/2020/01/22/russia-at-united-nations-law-sovereignty-and-legitimacy-pub-80753.
Rowland, Daniel B. *God, Tsar, and People: The Political Culture of Early Modern Russia*. Ithaca, NY: Cornell Scholarship Online, 2021.
Sakwa, Richard. *The Putin Paradox*. London: I.B. Tauris, 2020.
Ševcova, L. F., and Antonina W. Bouis. *Lonely Power: Why Russia Has Failed to Become the West, and the West is Weary of Russia*. Washington, DC: Carnegie Endowment for International Peace, 2010.
Stoltzfus, Nathan, and Christopher Osmar. *The Power of Populism and People: Resistance and Protest in the Modern World*. London: Bloomsbury Academic, 2022.
Stoner, Kathryn. 'Introduction: Russia in Retrospect and in Prospect'. *Comparative Politics* 50, no. 3 (2018): 295–303.
Stoner, Kathryn. *Russia Resurrected: Its Power and Purpose in a New Global Order*. New York: Oxford University Press, 2021.
User. '364. China and Russia: Achieving Decision Dominance and Information Advantage'. *Mad Scientist Laboratory* (1 November 2021). Accessed 30 December 2021. https://madsciblog.tradoc.army.mil/364-china-and-russia-achieving-decision-dominance-and-information-advantage/.

8
POWER AND LEGITIMACY IN THE PEOPLE'S REPUBLIC OF CHINA

Michael Puett

8.1 Introduction

At first glance, the People's Republic of China might appear to be a jumble of contradictory forms of legitimation. A self-proclaimed communist state overseeing one of the most powerful capitalist economies in the world; a self-proclaimed Maoist ruler overseeing a meritocratic bureaucracy explicitly modelled on the imperial past; a communist party that is as likely to quote Confucius as Marx. But, when seen in terms of the development of Chinese political theory and in terms of the deeper history of Chinese political practice, the forms of political legitimacy in operation in China become more understandable. The goal of this chapter will be to explicate these forms of political legitimacy in China and discuss their larger implications.

8.2 History

Let us begin with notions of political legitimacy in earlier Chinese history, with a focus on those ideas and practices that have contemporary resonance and that are being appropriated by contemporary actors.

One of the most important notions in political theory in Chinese history is that of the Mandate of Heaven. This notion, which appears in documents from the Western Zhou dynasty (founded ca 11th century BCE), held that Heaven was a moral deity that ensured the legitimacy of the monarchy. Heaven would grant the mandate to rule to a virtuous figure. That figure would become the king as well as the founder of a dynasty, meaning that the kingship would be passed down from father to son within the same lineage. But, when a ruler from that lineage proved unworthy of the kingship, Heaven would withdraw the mandate and thus bring the dynasty to an end. Heaven would then grant the mandate to another figure, who would found the next dynasty.

The Zhou claimed that they ruled because they had received the Mandate of Heaven and that their overthrow of the previous dynasty, the Shang, had been given divine sanction. The vision of history entailed by the Mandate of Heaven theory was thus one of a dynastic cycle, in which one lineage would control the kingship as long as it maintained Heaven's favour.

Forged during the Bronze Age, the Mandate of Heaven very much assumed a world of hereditary power, in which all land and resources were controlled by aristocratic lineages. The mandate simply served as a check, ensuring that if the ruling lineage lost the support of Heaven (as manifested by a lack of support from the other aristocratic lineages), the kingship would move to another lineage.

Although based in a world of hereditary power and focused exclusively on the monarch, the concept would be expanded and altered over the next millennium. In particular, the concept played a crucial role in the bodies of political theory associated with Confucius. In the 4th century BCE, the political theorist Mencius – a follower of Confucius – argued that the people were the ones who, with their natures given to them by Heaven, would inherently be repulsed by a bad ruler and inherently drawn to a good figure. It was thus the people who should enforce the Mandate of Heaven by overthrowing a bad ruler and supporting a virtuous figure as the new ruler. Indeed, it was the duty of the population to do so.

But the concept fell into abeyance over the next several centuries. Over the course of the 4th through 2nd centuries BCE, during a period when China was divided into a series of competing states, a series of new institutions of statecraft were forged. The states started developing bureaucracies that would function on meritocratic principles – promoting officials based upon merit rather than high birth. Moreover, the goal of the bureaucracies was to undercut aristocratic control over land and resources. When successful, it would mean that the state, rather than the aristocracy, would be able to control these resources and utilise them for its own purposes. The state would also gain the power to create laws that would apply to all equally – aristocrats and commoners alike – and to build infrastructural projects that would cut across aristocratic lands.[1]

A key part of this governance involved the collection of data on resources – both human and material. The state would try to gain a census of the population of each area, the amount of grain produced in each area, the amount of the population that could be taken off the land to serve in the military, the amount of excess grain that would be needed to supply the army, types of infrastructure that needed to be built to allow the movement of supplies and population, etc.

The state that developed these forms of administrative statecraft most effectively was the Qin, which used the institutions to organise an extraordinary war machine that ultimately overwhelmed the other states. In 221 BCE, the Qin declared the beginning of the first empire in Chinese history. The ruler at the time – the self-proclaimed First Emperor of China – presented himself as rejecting the traditions of the past and creating an entirely new era. Among the traditions rejected was the Mandate of Heaven. Indeed, the claim was that the Qin would rule for 10,000 generations; there would never be another dynasty. Both the Mandate of Heaven and the resulting dynastic cycle were thus things of the past.

The Qin, however, fell shortly after the death of the First Emperor, and it was indeed replaced by another dynasty – the Han. After a tumultuous several decades, a ruler emerged named Han Wudi (Emperor Wu of the Han). Like all Han rulers, Emperor Wu kept the imperial title forged by the First Emperor and actively rebuilt the state institutions of the Qin. He also utilised these institutions to launch an enormous war with the Xiongnu empire in the northwest steppe region. In many ways, in other words, Han Wudi was modelling himself directly on the First Emperor.

But, to build legitimacy for the imperial state – something the Qin had failed to do, Han Wudi also claimed to have received the Mandate of Heaven, established academies for the study of the classics associated with Confucius, and claimed to support virtuous governance. This marked the beginning of what would become an odd, but historically extremely successful, amalgam of ideas and institutions.

At the top was a hereditary monarch, whose lineage would rule until the dynasty was overthrown. The monarch would oversee an imperial bureaucracy that ran the legal system, built infrastructure, and oversaw the military. The entire state – the monarch and bureaucracy alike – claimed to be governing with the support of the Mandate of Heaven, and, by implication, the entire state would collapse were the dynasty to be overthrown. Chinese political history would come to be defined by the resulting dynastic cycle, even though actual governance was predominantly undertaken by the imperial bureaucracy.

By the time one reaches the 14th century, the bureaucracy had come to be defined almost entirely as a meritocracy. With the significant exception of the hereditary monarch, almost all positions of power could only be obtained by passing a civil service examination aimed at testing one's commitment to learning and one's understanding of Confucian political thought. Even the children of aristocrats or wealthy merchants would have to be educated in order to pass the examination, and the hope was that they would thus be socialised into thinking more broadly about the political world rather acting in support of the interests of their background. Those who passed the examination would also be moved around constantly in order to prevent the officials from getting too connected to local networks of power. The goal of these institutional mechanisms was to divorce political power from wealth – regardless of whether that wealth had been obtained through heredity or merchant activity.[2]

The criteria by which the state would be held accountable were based to a significant degree on this autonomy from wealthy interests. Officials were expected to be non-corrupt, responsive to the population, and acting on behalf of the entire population, as opposed to narrow, wealthy interests. The state was also expected to be effective in building infrastructure, running the legal system, and responding to natural disasters.[3] These two sets of issues were often seen as inter-related: a failure to be effective was usually ascribed to the officials being corrupt and non-responsive. Strong critiques along these lines often presaged the fall of a dynasty.

8.3 Twentieth Century

The fall of the imperial system in the 20th century appeared at the time to bring an end to all of what we have been discussing so far. Certainly the most extreme moment in this rejection of the past occurred with the formation of the People's Republic of China in 1949. Mao explicitly associated pre-20th-century China with a traditional, feudal world that needed to be completely overcome. Indeed, Mao would compare himself with the First Emperor, saying that the biggest difference between the two was that Mao would succeed in fully rejecting the past, whereas the First Emperor had ultimately failed to do so.

Such a rejection became a key part of Mao's regime. The Cultural Revolution, for example, involved a claim that the Communist Party was becoming like the old imperial bureaucracy, and Mao called upon the people to rise up and tear down the party. Mao's vision, in other words, was of a permanent revolution by the people – a revolution that would never be followed by the creation of a new dynasty.

This vision would become a lasting legacy of Mao. Over the course of the 1980s, China embarked on rebuilding the state apparatus and promoting the market. In the student protests of 1989, one of the key criticisms was that the party was becoming corrupt and non-responsive to the people. Many of the students wore Mao buttons during the protests – a clear reference to Mao's calls on the people to stand up to corrupt officials.

It may well have been those same associations of the student demonstrations with the echoes of the Cultural Revolution that led Deng Xiaoping to suppress the protests brutally. The party continued with its efforts to rebuild the administrative state and embarked as well on a strong policy of state capitalism – supporting economic growth through major state investments in infrastructure and industrial policy. The result was a period of tremendous economic growth that transformed China into a dominant economic power.

But, by the beginning of the 21st century, this very success had become an object of concern. Wealth inequality in China had started growing to alarming levels, officials were increasingly seen as corrupt, and the state was seen as increasingly controlled by corporate interests.

8.4 The Rise of Xi Jinping

In response to these concerns, a new left began emerging in the party making explicit reference to Mao. Early on, the most successful figure to take on the Mao mantle was Bo Xilai, the official in charge of the city of Chongqing. Bo Xilai presented himself as standing against corruption and standing up to powerful corporate interests on behalf of the people. He also began developing a cult of personality clearly modelled on that of Mao.

Another figure started taking up the Maoist mantle as well: Xi Jinping. Although less charismatic than Bo Xilai, Xi had clearly mastered the politics of the party. After Bo Xilai was charged with corruption, Xi Jinping became the most important figure in the party claiming the Maoist legacy.

But, unlike Mao (and unlike Bo Xilai), Xi Jinping's approach has involved a dramatic increase in the power of the state bureaucracy, precisely out of the argument that a strong, effective state is required to stand up to corruption and corporate interests and to break down income inequality. Xi Jinping's move, in other words, has been to re-create the assertion of a strong divorce between political power and economic wealth that had been a goal of pre-20th-century Chinese forms of governance.

Accordingly, one of the first emphases of Xi Jinping was a much-publicised anti-corruption campaign. The goal was to address directly the growing sense that the party had once again become corrupt. But Xi undertook this anti-corruption campaign not by calling on the people to overthrow party officials but rather through a strengthening of the state apparatus itself.

Moreover, Xi Jinping has also strongly emphasised the recreation of the meritocratic underpinnings of the party. Although Xi has not re-introduced the civil service examination, he has built upon the existing college examination system to do something very similar. Admission into colleges in China is based upon an intense entrance examination. Those who test highest are moved to the best universities – such as Tsinghua University. Those students who then do extremely well at Tsinghua are invited to join the party. The result, as the party strongly emphasises, is a party composed of an educated, meritocratic elite, rather than a wealthy elite.[4]

Xi Jinping is thus very much presenting himself as a Maoist response to the perceptions of a China overly controlled by the market during the 1990s. But Xi is doing so not through a permanent revolution by the population but rather by re-creating many of the political ideas and institutions of the pre-20th-century period. The very bureaucratic institutions that Mao saw as holding back the population are being presented by Xi as that which can stand up to the growing power of corporate interests.

If Mao compared himself to the First Emperor, Xi Jinping is in a sense playing Han Wudi to Mao's First Emperor. Han Wudi built on the First Emperor's creations, but also consolidated his innovations by synthesising them with past practices. Xi Jinping is doing much the same. Xi is thus a Maoist figure overseeing an administrative state directly modelled upon the very pre-imperial meritocratic bureaucracy Mao sought to destroy.

I mentioned above that the China of Xi Jinping might seem to the outside like a series of contradictions. But, by looking at the historical background to these ideas and practices and by seeing their current resonance and associations it becomes clear how Xi Jinping's synthesis makes sense.

8.5 Xi Jinping's China

The resulting order is a surprising re-creation of many of the earlier forms of governance from imperial China. Instead of a single lineage, the dynasty is now defined by the party. And instead of a civil service examination determining entrance into the bureaucracy, entrance to the bureaucracy is determined by a combination of the college entrance examination and grades in college. But the claims of a bureaucracy composed of an educated elite and divorced from moneyed interests very much play upon earlier ideas and practices.

The resulting bureaucracy is focused upon major infrastructure projects and major state investments in specific areas of strategic and economic interest – most significantly technology. China is positioning itself as the next leader in engineering infrastructure and technology. It is also becoming the leader in utilising technology for governance as well. We noted above how focused the imperial bureaucracy had been on utilising data to organise human and material resources. This is very much the case in the current regime as well, only now that data organisation is being worked through the use of algorithms. Increasingly, algorithms are being used to determine everything from surveillance to the workings of public infrastructure. China is also quickly becoming the leader in green technology, geoengineering, and genetic engineering.

To explain the significance of these technological developments for China's legitimation, it will be helpful to turn to the question of how China is positioning itself in the international arena.

8.6 The International Order

Thus far, we have been discussing China's mode of political legitimation within the domestic sphere. But Xi Jinping is also very concerned with the international arena as well. China is explicitly presenting itself in opposition to the political economy of the United States and in opposition to the international system run by the United States.

A commonly made argument in China is that the system of governance in the United States is one in which a neoliberal economic order has been allowed to run fully for several decades. The result has been the growth of massive income inequality with minimal social mobility, despite US claims to being a meritocracy. Moreover, because of the tremendous income inequality, wealthy figures and corporations have de facto been allowed to play an outsize role in determining government policy.

The result is a form of governance that works for and is to a significant degree controlled by major corporate interests. A further result is that governance is highly ineffective, since it is in practice designed to work for such a narrow set of interests and is therefore incapable of confronting the major issues of the day. It is a system of governance that by definition cannot seriously address income inequality, since the governing institutions are largely controlled by wealthy interests. And it cannot address climate change, since the corporate interests that led to environmental destruction by definition would not support policies that would undercut their own profits.

The further argument is that the current US form of political economy has largely been exported to the world as the normative model. Indeed, the implicit claim of Xi Jinping's government is that the Communist Party in China overly embraced the neoliberal policies of the United States during the 1990s. Xi Jinping's response to the problems in China of economic inequality and corruption is thus also a response to the political economy that the United States embodies and has been exporting to the world.[5]

But the critique of the current international order goes further than just this. A recurrent claim in China is also that the existing world order – including most international law and most institutions of global governance – is a product of the imperial system of Great Britain and its successor, the United States. Under the guise of "free markets," the argument goes, a system is being run that effectively enriches American corporate interests at the expense of the rest of the world. The kind of income inequality that the US political economy creates domestically is thus also being replicated in the international order as well, with the rest of humanity being impoverished at the expense of American corporations.

Along with the impoverishment of the rest of the world, the reigning ideology of economics and statecraft embodied in the United States and held as normative for the world is presented in China as one that has created global climate change. Here again, the US political economy has created the problem and is incapable of solving it.

The model that China is presenting domestically to solve its own problems is thus one that it is also presenting as an alternate model for the world in opposition to the neoliberal system of the United States. China is presenting itself not simply as the next world power – a significant claim in itself – but as the world power that will bring an end to the entire Anglo-American imperial system that has dominated the international order for the past two centuries.

8.7 Potentials and Challenges

How likely is it that China will accomplish these goals? To begin to answer this, let us note the places where China may have a chance of succeeding, then turn to where it will be facing very significant challenges, and finally turn to the implications these potentials and challenges might have for the international order.

Certainly the clearest opening that exists for China's attempted international positioning as the world's next superpower is being created by recent failures on the part of the United States. Many of the critiques being made by China have a potential to resonate globally for the simple reason that there is a great deal of truth to them. The United States has been unable to provide any credible leadership on climate change and seems unlikely to do so in the foreseeable future. Income inequality in the United States is extremely high, and no significant government policies have been enacted to address it. The perception that US governmental institutions are controlled by corporate interests has led to significant populist protests in America that even threaten the democratic system itself. The United States is hardly at its strongest position as a world leader.

Many of these same points can be made when moving from the domestic situation in the United States to the international order more broadly. Certainly the post-World War II liberal international order created by and largely run by the United States has rarely seemed weaker.

All of this makes a possible challenge to the current world order a realistic possibility. And certainly many of the specific responses that China is offering are clearly relevant to the current problems. The emphasis in Chinese political theory on creating a divorce between political power and economic interests, as well as the centuries of political experimentation in how to implement such a vision, fully deserve to be taken deeply seriously in global discussions.

But the success of the current model being offered by China – both domestically and internationally – will depend to a significant degree on its effectiveness in addressing the problems it emphasises so strongly.

To begin with the domestic space. Much of the domestic support in China for the government over the past two decades has emerged from the tremendous economic growth overseen by the state and in part forged through its infrastructure and investment projects. But economic growth at that level is clearly unsustainable. What will happen as economic growth slows, perhaps punctuated with significant financial crises from over-investments in specific industries (particularly construction)?

Income inequality and pollution in China are indeed alarmingly high, and the government is promising to alleviate these. But will China be able to address these effectively? Especially if doing so may lead in the short term to an even further slowing of the economy?

Even if it can prove an ability to address these problems, will China be able to gain the trust of other nations? Given the intense nationalism that exists in China, an effective state governance system that leads to a continued growth in standard of living and a growing prominence on the world stage would be likely to continue to generate strong domestic support. But that may not be enough to gain support internationally as a power that other states would be willing to rally behind in opposition to the United States. In East Asia itself, China is viewed with great suspicion by many states other than North Korea. Outside of East Asia, China has some support, but primarily as the most effective current rival to the United States, rather than as a long-term ally.

But even if the extreme position – of China as the next world power reorienting the international order – seems unlikely in the immediate future, the implications of China's current political positioning are nonetheless significant.

8.8 Challenges to the Current International Order

One of the hallmarks of liberal thinking as promoted by the United States since World War II has been that democracy and capitalism are inherently related. The argument has been that the United States, by promoting a global economic system, would help create the emergence of a middle class in each society, and that middle class would in turn push for the creation of a democracy. Indeed, this is precisely the way China has been approached by the United States since the 1980s: the assumption was that, by promoting economic liberalisation, China would inevitably become more and more like the United States.

It is not simply that this has not happened in China. If China can succeed in maintaining a strong economic system while also maintaining a strong managerial state – building, in other words, a successful form of authoritarian state capitalism – it could indeed present a model that would be tempting in many areas of the world. Most obviously, it provides a model for authoritarian states, now with levels of technology for effective surveillance and human engineering that would have been impossible even a few years ago.

But it also provides a vision for how states can use meritocratic mechanisms to divorce political power from corporate interests and thus open at least the possibility of dealing with issues like income inequality. Moreover, it provides a possible approach as well as a growing body of technology for dealing with climate change. China's approach to this issue will probably continue to be through geoengineering and new technologies for green infrastructure. For all the very serious concerns that geoengineering may raise, it is easy to imagine a scenario where it would become an increasingly common approach for attempting to deal with climate change, if only for a lack of other viable options. In all of these areas, China is likely to play a very significant role in the world to come.

8.9 Conclusions

Until quite recently, the dominant way of reading China occurred within a common Euro-American modernity framework. China was seen as having been controlled by a "traditional" state that inhibited economic growth – a traditional state that China had never completely thrown off. The assumption was that economic growth in China would inevitably lead to the emergence of a middle class and that such a rising middle class would in turn call for an American-style system of democratic governance and the gradual withering away of the "traditional" authoritarian state. China would thus become "modern" – understood as American-style democracy and capitalism.

But this is a misreading of China's past, a misreading of China's present, and very likely a misreading of things to come. Understanding ideas and practices from China's past allows us to see the development of a distinctive political culture that is actively being built upon and appropriated today. Such an understanding can allow us to see how political legitimation is operating in China today and what implications these forms of political legitimation might have, both domestically and in the international order. Given the significant role that China is likely to be playing in the decades to come, such an attempt will well repay the effort.

Notes

1 The theory for this approach is laid out clearly in the 3rd-century work, *The Book of Lord Shang*. For an outstanding translation, see Yuri Pines, *The Book of Lord Shang: Apologetics of State Power in Early China* (New York: Columbia University Press, 2019).
2 Benjamin A. Elman, *Civil Examinations and Meritocracy in Late Imperial China* (Cambridge: Harvard University Press, 2013).
3 For an excellent discussion of the late imperial Chinese administrative state, see R. Bin Wong, 'Coping with Poverty and Famine: Material Welfare, Public Goods, and Chinese Approaches to Governance,' in Masayuki Tanimoto and R. Bin Wong (Eds), *Public Goods Provision in the Early Modern Economy: Comparative Perspectives from Japan, China, and Europe* (Berkeley: University of California Press, 2019).
4 Chenyang Li and Hong Xiao, 'China's Meritocratic Examinations and the Ideal of Virtuous Talents', in Daniel A. Bell and Chenyang Li (Eds), *The East Asian Challenge for Democracy: Political Meritocracy in Comparative Perspective* (Cambridge: Cambridge University Press, 2013), 340–362.
5 For a helpful compendium of the speeches and official pronouncements of Xi Jinping, see *Xi Jinping: The Governance of China*, three volumes (Beijing: Foreign Languages Press, 2020). For an excellent study of Xi Jinping in relation to previous rulers of the Party, see David Shambaugh, *China's Leaders: From Mao to Now* (Cambridge: Polity Press, 2021).

Bibliography

Elman, Benjamin A. *Civil Examinations and Meritocracy in Late Imperial China*. Cambridge: Harvard University Press, 2013.
Jinping, Xi. *Xi Jinping: The Governance of China*. Beijing: Foreign Languages Press, 2020.
Li, Chenyang, and Hong Xiao. 'China's Meritocratic Examinations and the Ideal of Virtuous Talents'. In *The East Asian Challenge for Democracy: Political Meritocracy in Comparative Perspective*, edited by Daniel A. Bell and Chenyang Li. Cambridge: Cambridge University Press, 2013.
Pines, Yuri (trans.). *The Book of Lord Shang: Apologetics of State Power in Early China*. New York: Columbia University Press, 2019.
Shambaugh, David. *China's Leaders: From Mao to Now*. Cambridge: Polity Press, 2021.
Wong, R. Bin. 'Coping With Poverty and Famine: Material Welfare, Public Goods, and Chinese Approaches to Governance'. In *Public Goods Provision in the Early Modern Economy: Comparative Perspectives From Japan, China, and Europe*, edited by Masayuki Tanimoto and R. Bin Wong. Berkeley: University of California Press, 2019.

9
LEGITIMACY AND "A GLOBAL COMMUNITY OF SHARED FUTURE"[1]

Wang Yiwei

> A human community with a shared future implies that the destiny and future of each and every nation and country are tied tightly together. This means we stick together through thick and thin, stand together through good and bad, and work to build this planet of ours into one large harmonious family and to realise humankind's aspiration for a better life.[2]
>
> – President Xi Jinping

9.1 Introduction

The concept of "A Global Community of Shared Future" (*ren lei ming yun gong tong ti*, GCSF) has become a headline leading trend of the times and human progress, providing a vision of legitimacy based on traditional Chinese culture which has significant implications for the world. In this chapter, I propose to understand the vision behind GCSF from three dimensions – the time dimension, space dimension, and logic dimension. GCSF is a process rather than a static state. I argue that GCSF is to be understood from the perspectives of history, reality, and the future. Initially, the GCSF focuses on neighbouring countries, then developing countries, and finally seeks to include all people worldwide. Besides, the shared future is based on an independent and connected future. Common targets, shared responsibilities, and a common identity are necessary for laying the foundations for GCSF. In the process, the chapter reflects on questions of political legitimacy by examining the shared future of capitalism and socialism with "one country, two systems" as practised in Hong Kong, embodying the philosophy behind GCSF.

The chapter intends to explain the rationale and legitimacy of GCSF. The concept has been advocated by President Xi Jinping and has become the "banner" of China's foreign policy. It is the phrase that summarises Xi Jinping's thoughts on diplomacy. At the CPC and World Political Parties Summit, Xi said:

> Today, human society once again finds itself at a historic crossroads. It is about hostile confrontation or mutual respect, exclusiveness and decoupling or openness and co-operation, zero-sum game or win-win results. The choice is in our hands, and the responsibility falls on our shoulders. The human race is an integral community, and the planet Earth is its homeland. In the face of common challenges, no person or country can remain insulated.[3]

GCSF was proposed to promote these positive values. The GCSF indicates China's vision for domestic and global governance. Legitimacy comes from people and begins from good domestic governance. The vision originated from China's traditional culture and reflected China's confidence in its culture[4] and institutions and mirrors China's pursuit of normative power in the world.[5] It claims that historically, legitimacy originated from the continuity of culture, norms, policies, and human history. Spatially, domestic, regional, and global governance shall be connected and serve the needs of people. Logically, the "shared future" of the global community is an attempt to advance to an independent future, a connected future, and finally, an integrated and shared future. In this course, common targets, common responsibilities, and a common identity should be framed.

9.2 GCSF and Three-Dimensional Visions of Legitimacy

The Communique of the 6th plenary session of the 19th CPC Central Committee notes:

> The Chinese nation has achieved the tremendous transformation from standing up and growing prosperous to becoming strong ... We must work to develop a new type of international relations, promote the building of a human community with a shared future, champion the shared human values of peace, development, fairness, justice, democracy, and freedom, and steer the tide of human progress.[6]

The understanding of GCSF should recognise its historical context, practical measures, geographical locations, and logical phases. GCSF being a multi-dimensional concept means we need multiple perspectives to grasp it.

9.2.1 Time Dimension

GCSF reflects the traditional view of China that legitimacy comes from the well-being of people. It is the recognition of people that provides a foundation for the government, and the latter must serve the former. As an important Confucian philosopher, Xunzi said, "The governor is like a ship and the people water. The water supporting a ship can also upset it." The governor must obey the rule and order of *Tian* (heaven). But as it is invisible, *Tian's* will be exhibited by the people. Hence, legitimacy comes from *Tian*. But in practice, people's will is the basis of the legitimacy of any authority. GCSF inherits this vision and modernises it. The modernisation result of it is the whole-process democracy, which reflects that contemporary China's governance structure still holds the traditional vision. Such continuity indicates the time perspective of GCSF – one that connects the past, present, and future.

Traditionally, the worldview of the Chinese is influenced by three types of differently orientated thinking: Buddhism's thoughts of Karma lead to the concern of yesterday; the official orthodoxy, Confucianism, cares about today; Taoism pays attention to the future. These views continue to have an impact on China's foreign policy. The chronological dimension is about the origins, position, and targets of GCSF, which means history, reality, and future. We consider GCSF as an idea shaped by both Chinese and Western traditions and history. It provides specific guidelines for the contemporary world. Ultimately, the concept addresses future challenges in the world.

We should understand GCSF in the context of history. GCSF tries to activate shared traditions of lasting peace and common security. Legitimacy comes from its origins. It is widely accepted that the foundation of GCSF is a combination of Chinese traditional culture and Western civilisation. GCSF is rooted in China's culture of harmony (he-he), which again is based on the concept of tianxia (all under heaven), an inclusive worldview that is deeply rooted in Chinese philosophy and is conceptually linked to Marxism. The concept of GCSF is also based on China's foreign policies in the past decades, such as the Five Principles of Peaceful Coexistence. Notably, it is a move away from Mao's "three-world theory" to the concept of the world as a common community. GCSF recognises established Western values, especially the sovereignty principles of the Westphalian system, international humanitarianism, and the principles in the UN charter.

Apart from that, GCSF has roots in the ancient, modern, and contemporary history of China, the West, and humankind. The ancient world system was multi-centric and diverse, with the connections between different international sub-systems and civilisations being unstable. In this sense, GCSF can be seen as a restoration of the decentralised world in an interconnected age. The fact that both Eastern and Western traditions and history are the basis of GCSF reveals its intention to shape common values, which are indispensable to an interconnected, peaceful, and secure world.

GCSF is also a proposal for the contemporary world to shape common prosperity and an inclusive international system. GCSF answers questions about the legitimacy of China's rise. With its strong national capabilities, China is increasingly acting vigorously in the international arena. GCSF, as described in Xi's speech at the UN, has five pillars.

1. Politically, the aim is to build an equal and trustworthy partnership, in which a new approach to state-to-state relations, dialogue, and mutual understanding is required.
2. In the security realm, it advocates a security vision that is just based on mutual consultation and pursues common, comprehensive, co-operative, and sustainable security.
3. In the economic realm, it calls for building a world of shared prosperity through win-win co-operation. It advocates interdependent development without asymmetry.
4. In the cultural domain, it recognises the need to increase inter-civilisational exchanges to promote harmony and inclusiveness and to respect differences.
5. Ecologically, to make the world clean and beautiful by pursuing green and low-carbon development.

These five pillars can be better understood by examining China's domestic politics. In the report of the 18th National Congress of CPC, "the Five-Sphere Integrated Plan" was established. During Xi Jinping's term, GCSF has been labelled as the principal strategy for building socialism with Chinese characteristics. The five spheres are identical to the five pillars of GCSF. All this reflects China's view on governance – integration of national governance, regional, and global governance. As GCSF tries to establish a decentralised network, it calls for co-ordinated domestic governance of countries, which is related to the logical dimension below.

GCSF is a proposal for the future, as it envisages building a green and sustainable world, seeking dynamic global consensus in the artificial intelligence (AI) revolution and global commons. Industrial Revolution 4.0 has already begun, with AI, big data, and the Internet of Things reshaping human society and humans themselves. As mentioned before, it is argued that the world in the future will be a decentralised one, and what GCSF seeks is just a decentralised partner network. The spirits of GCSF, expressed in frequently mentioned phrases such as mutual respect, equality, and consultation, are not political clichés but oriented to the needs of the future.

In emerging areas of governance, such as the high seas, outer space, cyber and polar areas, GCSF means that they should not be guided by jungle rule as traditional fields have been. Common development is crucial for the stability of the world in the future. For example, now artificial intelligence is rapidly developing, but the fact is that about 840 million people do not even have access to electricity.[7] They may be further marginalised with the development of AI. Extremism might be intensified as disparities increase. GCSF attempts to avoid tragedy in the future and pursue world justice. Again, such efforts can also be found in China's domestic policy of eliminating poverty.

The emphasis here is the word "common," which will be further discussed in this chapter. GCSF is a way to solve common challenges through the common values of different cultures. Accordingly, it creates new values for humankind.

At the general debate of the 70th Session of the UN General Assembly, Xi mentioned that "the greatest ideal is to create a world truly shared by all. Peace, development, equity, justice, democracy and freedom are common values of all mankind and the lofty goals of the United Nations."[8]

GCSF focuses on the sustainability of human civilisation. It promotes the world order defined by civilisation and a holistic view of human beings, which differs from a world order defined on the basis of narrow-minded nationalistic and ideological perspectives. A new type of international relations and "green" development model is necessary. In China's context, "green" implies more than the word "eco-friendly" in Europe's context. Even finance and lifestyle can be "green." People tend to interpret these ideas as China's ambition to establish a new order. But in fact, they are not coined simply for the current international situation, but for what will inevitably come in the future.

GCSF is the projection of China's domestic vision of legitimacy to the world. People are the basis of domestic governance as well as global governance. Traditionally, in China, diplomacy and domestic governance come from the same philosophy. This implies that domestic, regional, and global governance should be integrated and reflect the same legitimacy vision, which revolves around the people's approval. It is a process that begins in the domestic realm and gradually moves into regional and international spaces. The process is related to the traditional worldview of the Chinese people. According to sociologist Fei Xiaotong, traditionally, the Chinese worldview is "a ripple model." Many Chinese see social interactions as ripples in a lake that move out in circles, impacting close friends/family first and subsequently the wider world.[9] This view still holds today in China. China's neighbouring regions constitute the primary focus of the GCSF because it critically affects its security and development. Then it is extended to all the developing countries, with a focus on countries of the South. A Global Community of Shared Future is the ultimate stage.

First, a community of shared future starts from neighbouring countries. Fourteen continental countries border China, which means that a stable regional order is crucial for Beijing. China can survive and thrive in a stable regional environment. The first step of GCSF was the community of shared future between China and Pakistan, and ASEAN. The Belt and Road Initiative (BRI) is crucial to strengthen China's regional co-operation with these neighbours.

The second stage is a community of shared future with developing countries, namely countries of the South. China claims that the developing countries are naturally in a community of shared future, and they are the primary participants of GCSF. China officially declares that it has the "four confidences" (*si ge zi xin*) in its path, institutions, theories, and culture. GCSF hopes to build such confidence in other developing countries to work for a new future. At the 7th BRICS summit in Ufa, Russia, Xi said:

> International economic rules need constant updating in order to reflect changes in global growth patterns and ensure that a country's responsibilities

are commensurate with its capabilities. We need to work together to enhance the stature and role of the BRICS countries in the global governance system and help shape the international economic order in a way that conforms to the historical trend of rising emerging markets and developing countries.[10]

Third, to make it an internationally accepted concept, President Xi Jinping, in his speeches to the UN in New York and Geneva, and subsequently on almost every international occasion, highlighted the idea of GCSF. GCSF indicates that developing countries are the best partners for China to establish a new pattern in the world. Hence, China will work closely with them. Currently, the problems of the world have originated partly from disruptions in the international order.[11] GCSF intends to propose a new model and make it more inclusive, not to change it.

GCSF also includes governance in emerging fields. Initially, GCSF focuses on traditional areas. Subsequently, it covers the virtual world, such as a community with a shared future in cyberspace. More domains, such as security and trade, to the emerging ones such as deep sea, polar areas, and outer space will be included in the GCSF. Instead of a zero-sum game, China advocates that the guiding principles such as peace, sovereignty, mutual benefit, and common governance will define GCSF governance.

9.2.2 Logical Dimension

The implications of legitimacy indicate the logic of GCSF: If a country's vision of legitimacy can be legitimised globally, then any country's vision can be legitimised. Thus, independent of a country's development model, a shared future can be harmoniously created. The logic is that GCSF seeks to gradually chip away at the notions of national interests and values to construct a common identity. There are three stages to building a common identity.

The first is to build an independent future. China advocates a trustworthy security partnership, which is different from the bilateral alliance system, where countries rely on the US for security and China for economic prosperity. GCSF embodies China's wish that every country should reduce its reliance on the US and the West. For instance, Xi Jinping stated that "the core of GCSF is that the future of a country should be decided by its people, international rules be proposed by all, international affairs be managed together, and the fruits of development be shared by all countries."[12] President Xi Jinping's comments suggest the need to move away from the alliance system. Similarly, BRI promotes independent development, which is different from the EU's concept of transferring sovereignty.

Second, to build a connected future, the independent future of countries should be connected to evolve to a higher level of community. Co-ordinated security and co-ordinated economies can only be achieved when the efforts of countries to develop themselves are respected. It also requires interconnectivity, and the role of BRI is crucial. The core of BRI is to facilitate infrastructure construction and interconnectivity, enhance the complementarity and synergy between the policies and strategies of different countries, deepen practical co-operation, co-ordinate development in other regions and fields, and achieve prosperity together.

The third is to build a shared future and emphasise common ground while resolving differences. Although the world is diverse, there are common memories, common situations, and a common identity, and hence, a common future can be pursued. The concept of GCSF contains the ideas of joint internet, sympathy for all, common values, collective responsibilities, and mutual benefit. Accordingly, BRI emphasises mutual assistance, equality, a search for commonality amidst differences, inclusiveness, and dialogue. It differs from America's exclusive alliance system, as China values openness, inclusiveness, harmony, and co-existence.

Three common values must be established during the process – namely, common targets, common responsibilities, and finally, a common identity. Common targets are to reduce the argument about globalisation. Since there is a pushback against globalisation, there is greater uncertainty in world politics. GCSF's solution is to create common targets for countries to pursue together. Common responsibilities are to solve the conflict of interests between countries to achieve joint development and peace. A significant value is a common identity to narrow the gap between values. GCSF seeks to find common values and avoid the confrontation of ideologies and the so-called clash of civilisations.

9.3 Hong Kong: Practice of the Logic behind GCSF

As a special administrative region of China, the governance of Hong Kong reflects the logic behind GCSF's vision of legitimacy. It is a logic that recognises that the differences in institutions and civilisation can be harmonised, and they can coexist. As Xi said at the Conference marking the 50th Anniversary of the Restoration of the Lawful Seat of the People's Republic of China,

> To build a community with a shared future for mankind is not to replace one system or civilisation with another. Instead, it is about countries with different social systems, ideologies, histories, cultures and levels of development coming together for shared interests, shared rights and shared responsibilities in global affairs, and creating the greatest synergy for building a better world.[13]

Hong Kong is a perfect signal from China to the world that capitalism and socialism can peacefully thrive in the same system. It is the approval of the people that defines the legitimacy of political institutions and development models. Hence, though the developments in Hong Kong constitute domestic affairs, recent developments reflect China's philosophy of harmony behind GCSF, which has guided China's policy for thousands of years.

9.4 Conclusion

To sum up, GCSF operates at three levels. First, it is an approach for a rapidly developing China to get along with the world. It indicates that China's objectives are not to overtake the United States or restore the position of Han or Tang dynasties but to build a global community of shared future. It is, therefore, written into the Constitution of China. Second, it is the "China proposal" to address the world's contemporary challenges in an interconnected world strengthened by the Belt and Road Initiative. Now the GCSF is also part of the Constitution of the CPC. Third, it is intended to find the righteous path for humankind. The Communique of the 6th plenary session of the 19th CPC Central Committee stated that "the concept of a global community of shared future has become a banner leading trends of the times and human progress." In fact, the concept of "a community of shared future for all humankind" was included in a UN resolution, which indicates its growing salience in international politics.

Now, China is exhibiting its vision of legitimacy based on its own culture. GCSF is trying to combine three things into an integrated structure: Chinese traditions, Western traditions, and Marxism traditions. The GCSF also attempts to solve a paradox: If China always stresses that it does not interfere in the domestic affairs of others nations, then how can it claim that it needs to shoulder more international responsibilities? Here, we see the role of GCSF. It is rebuilding the Chinese Communist Party from revolution to construction, from internationalism to globalism.

This chapter posits that GCSF reveals a new vision of legitimacy based on traditional Chinese culture. In time, the spatial and logic dimensions GCSF ensures that legitimacy is based on popular will. GCSF seeks to build conceptual linkages between Western and Chinese history/traditions and the history of human beings. It is practical and is future oriented. Spatial governance – domestic, regional, and global –follows the above principles and the process is gradual. GCSF starts from the neighbouring areas of China and is extended to developing countries because they share a similar history and worldview. A Global Community of Shared Future is the last stage in the whole process. The vision implies making countries independent, connecting them together and making them coexist. In the process, the GCSF intends to create a new common identity of "we-ness" and a new world civilisation of great harmony.

Notes

1 "A Global Community of Shared Future" (人类命运共同体) was also translated as "a Community of Shared Future for Mankind" and "Human Community with a

Shared Future," and used to be translated as "Community of Common Destiny for Humankind/Mankind."
2 Xi Jinping, *On Building a Human Community with a Shared Future* (Beijing: Central Compilation & Translation Press, 2019), 521.
3 Xi Jinping, 'Strengthening Co-operation Among Political Parties to Jointly Pursue the People's Wellbeing', *CPC and World Political Parties Summit* (Beijing, 7 July 2007).
4 Sun Jisheng, 'zhong guo ji hua yu quan de su zao yu ti sheng lu jing – yi dang de shi ba da yi lai de zhong guo wai jiao shi jian wei li [China's Approach to Shape and Improve Its International Discursive Power: Diplomatic Practice Since the 18th Party Congress as an Example]', *World Economics and Politics* (7 July 2017).
5 Emilian Kavalski, 'The Struggle for Recognition of Normative Powers: Normative Power Europe and Normative Power China in Context', *Co-operation and Conflict* (4 June 2013).
6 Xinhua, 'Full Text: Communique of 6th Plenary Session of 19th CPC Central Committee' (11 November 2021).
7 IEA, World Energy Outlook 2018, IEA (2018). https://www.iea.org/reports/world-energy-outlook-2018
8 Xi Jinping, 'Working Together to Forge a New Partnership of Win-Win Co-Operation and Create a Global Community of Shared Future', *The General Debate of the 70th Session of the UN General Assembly* (28 September 2015).
9 Fei Xiaotong, *Earthbound China* (Shanghai: Shang People's Press, 2006), 24.
10 Xi Jinping, 'Building Partnership Together Towards a Bright Future', *7th BRICS summit in Ufa, Russia* (9 July 2015).
11 G. John Ikenberry, 'The Plot Against American Foreign Policy: Can The Liberal Order Survive', *Foreign Affairs* (2017).
12 Xi Jinping, 'Work Together to Build a Global Community of Shared Future', *United Nations Office at Geneva* (18 January 2017).
13 Xi Jinping, Remarks at Conference Marking 50th Anniversary of Restoration of People's Republic of China's Lawful Seat in UN, Beijing (25 October 2021).

Bibliography

Ikenberry, G. John. 'The Plot Against American Foreign Policy: Can the Liberal Order Survive?' *Foreign Affairs* (2017).
Jinping, Xi. 'Building Partnership Together Toward a Bright Future'. *7th BRICS Summit in UFA, Russia* (July 9, 2015).
Jinping, Xi. 'Strengthening Co-operation Among Political Parties to Jointly Pursue the People's Wellbeing'. *CPC and World Political Parties Summit* (Beijing, July 7, 2007).
Jinping, Xi. 'Work Together to Build a Global Community of Shared Future'. *United Nations Office at Geneva* (January 18, 2017).
Jisheng, Sun. 'zhong guo guo ji hua yu quan de su zao yu ti sheng lu jing—Yi dang de shi ba da yi lai de zhong guo wai jiao shi jian wei li [China's Approach to Shape and Improve Its International Discursive Power: Diplomatic Practice Since the 18th Party Congress as an Example]'. *World Economics and Politics* (July 7, 2017).
Kavalski, Emilian. 'The Struggle for Recognition of Normative Powers: Normative Power Europe and Normative Power China in Context'. *Cooperation and Conflict* (June 4, 2013).
Xinhua. 'Full Text: Communique of 6th Plenary Session of 19th CPC Central Committee' (November 11, 2021).

10
TRIBALISM AND THE LIMITS OF LIBERALISM

A (Conservative) Japanese Perspective on Legitimacy in World Politics

Tadashi Anno

10.1 Introduction

World politics today is characterised by growing instability, rising military tensions, and increasing challenge to the legitimacy of the existing international order. In this short chapter, I argue that a major reason for the instability and diminishing legitimacy of the international order lies in what might be called the overreach of liberalism. Liberalism is the reigning idea of the modern world.[1] It has achieved tremendous success and won hundreds of millions if not billions of adherents by protecting individual rights from arbitrary power, and by unleashing the creative and enterprising qualities in individual human beings. Liberalism has also helped create a more peaceful and prosperous world by developing international law and organisations, by promoting economic cooperation, and by advancing trust among liberal democracies. Small wonder liberalism has come to be regarded as a key principle of political legitimacy not only for domestic regimes but also for the international order.

Despite its many strengths, however, I argue that liberalism taken by itself cannot be the basis of a stable social order, either within the state or internationally. Liberalism achieves best results when it serves as a principle of reform for an already existing order. Thus, post-Cold War attempts to reconstitute the international order based on a universalistic interpretation of liberalism have destabilised the existing order. The instability has been amplified by the over-optimistic belief in the neutrality and universality of liberalism, which has led liberal states to attempt an expansion of the liberal order, arousing negative reactions from many in the non-western world. Politics is at its root an activity characterised by tribalism.[2] While it is possible to make our tribal politics more liberal, we cannot replace tribalism with thoroughgoing liberalism.[3] In the rest of this chapter, I will first briefly trace the evolution of the liberal international order and then analyse how an "overreach" of liberalism in the post-Cold War era led to instability and crisis of this order.

10.2 The Evolution of the Liberal International Order: Layers of Legitimacy in IR

The central challenge for any international order is how to ensure some measure of orderliness among states with widely divergent values and cultures. Before the global expansion of Europe, world politics was dominated by "universal empires," whose authority theoretically extended to the entire known world. Imperial China, the Islamic Caliphate, and the Byzantine Empire were prime examples. Universal empires sought to establish order over an expansive region beyond immediate territories of the state by subordinating peripheral regions to a single, imperial authority – in theory, if not in reality. By contrast, the modern international order originates from the failure of an attempt to build an "imperial" order in Europe. Protracted religious wars were terminated based on the principle that multiple states enjoy equal claim to justice and sovereignty. The principle of "multiple sovereignty" was well-suited for facilitating coexistence among states with divergent values and cultures.[4] This principle, or what I have termed "sovereignty values," to this day constitutes the most foundational layer in the principles of legitimacy in world politics.[5]

Yet, the modern international order has faced multiple criticisms as it spread from Europe to the rest of the world, and reactions to such criticisms have generated additional principles of political legitimacy. For our purposes, three criticisms are most relevant. First, granting sovereign power to states and to their monarchical rulers may have been necessary to end a state of civil war in Europe, but sovereign authority of the state could easily turn into a threat to the rights and freedoms of the people. Liberalism arose to check the excessive and arbitrary power of the state and to guarantee individual freedom and dignity. Until the 19th century, however, liberalism remained mostly a principle of domestic political legitimacy.

Second, while state sovereignty brought peace within state borders, and facilitated coexistence of states with conflicting claims of "justice," the anarchical character of the Westphalian system meant that the relationship among states was prone to warfare. The critique of the war-prone character of the Westphalian system intensified in the early 20th century, when total wars resulted in the deaths of tens of millions, including non-combatants. Third, while the system of sovereign states presupposed the coexistence of "multiple justices" within Europe, the expansion of that system to non-European areas took place mostly on the basis of colonial domination and imposition of "unequal treaties," reflecting the assertion of the superiority of European civilisation over the rest of the world.[6] While the claim of superiority of European/western civilisation was accepted by many outside the West, colonial domination and racial discrimination eventually aroused widespread resistance against the West. In the early 20th century, the intense rivalry among western great powers became merged with non-western revolt against the West and exploded in a major conflagration. This crisis of the international order led to the de-legitimation of aggressive wars and of colonial rule, which constitutes the second most fundamental layer in the principles of legitimacy in world politics ("non-aggression values").

Liberalism first emerged on the international political scene as a major force after World War I, when Woodrow Wilson proposed a liberal reform of the international order. Liberalism had emerged as the dominant ideology in the domestic politics and economy of western states by the mid-19th century, but its influence on foreign policy remained limited. International politics, still centred on Europe, continued to be dominated by state sovereignty and the balance of power. But the Great War destroyed the confidence of the European elites in the old system and opened up the political space for new ideas to step in.[7] Wilsonian liberalism, along with Leninism, emerged as new, competing principles of legitimacy for reorganising world politics in response to the dual crises of great-power war and revolt of the non-West.

From its inception, the US saw itself as a "land of liberty" free from the European diseases of "tyranny and incessant warfare." Contrary to the moral relativism inherent in the European sovereign states system, Americans believed that their country was a "city upon a hill," whose mission was to show the way to the rest of humanity.[8] Standing squarely in this tradition, Wilson argued that the crisis of the Eurocentric international order would be resolved by America's liberal ideas. Despite its ambiguities and compromises, Wilson's vision pointed to a liberal international order in which nations, exercising their right of self-determination as well as democratic control over their foreign policies, assembled to form international organisations and were bound together by close economic ties.

The post-World War I attempt to reform the international order along liberal lines proved singularly unsuccessful. By contrast, the US-led post-World War II attempt to build a liberal international order proved much more successful. Some of the reasons for this success will be discussed later. Here, suffice it to say that decolonisation of the 1950s and 1960s removed the biggest sore spot in the legitimacy of a liberal international order and undermined the argument of the Leninist critics, who had charged that capitalism cannot survive except through imperialist expansion. The declining credibility of Marxism, coupled with the military and moral defeat of right-wing dictatorships, served to strengthen the legitimacy of liberalism. Liberal, western values (whose key components are respect for individual rights, political democracy, market economy, plus friendship and economic cooperation among liberal democracies) became the third layer in the principles of international political legitimacy.

With the end of the Cold War, the liberal international order appeared triumphant, ready to conquer the rest of the world. Liberal values, which had been confined largely to the western camp, now appeared to have become universal values. Yet, some 30 years later, the picture looks very different. In my view, the current crisis is largely a product of the weaknesses of liberalism as an organising principle for international order, and of the failure of many liberals to take them into account. Specifically, I focus on three weaknesses: the illusion of universality, underestimation of the role of coercive power, and undermining of the system of sovereign nation-states. These weaknesses, in combination, have led to a triple crisis, including the revenge of power politics, instability in the West, and pushback from the rest.

10.3 The Overreach of Liberalism and the Crisis of the International Order

10.3.1 The Illusion of Universality

Historically, ideas which later crystallised as liberalism developed as assertions of the rights and freedoms of privileged estates in certain European states. Since the Enlightenment period, however, liberalism took a universalistic turn. Instead of the rights of the nobility or of Englishmen, liberals increasingly spoke of the "rights of man." This instilled a strong element of universalism in liberal thought, which stood in tension with the sovereign state. If individual rights were universal, the legitimacy of the existence of separate states was questionable. In practice, of course, most liberals took the sovereign states system for granted. But whereas sovereignty meant that states were free to choose their own political system, liberalism implied that only liberal states were fully legitimate.

Such universalistic aspirations of liberalism did not manifest themselves immediately. Enlightenment did not require that every individual and every state be given equal freedom right away. In the Enlightenment worldview, freedom and rights of men were justified by the universality of reason. But in reality, reason was regarded as unevenly developed, depending on race, ethnicity, gender, and other variable. Thus, the Enlightenment worldview justified the rule by the "civilised" humanity over the supposedly "uncivilised," including European colonial rule over the rest of the world.

By the second half of the 20th century, this international version of enlightened despotism was de-legitimised, as the "self-determination of peoples" became the order of the day. At a practical level, de-colonisation meant the victory of state sovereignty over claims of Enlightenment universalism. The world became politically and culturally more diverse with the entry of dozens of ex-colonial states into the international society. Yet, this did not extinguish the belief in the universal validity of liberalism. Theoretically, the declaration that all peoples are ready for self-rule meant that there was one less reason why liberalism should not be universalised immediately.

Liberals were not blind to the importance of cultural differences. But by the early 21st century, under the impact of globalisation, culture was being reconceptualised by many analysts as something malleable, changeable, and subject to individual choice and hybridisation, instead of being an all-encompassing, stable, and tightly organised structure which mould people's thought and behaviour.[9] Individual freedom coupled with global communication would tear down the Chinese Walls of cultural differences. The 1993 Vienna Declaration of the World Conference on Human Rights stated that "it is the duty of States, regardless of their political, economic, and cultural systems, to promote and to protect all human rights and fundamental freedoms."[10]

Given this background, it was perhaps natural that, with the end of the Cold War, many liberals hoped that liberal democracy would become the global political standard and that they made strenuous efforts in that direction. Lengthy preparation was no longer considered prerequisite to democratic change; one needed only to bring down the existing authoritarian government. Some called for regime change imposed from above through military force. Others preferred to assist indigenous democratic revolutions by training activists in the technique of peaceful popular protest. Still others advocated a more patient approach, sending advisors to help existing governments, or working with the civil society sector. Regardless of the variety in approaches, the universality of liberal democracy and the justifiability of foreign assistance for its realisation were taken for granted.

Yet, despite its broad appeal, claim of universal validity, and appearance of neutrality, the universality of liberalism is questionable on three counts. First, liberalism is a partisan ideology in its unswerving commitment to individual liberty and autonomy. While liberalism seeks to provide a "neutral" platform on the basis of which individuals with diverse beliefs and values can pursue their own vision of "the good life,"[11] liberal neutrality applies only to those conceptions of the human good which accept the freedom and autonomy of individuals as the ground rule.[12] Dismantling an existing authoritarian government may lead to successful democratisation in a society which has embraced (or is ready to embrace) the value of individual freedom and autonomy, and where there is a pre-existing consensus that the society should form a unified political community. But the same act might simply lead to chaos where requisite conditions are lacking.[13]

Second, the liberal search for a "neutral platform" where everyone can pursue his/her vision of the good life on an equal footing may prove ultimately illusory. Liberal institutions still need to be built upon the basis of what Will Kymlicka calls "societal culture" – a shared vocabulary of tradition and convention which provides members with meaningful ways of life across the full range of human activities.[14] And while a societal culture can encompass a wide variety of religious beliefs, political ideologies, and lifestyles, it cannot be neutral because it has to build on a shared language and on a set of shared traditions and conventions. To the extent that "societal culture" cannot be neutral, the playing field is not entirely level for diverse citizens of liberal states, especially for historically discriminated minorities. Thus, it is not surprising that liberal democratic societies in recent decades have witnessed the rise of "identity politics." If liberal institutions based on individualist assumptions have difficulty addressing the question of minority rights within predominantly liberal societies, this casts more doubt on the universalisability of liberalism globally.

Third, the universalistic aspirations of liberalism do not prevent it from being implicated in the struggle for status and recognition in the international society. The claim on the universal validity of liberalism may be rooted in a genuine belief in liberalism's intrinsic value for all human beings. Yet sometimes, liberalism and democracy are promoted as "western values" by the same Westerners who claim their universality.[15] It is natural that people see such values as "western," for it was indeed in the western world that those values were first articulated and practised in their modern forms. Yet ostentatious claims of collective "ownership" over principles can transform supposedly universal values into tribal totems. If liberal democracy is a universal value, all states should embrace them. But if it is advertised as a "western" value, it was natural that some began to assert that "Asian values" are more suitable for Asian states.

In short, while liberalism is universalistic in its orientation, its reach is not quite universal; it can work only in the context of stable polities ready to accept the assumptions of individualism. The assumption of universality of liberalism has led western states to ambitious projects of liberal enlargement in the post-Cold War era. But when imposed upon societies without the requisite conditions, such attempts were prone to generate confusion, resentment, hostility, or sheer chaos. Resentment or pushback from the non-western states may not have mattered much if liberal, western states had overwhelming power advantage. But the power balance was shifting while liberal thinking preferred not to pay attention to questions of power.

10.3.2 Underestimation of the Role of Coercive Power

Social orders including international orders can achieve stability only with the backing of coercive power. This is not to say that power alone is sufficient, but neither is legitimacy. For one thing, even a social order that is legitimate in the eyes of most may still face violent challenges from the disgruntled few. For another, even those who consider the order legitimate may be tempted to achieve unilateral advantage by challenging the order, using force if necessary. Thus, to be stable, a social order requires the reliable backing of power in addition to legitimacy.

Generally speaking, liberalism has de-emphasised the element of power in the construction of social order, seeing in coercive power (especially one unregulated by law) a grave danger to individual liberty.[16] In the field of international relations, too, liberal theorists have paid comparatively small attention to the role of power. Instead, they have explored how the role of force in international relations might be minimised through international law, economic interdependence, or cooperation among democracies. While it is entirely reasonable that liberals have sought to limit the role of force, at times this has led to an underestimation of the role of power. Undoubtedly, one major factor in the failure of the interwar liberal international order was the lack of an effective backing of coercive power, which may be attributed partly to the weakness of liberal international relations theory in *recognising the necessity* of power.[17]

Liberalism also faces difficulty *procuring* the coercive power needed for the defence of liberal societies from domestic and external challenges. Defending society from violent challenges requires that some of its members risk their own lives when needed. But to the extent that liberalism emphasises the universality of individual rights, including the right to life, liberalism alone is hardly sufficient to motivate citizens to undertake the obligations of national defence (or policing violent crimes).[18]

Obviously, from ancient Athens to today's US, liberal states have not necessarily been lacking in military prowess. One might argue that liberal, democratic states are *more* capable than their authoritarian competitors of mobilising citizens' loyalty and thus are better equipped for national defence. The defence capability of liberal states is further enhanced by the advantages in wealth, technology, and alliance diplomacy which liberal states often enjoy. Yet it is not liberalism itself but rather patriotism that provides liberal states with the *moral* resources for national defence. Liberal states may enjoy strong patriotic support of their citizens. But liberalism does not provide compelling reasons why individuals should tie their fate to that of a particular nation, especially in adversity. If anything, liberalism tends to weaken such ties, because it emphasises the element of choice in individuals' relations with the state.

Given these considerations, the stability of the US-led liberal international order in the post-World War II era must be regarded as a product of exceptionally favourable and not easily replicated circumstances. As mentioned earlier, the US has regarded itself as a special nation with a global mission to spread liberty worldwide. Events of the 1930s and 1940s convinced the American leadership and the public that American security and interests cannot be protected without US commitment to the defence of a liberal international order. Further, Americans were ready to make sacrifices out of patriotism for that purpose. The idea of America's universal mission coupled with the willingness to sacrifice did much to prop up the liberal international order during the Cold War era.

With the end of the Cold War, an optimistic outlook returned to western liberal thinking about military power. While small rogue states remained, the big rivals seemed to have disappeared; Russia was democratising, and China had fully embraced the market economy, which in the long run was believed certain to bring about democratisation. With all or most great powers embracing liberal democracy and the global market economy, the chances of major-power wars would be almost nil.

Naturally, this did not lead to disarmament of the West (or of the US in particular). While the collapse of the USSR allowed NATO member states to decrease their combined military spending by 28 per cent between 1987 and 1998,[19] the post-Cold War US strategy aimed to consolidate US military dominance for decades to come.[20] What is remarkable, though, is the fact that the expectation was widespread that long-term US primacy would be accomplished without evoking negative reactions from other major powers. The US is a liberal hegemon which seeks no territorial aggrandisement, and which has the capacity to bind itself in international institutions and to exercise its power with restraint, or so it was argued.[21] Thus, there was no reason why American and more generally western military power should threaten the security of other states. Because economic development eventually brings about the liberalisation of the political system, it was hardly likely that the global balance of power would shift in favour of authoritarian states.

But things turned out quite differently. A favourable balance of power, coupled with the assumption of universality of liberalism, led the US and its allies to engage in an ambitious project of liberal expansion. Attempts to export liberal democracy by force caused chaos in the Middle East, and trapped the US in protracted warfare, sapping material resources as well as domestic support for international leadership role. Both Russia and China turned their backs on democratisation, achieved economic growth through participation in the capitalist market economy, and invested a significant portion of their newfound wealth in military buildup. Yet, distracted by the "war against terror" and clinging to the liberal vision of a post-realist world, western liberal democracies were slow to refocus their strategic priorities. Russian invasion of Crimea and Chinese expansion in the South China Sea served as rude wake-up calls. But by that time, a new crisis was festering inside liberal western states.

10.3.3 Undermining the Framework of Sovereign Nation-States

Due to its universalistic character, liberalism stands in tense relationship with the system of sovereign nation-states. Liberalism acknowledges that a state is necessary to ensure the rights and freedoms of individuals. Yet, it is not easy to legitimise *existing national/state boundaries* based on a liberal political theory.[22] The two world wars of the early 20th century had already cast a spell of doubt over nation-states, especially among intellectuals.[23] After the end of the Cold War, this trend accelerated; "obsolescence of national borders" became an article of faith among many western intellectuals. In addition to economic openness, which exposed workers in rich countries to competition from workers in the developing world, borders of western states were opened wide for immigration, resulting in a significant hike in the share of immigrant population.[24]

Rapid change in the composition of the population destabilises established views of national identity. This is certainly true in nations whose identity has been defined in racial or ethnic terms. Even in "civic nations," the existing majority often perceive such changes as a threat. It may be possible to dismiss the "threat" perceived by the racial/ethnic majority as arising from the loss of undue privileges. Yet, for some segments of the majority, any privileges accruing from race or ethnicity may pale before their economic marginalisation and lack of cultural capital. It is not surprising that such people protested the elite-led project of globalisation.

From the viewpoint of universalistic liberalism, such protests may appear both unreasonable and pointless. There is no compelling reason why citizens should be favoured over non-citizen immigrants or potential immigrants. Moreover, a transnational, "civic identity"[25] will perhaps replace national identity in the long run, so "backward-looking" political forces may simply be left to rot in the garbage heap of history. Yet the neglect and rhetorical denigration of a significant portion of a nation's economic and cultural underclass stand in curious tension with the pervasive rhetoric of "inclusion."

Politics is often characterised by "tribal" behaviour. Conflicts over issues may normally be resolved by rational discussions, mutually acceptable compromises, or through tug-of-war among competing interests. But when stakes are high, and when conflicts intensify to a certain level, lines are drawn between "friends" and "enemies," and each side begins to behave in a more tribal manner. When this happens, morality, science, economic ties, and religious teachings – all are prone to be mobilised and reconstructed to serve political ends.[26] Each tribe monitors the loyalty of its members and punishes or expels "traitors." A central goal of liberalism is to prevent such tribal behaviour from running amok, trampling individual rights and liberties in the process.

Yet, what complicates the problem is that, once caught in the gravitational field of tribal politics, even progressive and humane ideas can become the totem for a political tribe, and in that capacity, function as exclusionary and bellicose ideologies. Opposition to the exploitation of workers, when it was turned into a political totem, could serve to mobilise hatred of the class enemy as well as to justify extermination of suspected "traitors" within the working class. It is evident that ideas such as racism and religious fundamentalism easily generate such tribal behaviour. But even seemingly innocuous ideas such as "protecting minorities" and "promoting diversity" are not exempt from similar dangers *if* they become the banner of tribal struggle against "enemy" forces.

Putting the matter differently, I submit that, in the world of politics, which is easily prone to tribalism, values such as racial equality or protection of minority rights are most likely to be respected *if they become embedded in the collective identity of entire societies* ("large tribes"). Even individuals who hold prejudicial views of minority groups may at least pretend to respect such values, if protecting minority rights is part of the identity of their "larger tribe," and if conformity with such values is important to enhance one's own status within that tribe.

This implies that values which cannot achieve "consensual" status within a particular society (large tribe) are unlikely to be observed reliably in that society. "Consensual" values often reflect the values of dominant groups, while minority groups usually find themselves in structurally disadvantaged positions. In such cases, minority groups can hardly expect to improve their position in society except through political struggle, and the resort to "us-versus-them" rhetoric is unavoidable. Nevertheless, it is my argument that, in the case of democratic polities, such struggles are likely to achieve the best long-term results if they are presented not primarily as a power struggle of the oppressed against the oppressors, but rather as an appeal to the sense of justice of the "larger tribe."

10.4 Conclusion

If we are to believe the findings of evolutionary psychology, human beings have evolved as tribal animals.[27] Social orders formed by human beings are not exactly the products of contracts among autonomous individuals, as liberal political theories hypothesise. Rather, they are shaped by the tribal nature of humans. This is not to say that politics is wholly determined by biology, or that our search for a better social and political order is futile. Though humans are tribal animals, "tribes" can be formed based on a variety of criteria. And how people relate to each other within their own tribes, and whether cooperation, competition, or conflict dominates the relationship among tribes vary widely depending on the cultures, ideas, and institutions on the basis of which tribes are formed, organised, and carry out relations among themselves.

Liberalism launched a new era in the history of human civilisation by focusing on the autonomy of individual human beings, by bringing together diverse individuals under common ideals of freedom and equality, and by unleashing their creativity. Although liberalism currently faces a major crisis and fundamental criticisms,[28] it is unlikely that its principles and achievements will be easily discarded. Liberalism will no doubt remain a central element in any plausible theory of legitimacy in world politics for the foreseeable future. Yet, given that human beings are still divided into states and nations, and given that those tribal entities still provide important anchors for people's identities, attempts to undermine such frameworks and to reorganise world politics along transnational lines are likely to produce more conflict and less freedom. Also, while it is natural for domestic underprivileged groups to assert their own "tribal" identities, better long-term results in liberal democratic societies may be achieved from politics of the "common good," which seeks to appeal to the "better angels" of the larger tribes' nature.

A social order is oriented towards the realisation of a particular set of values, from which it derives legitimacy. The strong appeal that the liberal international order has enjoyed in the past derived in no small part from the belief in the universal validity of liberalism. The liberal international order today faces not only instability within, but also military challenges from without. Under such conditions, some may worry that raising questions about the universality of liberal values might itself contribute to the weakening of the already shaky ties among liberal democracies and shift the global balance of power in favour of authoritarian challengers. Yet, to argue that liberal values should be embedded in the framework of historically evolved communities need not be regarded as a step backward. My only plea to liberals is to have patience for the recalcitrance of human nature and to appreciate once again the extent to which individual freedom depends on the framework of stable social and political orders, which in today's world is still underpinned by nations, states, or their confederations.

Now that the post-Cold War dream of a universal liberal order is gone, any liberal international order would have to be built as a patchwork quilt of like-minded liberal democracies and friendly nations. In the face of flagrant violation of the basic norm of non-aggression, the top priority of liberal democracies today should be to salvage what is left of an international order in which international disputes are resolved peacefully. While liberal democracies should, in partnership with friendly states, continue to pursue their attempt to build and to strengthen the liberal international order, they should do so in a way that is compatible with the maintenance of domestic socio-political stability. And in dealing with non-liberal states, our belief in liberal values must be tempered by a measure of respect for different cultures and traditions and by humility about our own fallibility. Such a cautious, unobtrusive approach is more likely to restore stability in liberal states and to win more friends for the liberal international order around the world. In the longer term, such an approach may also facilitate a true dialogue among different civilisations concerning the meaning of freedom – and more broadly about conceptions of the human good.[29]

Notes

1 I understand liberalism as an intellectual/political stance which regards the pursuit of individual freedom and dignity through the defence of individual rights as the highest principle of public policy.
2 By tribalism I mean the seemingly innate tendency of individual human beings to identify themselves as members of a particular group in competition with other groups, and to act qua members of that group. Tribalism induces people to make sharp distinctions between the ingroup and the outgroup, to believe the former is superior, and to denigrate or even attack the latter. On tribalism, see Amy Chua, *Political Tribes: Group Instinct and the Fate of Nations* (New York: Penguin, 2018).
3 My viewpoint is conservative in expressing scepticism about the possibility of reconstructing the entire structure of world politics according to consistent, rational principles. It also reflects modern Japan's historical experience in that, while acknowledging the strengths and benefits of liberalism, it is informed by the sense that liberalism is a particular way of life that presupposes certain cultural underpinnings which are not universally shared.
4 Henry Kissinger, *World Order: Reflections on the Character of Nations and the Course of History* (New York: Penguin, 2014), 6–7.
5 Tadashi Anno, 'Values in Japanese Foreign Policy: Between "Universal Values" and the Search for Cultural Pluralism,' in Krishnan Srinivasan et al. (ed.), *Values in Foreign Policy: Investigating Ideals and Interests* (New York: Romwan & Littlefield, 2019), 228–229.
6 Hedley Bull and Adam Watson (eds.), *The Expansion of the International Society* (Oxford: The Clarendon Press, 1984).
7 A.J.P. Taylor, *The Origins of the Second World War* (London: H. Hamilton, 1961), 30.
8 Samuel P Huntington, 'American Ideals versus American Institutions', *Political Science Quarterly* (Spring 1982): 1–37.
9 Mary Margaret Steedly, 'The State of Culture Theory in the Anthropology of Southeast Asia', *Annual Review of Anthropology* 28 (1999): 440–444.

10 See the website of the Office of the UN High Commissioner for Human Rights: https://www.ohchr.org/EN/ProfessionalInterest/Pages/Vienna.aspx (last accessed 17 April 2022).
11 Michael Sandel, *Liberalism and the Limits of Justice*, 2nd edition (Princeton: Princeton University Press, 1998).
12 Will Kymlicka, *Multicultural Citizenship: A Liberal Theory of Minority Rights* (Oxford University Press, 1995), 152–172.
13 Roland Paris, *At War's End: Building Peace after Civil Conflict* (Cambridge University Press, 2004), 235–236.
14 Will Kymlicka, *Multicultural Citizenship*, 83.
15 David Sadler, 'Defending the West: Ideology and Foreign Policy during the Cold War', in Philip John Davis (ed.), *Representing and Imagining America* (Edinburgh: Edinburgh University Press, 1996), 215–216.
16 Roland Paris, *At War's End*, 40.
17 E.H. Carr, *The Twenty Years' Crisis 1919–1939: An Introduction to the Study of International Relations* (New York: Harper & Row, 1946), 50–62.
18 April Carter, 'Liberalism and the Obligation to Military Service', *Political Studies* (March 1998): 68–81.
19 *SIPRI Military Expenditure Database*, https://www.sipri.org/databases/milex (last accessed 17 April 2022).
20 Hal Brands, 'Choosing Primacy: US Strategy and Global Order at the Dawn of the Post-Cold War Era', *Texas National Security Review* 1, no. 2 (2018): 8–33.
21 Ikenberry, John, G. (ed.), *America Unrivaled: The Future of Balance of Power* (Cornell University Press, 2002).
22 Stephen Holmes, *Passions and Constraint: On the Theory of Liberal Democracy* (University of Chicago Press, 1995), 39.
23 R.R. Reno, *Return of the Strong Gods: Nationalism, Populism, and the Future of the West* (Washington, DC: Regnery Gateway, 2019), 1–31.
24 The share of foreign-born population in the combined population of G7 countries increased from 6.97 per cent in 1990 to 12.00 per cent by 2015. Calculated from World Bank data on international migrant stock: https://data.worldbank.org/indicator/SM.POP.TOTL.ZS (last accessed April 17, 2022).
25 The concept is borrowed from Daniel Deudney and G. John Ikenberry, 'The Nature and Sources of Liberal International Order', *Review of International Studies* (April 1999): 192–195.
26 Carl Schmitt, *The Concept of the Political* (Chicago: University of Chicago Press, 1996), 25–27.
27 Jonathan Haidt, *The Righteous Mind: Why Good People Are Divided by Politics and Religion* (New York: Pantheon, 2012), 161–165; Joshua Greene, *Moral Tribes: Emotion, Reason, and the Gap between Us and Them* (New York: Penguin, 2013), 49–69.
28 Patrick Deneen, *Why Liberalism Failed* (Yale University Press, 2018).
29 Yasusuke Murakami, *An Anti-Classical Political-Economic Analysis: A Vision for the Twenty-First Century* (Stanford: Stanford University Press, 1997).

Bibliography

Anno, Tadashi. "Values in Japanese Foreign Policy: Between 'Universal Values' and the Search for Cultural Pluralism." In *Values in Foreign Policy: Investigating Ideals and Interests*, edited by Krishnan Srinivasan, James Mayall, and Sanjay Pulipaka. New York: Romwan & Littlefield, 2019, 227–249.
Brands, Hal. "Choosing Primacy: US Strategy and Global Order at the Dawn of the Post-Cold War Era." *Texas National Security Review* 1, no. 2 (2018): 8–33.

Bull, Hedley, and Adam Watson, eds. *The Expansion of the International Society*. Oxford: The Clarendon Press, 1984.

Carr, E. H. *The Twenty Years' Crisis 1919–1939: An Introduction to the Study of International Relations*. New York: Harper & Row, 1946.

Carter, April. "Liberalism and the Obligation to Military Service." *Political Studies* (March 1998): 68–81.

Chua, Amy. *Political Tribes: Group Instinct and the Fate of Nations*. New York: Penguin, 2018.

Deneen, Patrick. *Why Liberalism Failed*. New Haven, CT: Yale University Press, 2018.

Deudney, Daniel, and G. John Ikenberry. "The Nature and Sources of Liberal International Order." *Review of International Studies* (April 1999): 179–196.

Greene, Joshua. *Moral Tribes: Emotion, Reason, and the Gap Between Us and Them*. New York: Penguin, 2013.

Haidt, Jonathan. *The Righteous Mind: Why Good People Are Divided by Politics and Religion*. New York: Pantheon, 2012.

Holmes, Stephen. *Passions and Constraint: On the Theory of Liberal Democracy*. Chicago, IL: University of Chicago Press, 1995.

Huntington, Samuel P. "American Ideals Versus American Institutions." *Political Science Quarterly* (Spring 1982): 1–37.

Ikenberry, G. John, ed. *America Unrivaled: The Future of Balance of Power*. Ithaca, NY: Cornell University Press, 2002.

Kissinger, Henry. *World Order: Reflections on the Character of Nations and the Course of History*. New York: Penguin, 2014.

Kymlicka, Will. *Multicultural Citizenship: A Liberal Theory of Minority Rights*. Oxford: Oxford University Press, 1995.

Murakami, Yasusuke. *An Anti-Classical Political-Economic Analysis: A Vision for the Twenty-First Century*. Stanford, CA: Stanford University Press, 1997.

Paris, Roland. *At War's End: Building Peace After Civil Conflict*. Cambridge: Cambridge University Press, 2004.

Reno, R. R. *Return of the Strong Gods: Nationalism, Populism, and the Future of the West*. Washington, DC: Regnery Gateway, 2019.

Sadler, David. "Defending the West: Ideology and Foreign Policy During the Cold War." In *Representing and Imagining America*, edited by Philip John Davis. Edinburgh: Edinburgh University Press, 1996, 210–220.

Sandel, Michael. *Liberalism and the Limits of Justice*, 2nd edition. Princeton, NJ: Princeton University Press, 1998.

Schmitt, Carl. *The Concept of the Political*. Chicago, IL: University of Chicago Press, 1996.

Steedly, Mary Margaret. "The State of Culture Theory in the Anthropology of Southeast Asia." *Annual Review of Anthropology* 28 (1999): 431–454.

Taylor, A. J. P. *The Origins of the Second World War*. London: H. Hamilton, 1961.

11
AUTOCRACY, INSTITUTIONAL WEAKNESS, AND LATIN AMERICAN CONCEPT OF LEGITIMACY

Deepak Bhojwani

11.1 Introduction

Latin America[1] is a disparate region comprising around 20 nation-states whose geographical isolation exceeds that of North America. The latter made its global political presence felt only in the 20th century, the former has yet to make its mark. Cynics endorse the opinion of French President Charles de Gaulle on whether Brazil was the country of the future: "… and always will be."[2]

Most Latin American nations gained their independence in the early 19th century, long before their Asian and African counterparts. In Latin America, the elites that seized power and retained it after the colonial retreat were descendants of the colonial rulers or subsequent migrants from Europe. In Asia, the indigenous populations assumed power, as in most of Africa. Latin America was hence oriented politically and economically towards Europe, and later the United States. Though Asian and African regimes too depended economically on the western powers, they came into their own over a century after Latin American nations, in a world debilitated by two world wars and impacted by conflicting ideologies. Many followed a more independent policy in their relations with the western and socialist blocs.[3]

Latin America's conquest and colonisation by Spain and Portugal was violent, the decimation of the indigenous races in most of the region leading to the import and enslavement of hundreds of thousands of Africans. Social tensions were latent but inherent. Independence was mostly achieved by violent insurrection (with the notable exception of Brazil), enabling the militarisation and empowerment of the local "creole"[4] community. The hangover from the colonial era led to the formation of paternalistic societies in most cases. In many instances, local strongmen or *"caudillos"* assumed political power, sometimes giving way to rule by the armed forces, spurred by border conflicts and revanchist

DOI: 10.4324/9781003385233-11

ventures. The concept and essence of legitimacy in this region were initially based on the exercise of the military – and consequent political – power in the 19th century, refined over the twentieth by the dictates of international law and practice, as well as the evolution of civil society and democratic models of governance.

11.2 The Foundations of Autocracy and Ideological Struggle

Although Latin American freedom fighters were motivated by European republican ideals, they did not manage to get the new-born nations to coalesce around the founding principles of the American and French revolutions. Even Simon Bolivar, the Liberator of most of South America, failed in his attempt to unite the countries he liberated[5] and the region split up into nation-states with their own peculiarities. Ideological and political differences still get in the way of the political cohesion that has enabled the European Union and ASEAN to promote common ideals and goals. This enables even elected leaders and political parties to subvert national laws and debilitate institutions to exercise power.

The absence, or weakness, of conventional political institutions in post-colonial Latin America enabled the Catholic Church to consolidate its hold on the populations. While this helped ruling elites maintain legitimacy in many cases, the doctrine of *Liberation Theology*[6] propounded by some progressive priests posed a challenge to several regimes and inspired some modern left-wing political movements.

The advent of left-wing and communist ideologies survived repression of the Mexican Communist Party (founded in 1919, with India's M. N. Roy as a member). Leftist ideologues like Jose Marti of Cuba, Jose Vasconcelos of Mexico, Victor Haya de la Torre and Mariategui of Peru, Augusto Sandino of Nicaragua, Farabundo Marti of El Salvador, and others became role models. Notable in this struggle was the tenacity of armed insurrection movements in Colombia (FARC), Peru (Shining Path), Mexico (Zapata and Pancho Villa), and Nicaragua (Sandinistas). Most of these were eliminated or contained, but their vestiges continue to present political dilemmas today. The left came into its own with the Cuban revolution in 1959. The communist regime provided an anchor – and an icon in Fidel Castro – for Hugo Chavez in Venezuela, Raphael Correa in Ecuador, Evo Morales in Bolivia, and Daniel Ortega in Nicaragua, among others. This ideological divide prevails and accentuates the continuing struggle for the legitimacy of political, social, and economic policy in Latin America. As explained earlier, political legitimacy in Latin America stemmed initially from the ability to capture and retain power through strength – primarily military – which then bestowed a certain legacy on the personalities of leaders and their families or chosen successors. This paradigm was challenged, sometimes by leftist ideologues but also by military generals who overthrew regimes which had lost steam politically or otherwise became inconvenient to certain vested interests, not always local.

In most cases the genesis of these ideological confrontations lies in the history of dictatorship, military rule, and foreign intervention that plagued the region for over a century. The dictatorship of Porfirio Diaz in Mexico; the violence in Colombia in the mid-20th century; the 1964 military coup in Brazil; military rule in Argentina from 1976 till 1983; the tumultuous uprisings in Central America; the assassination of President Salvador Allende in Chile in 1970; and subsequent dictatorship of Augusto Pinochet till 1988 were some of the more egregious events in Latin America's history.

The role of external powers, principally Europe and the US, was nefarious in many ways. From the declaration of the Monroe Doctrine in 1823[7] to the Cold War and subsequent contention between the US/Europe versus Russia and China, Latin America has been buffeted by forces it has been unable to resist. In many instances, political leaders have chosen to collaborate with foreign interests, out of helplessness or for political gain. The 20th century was littered with invasions, regime change, assassinations, and other instances of political engineering to keep Latin American regimes in line with the interests of the power concerned. In this century, some regimes have challenged US power with political and economic support from Russia and China. This collaboration sometimes involved mortgaging of national interest and autonomy and the skirting of democratic responsibilities.

Despite the virtual absence of any territorial or foreign military threat, the armed forces are not firmly in the barracks. Costa Rica is the only country without an army (since 1948). In Brazil, attempts by the left to highlight the excesses of 20th-century military rule have been downplayed successfully by a military establishment that currently holds the Vice Presidency and ten Cabinet posts under President Bolsonaro. Mexico's armed forces have put successive regimes on notice, helped by the threat of drug cartels.[8] Colombia's military has been empowered over decades by US political, military, and financial backing of the war against the FARC. Paraguay's armed forces have seen off leftist regimes, as have the Argentine forces. Left-wing governments in Ecuador, Peru, Bolivia, and Central America have accepted the inevitability of the armed forces: Rafael Correa put the navy in charge of the Ecuador state oil company; Evo Morales stepped down in 2019 after winning the Bolivian elections, on the urging of the army. Chile's armed forces are more disciplined and respected, and their political power will probably diminish further with the promulgation of a new constitution in 2022.

Apart from ample budget allocations, the power of the Latin American armed forces also abides because they control the police forces, which deal with organised crime and other local security threats. In a region where public and civic services are often found wanting, they also manage functions such as disaster management, pandemic control, and immigration.

11.3 Institutional Weakness in Latin America

Although democracy in Latin America has survived challenges from the armed forces, autocrats, and "revolutionaries," its principal challenge – the lack of strong institutions – works to the detriment of governance all over the region. Most of the nations have elected parliaments which can serve as checks on powers of the presidency and executive. Too often however, the political party system emasculates parliamentary oversight. If the executive succeeds in achieving a parliamentary majority – as in El Salvador – or controlling it – as in Cuba, Nicaragua, or Venezuela – elected representatives are little more than political appointees. If the parliamentary majority is in opposition, it often forces elected presidents to sacrifice crucial policies and reforms to satisfy vested political interests, as in the case of Peru or Argentina.

On 5 April 1992, Peru's President Alberto Fujimori dissolved the constitution, shut down the opposition-controlled Congress, and "reorganised" the judicial branch, eliminating all constitutional checks and balances. The constitution was rewritten, and he was re-elected – not entirely fairly – in 1995. His supporters won control of Congress, allowing Fujimori to pack the Supreme Court and the electoral authorities. Fujimori inherited hyperinflation and a brutal Maoist insurgency. His approval rating was 80 per cent after the coup, partly because most Peruvians wanted a fresh start. His success in ending hyperinflation and defeating the Shining Path enabled him to gain international support – or acquiescence – for fighting left-wing guerrillas and the drug trade. Though Fujimori was eventually convicted and served his sentence, his daughter Keiko is the principal opposition figure in Peru. She lost the recent presidential election narrowly but commands considerable clout in Congress, which threatens to impeach the left-wing President Pedro Castillo.

Brazil's President Bolsonaro was indicted in October 2021 by the Supreme Court for 11 offences relating to his handling of the COVID pandemic, but will probably not be impeached, despite support for this within Congress and without. Argentina's economic calamity has been compounded by polarised politics that prevents attempts at reform even as the state stares at bankruptcy. Recent legislative elections have maintained a tenuous balance between contending political coalitions but revealed the fragile political hold of the executive.[9] Venezuela's opposition-dominated parliament was superseded by executive fiat in 2016. In November 2021, the ruling party PSUV obtained a majority in elections certified as fair by European Union observers. Some opposition politicians now accept their minority status, perpetuating the power grab by the Maduro regime, whose backbone is the armed forces and which has stacked the judiciary and the electoral tribunal with his supporters.

In Central America, strong leaders elected by populations exhausted by poverty and insecurity have strengthened their hold. In February 2021, El Salvador's President Nayib Bukele leveraged a two-thirds majority in Congress to replace the country's top judges and attorney general with loyalists, gaining control over all three branches of the government. His popularity persists because criminality has decreased. The International Commission against Impunity in Guatemala (Spanish acronym CICIG), under an agreement between the United Nations and Guatemala, successfully investigated and prosecuted serious crimes in Guatemala since 2006. In January 2019, President Jimmy Morales, under investigation for campaign finance violations, terminated the agreement alleging CICIG's participation in illegal acts, abuse of authority, and acts against the constitution. Nicaragua's presidential election in November 2021 was widely condemned for the way President Daniel Ortega, permitted to stand for unconstitutional re-election by a pliant Supreme Court, jailed all credible opponents months before, but his hold over the country's institutions is intact.[10] Democracy in Honduras was interrupted by a blatant coup in June 2009, removing left-wing President Manuel Zelaya. The subsequent political co-existence accepted by the left ruptured institutional legitimacy in a country reputed as the homicide capital of the world and a major narcotics transit hub. President Juan Orlando Hernandez manipulated the Supreme Court to permit his (unconstitutional) re-election in 2017, an event widely condemned for fraud and violence, catalogued in a scathing report by the UN Human Rights Commission.[11] He is wanted by the US on drug trafficking charges. Zelaya's wife, Xiomara Castro was elected President in November 2021 and is expected to reverse several domestic and international policies of her predecessor.

The principal institutions which could exercise control over governments – the parliament, the judiciary, the electoral tribunals – are all too frequently subordinated to the government of the day, as in the instances cited above. Bureaucrats in Latin America are seldom independently recruited and sustained through impartial procedures independent of the government of the day. In Latin America, the culture of nepotism is alimented by the power of the executive to appoint and replace bureaucrats and officials with little parliamentary or other oversight. Policy is therefore mostly at the mercy of politicians. The favour of public office – often with substantial pensionary benefits – is understandably reciprocated by "public servants" keenly aware of the mortality of their tenures.

The media in most of the region has been vibrant, though significant networks are in the hands of powerful business interests such as Globo Group in Brazil, Albavision in Mexico, and Grupo Clarin in Argentina. Though powerful media houses carry clout, they have been on occasion accused of collaborating with the political leadership, or surrendering their power to call it to account.[12] There have been notable exceptions, such as Tal Cual in Venezuela, but too few to challenge the establishment or draw attention away from the mainstream media controlled by big business houses. At the other end of the spectrum, intrepid journalists all over the region have faced censorship, attacks, and even death.

11.4 The Exercise of Power

The concentration of power in most Latin American regimes is a consequence of the post-independence evolution, when nation-states were in process of formation. The centralised nature of most of these political economies enables leaders, once elected – or in power – to dictate terms with little resistance. Even a gigantic state like Brazil has concentrated power in the presidency, with governors of states frequently outmanoeuvred by the federal government on all but local issues. This concentration of power in turn magnetises the presidency, compelling supportive political forces to coalesce around potential leaders, attracting financial and business support that create the centripetal momentum that helped the Institutional Revolutionary Party (PRI) rule Mexico for 70 years; Peronism to survive in Argentina for decades; and conservative forces to retain the presidency of Colombia.

Latin American leaders are seldom colourless. Several have been demagogues or become so on the job. Durable autocrats like Fidel Castro in Cuba, Hugo Chavez (whose spirit endures after his death in 2013) in Venezuela, Daniel Ortega in Nicaragua have combined personal charisma with clever social manipulation. Once in control, such leaders have organised their regimes around concentric circles of support, principally the armed forces, but also an elaborate state apparatus of bureaucratic and systemic controls, the most sophisticated examples being Cuba and Venezuela. In these countries, ideological contention has been suppressed by regimes led by individuals, backed by the armed forces and police, and represented by single parties which dominate debate and decision-making in rubber-stamp parliaments. Their legitimacy – so-called because the international community has little choice but to deal with them – is based on their durability. Other regimes which have emulated the success of Cuba have, in lesser or greater degree, suffered from a lack of consistency in leadership qualities and determination, or faced early headwinds in their quest for continuity. Examples are Bolivia where Evo Morales appeared invincible but was forced to resign by the military after demonstrations in 2019, provoked by the right. He returned two years later but his successor (his former Vice President) may not be in a position to perpetuate his legacy in a country riven by contradictions. Rafael Correa in Ecuador similarly had to retreat to Belgium when his successor dismantled his policies and pursued him legally. Yet others have managed to stay in power through "engineered consent."[13]

Some regimes, notably Costa Rica and Chile, have shown that Latin America can sustain durable democracy. The former, surrounded by equally small states at the mercy of organised crime, narcotics trade, crushing poverty, and disparity, is an oasis where peaceful transfer of power is relatively free of political scandal. Chile, the most prosperous economy, and a member of the Organisation for Economic Co-operation and Development (OECD), has been a conservative bulwark in a region where ideological sands keep shifting. Inequality of opportunity, economic issues, and social justice have been the focus of protests for years. In 2019 massive protests forced the government to concede a referendum. Chileans voted overwhelmingly to set up a Constituent Assembly to replace the 1990 hangover from the Pinochet dictatorship. The Assembly – 78 men and 77 women – headed by an indigenous Mapuche woman is expected to deliver a radically changed Magna Carta. The business-friendly parties of the right and centre are already gearing up for change but have recognised the depth of popular feeling. Former Chilean President Michelle Bachelet (currently UN High

Commissioner for Human Rights) had members of the Communist Party in her Cabinet. President Sebastian Pinera went out under a cloud after revelations of wrongdoing by his family in the Pandora Papers, though the Senate voted against his impeachment.

The election of left-wing and populist leaders across the region has the US and Europe worried. The levers of power are skilfully manipulated by autocratic and leftist leaders alike. In a multipolar world, as Russia and China fish in troubled waters, the US and Europe see their economic and political bases weaken. The latter focuses on issues which Latin American regimes do not prioritise: narco-traffic, immigration, labour laws, environment. China dominates trade in the region and its investments – under the rubric of the Belt and Road Initiative – have not just attracted attention. Some right-wing and centrist regimes – Panama, Costa Rica, El Salvador, Dominican Republic – have switched recognition to China from Taiwan. Russian political and military backing bolsters autocratic regimes in Cuba, Venezuela, Nicaragua, and leftist Bolivia. In the Organisation of American States (OAS), there is a critical number of regimes whose number is sufficient to challenge the erstwhile domination of the US.

11.5 Conclusion

The imperfections outlined above do not tell the full story. Latin Americans may appear cynical about their political institutions, but they have not given up on their destiny. Most Latin Americans live in middle-income economies, although inequality and poverty levels have increased, in cyclical terms due to the COVID pandemic, but also structurally due to the inability of the ruling classes to deal with the crises besetting the region. Popular movements in Chile, Colombia, Bolivia, Brazil, Argentina, and elsewhere are forcing governments to reassess their policies.

Latin American political crises are often traced to corruption and lack of adequate institutions that can act as a check on unbridled power. There is also an interplay between the ideological forces of the right, which more often than not are a hangover from the post-colonial past, and the relatively recent, ideologically driven reaction from the left. The latter can be accused of demagoguery and populism, which have propelled charismatic leaders to power and office but fuel the ambition that hardens their rule, making them turn to autocratic instruments of governance to sustain their power base. There are indications that some left-leaning politicians can work with institutional structures of governance, irrespective of ideology. This could be the case of President Gabriel Boric in Chile, and possibly Lula da Silva, if he wins the election in Brazil in 2022, a distinct possibility.

The promise of a better standard of living, better governance, and social security can only be delivered by institutions that respond to democratic needs, even as they call leaders to account. On both measures, Latin American democracies have been found wanting. The promise of "participatory democracy"[14] held out by some populist leaders like Hugo Chavez in Venezuela, to replace the allegedly oligarchical system of "representative democracy," seems to have stifled the currents of democratic convention which would allow opposing voices a shot at government. In most cases, the promise of participatory democracy was used to sideline traditional political parties – which usually had themselves to blame for their political mortality – and replace them with political parties totally loyal to the regime, sometimes backed by extra-constitutional agencies or militias to provide muscle to the autocrat.

In a region so richly endowed with natural resources, poor governance has had disastrous consequences. A prime example is Venezuela, with the richest hydrocarbon deposits in the world but a rapidly shrinking economy in the hands of a despotic regime. Other countries in the region have either squandered valuable resources or had them stolen by corrupt regimes. The lack of public accountability in Brazil has encouraged massive deforestation of the Amazon rainforest by agricultural and timber lobbies. Illegal exploitation of mineral resources in Colombia, Peru, Bolivia, and elsewhere has given rise to vested interests which prevent the formalisation of the economy to benefit the majority. In addition, massive contracts and large investments have been manipulated by bribing high officials, even presidents. The case of Odebrecht is one of the most glaring, and the downfall of several heads of state and government.[15]

A major threat to governance in the region is the prevalence of the illegal narcotics trade and associated organised crime networks. Starting with the cultivation of coca leaves and chemical conversion into cocaine in the early 20th century, the drug trade has morphed into a multi-billion-dollar industry which has subverted and suborned government agencies, created layers of networks that produce, transport, and distribute illicit drugs and launder the proceeds of this industry to an extent which even the powerful US establishment has been unable to contain.

Latin America has dealt with several challenges left over by history such as ethnic and racial tensions, a quasi-feudal political economy, inadequate human resource development, economic inequality, and manipulation by global powers. It has achieved admirable levels of progress, although innate structural features have held it back. The relative absence of armed conflict over the past century, shunning of the global arms race, and a generally pacific dispensation are broadly characteristic of inter-state relations. Internal politics and the proclivity to power, on the other hand, have distorted even well-meaning attempts and initiatives at governance. Lack of accountability in many cases, immunity from prosecution in others, have been the clothes worn by many a Latin American emperor.

A wave of international initiatives for better governance, an increasingly integrated global economy, combined with the desire for legitimacy, or the possibility of admission to prestigious international forums – such as the OECD[16] – can propel future leaders to integrate and support systems of institutional governance to ensure accountability. The best bet for such outcomes is the dynamism of democracy and the determination of Latin Americans to achieve their manifest destiny.

Notes

1 For this study, Latin America refers to the former Hispanic and Portuguese colonies of South and Central America and the Caribbean but excludes the Caribbean ex-colonies of the UK, France, and others.
2 Nicholas Vardy, 'The Global Guru: The Country of the Future', *Eagle Financial Publications* (18 June 2014).
3 Deepak Bhojwani, *Latin America, the Caribbean and India: Promise and Challenge* (New Delhi: Pentagon Press, 2015), 105–106.
4 The original Spanish term "Criollo" applies to descendants of the conquerors and immigrants, distinct from those born on the Iberian peninsula.
5 Odeen Ishmael, 'Influencing the Democratic Process in the Americas: A Tribute to Simon Bolivar', *Guyana News and Information* (2002). http://www.guyana.org/speeches/ishmael_bolivar.html
6 Philip Berryman, *Liberation Theology: Essential Facts about the Revolutionary Movement in Latin America and Beyond* (New York: Pantheon Books, 1987).
7 On 2 December 1823, US President James Monroe declared that the Old World and New World had different systems and must remain distinct spheres. US recognised and would not interfere with existing colonies and dependencies in the Western Hemisphere, which was closed to future colonisation; any attempt by a European power to oppress or control any nation in the Western Hemisphere would be viewed as a hostile act against the United States.
8 The US arrested General Salvador Cienfuegos, the former Defence Minister of Mexico, and notorious godfather of Mexican drug cartels, in October 2020. Mexico's military threatened to suspend cooperation with the US Drug Enforcement Administration and he was repatriated to Mexico. In January 2021 Mexico's Attorney General dropped all charges against him.
9 Bruno Binetti and Gaston Ocampo, 'Few Changes After Argentina's Legislative Elections', *InterAmerican Dialogue* (19 November 2021).
10 A resolution of the Foreign Ministers of the OAS soon after the election, condemning President Ortega's anti-democratic actions was supported by 25 countries, opposed only by Nicaragua, with 7 abstentions.
11 'Accountability for human rights violations committed in the context of the 2017 elections in Honduras: Progress and challenges', *Report of the United Nations High Commissioner for Human Rights* (January 2020). https://www.ohchr.org/Documents/Countries/HN/2017ReportElectionsHRViolations_Honduras_EN.pdf
12 Don Podesta, 'Media in Latin America: A Path Forward', *Centre for International Media Assistance* (January 2016).
13 Edward Bernays in his book *Propaganda* outlines the need for "engineering consent … the conscious and intelligent manipulation of the organized habits and opinions of the masses … regimenting the public mind." See Edward L Bernays, *Propaganda* (New York: H. Liveright, 1928).
14 Participatory democracy tends to advocate greater citizen participation and more direct representation than traditional representative democracy. The theory of participatory democracy was developed by Jean-Jacques Rousseau and later promoted by J. S. Mill and G. D. H. Cole, who argued that political participation is indispensable for the realisation of a just society.
15 'Odebrecht case: Politicians Worldwide Suspected in Bribery Scandal', *BBC* (17 April 2019). https://www.bbc.com/news/world-latin-america-41109132

16 'The OECD and Latin America and the Caribbean', *Report of the OECD* (November 2021). https://www.oecd.org/latin-america/

Bibliography

'Accountability for Human Rights Violations Committed in the Context of the 2017 Elections in Honduras: Progress and Challenges'. *Report of the United Nations High Commissioner for Human Rights* (January 2020). https://www.ohchr.org/Documents/Countries/HN/2017ReportElectionsHRViolations_Honduras_EN.pdf.

Anderson, Benedict. *Imagined Communities*. London: Verso, 2006.

Berryman, Philip. *Liberation Theology: Essential Facts About the Revolutionary Movement in Latin America and Beyond*. New York: Pantheon Books, 1987.

Bhojwani, Deepak. *Latin America, the Caribbean and India: Promise and Challenge*. New Delhi: Pentagon Press, 2015.

Bruno, Binetti, and Gaston Ocampo. 'Few Changes After Argentina's Legislative Elections'. *InterAmerican Dialogue* (19 November 2021).

Ishmael, Odeen. 'Influencing the Democratic Process in the Americas: A Tribute to Simon Bolivar'. *Guyana News and Information* (2002). http://www.guyana.org/Speeches/ishmael_bolivar.html.

Podesta, Don. 'Media in Latin America: A Path Forward'. *Centre for International Media Assistance* (January 2016).

'The OECD and Latin America and the Caribbean'. *Report of the OECD* (November 2021). https://www.oecd.org/latin-america/.

Vardy, Nicholas. 'The Global Guru: The Country of the Future'. Eagle Financial Publications (18 June 2014).

12
POWER AND LEGITIMACY: A 21ST-CENTURY PERSPECTIVE ON AFRICA

Bhatia

1 Introduction

This book's central theme – power and legitimacy – touches the very heart of key issues of governance and development in Africa. A continent comprising 54 countries, with over 17 per cent of the world population, contributes barely 3 per cent to the global GDP, even though it is endowed with a rich treasure of hydrocarbons, minerals, other natural resources, and a vast young populace. In spite of a handful of success stories, Africa continues to be at the lower ladder of economic development 60 years after its decolonisation began. Clearly, this has much to do with its long colonial subjugation and exploitation by European powers as well as the continent's failure to shape itself well in politico-economic terms during the post-colonial phase of its history. Africa's underperformance is due to its own weaknesses, its colonial past, the neo-colonialism to which it was subjected, and a mix of compulsions created by global geopolitics.

Rajen Harshe is right to emphasise the value of a holistic perspective on Africa, urging that "the intricately intertwined phases involving colonial, anti-colonial and post-colonial realities need to be observed and analyzed in a continuum in any attempt to understand politics, political economy and the history of African states and societies."[1] An endeavour to offer interpretations on how power is exercised by rulers with or without the consent of the governed – and therefore, legitimately or illegitimately – impels us to dig deep into Africa's past as a prelude to examining its present and future. The "darkness" associated with the continent refers to a persisting myth that Africans were uncivilised people who lived in jungles before European colonialists arrived. Above all, this myth reflects the outsider's ignorance about Africa. In many parts of pre-colonial or traditional Africa, there was tranquillity, social harmony, and accountable local governance. This comes through in the writings of some western and African historians. Bernard Matolino emphasises accurately, "The point here is not to praise a certain glorious African past but to point out the reality that Africa has had, in the past, institutions which have worked effectively as guardians of political power."[2]

Kwame Nkrumah who spearheaded national rejuvenation in his country – Ghana – and led the movement for Pan-Africanism, played a seminal role in creating pride in Africa's past. That legacy was marked by traditional social, communal, and family values as well as by rulers or local chiefs who were not despotic in many cases but ruled or served with the counsel of their advisers or elders. They could be replaced if they lost the confidence and support of their tribal communities.

How colonialism came to dominate and damage traditional African society was best described by Archbishop Desmond Tutu who observed:

> When the missionaries came to Africa, they had the Bible and we had the land. They said, "Let us pray." We closed our eyes. When we opened them, we had the Bible and they had the land.[3]

Against an obviously complex backdrop, this chapter begins the story in 2021 when news headlines from Africa were once again about coups executed in violation of laws and constitutions as well as participation by some African leaders in the Summit for Democracy, convened by US President Joseph Biden. It then moves on to examine a set of several relevant issues, trends, and developments in the past two decades of the 21st century, which have a direct bearing on this book's theme. In the end, the chapter draws a few conclusions and pointers as regards the future.

12.2 Coups Are Back?

Africa has been far too familiar with the change of government brought through a coup d'état which, by definition, is an illegitimate act. Article 30 of the Constitutive Act of the African Union (AU) explicitly states that "Governments which shall come to power through unconstitutional means shall not be allowed to participate in the activities of the Union."[4] Validation later through a change in law or constitution, and on the basis of the economic argument – that the post-coup regime improved economic conditions of the people – is generally found to be unacceptable. Throughout the post-colonial period in the previous century, a large number of coups took place in Africa, but they were reduced to a trickle in the first two decades of the 21st century. The past two decades witnessed the assertion of democracy and constitutionalism. The African Union's Lomé Convention of 1999 and the Africa Charter on Democracy, Elections and Governance made it clear that the continent should prohibit, reject, and condemn unconstitutional changes of government in any member state as a serious threat to stability, peace, security, and development.

The year 2021, however, revealed a different trend as coups took place in Mali, Chad, Guinea, and Sudan. Their triggers, patterns of evolution, and outcomes varied. In Chad, the military seized power after the demise of President Idriss Déby in clashes with rebels in April 2021. Subsequently, his 37-year-old son Mahamat Idriss Déby, a military commander, was appointed as the interim president and the constitution was suspended. Chad's neighbouring countries supported the coup, thereby creating a serious dilemma for the AU. Eventually, AU's Peace and Security Council (PSC) was forced to craft a middle path. It endorsed Chad's transitional military council, subject to a set of conditions. The PSC decision raised "questions in terms of its rationale, implementation and implications," as Paul-Simon Handy and Félicité Djilo argued cogently.[5] It is noteworthy that the AU has suspended every member state where the military seized power since 2004, except Chad.[6]

The military takeover in Mali by 37-year-old Colonel Assimi Goita led to the overthrow of the civilian president in August 2020 and to the removal of the civilian transition team in June 2021. This invited the suspension of Mali from the Economic Community of West African States (ECOWAS) and the AU. The coup in Guinea was executed by Col. Mamady Doumbouya in September 2021, who overthrew the government of President Alpha Conde. The new leader announced that he had no choice but to seize power because of the rampant corruption, infringement of human rights, and discontent against poor economic management. It was a familiar argument. As Judd Devermont explained, President Conde's "decision to amend the constitution to run for a third term and recent missteps on the economy set the stage for the military putsch."[7] Sudan saw two coup attempts in 2021, the first in September that failed and the second in October which succeeded when General Abdel Fattah Burhan dissolved the civilian arm of the transitional government and took full control. Later, however, he was forced by popular protests to re-install Abdalla Hamdok as the prime minister. The AU which had expressed deep dismay over the coup apparently played a significant role in diluting its impact. Ironically, mass protests in the streets erupted again which led Hamdok to tender his resignation on 2 January 2022. It was another setback to Sudan's fragile endeavours to arrange a transition to civilian rule and democracy. PM Hamdok stressed that the nation faced "a dangerous turning point that threatens its whole survival."[8]

> In Niger, a coup was thwarted in March 2021 just before the presidential inauguration.

Whether coups represent an established new trend in Africa is a question that will be answered by developments in the next two or three years. Meanwhile, experts point out that while pockets of concern exist, democracy has been flourishing in many other parts of the continent. The spread of technology, especially the internet and social media platforms, the discontent with the vaccine inequity in the COVID-19 era, and the general dissatisfaction with the level and quality of socio-economic development impel Africans, particularly the youth, to crave for more – not less – democratic governance. As Ronek Gopaldas posited:

> As Africa navigates internal and external threats to democracy, the pressing issue is not the system of governance but the quality of leadership. Leadership vacuums create fertile grounds for anti-democratic tendencies and disorderly regime changes.[9]

In many African countries, the ruling leaders often came from the military. According to some reports, in 2021, "there were 21 former military men in power in Africa — including in Angola, Chad, Egypt, Ethiopia, Nigeria, Uganda, Rwanda, Sudan, South Sudan and Zimbabwe."[10] The increased incidence of coups and military presence in the governance process in Africa in 2021 coincided with the growing concern regarding the state of democracy everywhere and indeed with a perceived legitimacy crisis in many parts of the world.

12.3 Summit for Democracy

The Summit for Democracy, hosted by President Biden in video format from 9 to 10 December 2021, was widely assailed by critics as an empty gesture by a domestically embattled leader and as an ideological ploy to raise pressure on America's strategic adversaries – China and Russia. Nevertheless, it served a useful purpose, in this author's assessment, by highlighting three major faultlines in modern governance: authoritarianism of many rulers, escalating corruption, and dangers to human rights.[11] The summit served as a valuable forum to address the trio of issues and more specifically the issues of legitimacy.

The list of invitees to the summit was problematic. It triggered controversy. Of the 113 countries chosen, 69 per cent were assessed to be "Free", 28 per cent "Partly Free," and 3 per cent "Not Free," according to a study by Carnegie Endowment.[12] Seventeen countries from Africa were invited,[13] including deficient democracies like Angola and the Democratic Republic of Congo (DRC). South Africa declined to attend, possibly due to a combination of diplomatic reasons listed by Peter Fabricius, a reputed South African journalist.[14]

In principle, all African countries ratified the Constitutive Act of the AU, which condemns authoritarianism as illegitimate and affirms freedoms and other democratic goals. The adoption letter of the African Charter on Democracy, Elections and Governance cleared the way for operationalising this commitment. In practice, people show a preference for democracy and popular rule, despite the fact that elites and rulers often end up disappointing them by turning autocratic or corrupt or a threat to human rights – or all of this. In one of the more notable and candid speeches delivered at the summit, Nigerian President Muhammadu Buhari stated that democracy remained "the most popular and universally recognized way of governance thus far," while adding that "more is required from us as members of democratic societies." His plea to "build back better democratic institutions and sustainable democratic values" applied not only to his country but also to Africa and the world in general.[15]

In a thoughtful assessment entitled "An Opportunity Missed for Democratic Renewal in Africa," Eghosa E. Osaghae, director-general of the Nigerian Institute of International Affairs, elaborated on the issue concerning "the looming danger of democratic reversals in Africa."[16] The real challenge Africa faced was how to make democracy work for ordinary citizens, how to enhance the accountability of leaders, and how to strengthen state capacities to ensure security, growth, and prosperity. "Democracy," he noted, "requires a level of capacitation that is both clearly lacking and beyond the grasp of African citizens and civil society." He added: "This is the help needed, not regime change that seeks to change the countries into what outside powers want, but what Africans themselves determine as democracy that works for them."[17]

12.4 Legitimacy in the African Context

When colonialism arrived in Africa, it did so without any legitimacy, regardless of false rationalisations such as the theory of "the white man's burden." The colonial rule simply imposed itself on the people without their consent. It stemmed from the basic premise of "Might is Right." The drawing of colonial frontiers based on the imported notion of a nation-state was also arbitrary and without people's concurrence. Centuries of subjugation, exploitation, and injustice followed. Eventually, the winds of enlightenment, freedoms, and liberation reached African shores, inspired by what early African intellectuals and their allies in Europe, the US, and Asia strove for.

The 1960s saw many African states attaining independence. But soon they discovered that political independence was not enough. Without economic freedom and essential conditions in place for development, democratic states were like skeletons without life. The Age of Hope represented by the 1960s gave way to the Lost Decades of the 1970s to 1990s.[18] Africa was further ravaged by neo-colonial and imperialist tendencies, accentuated by the Cold War compulsions where the two superpowers – the US and the USSR – put a premium on the loyalty of an ally, regardless of the quality of rule he offered to his citizens. As a well-known American maxim went regarding an ally, "We know he is an SOB, but he is our SOB!"[19] Interests of the poor populace stood sacrificed at the altar of geopolitics.

Africa's real renewal began as the 21st century opened and as the Organisation of African Unity (OAU) gave way to the AU and new institutional mechanisms such as the New Partnership for Africa's Development (NEPAD) and the African Peer Review Mechanism (APRM). Democracy, accountability, human rights, and sound economic governance were now the new elements in Africa's political lexicon. The vision of "Africa 2063" took hold of people's imagination. Two of its components have been: "An Africa of good governance, democracy, respect for human rights, justice and the rule of law," and "An Africa, whose development is people-driven, relying on the potential of African people, especially its women and youth and caring for children."[20] Africa's rulers and people continue to strive to achieve these goals, even as their journey is often hazardous, and the outcome of their endeavours is mixed and uneven. Inevitably, the trajectory of their democracy can be neither linear nor smooth. But in most parts, it continues – and that is important.

Another basis of hope was provided in a policy brief entitled *African futures: key trends to 2035*, which was published by the Institute for Security Studies (ISS) of South Africa in August 2017.[21] Based on deep research and study, it projected what Africa might look like in the mid-2030s. It indicated that the number of democracies was likely to increase and the levels of democracy were expected to continue to improve, though slowly and from a relatively low base. The study concluded, "Africa's story reveals a positive trend. Yet the trend is neither stable nor even." For governance to be imbued with legitimacy and democratic culture, its institutions need to be strengthened; its leaders have to perform better; and its people should experience faster and more inclusive economic development in the short to medium term.

A close review of writings by African authors and foreign experts on African affairs reveals a set of notable perceptions and observations on the role of legitimacy in governance in Africa. First, elections held in accordance with a nation's constitution bestow legitimacy on the elected government, but it can only be sustained through a good rule that runs in harmony with the popular will. This comes only if the ruler adopts an inclusive approach rather than a narrow one focused on promoting the welfare of his tribe or political constituency only. Michael G. Schatzberg concluded, "Political legitimacy in much of sub-Saharan Africa is based on tacit normative idea that government stands in the same relationship to its citizens as a father does to his children."[22] An essential belief is that paternal (or political – my addition) authority is "legitimate as long as the implicit understanding of rights and duties contained in the moral matrix is not violated."[23]

Second, a military coup or a popular rebellion begins its journey steeped in illegitimacy, but over time it sometimes gains grudging popular acceptance. Third, as regards the noticeable trend of African states' participation in Peacekeeping Operations (PKOs) on the continent, is there a link between this participation and the nature of the regime in question? Jonah Victor argued that repressive governments tended to take part in PKOs "as a strategy for bolstering regime survival."[24] This gave them the opportunity to keep their militaries fruitfully engaged abroad, thereby safeguarding against their interference in domestic politics, and it also enabled them to win the approval and favours of their foreign partners. The broad conclusion of his empirical study was that "the state that will contribute to regional peacekeeping is a poor, less repressive, former British colony with low state legitimacy and a large military."[25] Fourth, studying the role of Africa's Regional Organisations (ROs) and the AU or ECOWAS throws up interesting insights as well as gaps in current research. A 2018 study by

Simone Schnabel argued that "a bottom-up perspective on legitimacy of regional organizations could feed into novel theorizing of the meaning and function of legitimacy beyond the nation-state that deliberately draws on and theorizes from non-western experiences."[26] Finally, people in Africa reject the binary choice between democracy or good economic governance. They want both, and when this is denied, instability, violence, and turmoil become unavoidable. A recurring theme among scholars on democracy in Africa has been that its success is dependent on creating and sustaining suitable institutions that work properly, linking the ruler meaningfully with the ruled. This was practised in many parts of pre-colonial Africa. Those forums and practices of consultation with people should be remembered and recreated. Then authority will enjoy greater legitimacy. "Thus," wrote Bernard Matolino, "one finds precedence in traditional Africa which ought to serve as an informant to modern Africa on the importance and functioning of institutions."[27]

12.5 Role of International Partners

While all friends of Africa today may vouch for its need for independence and agency, the reality of globalisation compels us to recognise that many – perhaps most – countries are handicapped in exercising complete autonomy in decision-making. Therefore, the foreign countries that offer development and humanitarian assistance, capital, technology, goods, and markets to Africa are in a position to exert themselves to ensure that legitimacy and consent of the people should continuously stamp governance models.

The western camp brought the values and institutions of modern democracy to the continent. But it, especially its European component, was marred by a terrible colonial past. Neo-colonial impulses and policies served as another constraint that created an alliance of vested interests between the aid-givers and privileged cliques in aid-receiving countries. This ensured that often large parts of the population remained unaffected by development and democracy. In this backdrop entered China in the last decade of the 20th century and quickly broadened its footprint in the past two decades. The Chinese model promised non-interference in internal affairs, while offering its generous aid, with no strings attached. The result, however, turned out to be different: the engagement of China as an authoritarian one party-state brought some good in the form of infrastructure and higher prices for African commodities, but it also introduced increased corruption, Chinese labour, environmental degradation, and hefty debts which, if not paid on time, could result in the loss of national assets. And the so-called Beijing Consensus cared little for legitimacy and accountability of rulers.

Africa then has had the benefit of a third choice presented by (largely) Asian democracies: India, Japan, Indonesia, Australia, and others. Without the taint of a colonial burden and with a good track record of democracies that work, Asia offered – and offers – an attractive option that evoked increasing acceptance.

India undoubtedly figures in the front rank among these nations: "Democracy with Development" has been a strong calling card in multiple African capitals. For this third option to succeed more than it has in recent years, some introspection, however, is essential. The democracy on offer should be a little less noisy and socially more cohesive. Besides, it must learn to deliver, better and faster, the fruits of economic development. Addressing the Ugandan parliament – and by implication the whole continent – Indian Prime Minister Narendra Modi listed ten fundamental principles that guided India's Africa policy, stressing that "our development partnership will be guided by your priorities."[28] This must be kept in view by all those who truly care for the welfare of African people.

12.6 Conclusion

The foregoing analysis clearly suggests that the Africa of today clamours for legitimacy in governance and realises that a choice between democracy and authoritarianism is a false one. It prefers democratic governance that engages people; guarantees their freedoms, human rights, and reduced corruption; and makes their rulers accountable. At the same time, Africa cannot do without a development framework that creates local industry; more innovation, investment, and employment; better education and health facilities; greater access to modern technology; and accelerated achievement of UN Sustainable Development Goals. Equity, justice, and inclusiveness need to be built into this formula in a practical way. Its success will also depend on ensuring necessary conditions for peace, security, and stability. Africans need all of this and more.

In sum, Africa needs a holistic and legitimate governance system with "African characteristics." Its institutions should be inspired not by American, French, Japanese, and Indian values, but by the norms, beliefs, traditions, and values preferred by the African people. The shift should take into account their traditional as well as contemporary ethos. Only then legitimacy will sustain itself, turning Africa into a more effective and worthy player on the international stage.

Notes

1 Rajen Harshe, *Africa in World Affairs* (Oxon: Routledge, 2019), 36.
2 For example, as mentioned by Godffrey Sogolo and cited by Bernard Matolino: The ancient empires and city-states of Ghana, Songhai, Benin, the civilisations of Kilwa and Zimbabwe, and the relics of ancient civilisations of Northern Africa provide abundant evidence of the African past, in Bernard Matolino, 'Quandaries of Legitimacy', *Theoria: A Journal of Social and Political Theory* 57, no. 123 (June 2010): 52–76. https://www.jstor.org/stable/41802471
3 These words were heard by this author at an event pertaining to Mahatma Gandhi, which was organised in Cape Town, South Africa, in December 2017.
4 'Constitutive Act of the African Union', *African Union* (11 July 2000). https://au.int/sites/default/files/pages/34873-file-constitutiveact_en.pdf

5 Paul-Simon Handy and Félicité Djilo, 'AU Balancing Act on Chad's Coup Sets a Disturbing Precedent', *Institute for Security Studies* (2 June 2021). https://issafrica.org/iss-today/au-balancing-act-on-chads-coup-sets-a-disturbing-precedent
6 Since February 2021 the AU has suspended four countries – Mali, Guinea, Sudan, and Burkina Faso – over military coups. See: 'African Union condemns 'wave' of military coups', *DW* (6 February 2022) https://www.dw.com/en/african-union-condemns-wave-of-military-coups/a-60678794
7 Judd Devermont, 'Guinea: The Causes and Consequences of West Africa's Latest Coup', *Centre for Strategic and International Studies* (8 September 2021). https://www.csis.org/analysis/guinea-causes-and-consequences-west-africas-latest-coup
8 'Sudan coup: Prime Minister Abdalla Hamdok Resigns after Mass Protests', *BBC News* (4 January 2022). https://www.bbc.com/news/world-africa-59855246
9 Ronek Gopaldas, 'Democracy in Decline in Africa? Not so Fast', *Institute for Security Studies* (4 November 2021). https://issafrica.org/iss-today/democracy-in-decline-in-africa-not-so-fast
10 David Pilling, 'Democracy in Africa is in Retreat', *Financial Times* (23 December 2020).
11 For basic details about the summit, see Suhasini Haidar, 'Worldview with Suhasini Haidar | Summit for Democracy', *The Hindu* (18 December 2021). https://www.thehindu.com/news/international/worldview-with-suhasini-haidar-summit-for-democracy/article37984530.ece
12 Steven Feldstein, 'Who's In and Who's Out from Biden's Democracy Summit', *Carnegie Endowment for International Peace* (22 November 2021). https://carnegieendowment.org/2021/11/22/who-s-in-and-who-s-out-from-biden-s-democracy-summit-pub-85822
13 The list of African countries invited were the following: Angola, Botswana, Cape Verde, DR of Congo, Ghana, Kenya, Liberia, Malawi, Mauritius, Namibia, Niger, Nigeria, São Tomé and Príncipe, Senegal, Seychelles, South Africa, Zambia. South Africa declined to attend.
14 Peter Fabricius, 'Ramaphosa Gives US President's Democracy Summit the Cold Shoulder', *Daily Maverick* (10 December 2021). https://www.dailymaverick.co.za/article/2021-12-10-ramaphosa-gives-us-presidents-democracy-summit-the-cold-shoulder/
15 'Address by President Buhari at the Virtual Summit for Democracy Organised by President Joe Biden of USA', *The State House, Abuja* (December 9, 2021) https://statehouse.gov.ng/news/address-by-president-buhari-at-the-virtual-summit-for-democracy-organised-by-president-joe-biden-of-usa/
16 Eghosa E. Osaghae, 'An Opportunity Missed for Democratic Renewal in Africa', *Council of Councils* (16 December 2021). https://www.cfr.org/councilofcouncils/global-memos/global-perspectives-bidens-democracy-summit
17 Ibid. (16 December 2021).
18 Rajiv Bhatia, *India-Africa Relations: Changing Horizons* (Oxon: Routledge, 2022). For more details, please see Chapter 1 – 'Africa in Transition.'
19 Kevin Drum, '"But He's Our Son of a Bitch"', *Washington Monthly* (16 May 2006). https://washingtonmonthly.com/2006/05/16/but-hes-our-son-of-a-bitch/
20 'Agenda 2063, African Union Commission, 2015'. *African Union Commission*. https://au.int/sites/default/files/documents/36204-doc-agenda2063_popular_version_en.pdf (accessed on 4 January 2022).
21 Julia Bello-Schünemann, Jakkie Cilliers, Zachary Donnenfeld, Ciara Aucoin and Alex Porter, 'African Futures: Key Trends to 2035', *Institute for Security Studies Policy Brief* 105 (August 2017): 1. https://issafrica.s3.amazonaws.com/site/uploads/policy-brief105.pdf
22 Michael G. Schatzberg, 'Power, Legitimacy and 'democratisation' in Africa', *Africa: Journal of the International African Institute* 63, no. 4 (1993): 445–461.
23 Ibid., 455.

24 Jonah Victor, 'African Peacekeeping in Africa: Warlord Politics, Defense Economics, and State Legitimacy', *Journal of Peace Research* 47, no. 2 (March 2010): 217–229.
25 Ibid., 227.
26 Simone Schnabel, 'African Regional Organizations Seen from Below: Theorizing Legitimacy Beyond the European Nation-State', *Peace Research Institute Frankfurt* (September 2018). http://www.jstor.com/stable/resrep19886
27 Bernard Matolino, 'Quandaries of Legitimacy', *Theoria: A Journal of Social and Political Theory* 57, no. 123 (June 2010): 52–76.
28 'Prime Minister's Address at Parliament of Uganda During His State Visit to Uganda', *Ministry of External Affairs* (25 July 2018). https://mea.gov.in/Speeches-Statements.htm?dtl/30152/Prime+Ministers+address+at+Parliament+of+Uganda +during+his+State+Visit+to+Uganda

Bibliography

'Address by President Buhari at the Virtual Summit for Democracy Organised by President Joe Biden of USA'. *The State House, Abuja* (9 December 2021). https://statehouse.gov.ng/news/address-by-president-buhari-at-the-virtual-summit-for-democracy-organised-by-president-joe-biden-of-usa/.

Bello-Schünemann, Julia, Jakkie Cilliers, Zachary Donnenfeld, Ciara Aucoin, and Alex Porter, 'African Futures: Key Trends to 2035'. *Institute for Security Studies Policy Brief* 105 (August 2017). https://issafrica.s3.amazonaws.com/site/uploads/policybrief105.pdf.

Bhatia, Rajiv. *India-Africa Relations: Changing Horizons*. Oxon: Routledge, 2022.

Devermont, Judd. 'Guinea: The Causes and Consequences of West Africa's Latest Coup'. *Centre for Strategic and International Studies* (8 September 2021). https://www.csis.org/analysis/guinea-causes-and-consequences-west-africas-latest-coup.

Fabricius, Peter. 'Ramaphosa Gives US President's Democracy Summit the Cold Shoulder'. *Daily Maverick* (10 December 2021). https://www.dailymaverick.co.za/article/2021-12-10-ramaphosa-gives-us-presidents-democracy-summit-the-cold-shoulder/.

Feldstein, Steven. 'Who's In and Who's Out From Biden's Democracy Summit'. *Carnegie Endowment for International Peace* (22 November 2021). https://carnegieendowment.org/2021/11/22/who-s-in-and-who-s-out-from-biden-s-democracy-summit-pub-85822.

Gopaldas, Ronek. 'Democracy in Decline in Africa? Not So Far'. *Institute for Security Studies* (4 November 2021). https://issafrica.org/iss-today/democracy-in-decline-in-africa-not-so-fast.

Haidar, Suhasini. 'Worldview With Suhasini Haidar|Summit for Democracy'. *The Hindu* (18 December 2021). https://www.thehindu.com/news/international/worldview-with-suhasini-haidar-summit-for-democracy/article37984530.ece.

Harshe, Rajen. *Africa in World Affairs*. Oxon: Routledge, 2019.

Matolino, Bernard. 'Quandaries of Legitimacy'. *Theoria: A Journal of Social and Political Theory* 57, no. 123 (June 2010): 52–76. https://www.jstor.org/stable/41802471.

Osaghae, Eghosa E. 'An Opportunity Missed for Democratic Renewal in Africa'. *Council of Councils* (16 December 2021). https://www.cfr.org/councilofcouncils/global-memos/global-perspectives-bidens-democracy-summit.

Paul-Simon, Handy, and Félicité Djilo. 'AU Balancing Act on Chad's Coup Sets a Disturbing Precedent'. *Institute for Security Studies*(2 June 2021). https://issafrica.org/iss-today/au-balancing-act-on-chads-coup-sets-a-disturbing-precedent.

'Prime Minister's Address at Parliament of Uganda During His State Visit to Uganda'. *Ministry of External Affairs, Government of India* (25 July 2018).

Schatzberg, Michael G. 'Power, Legitimacy and 'Democratisation' in Africa'. *Africa: Journal of the International African Institute* 63, no. 4 (1993): 445–461.

Schnabel, Simone. 'African Regional Organizations Seen From Below: Theorizing Legitimacy Beyond the European Nation-State'. *Peace Research Institute Frankfurt* (September 2018).

'Sudan Coup: Prime Minister Abdalla Hamdok Resigns After Mass Protests'. *BBC News* (4 January 2022). https://www.bbc.com/news/world-africa-59855246.

Victor, Jonah. 'African Peacekeeping in Africa: Warlord Politics, Defense Economics, and State Legitimacy'. *Journal of Peace Research* 47, no. 2 (March 2010): 217–229.

13
AUTHORITARIANISM, RESISTANCE, AND LEGITIMACY IN THE WEST ASIAN POLITICAL ORDER

Talmiz Ahmad

13.1 Introduction

Over 25 years ago, a distinguished writer on the West Asian[1] political economy, Nazih Ayubi, pointed out that, "although most Arab states are 'hard' states, and, indeed, many of them are 'fierce' states, few of them are really 'strong' states." He illustrated this observation by noting that the state was "lamentably feeble" in collecting taxes, winning wars, or forging an ideology or a power bloc that would take it beyond coercion into the "moral and intellectual sphere."[2]

West Asia today presents a picture of widespread domestic and inter-state conflict, with powerful non-state actors rampaging through vast territories, galvanised by messages of intolerance and hate. Besides this, West Asia is the playground for Western nations that provide most of the weaponry used in the region, agitate for lucrative commercial contracts, and unleash their armed forces when their national interests and hegemonic positions are challenged.

The principal source of this political malaise lies in the absence of legitimacy for regional political leaderships in the perception of the populace ruled by them. Though leaders regularly frame diverse bases to obtain popular support, their default instrument to sustain their rule is coercion which evokes periodic outbursts of resistance to their tyrannical authority. This chapter will examine the persistent failure of the West Asian political order to obtain legitimacy and popular support and discuss whether any significant changes in this parlous scenario are likely in the near future. The chapter will also map the origins of Islam and trace its trajectory to our times, alongside other influences that have become resonant in different periods.

DOI: 10.4324/9781003385233-13

13.2 Early Islamic Polities

The message of Prophet Mohammed in the early 7th century was revolutionary in that it challenged the shape of contemporary society and the political order and provided new bases for the assertion of legitimacy by the ruler of the emerging polity. His message of a universal Muslim community that transcended family, clan, and tribe subverted the core personal affiliations of those who accepted his message and compelled them to share links not just with Arabs outside their kinship ties, but later, also with alien, non-Arab communities across West Asia based on their shared faith.

Mohammed was succeeded by the "Rightly guided caliphs" – Abu Bakr, Omar, Othman, and Ali. The first, Abu Bakr, was the prophet's closest associate, and one of the first to accept the message of Islam after Khadija, Mohammed's wife, and the father of the prophet's favourite wife, Ayesha. However, he sought legitimacy for his leadership of the community based on his status as the departed prophet's closest associate and his own acknowledged piety and commitment to the faith.

In his historic acceptance speech, Abu Bakr assured his community: "We do not fail to consult you with regard to political matters and we do not adjudicate matters without you." He also sought the community's guidance: "Indeed, I am a follower, not an innovator; if I perform well, then help me, and if I should deviate, correct me."[3] This appeal enshrined the concept of *shura* (consultation) and the idea of conditional allegiance (*bayat*) into Islamic political theory which was frequently invoked in later years to shape resistance to tyranny. Abu Bakr's claim to the caliphate was accepted by popular acclamation. The community selected the next caliphs ("deputies") on similar bases, though their fitness to lead was supported by their ties of kinship with the prophet.

As Muslim territories expanded in size, the prophet's family and tribal kins were embroiled in rival claims to leadership. The Omayyads (661–750), who came to power following these fratricidal competitions, moved away from several norms that had defined the first four caliphates. They based their dynastic claim to head the Muslim community on tribal kinship with the prophet and their noble lineage rather than personal merit. They discriminated against non-Arabs who had become Muslims, contradicting a fundamental tenet of the new faith. They also assumed the grandiose title, *Khalifat Allah* ("Deputy of God"), rejecting the more modest *Khalifat Rasul Allah* ("Deputy of the Messenger of God") that the first four caliphs had chosen.

13.3 Early Islamic Political Thought

The Abbasid period (750–1258) saw some important developments in Islamic law, jurisprudence, and political thought through the writings of major intellectuals of that era who discussed issues of political legitimacy and authority. Two developments of doctrinal significance were: one, the finalisation of the *Hadith* collections, i.e., "traditions" relating to the words and actions of the prophet as transmitted by a chain of witnesses that went back to the prophet's family and companions. The other was the emergence of four schools of Sunni Islam (*madhhabs*), each named after the teachings of a scholar – Hanafi, Maliki, Shafai, and Hanbali. The Koran, the Hadith, and the four schools of Islamic law taken together constitute the *Sharia* ("the path"), the corpus of Islamic doctrine and jurisprudence. This law was imparted contemporary resonance by scholars and jurists by using *ijtihad* (reasoning) which is supported by the approved tools of *qiyas* (analogy) and *ijma* (consensus) to explain the meaning, intent, and contemporary application of Islamic law. Rulings in specific court cases were made by *qadis* (judges) who enjoyed considerable independence. They were rarely bound by the strict letter of the law; their pronouncements were usually founded on two considerations: *maslaha* (public good) and *siyasa shariyya* (the "spirit of the Sharia").[4] These concepts imparted considerable flexibility to judges in their rulings and ensured that law continued to be a vibrant and relevant part of contemporary society and political order.

The Sharia dealt largely with matters pertaining to religious doctrine and personal conduct; it provides very little in regard to political theory or statecraft. Thus, scholars had to carefully draw norms and rules relating to governance through *ijtihad*. The Omayyads, for instance, justified dynastic rule by invoking the Koranic verse: "Obey God and the Messenger, and those possessing authority among you." But their simplistic interpretation of the verse had few takers among contemporary scholars. The latter asserted that the reference to "those possessing authority" was to persons with knowledge, independent reasoning, and a deep understanding of religious precepts; most Omayyad caliphs were seriously wanting in this regard.[5]

The Abbasids continued the pattern of centralised monarchy, inventing the term *dawla* to describe dynasty, regime, and the state. It literally meant a "turn of fortune," suggesting that a ruler's success in taking and holding power was a sign of divine grace, making the ruler worthy of popular support. Abbasid rulers claimed their position on the basis of divine authority to continue the work of the prophet; Muslims must therefore assist the caliphs in the fulfilment of their political and moral responsibilities. An extension of this assertion was that the ruler had to be accepted even if he was tyrannical.[6]

From the early 11th century, the political authority of the Abbasids was taken over by the Saljuk Turks, though the former continued to exercise caliphal authority. Thus, the political centre of Islam saw a new situation in state order – a Sunni political dynasty ruling alongside a Sunni caliph, leading to a divide in the expression of political-military authority on the one hand and doctrinal authority on the other.

The issues the scholars grappled with at this time were: the caliphate, legitimate political authority, obedience to authority, and constraints on the ruler. Scholars accepted the political reality of early Abbasid authority and recognised their supreme position in religious and political matters. They also accepted the incumbent on the throne, without attempting to measure his fitness on the basis of specific qualifications. Prominent scholars, such as Ibn Hanbal (780–855) and al-Ashari (874–936), advocated the need for absolute obedience to the ruler, the only limits being the ruler's apostasy.[7]

The Mongol invasions in West Asia from 1206 wreaked devastation across Muslim lands, culminating in the destruction of the Abbasid caliphate in 1258. The subsequent experience of political disruption and personal privation made the scholar Ahmad ibn Taymiyya (1263–1328) desperate to seek order from a strong ruler enforcing the doctrines of Islam with utmost rigidity. He rejected "innovation" (*bida*) not just Shiism and Sufism but also interpreted Sunni precepts narrowly to remove extraneous influences from pre-Muslim and non-Muslim sources.

13.4 *Al Nahda* ("Renaissance") in West Asia

In the 16th century, almost all the Arab lands in West Asia and North Africa became part of the Ottoman Empire (1290–1921). From the beginning of the 19th century, the empire and particularly Egypt confronted a new challenge – the steady encroachment, political and economic, of Western powers that, in the course of the century, deprived the empire of its autonomy and subjected large parts of its Arab territories to direct colonial subjugation.

This was a period of extraordinary turmoil for the Muslim people – for the first time in several centuries they faced the prospect of a comprehensive defeat at the hands of Western powers which were armed by advances in science and technology and a political order founded on popular participation. This assault from the West led to an extraordinary intellectual ferment, with many Egyptian scholars taking the lead. Given the substance, variety and strength of the reforms they advocated, the 19th century is referred to as *Al Nahda*, "Renaissance."

As they reflected on Muslim defeat, Arab intellectuals sought in pristine Islam the panacea for their predicament. The traditionalists among them advocated a "return to Islam," an Islam that most closely reflected the ideal society in Madinah headed by Prophet Mohammed. But their modern-day polity did not seek to replicate the old order – it was from the core principles of Islam that they teased out the foundations of a new order, one that would be based on *shura* (consultation) and whose norms would emerge from the hoary principle of *maslaha*, public welfare.

Egyptian scholar Mohammed Abduh (1850–1905) and his student Rashid Rida (1865–1935) were the most influential presence in this ferment. They advocated the need for Sharia to be in tune with contemporary times through the use of *ijtihad* and *qiyas* (analogical reasoning) and placed *maslaha* at the heart of the reformed political order. Drawing on Islamic tradition, Rida found his just ruler in the institution of the caliph. However, the caliph envisaged by him was not an absolute ruler, nor even a temporal one. Learned in Islamic law, he would be the supreme religious authority and guide, whose interpretations of the law would prevail in matters of public interest.[8] However, this enthusiasm for reform fell on the unfertile soil of ruthless colonial domination of Britain and France. Thus, on the eve of World War I, the British controlled Egypt and Sudan and the Sheikhdoms of the Persian Gulf, while France had colonised most of North Africa. Al Nahda withered away before the hot winds of the imperialist enterprise.

13.5 The Arab Monarchies

The Arab states in West Asia and North Africa obtained their present-day form in two stages – after World War I and after World War II. Just after World War I, five states were carved out of the Ottoman territories in West Asia and placed under the control of Western powers – Iraq, Jordan, and Palestine came under British control, while France took over Syria and from it carved out the Christian-majority enclave of Lebanon. In North Africa, Egypt and Sudan were under British influence, while France took control of Tunisia, Algeria, and Morocco. Libya was under Italian authority. National boundaries were drawn to serve imperial interests and had little regard for the traditional affiliations of the people affected by these cartographic manipulations. Puppet rulers were placed to head most of these new states.

The second stage in the shaping of Arab state order occurred after World War II when several monarchs planted in different countries by Western powers were overthrown by the armed forces and republics were set up across many parts of West Asia and North Africa. The revolution in Egypt in 1952 was followed by similar events in Iraq (1958), Yemen (1962), Syria (1963), and Libya (1970). Algeria became free as a result of a long and bloody struggle against France in 1962.[9]

Finally, in 1968, Britain announced that it would be withdrawing from its colonies "East of Suez" over the next couple of years. In the Arab world, this affected the Gulf Sheikhdoms. Following a prolonged process of negotiations among local leaders, Oman emerged as a sultanate in 1970, while seven sheikhdoms voted to join the United Arab Emirates that emerged as a federal polity in December 1971. Bahrain, Qatar, and Kuwait remained separate sovereign entities. The "legitimacy" of the "royal" families that emerged to head these nascent states was largely a product of their ties with Britain. The latter, represented by officers from British India, had dominated the political and economic affairs of the region over nearly two centuries through treaty arrangements, with its authority being ensured by the presence of armed forces and the British navy.[10]

The Kingdom of Saudi Arabia acquired its present shape as a result of conquests across the Arabian Peninsula between 1902 and 1925 by Abdulaziz Al-Saud. He was the scion of the family that had created two earlier "states" in central Arabia in the 18th and 19th centuries. These early states were unique in the Arabian Peninsula in that they were imbued with a faith-based ideology – Wahhabiyya – that was enshrined in the teachings of the 18th-century cleric from central Arabia, Sheikh Mohammed ibn Abdul Wahhab (1703–1792).

In 1744, the sheikh entered into a covenant with a prominent local chieftain of Najd, Mohammed bin Saud (1687–1767) which provided that, in the territories conquered by the Al-Saud family, the religious and moral precepts of the sheikh would be enforced, while the Al-Saud would be responsible for political and military matters.

Thus, from this date, the Saudi states have reflected this religio-political character which has distinguished them from other regional political entities in the peninsula that have been shaped by colonial interventions. In 1932, Abdulaziz Al-Saud, after bringing large parts of the peninsula under his control, formally proclaimed the establishment of the "Kingdom of Saudi Arabia," with himself as the king. He set up a hereditary monarchy, but the ruling family has legitimised its claim to the throne on the basis of its affiliation with the tenets of Wahhabiyya which, the family asserts, is the true doctrine of Islam.

The six states in the Gulf depend on partnerships with Western powers for their security. From the 1970s, all of these monarchies have maintained deep political, military, and economic ties with the US. The Gulf Sheikhdoms are uniquely placed in domestic and regional affairs as they own about 45 per cent of global oil reserves – a situation that has enhanced the capacity of the ruling families to retain power at home and retain their value as allies of the US through lucrative defence and commercial contracts. In effect, the interests of the "state" and the ruling family are conflated. This has earned them the appellation of "rentier states" – a political and economic order that lives off natural resources, with revenues flowing in from the global marketplace.

The monarchies are said to have entered into a "social contract" with their citizens – total loyalty and obedience to the monarch in return for state-funded education and health facilities, subsidies on items for daily living, guaranteed employment in the state sector, and generous state support for important purposes – housing and marriages. Usually, Gulf monarchies are benign – their resources enable them to co-opt most sections of their population as upholders of the ruling order. However, the capacity and instruments of coercion are also readily available (and used) to handle the particularly obstinate and recalcitrant dissidents. The state security apparatus is equipped with state-of-the-art surveillance technologies that closely monitor every word, movement, association, and action of all residents at all times and take stern action at appropriate times.

The other two kingdoms in the region are Jordan and Morocco. The ruling family of Jordan was installed in the country after World War I by Britain, when the country became part of the British "mandate" in 1923. The royal family claims descent from Prophet Mohammed, but Britain, in the words of Nazih Ayubi, was "not only the creator and protector of its [Jordan's] king, but, to a large extent, financier and commander of its armed forces."[11] Thus, the monarchy rules the country not on the basis of legitimacy derived from its familial affiliation with the prophet, but due to sustained political, military, and economic support provided by Western powers.

The royal family of Morocco, the Alaouite dynasty, has ruled the country for four centuries. Its members are also direct descendants of the prophet. The rulers constitutionally enjoy the caliphal title, Amir al-Momineen ("Commander of the Faithful"), and formally head the Maliki school of Sunni Islam. In recent years, the royal family has consolidated its legitimacy through its role in freeing the country from French control and heading a quasi-democratic political order that focuses on national reconciliation and development.

13.6 The Arab Republics

Nazih Ayubi, in 1995, described the Arab republics as "populist-corporatist regimes."[12] Another authority on West Asian politics, Mehran Kamrava, writing nearly 25 years later, said the states are defined by "corporatist populism."[13] The term "corporatism" used in the context of the Arab republics refers to the diverse associations that are state-sponsored, bring together persons who share an identity or special interest, and then can be mobilised to support the regime when required, particularly through mass demonstrations. Not surprisingly, their analysis of the Arab state order, though separated by a quarter of a century, is remarkably similar.

The Arab republican order consists of three poles: the president, the army, and the party. The leader seeks legitimacy through emotional appeals to his people by speaking of "unity" (based either on the nation or "Arabness") and promising technology-based "modernisation" for the middle classes and ambitious welfare schemes for the poor. The legitimacy of the political order is sought to be further enhanced by clothing it emotively in a "pseudo-ideology" – though Egypt's Gamal Abdel Nasser paid lip-service to socialism, it was the rhetoric of "Arab nationalism" which aroused wild enthusiasms across West Asia and North Africa until defeat in the 1967 war ground it into dust. For Saddam Hussein in Iraq, the "ideology" was Ba'athism – a movement that brought together Arab nationalism and socialism. But what was most evocative about the ideology were its ringing slogans – "*Wahda, Hurriya, Ishtarakia*" (Unity, Freedom, Socialism) and "*Umma Arabiya Wahda, Dhaath Risala Khalida*" ("The Arab People are One, that is our Eternal Message").

Mehran Kamrava has identified three phases in the shaping of the Arab republican state order: state-building, state consolidation, and state atrophy.[14] The 1950s was the first phase of state-building; this was a period of optimism and idealism – the revolutionaries were imbued with a sense of historic mission, sought popular support through mass demonstrations, projected an over-arching ideology, and promised state-guided national development and ambitious welfare schemes for the poor. Key institutions of the state order were set up – national assembly, elections, judiciary, and the civil service. During this period, the armed forces were built up and became the "spine of the regime." The regimes tacitly imposed on their people a "social contract" promising education, health, subsidies, and state employment to its people in exchange of compliance with the state diktat.

In the consolidation phase in the 1960–1970s, presidents built around themselves a narrow support base of "cronies" who assumed control of industrial assets and were awarded the bulk of the contracts for national projects. This cabal had a shared interest in regime longevity and the survival of the existing state order. In the 1980s, the deficiencies in state order made themselves felt – economic pressures due to falling oil prices, coupled with raging unemployment, particularly among the educated; the increasing burden of state subsidies; the debt burden incurred to pay for the subsidies, which aggravated by having to pay for debt services; neo-liberal economic policies imposed by the IMF; and the World Bank that called for cuts in state expenditures, deregulation, and privatisation of business – all of which undermined the "ruling bargains."

From the 1990s onwards, we see the phase of state atrophy. This was when the inherent weaknesses of state order became apparent – state institutions such as the assembly and the judiciary had lost all credibility and elections had become farcical. The armed forces and the security services became the principal pillars of state order and created a "deeply rooted culture of fear" among the people.[15] This was accompanied by a cult of personality around the leaders who "had uncanny survival instincts, as well as a voracious appetite for both power and cruelty which enabled them ... to hold on to office." As most leaders began to groom their sons as successors, the leaderships became "monarchical presidencies."[16]

13.7 Iran: From Monarchy to Islamic Republic

Iran shares a long and complex history with its West Asian neighbours. At the centre of world politics and civilisation for several centuries, Iran was defeated by Arab armies at the Battle of Qadisiyya in AD 637. As Arab power declined in West Asia, the Persians reasserted themselves as independent polities, culminating with the Safavid dynasty (1501–1736), which was a rival of the neighbouring Ottoman Empire. The two major Islamic realms were not only divided ethnically as Turk and Persian; they also, from 1501, got separated doctrinally, when Shah Ismail I (1487–1524) declared Twelver Shiism as the official faith of the Persian empire. Thus, the Safavids put in place a new source of legitimacy for their rule – their affiliation with Shia Islam that set them off against the Ottoman sultans who, as caliphs, claimed leadership of the global Muslim community.

The Safavids also imbued new doctrinal and political principles into the Islamic order that were unique to Iran – Shia Islam, unlike its Sunni counterpart, had an organised clergy that, during the succeeding Qajar dynasty (1785–1925), shaped an integrated hierarchical structure for itself based on the level of learning of the clerics concerned. The first manifestation of clerical activism were agitations in Iran in 1905–1906 against royal weakness in the face of Western demands. These demonstrations yielded an elected assembly and the country's first constitution. The constitution declared that the ruler derived his authority from the people and ruled as a trustee of the peoples' interests. It also recognised the status of the clergy through the powers given to clerical courts and their right to scrutinise legislation to ensure its conformity with Sharia. Though the assembly was forcibly closed in 1908 by the monarch, the constitution endured as a model and was later regularly invoked to rebuke autocratic rulers. The Qajars were replaced by a new ruler – Reza Shah Pahlavi – a former colonel who set up a new dynasty in Iran in 1925. The Western powers deposed him in 1941 for his proximity to Germany in World War II and placed his son, Mohammed Reza Shah, on the throne.

After World War II, Iran, suffused in nationalist fervour, asserted its interest in constitutional monarchy, a democratic order and independence from foreign influence; these interests were specifically centred on the nationalisation of the oil industry. However, a coup engineered by a British–US coalition in 1953 overthrew the country's democratically elected government, headed by Mohammed Mossadeq, and placed Iran under authoritarian rule for the next 26 years. Mohammed Reza Shah sought popular support through a wide-ranging reform programme but also secured his rule through the strengthening of the armed forces and the security services. In the process, he also alienated the clergy by excluding clerics from their traditional role of scrutinising legislation. Seeking to free himself from clerical restraint, the shah sought legitimacy from Iran's pre-Islamic traditions. Thus, in 1971, he commemorated, in Persepolis, 2,500 years of the Iranian monarchy going back to Cyrus the Great, and later replacing the Islamic Hegira calendar with one dating back to Cyrus. In his search for legitimacy outside Islam, the shah also focused on the "Aryan" identity of the Persian people – this highlighted Iran's "superior civilisation, language, and culture, and [was] filled with a sense of supremacy toward neighbouring nations and cultures."[17]

Opposition to the shah's authoritarian rule was led by a popular and influential cleric, Ayatollah Ruhollah Khomeini. Khomeini castigated the monarch for mass corruption, rigging of elections, and proximity to foreign powers, especially Israel, all of which resonated well with the masses. Though deported in 1964, Khomeini carried on his campaign from Najaf in Iraq, with his words reaching Iran through audio tapes.

Through over a year of public agitations in 1978, a diverse group of opponents – clerical, constitutionalists, socialists, and Marxists who believed in armed struggle – united to bring down the shah's rule in January 1979. But the republic that emerged acquired the unique character of an "Islamic" republic – which was not preordained by the revolution. This was almost entirely the handiwork of Khomeini, whose personal commitment, intellectual innovativeness, political skill, and – when required – ruthlessness gave the country a new name, the "Islamic Republic of Iran," and a new constitution that institutionalised Islam and the sovereignty of God in the nascent political order. Thus, the revolution in Iran legitimised itself on the basis of the country's "Iran-Islamic" identity against the shah's exclusive national Iranian identity.[18]

Khomeini's personal contribution to the constitution was the concept of "vilayet-e-faqih" – the "guardianship of Islamic Law." Khomeini argued that, since Muslim societies were governed by Sharia, in the Shia polity, in the absence of the "Hidden Imam" (the 12th imam who went into occultation in AD 939, and who will return as the awaited Mahdi or Messiah and establish the kingdom of God on earth), only one learned in Islamic law could interpret the law and guide its application in the political order. Such a person could not be a hereditary monarch, but only a cleric elected by the ulama as the "Supreme Leader" ("rahbar"). The Iranian constitution created the office of Supreme Leader with sweeping powers – the appointment of heads of the armed forces, ordering military mobilisation, declaring war and peace, and vetting candidates for the presidency. Thus, the constitution enshrined direct rule by the clergy, in place of its traditional role as counsellor and admonisher.

It also recognised the Islamic Revolution Guard Corps (IRGC) as the guardian of the revolution, with responsibility for the protection of national borders and the waters of the Persian Gulf. The constitution had another part – it provided for direct elections to the presidency and the national assembly and gave all the rights that are available to citizens in a normal democracy. However, clerical authority and power remain the central features of the constitution.

The Iran–Iraq war (1980–1988), initiated by Iraq's president Saddam Hussein to overthrow the Iranian revolution, had the opposite effect – it engendered in Iranians a deep sense of national unity and national pride due to their success in repelling the aggression and keeping their territory intact. It also consolidated the Islamic revolution in the country. Khomeini pointed out that the Iranian people had "struggled against tyranny, and the oppression of stagnation and backwardness" and had upheld "the ideals of Mohammed's Islam in place of the ideals of … American Islam." Twenty years after the war with Iraq ended, there was a major effort made in Iran by large sections of the middle class to reform their clergy-controlled political order. In June 2009, the sitting president, Mahmoud Ahmadinejad, was challenged by two reformist candidates – Mir Hossein Mousavi and Mehdi Karroubi. The latter sought greater democracy in the political order, but within the framework of the existing constitution. The election results, which favoured Ahmadinejad, were viewed as fraudulent and led to hundreds of thousands of people taking to the streets, asking: "Where is my vote?" However, the hard crackdown by the government and the upholding of the election results diluted popular fervour, though protests, referred to as the Green Movement, continued for some more weeks.

Arshin Adib-Moghaddam has explained that the Islamic Republic "is not a monolith" and that the country's "pluralistic momentum" means there is "critique, defiance and opposition," which has ensured that politicians of diverse ideological persuasions remain sensitive to popular wishes.[19] Thus, the agitations of 2009 were followed by nationwide demonstrations in late 2017 and November 2019; these largely consisted of workers and the lower-income segment who bitterly criticised the government for their economic distress. A little later, in January 2020, Iranians went back to the streets after the accidental shooting down of the Ukraine Airlines civilian aircraft by the IRGC. They rejected the attempts at cover-up and denial by this powerful entity; a students' statement called for "a return to popular politics" and the acceptance that the rights of security, freedom, and equality are not just for the elite but are "inalienable and for all people."[20]

Thus, the dynamics of Iranian politics continues to reflect the enduring search for fresh bases for legitimacy that will accommodate the ideological concerns of rulers as well as the popular aspirations for freedom and justice contained in the country's pluralistic ethos. Having briefly discussed the Islamisation of political order in Iran, the next section will examine the efforts of Islamic thought and movements to shape politics in neighbouring Arab states.

13.8 "Islam" in the Political Order

The most powerful platform for dissent in West Asia in the 20th century has been the Muslim Brotherhood. It originated in Egypt in 1928 as a cultural movement, led by Hassan al-Banna (1906–1949), to protect Muslims from the allures of secularism and materialism offered by the West. Hassan al-Banna's principal concern was that Western influences in the Muslim world had "corrupted and perverted" the Muslims' religious, social, and cultural thought and institutions. He saw the panacea for the community in a "return to Islam" – the Islam of the early period of the "Rightly guided" caliphs. After the period of the first four caliphs, al-Banna noted that their successors' rule consisted of kingship, dynastic rule, arbitrary rule, tribalism, factionalism, and gross corruption. This internal debilitation enabled the enemies of Islam – the Western powers – to wreck the Islamic State order, a defeat that was facilitated by the ulama (Islamic scholars) "who observed and heard and did nothing."[21] The solution for the Muslims' predicament was to return to the Islamic order based on Sharia – the tenets of the Koran and the Hadith and with fresh interpretations by learned scholars. The Sharia would provide the norms for the reformed Islamic society that would be based on public welfare. In this Islamic society, there would be no divide between church and state since Islam provides for a "unity of life." But the Islamic State would not be a theocracy – the authority to rule would come from "the people" and would be contingent on the ruler obeying and implementing the Sharia and ruling on the basis of *shura* (consultation).[22]

By the 1950s, the Brotherhood had acquired a pan-Arab presence and was viewed as a threat by the emerging revolutionary regimes as it advocated grassroots activist political participation to obtain an Islamic polity. It was brutally suppressed by Nasser and his successors Anwar Sadat and Hosni Mubarak. In Syria, in 1982, the Syrian president, Hafez al-Assad, launched a massive military assault on the Brotherhood in Hama in which several thousand of its members were killed. Despite state repression, the Brotherhood has spawned a number of remarkable intellectuals who, following in the footsteps of their predecessors, have made a major effort to harmonise the principles of Islam with those of parliamentary democracy. Four of these scholars – Yusuf al-Qaradawi (b 1926),

Tariq al-Bishri (b 1933), Kamal Abdul Majd (b 1930), and Mohammed Salem al-Awwa (b 1942) – expounded their views towards the end of the last century, achieving collectively what Bruce Rutherford has called "a coherent view of Islamic constitutionalism."[23]

Their central assertion is that the "renewal of Sharia is essential for reviving the dignity and strength of the Muslim world."[24] Like their predecessors, they insist on the accountability of the ruler and the importance of *shura* (consultation). The political order should have parliaments, political parties, free elections, and provide full protection of rights for all citizens, including women and non-Muslims. Peoples' participation in the selection of their leader is enshrined in Islamic tradition as is the idea of elections – Islamic law requires that all those who have knowledge of a particular matter under litigation are obliged to testify; by analogy, voting is the individual's testimony about the fitness of the candidate for leadership.

It should be noted that these modernist interventions in Islamic discourse have so far met the same fate as the works of the scholars a century ago – then their thoughts had no resonance with the colonial powers which were taking over the Arab world; now, the Arab authoritarian order also does not offer fertile soil for these ideas to take root and flourish. But, while the Brotherhood advocated peaceful political activism, an alternative approach to imparting legitimacy to the regional political order from within the doctrines of Islam – an approach that asserted that the Islamic polity can and should be reformed through proactive violent action. This is discussed in the next section.

13.9 Radical Islam as Source of Resistance

The Arab republics that emerged as a result of revolutions espoused nationalism, socialism, and secularism as their central defining principles and, in terms of global politics, upheld non-alignment, though, in the Cold War they had close economic and military links with the Soviet bloc. The monarchies, led by Saudi Arabia, were largely anchored in Islam and were part of the Western alliance. This ideological divide ended with the defeat of Egypt and Syria in the 1967 war, when the pendulum of influence in the Arab world shifted in favour of Saudi Arabia. The latter institutionalised its leadership of the Arab and Islamic worlds by convening the Islamic Summit in Rabat in 1969 and then setting up the Organisation of the Islamic Conference in Jeddah in 1972. Western powers viewed Islam as a "natural ally" against "godless communism."

While the kingdom utilised pan-Islamism to serve its political interests, the faith was also used by Arab intellectuals to shape a radical ideology of resistance to state tyranny and Western nations viewed as enemies of the faith. The Egyptian intellectual, Sayyid Qutb (1906–1966), called for a God-centred society in which faith would be "an all-embracing and total revolution against the sovereignty of man."[25] This message of resistance and revolution was elaborated by the Palestinian scholar, Abdullah Azzam (1941–1989), who proclaimed that jihad, the divinely sanctioned war on the enemies of Islam, was the first duty of all Muslims. Following the "victory" of jihad in Afghanistan, it became a powerful instrument of opposition against all existing Arab regimes and their replacement by states founded on Islamic principles. The lead role in this endeavour was played by Al-Qaeda, whose assaults on the enemies of the faith culminated in the 9/11 attacks on the US mainland. After the US assault on Al-Qaeda in Afghanistan post 9/11, the organisation decentralised and now functions through local affiliates in different parts of West Asia and North Africa. After the US-led attack on Iraq in 2003, the country became a fertile ground for radical politics as sections of its Sunni community joined jihadi groups in defence of their interests against the US privileging the Shia community in the re-shaped state order. From civil conflict and state breakdown in Iraq, emerged a new jihadi organisation that, from 2013, called itself the Islamic State of Iraq and Syria (ISIS). Its leader, Abu Bakr al-Baghdadi, proclaimed a new vision of state order in West Asia – in July 2014, he announced the setting up of a proto-state, the "Islamic State" (IS), that straddled large parts of Iraq and Syria that was headed by him as caliph, the first to hold this position since it was abolished in Turkey in 1924. The destruction of the IS in 2018 has made its surviving members into "lone-wolves" who regularly carry out lethal attacks across the region and even, on occasion, in Europe.

The authoritarian order in West Asia has also faced domestic opposition from intellectuals and dissident movements. In Saudi Arabia, in the 1990s, an Islamic movement emerged from within the Wahhabi fold, the *Sahwa* ("Awakening"). It demanded a comprehensive reform of the Saudi order, with a constitution, a limited monarchy, political parties, elections, a national assembly free of royal control, and guaranteed human rights.[26] Most of its leaders served long jail sentences and were compelled to withdraw from political life. However, the movement continues to make its presence felt on social media and demand wide-ranging reforms. Over the last decade, the Arabs have made one more effort to reform their political order and make it legitimate and responsive to their needs and aspirations – this ongoing effort is referred to as the "Arab Spring."

13.10 The Arab Spring Uprisings

The public agitations that overwhelmed the Arab world from 2011 onwards took rulers, diplomats, and scholars by surprise. This popular anger and the absence of fear before the firepower of the incumbent regimes brought down four rulers who had been in position for 25 years or more – those of Tunisia, Egypt, Yemen, and Libya.[27] What were the agitators calling for? Despite country-specific demands, they were bound by their call for freedom, democracy, and personal dignity. Again, almost all the demonstrations were peaceful with diverse participants – men and women, Muslims and Christians, Islamists and secularists, lower and middle classes, urban and rural communities – and despite deliberate provocations and intimidation from the rulers. The forces of counter-revolution then moved in quickly and, through blandishments of co-option, coupled with state violence, ensured that no more potentates fell. There was a second round of uprisings in 2018–2021 – in Sudan, Algeria, Iraq, and Lebanon – where they had not occurred earlier. In each case, the head of state or government was compelled to leave office under popular pressure.

The Arab Spring uprisings affirm that the "ruling bargain" that has kept Arab rulers in power in the republics and monarchies has broken down in the face of rising unemployment, poverty, and the food crisis due to massive increases in world food prices. There is also little doubt that long-standing rulers panicked before these expressions of public dissent from people whose subservience they had taken for granted. In response, Gulf monarchies showered their people with billions of dollars of sops – salary increases, enhanced unemployment benefits, and massive loans for housing and marriages.

But, finally, the principal instrument to curb these agitations was coercion – confirming what Ayubi had said all those years ago, that "the Arab state is … often violent *because* it is weak."[28] In Saudi Arabia and the UAE, several petitioners for reform were imprisoned. In Egypt, the armed forces, backed by Saudi Arabia and the UAE, overthrew the democratically elected government and re-installed a military dictatorship in the country that is more brutal than any of its predecessors.

The trajectory events in Morocco have been somewhat different. The greatest achievement of the monarchy in Morocco has been its ability to survive despite failures to meet popular aspirations and organised opposition from large sections of its population. The present ruler, King Mohammed VI, came to the throne in July 1999, after nearly four decades of authoritarian rule of his father, Hassan II. In the first decade, through several major reforms, the king gained considerable popularity, even earning the title, "King of the Poor."

The Arab Spring protests began in Rabat on 20 February 2011 and spread quickly to Casablanca, Marrakesh, Tangiers, and other cities. These agitations were led by self-organised youth, who used the word Al-Hogra ("Contempt") to describe their situation of exclusion, scorn, humiliation, and injustice. The king moved swiftly to defuse tensions by initiating constitutional changes, which were finalised by July 2011. The new constitution added the word "parliamentary," so that Morocco was now described as a "constitutional, democratic, parliamentary and social" monarchy. The new constitution provided for an empowered prime minister, freedom of the press and judicial reform, and limited royal appointments to 400, as against the earlier 1,200. The king's position, described as "sacrosanct" in the earlier constitution, now became "duly respected."[29] In the elections held in November that year, the Islamist Justice and Development party won a majority of the seats and formed the government.

The monarchy in Morocco, Kamrava has pointed out, "is seen as a unifying factor for all Moroccans and a central pillar of Moroccan national identity."[30] But the Arab Spring uprisings posed a unique challenge which the king handled most adroitly. He has projected himself as being committed to reform and responsive to his people's aspirations, though, in reality, no significant change has occurred in the political order. As Aziz Chahir has noted, Mohammed VI shares with his authoritarian father the "ideological origin that privileges the personification of government, the concentration of powers and political domination of opponents."[31]

13.11 Outlook for West Asian State Order

Given the oil revenues that are still available to them, the Gulf monarchies are pursuing novel initiatives to obtain fresh bases to legitimise their rule. The most dramatic and wide-ranging efforts in this regard are taking place in Saudi Arabia. In his rapid ascent to becoming crown prince in his early thirties, Crown Prince Mohammed bin Salman Al Saud (MBS) upended two fundamental principles that have guided royal family affairs for the last several decades – succession on the basis of seniority and maintaining the unity of the royal family. MBS has therefore sought to legitimise his claim to the throne with a programme of radical reform that will appeal to the youth of his country – 51 per cent of the Saudi population is below the age of 25 years. This new foundation for legitimacy replaces the kingdom's two hoary platforms – religious nationalism at home and pan-Islamism abroad – with what scholars are calling "hyper-nationalism."

The crown prince's reform programme consists of doing away with the restrictive social norms that have been enforced in the country for several decades in the name of Islam – women are now allowed to drive, mixed-gender gatherings in public places are permitted, public entertainment – events that were forbidden till recently, with violations inviting severe punishments.

The kingdom's "Vision-2030" programme, promulgated in April 2016, is aimed at preparing the country for a non-oil future. It holds out the prospect of a vibrant and exciting adventure which makes young people entrepreneurs and not state employees. This includes the kingdom celebrating its non-Muslim heritage by showcasing its ancient archaeological sites and also simultaneously pursuing a dazzling high-tech multi-billion project, the NEOM, a unique working/living environment based on state-of-the-art technology that, when completed, will straddle three countries – the kingdom, Jordan, and Egypt.

However, the kingdom's hyper-nationalism is most apparent in the steady securitisation of the political order and its activist approach to regional matters. A prominent Saudi academic declared that citizens who do not defend their country should be labelled "traitors" – thus, justifying the harsh clampdowns on dissidents and human rights activists at home and on critics of the country's regional policies – the war in Yemen or the blockade of Qatar. The country's leading royal family members, Islamic scholars, businesspersons, and human rights activists have suffered brutal and prolonged incarceration. This is largely to affirm "the centrality of the crown prince" in the nationalism project that resounds with such Trumpian slogans as "Saudi Arabia is Great" and "Saudi Arabia for Saudis."[32] This focus on nationalism is meant to achieve the silencing of all challenge and dissent. It is accompanied by the simultaneous exaltation of the prince through a robust branding campaign at home and abroad as a modern reformer, despite his association with the brutal killing of the Saudi dissident, Jamal Khashoggi, in Istanbul, in October 2018.

A major aspect of MBS's agenda is to re-invent Saudi Arabia's Islamic discourse and present it as modern and moderate; the earlier covenant in the mid-18th century between Sheikh Mohammed ibn Abdul Wahhab and the Al-Saud is being airbrushed, with the rise of the family being projected as entirely self-driven. The earlier restrictive norms in the country are being blamed on the pernicious influence of the Islamic revolution in Iran in 1979.[33] The shift away from pan-Islamism towards hyper-nationalism as the legitimising principle for the kingdom and its crown prince serves many useful purposes. One, it enables the kingdom to distance itself from the intrusive and coercive norms, enforced in the name of Islam, that had made Saudi Arabia a despised outlier in the regional and global order and had militated against its efforts to project itself as an attractive political, military, and economic partner. At the same time, the "reforms" have won the crown prince a solid support base among the youth who are enjoying their new-found freedom and remain allured by the prince's promise of a post-oil technology-based future. Two, the rejection of Saudi Arabia's affiliation with the harsh tenets of Wahhabiyya also enables the kingdom to deny any responsibility in the proliferation of radical Islam, despite the fact that the Wahhabi doctrines were influential in shaping jihadi discourse, and Saudi nationals, nurtured in such doctrines, were a major presence in both the Al-Qaeda and the Islamic State. Finally, the distancing from pan-Islamism enables the kingdom to face two competitions – an ideological challenge from the Muslim Brotherhood and its affiliates across West Asia, and the political challenges from Turkey and Iran for leadership of the Muslim world. This imparts greater flexibility to the country in making foreign policy choices – with even unpopular options being justified as being in the national interest.

Christopher Davidson has argued that both the crown prince of Saudi Arabia and Sheikh Mohammed bin Zayed, crown prince of Abu Dhabi and de facto head of the UAE, have moved from the traditional "sheikly rule" of the Gulf rulers – that provided for consultation and consensus-building – to autocratic-authoritarianism that he refers to as "sultanism," an extreme form of autocracy.[34] Saudi Arabia and the UAE, led by their respective "sultans," are today jointly engaged in an enterprise that takes them beyond authoritarian control over their own countries to manipulating the politics of neighbouring countries to ensure that the first shoots of political participation do not take root in fertile soil. In Egypt, in 2013, they had generously funded the movement to overthrow the government headed by Mohammed Morsi and reinstate military rule. Their concern obviously was that a successful Brotherhood administration, founded on the marriage of Islamic precepts with democratic norms, would become a model for other Arab countries and threaten their dynastic rule. Both of them had earlier also sent their troops into Bahrain in March 2011 to disrupt the reform movement that was then discussing with the Bahraini crown prince the shaping of a constitutional monarchy in that country. Here the concerns were that a democratic model in a fellow member of the Gulf Cooperation Council (GCC) would encourage similar popular movements in other GCC countries. Besides this, with Bahrain having a Shia majority, there were fears that Shia communities in other countries, particularly in Saudi Arabia where they suffer considerable discrimination, would demand reforms and a more active role in the national order. Above all, Saudi Arabia feared that Shia empowerment in Bahrain would bring Iranian influence into the heart of the GCC family.

In the early days of the Arab Spring, largely to neutralise domestic demands for reform, Saudi Arabia demonised Iran as a sectarian and hegemonic threat to the region. It sought to undermine Iranian interests by promoting regime change in Syria, an Iranian ally over 40 years, on the basis that President Bashar al-Assad belonged to the Alawi/Shia community. It saw a similar sectarian threat in Yemen where the Zaidi/Shia community had organised itself into a militia under the Houthi family to demand political and economic rights. The kingdom viewed the Houthis as affiliates of Iran and launched a fierce military campaign against Yemen in early 2015. In Libya, the lead role is being played by the UAE, backed by Egypt. The civil conflict, which led to the overthrow of the Gaddafi government and the killing of the president himself, has split the country into two governments – one in Tripoli that is linked to the Brotherhood and the other in Tobruk that is supported by the UAE to ensure that the Brotherhood would not take over the country.

13.12 Conclusion

This pattern of intervention to undermine popular aspirations in the wake of the Arab Spring uprisings has continued, most recently in Tunisia and Sudan, the two "success" stories from the first and second waves of the Arab Spring, respectively. Here, they have helped to reverse the processes that were taking the two countries towards a functioning democratic order. In Tunisia, this has been done through a constitutional coup engineered by the president, while in Sudan, the armed forces have again asserted their right to govern without democratic constraint.[35]

What then is the outlook for state order in the Arab world? Given the circumstances described above, no reform of the political order is likely. However, with weak state institutions, the spread of radicalised non-state militants, the burgeoning economic challenges, the proliferation of weaponry and the several unresolved regional disputes, the sustained commitment to authoritarian rule, and the malign role of Western powers in supporting authoritarian regimes – the region will remain unstable and insecure. And, as a scholar predicted years ago, its fragile state order will "[falter] at the first shock, and the carefully erected façade [will] crack open to reveal all manner of horrid monsters that many thought History had long since laid to rest."[36]

Notes

1. For the purposes of this chapter, West Asia has been defined as Arab-speaking Middle Eastern countries and Iran.
2. Nazih N. Ayubi, *Over-stating the Arab State: Politics and Society in the Middle East* (London: IB Tauris, 1995), ix.
3. Asma Afsaruddin, *The First Muslims: History and Memory* (Oxford: One World, 2009), 21, 123–124.
4. Knut S. Vikor, *Between God and the Sultan* (London: Hurst and Co, 2005), 190.
5. Asma Asfaruddin, *The First Muslims*, 124–125.
6. Antony Black, *The History of Islamic Political Thought: From the Prophet to the Present* (Edinburgh: Edinburgh University Press, 2012), 20.
7. Ibid., 84–85.
8. Albert Hourani, *Arabic Thought in the Liberal Age 1789-1939* (Cambridge: Cambridge University Press, 2011), 239–240.
9. The monarchy in Jordan, put in place by Britain in 1921, continues to this day.
10. Nazhi N. Ayubi, *Over-stating the Arab State*, 132.
11. Ibid., 114.
12. Ibid., 196.
13. Mehran Kamrava, *Inside the Arab State* (London: Hurst and Co, 2018), 11.
14. Ibid., 14.
15. Mehran Kamrava, *Inside the Arab State*, 29.
16. Ibid., 30–31.
17. Golnar Mehran, quoted in Arshin Adib-Moghaddam, *What is Iran? Domestic Politics and International Relations in Five Musical Pieces* (Cambridge: Cambridge University Press, 2021), 50.
18. Ibid.
19. Ibid., 66, 71.
20. Ibid., 77.
21. Richard P. Mitchell, *The Society of the Muslim Brothers* (Oxford: Oxford University Press, 1993), 212.
22. Ibid., 243.
23. Bruce K. Rutherford, 'What Do Egypt's Islamists Want?', in Mehrzad Boroujerdi (ed.), *Mirror for the Muslim Prince: Islam and the Theory of Statecraft* (Syracuse, NY: Syracuse University Press, 2013), 244.
24. Ibid., 245.
25. Gilles Kepel, *The Roots of Radical Islam* (London: Saqi Books, 2005), 258.
26. For details, see: Talmiz Ahmad, *The Islamist Challenge in West Asia: Doctrinal and Political Competitions after the Arab Spring* (New Delhi: Pentagon Press/ IDSA, 2013), 32-37.
27. For an overview of the Arab Spring, see: Talmiz Ahmad, 'The Enduring 'Arab Spring': Change and Resistance', *Indian and Foreign Affairs Journal* 15, No. 2 (April-June 2020): 91–107.
28. Nazhi N. Ayubi, *Over-stating the Arab State*, 450.
29. Kamrava, *Inside the Arab State*, 65–66.
30. Ibid., 66.
31. Aziz Chahir, "Morocco: Ten Reasons Why Mohammed VI's Reign Has Lasted 20 Years", *Middle East Eye* (29 August 2019).
32. Madawi Al-Rasheed, *The Son King: Reform and Repression in Saudi Arabia* (London: Hurst and Co, 2020), 158.
33. Madawi Al-Rasheed, "The New Populist Nationalism in Saudi Arabia: Imagined Utopia by Royal Decree", *LSE Blogs* (5 May 2020).
34. Christopher M. Davidson, *From Sheikhs to Sultanism: Statecraft and Authority in Saudi Arabia and the UAE* (London: Hurst and Co, 2021), 20.
35. Khalid al-Anani, 'Tunisia … in the footsteps of Arab authoritarianism', *Middle East Eye* (31 July 2021). https://www.tellerreport.com/life/2021-07-30-tunisia- in-the

-footsteps-of-arab-authoritarianism.HJ00CZfyY.html ; James M. Dorsey, "Sudan and the UAE: Pulling Sudanese Strings", *Modern Diplomacy* (3 November 2021). https://moderndiplomacy.eu/2021/11/03/ sudan-and-the-uae-pulling-sudanese-strings/

36 Nazhi N. Ayubi, *Over-stating the Arab State,* 448.

Bibliography

Afsaruddin, Asma. *The First Muslims: History and Memory.* Oxford: One World, 2009.

Al-Rasheed, Madawi. *The Son King: Reform and Repression in Saudi Arabia.* London: Hurst and Co, 2020.

Anscombe, Frederick F. *State, Faith, and Nation in Ottoman and Post-Ottoman Lands.* Cambridge: Cambridge University Press, 2014.

Ayubi, Nazih N. *Over-Stating the Arab State: Politics and Society in the Middle East.* London: IB Tauris, 1995.

Black, Antony. *The History of Islamic Political Thought: From the Prophet to the Present.* Edinburgh: Edinburgh University Press, 2012.

Davidson, Christopher M. *From Sheikhs to Sultanism: Statecraft and Authority in Saudi Arabia and the UAE.* London: Hurst and Co, 2021.

Elbadawi, Ibrahim, and Samir Makdisi. *Democratic Transitions in the Arab World.* Cambridge: Cambridge University Press, 2017.

Esposito, John L., Tamara Sonn, and John O Voll. *Islam and Democracy After the Arab Spring.* Oxford: Oxford University Press, 2016.

Kamrava, Mehran. *Inside the Arab State.* London: Hurst and Co, 2018.

Lapidus, Ira M. *Islamic Societies to the Nineteenth Century: A Global History.* New Delhi: Cambridge University Press, 2013.

Marina, and David Ottaway. *A Tale of Four Worlds: The Arab Region After the Uprisings.* London: Hurst and Co, 2019.

Rutherford, Bruce K. "What Do Egypt's Islamists Want?" In *Mirror for the Muslim Prince: Islam and the Theory of Statecraft,* edited by Mehrzad Boroujerdi. Syracuse, NY: Syracuse University Press, 2013.

Sadiki, Larbi. *The Search for Arab Democracy: Discourses and Counter-Discourses.* New York: Columbia University Press, 2004.

Vikor, Knut S. *Between God and the Sultan: A History of Islamic Law.* London: Hurst and Co, 2005.

14

POWER AND LEGITIMACY IN PAKISTAN AND BANGLADESH

To Be Muslim or Islamic?

Kingshuk Chatterjee and Devadeep Purohit

14.1 Introduction

Almost all countries of the Muslim world have tended to be afflicted by the dilemma whether to give to Islam a space in public life. Not many have managed to square this circle conclusively – those countries that have chosen to relegate Islam to the private sphere have come to encounter formidable opposition from votaries of Islamisation in public life (viz. Turkey, Algeria, and Iran before 1979); by contrast, countries where Islam has been assigned a substantial space in public life tend to witness demands for limiting it to the private sphere (viz. Islamic Republic of Iran, Kingdom of Saudi Arabia). This constant negotiation between protagonists and opponents of Islamisation has become virtually a signature feature of politics in the Muslim world from the 20th century. From literally the moment of their births in 1947 as "homeland for Muslims of the Indian subcontinent," both Pakistan and Bangladesh have been tormented by the same dilemma, and their political journeys since have not seen much successful resolution of this question. While Bangladesh has managed to overcome its status of being a basket case of economic underdevelopment, both Pakistan and Bangladesh have so far been flirting with failure in conclusively devising the matrix of power and legitimacy on which the two states can rest.

This chapter means to argue that despite their shared origins in the Indian subcontinent and suffering from a similar dilemma over their relationship with Islam, the prospective outcomes in Pakistan and Bangladesh seem to be quite different in the two cases – especially with respect to power and legitimacy. In case of Pakistan, the dilemma serves to undermine the dispensation of power in, and legitimacy of, the state in a way that poses a virtually existential threat and is almost guaranteed to engulf the country in social violence of considerable degree. Bangladesh, by contrast, appears headed for a kind of Islamisation from

DOI: 10.4324/9781003385233-14

the bottom up which might overwhelm the state unless this challenge is contested real hard, as it is still being done.

14.2 Situating Legitimacy in Pakistan and Bangladesh

Pakistan had come into being with the promise ostensibly of being the homeland of the Muslims of the Indian subcontinent, but it never quite measured up to that idea.[1] The state of Pakistan that came into being was split into two wings – a geographically larger West Pakistan and a much smaller (but nearly as populous) East Pakistan. That state was a multi-ethnic polyglot entity that had really very little in common among the people, but for having a predominantly Muslim population.[2] Even in terms of the Islam that was practised, there were wide variations between regions as much as there was between town and country.[3] Hence, the idea of Pakistan was *not self-evident*; it required to be defined *after* the partition actually took place in 1947 what it *meant* to be a homeland for the Muslims of the subcontinent.

The experience of Pakistan before 1971 clearly showed that state-building in Pakistan was not going to be an easy job. Punjabi domination of the ranks of the economic, administrative, and military elites would give that very populous section an upper hand in the state of Pakistan over the still more populous Bengalis of the East Wing, and the far-less populous Sindhris, Pathans, and the Baloch;[4] Muslims who had left India for Pakistan would make a distinct category of people known as the *mohajir* (immigrant) anyway.[5] It was thus important for the ruling class of Pakistan to devise a state structure that would accommodate all these various ethnic and speech groups, and to start with the political consensus that was devised envisaged the creation of a state for the *Muslims*, but *not* an Islamic state – i.e. one would be free to practise one's faith the way one pleased, but in the private sphere where it belonged. This line was consistent with the dominant section of the ruling elite of the new state, inspired by Islamic modernism.[6] It was further decided the state would choose Urdu as its official language, one that was not associated with either of the two dominant speech groups of the new state (i.e. Bengali and Punjabi), but one which had come to be associated with Muslim culture in the subcontinent over the previous half century or so. The institutional complex that came to be associated with the state – the Westminster style of parliamentary democracy, the professional military (drawn virtually *in toto* from the section of the British Indian military that was assigned to Pakistan), the bureaucracy, and the judiciary – were all carried over from the British Indian establishment by the same political class that had dominated Muslim political life before 1947 (not unlike India from which the new country was cleaved out). While the political arena made new room for many of the provincial elites to play a much larger role on the larger federal space, the military, the bureaucracy, and the judiciary represented the elements of continuity with what used to be the colonial establishment.[7]

Once the political class began to jostle for power in the federal legislature and constituent assembly, it swiftly turned into a struggle between the old (who favoured continuity with the colonial era) and the new (largely provincial forces, but also Islamists) political players – landing the constituent assembly in a quagmire over the questions of whether the framework of the colonial state (stronger centre and weaker provincial government; non-sectarian) need be retained at all.[8] This alarmed the bureaucracy and the military sufficiently to have them intercede with the task of constitution-making to ensure the preservation of the colonial institutional matrix (which preserved their own dominance over the system), bringing about the collusion between Punjabi politicians (mostly of the Muslim League) with Punjabi-dominated bureaucracy and the military that has come to characterise the Pakistani establishment. The provincial political classes thus began to show signs of centrifugalism right from the start. These struggles resulted in Pakistan taking almost a decade to come up with its first constitution in 1956, which satisfied virtually no one in the political landscape of the country, resulting in two more in 1962 and 1973 – the third one coming only after the strongest component among the centrifugal forces, East Pakistan, broke away from Pakistan and emerged as the sovereign country of Bangladesh.[9]

Military-bureaucratic centralisation in its embryonic stage severely undermined the attempts to create a democratic state in Pakistan, but the country had not been "won" by the military on the battlefield. It was the product of a major political upheaval, ostensibly in the name of cultural autonomy for the Muslims of the subcontinent, but actually on account of a veritable social upheaval militating against the prospective deadening centralisation that comprised the nation-building agenda of the Indian National Congress.[10] Hence, the artificial and the geographically, ethnically, and linguistically disparate country of Pakistan could not be brought into being unilaterally from above, ignoring the very people who helped bring it about from below. Legitimacy of the very exercise of state-building in Pakistan had thus necessarily to be derived from the people themselves and had to proceed in tandem with the project of nation-building. Given the intrinsic diversity of the country, the easiest instrument for tapping into the society had been chosen to be subcontinental Muslim culture, which many chose to interpret as being the same as Islam.[11] Political life in Pakistan thus necessarily had to be *representative* of its people, even when (ironically) its politics was not democratic in its character. Both the emergence of Bangladesh in 1971 and the subsequent trajectory of the state of Pakistan can be understood only in this context. Bangladesh was the product of a movement that sought *representation* of Bengali culture and refused to be smothered by the north Indian (predominantly Punjabi) courtly culture that the Pakistani state was pushing as *Muslim* culture, revolving around Urdu – a language spoken by less than 10 per cent of the population of the country, and totally alien to those in East Pakistan.[12]

There were others, though, who favoured submerging such cultural particularism beneath a homogenous "Islamic" frame – either because they understood the complexities of building a nation in the face of cultural diversity or because they found the courtly north Indian culture too elitist to be acceptable (or maybe both). The demand for the creation of a homogenised Islamic culture in the Islamic state of Pakistan thus emerged from the more traditional sections of the Pakistani people, enjoying considerable support from the urban underclass. Before 1971, such voices used to be raised essentially by politically marginal forces like the Jama'at-e Islami and Jami'at-e 'Ulema, with Maulana Maududi being its most famous protagonist.[13] Their counterparts in East Pakistan were determined to prevent the break-up of the country in 1971, and from these ranks came the *Razakars* of the *Muktijuddha* (Liberation War) of Bangladesh who helped the brutal attempts of the Pakistani military to subjugate the people of East Pakistan. After 1971, some of the stakeholders in the Pakistani military-bureaucratic-political establishment began to consider such Islamisation as precisely the kind of cement that the rump state of Pakistan needed to avoid further fragmentation.[14]

In the case of Bangladesh, after the euphoria of liberation began to give way to the realities of creating a new state, initially they resorted to the less-unfamiliar model of parliamentary democracy – but very soon recreated the fractiousness that characterised Pakistan's own experience in Bangladesh, and just like Pakistan abandoned it for a period of rule by the military.[15] This prompted quite similar questions about the location of power and legitimacy in the fledgling state that were being asked in Pakistan as well. Organisations like the Jama'at-e Islami, which had in 1971 stood against the *Muktijuddha* (War of Independence), reconciled themselves to the reality of Bangladesh, but have been active since in establishing the same kind of "homogenous" Islamic frame atop the Bengali identity that prevailed in 1971.[16] They are in the vanguard of the opposition to the secular Bengali values that are projected by the Awami League of the hero of the Mutijuddha, Sheikh Mujibur Rahman. Aligning with the Bangladesh National Party (BNP) of the other war hero General Ziaur Rahman, such conservative Islamist forces seek to bring about the sort of Islamisation that undermines the secular dispensation of the state in Bangladesh as it does in Pakistan.[17]

14.3 The Steady Unravelling of Pakistan

For most observers of Pakistan based outside the country, and for many others operating inside it, the state of Pakistan came into being in the name of Islam, hence the *idea* of Pakistan is *essentially* Islamic. However, there is little or no agreement about what that does or should entail. The loss of East Pakistan could easily have been considered (as many people indeed do) as giving the lie to the story that Muslims of the Indian subcontinent represent a Muslim nation any more than the non-Muslims could, simply on the strength of their religious identity masquerading as a civilisational or cultural monolith. But such an admission was considered to be posing an existential risk to the rump state left behind in 1971. The break-up of the country was put to good effect to instil among the countrymen a fear of further fragmentation (presumably engineered by the intrinsically hostile neighbour, India), and hence the constant vigil that needs to be exercised to prevent such an eventuality. It was this particular line of thinking that led to Pakistan being proclaimed as an Islamic Republic in the constitution of 1973.[18] All the regimes that have followed since, civilian or military, have tried to draw their legitimacy from the sense of insecurity that they themselves have cultivated incrementally. The power struggle between the civilian and military components of the state that Pakistani politics has witnessed right through the half-century since 1971 was always underlined by just such claims of making the state so capable. Hence, over the last half-century, national security and regime survival often appear to have trumped popular sovereignty as the source of political legitimacy in the country.[19]

Pakistan probably had its best opportunity yet of establishing civilian supremacy over the military in the years immediately following the break-up of the country, while the latter were still recovering from the debacle of 1971. Prima facie, the 1973 Constitution accommodated somewhat the provincial aspirations, and in its initial years the national government under Zulfiqar Ali Bhutto managed to redeem itself at home and abroad in a number of ways.[20] The Bhutto government also successfully cut the national bureaucracy (PCS) to size and carried out a veritable purge of the military command structure appointing a relatively less senior General Zia ul-Haq as the Chief of Staff in a bid to control the military, hoping that the obsequious *mohajir* would remain steadfastly loyal for elevation out of turn.[21] However, instead of consolidating democracy in the country, the ruling party was keener on perpetuating its own grasp on power at the centre. Its brazen attempts at electoral rigging (especially in Punjab) in 1977 discredited the government in public perception and helped mobilise the opposition at the centre and the provinces alike quite effectively behind the only common factor among the disparate forces – the banner of Islam.[22] The political and social turmoil that followed allowed the military to stand forth "in the interests of the nation" and toppled the civilian government in 1977 promising to hold democratic elections within six months.[23] The execution of the deposed prime minister clearly helped the military regain the upper hand in its struggle with the civilian establishment.[24]

The tenure of General Zia ul-Haq was possibly the single-most decisive factor in making the Pakistani military the formidable institution that it is today. The Soviet involvement in Afghanistan posed a major threat to Pakistani security (not least because USSR was an ally of India); hence, Pakistan became a conduit for American military and financial assistance to the Afghan Mujahideen only too gladly.[25] This increased the military establishment's resources exponentially, and began to turn Pakistan into a deep state, laying the foundations of the military-industrial complex that makes the Pakistani military "the only military with its own country."[26] Industries that were of military or strategic significance began to be brought under the control of the defence establishment, beginning the gradual penetration of the Pakistani military into the country's economy – far too formidable to be taken on by the civilian establishment.[27] Zia, who had by then elevated himself to the position of the president took advantage of the simmering conflict in Afghanistan to turn the parliamentary form of government into a presidential one by means of the Eight Amendment.

The Zia administration was also the first dispensation during which the Pakistani state actually accommodated the Islamist agenda in state policy, introducing Hadood legislation, making blasphemy a capital offence, elevating the legal-juridical status of the Shari'ah courts, and designating the state as the official recipient of *zakat*.[28] While some have attributed this onset of Islamisation of the Pakistani state to Zia's personal piety, others think the latter more likely to be symptomatic rather than causative. By the 1980s, a large section of the officer corps happened to be from among those who were born into independent Pakistan, with a large section of them coming from provincial, small-town traditionalist Muslim backgrounds. Such people of piety are believed to be the principal motors behind the policy of Islamisation undertaken by Zia. It is also possible that this Islamisation was not resorted to by the Zia administration out of any conviction, but rather owing to tactical considerations – to assert solidarity with Muslim brethren in Afghanistan, as also to deflect protagonists of political Islam who had risen in opposition to the Bhutto government, and had continued to gain ground by opposing military rule.[29] By the time the second military dictatorship in Pakistan came to an end in 1988 with Zia's death, political Islam had started to become an instrument both of Pakistani statecraft (viz. in Afghanistan and Kashmir), as also the politics of opposition.

14.4 The Relentless Rise of Political Islam in Pakistan

Right from its inception, votaries of political Islam have historically been marginal to the political life of Pakistan. In elections, at its most handsome showing, all the forces subscribing to political Islam have secured less than 10 per cent of the votes – which is taken by many as clear evidence that Pakistan is a state for Muslims, but not an Islamic one. From the 1980s, the tactical use of the Mujahideen in Afghanistan and Kashmir improved the profile of such organisations somewhat by lending *jihad* a kind of respectability and acceptability that Pakistani society never accorded till then. In the last two decades, the fortunes of political Islam have begun to change exponentially as they increasingly resort to violence, at low level and otherwise. So much so that it has begun to challenge the Pakistani establishment (civilian and military dispensations alike), and is strong enough to posit an Islamic alternative to the present dispensation, civilian or military.

Much of this remarkable ascendancy is arguably owing to Pakistani entanglement with the persistent turmoil in Afghanistan, which has witnessed two occupations and a deadly civil war.[30] With millions of Afghans seeking refuge in Pakistan over the last 40 years, there has been considerable change in the demographic character of much of the country. As the population of settlements adjacent to the frontier and those further afield have tended to increase manifold, the institutional infrastructure of the Pakistani state has failed to cater to their needs, or indeed be mindful of their requirements. The consequent disaffection among a large body of Pakistani people living in marginalised conditions has strengthened those votaries of political Islam who do not belong to the political mainstream. Such sections of the people severely disapproved of American entanglement in Afghanistan (which often had its repercussions on Pakistan as well), and despised the governments in Islamabad that failed to stand up for "fellow Muslims." Some of these organisations (such as the movement associated with Maulana Fazl ur-Rahman) seek to reform the Pakistani establishment by bringing pressure to bear on mainstream political parties (such as Imran Khan's *Tehreek-e Insaaf*); still others seek to overturn the entire establishment and replace it with an ill-defined and vague *Nizam-e Mustafa* (Islamic order).[31]

Hence, for the first time since its inception, the legitimacy of the state of Pakistan has begun to be questioned by a section of its own people which wasn't the case even in 1971. While the break-away of East Pakistan was accomplished with the objective of establishing of *khud-mukhtari* (self-rule, i.e. popular sovereignty), promised in 1947 but never delivered, the Islamist discourse completely dismisses *khud-mukhtari* as a smokescreen behind which the political class successfully perpetuate its grip on power and promote the interests of global financial capital.[32] The Islamists, ranging from the Tehreek-e Taliban-e Pakistan on the extreme end to the Jaish-e Muhammad, appear to be steadily winning over those sections of the people whom the state never reaches in times of distress, or appears to bother about even in normal times. The demand for the introduction of Shari'ah law in Swat valley of Khyber-Pakthunkhwah, which President Asif Ali Zardari was compelled to allow in 2009, has to be situated within this larger context.[33]

The steady rise of this wilfully subversive discourse could be argued to an extent to be the result of the contestation for power among the elites, which has undermined if not the state itself, then certainly the credibility of all the regimes that have held power in Pakistan, civilian or military, democratic or otherwise. The problem is that almost all the major stakeholders in the Pakistani establishment, at one point of time or the other, have courted forces or outfits associated with the Islamic sub-culture – the military has never shied away from resorting to these Islamists for tactical regions in Afghanistan and Kashmir; neither have the political elite been hesitant in approaching Islamist organisations in order to undermine their political adversaries.[34] The tactical co-opting of the Islamist lobby has emboldened the latter progressively and has almost imperceptibly been eroding the legitimacy of the Pakistani state. So much so that it is becoming difficult to speak of the abuses of blasphemy laws without jeopardy to life and limb – as the tragic assassination of Salman Taseer brought out.

The Pakistani state, however, has the resilience to stem this erosion of its legitimacy. The regime of Pervez Musharraf made this quite clear when they took out Islamist militants first in the heart of Lahore and then in parts at FATA and Khyber-Pakthunkhwah; civilian governments headed by Pakistan People's

Party, Muslim League (Nawaz), and Tehreek-e Insaaf alike have carried out intermittent operations against the Tehreek-e Taliban-e Pakistan; even Imran Khan fell out with the Tehreek-e Labbaik Pakistan in 2020 after years of tacit understanding. Whether further erosion of legitimacy of the state system would be possible or not would largely depend on the denial of future mileage to the Islamist lobby by the mainstream elites of Pakistani society.

14.5 Bangladesh's Short-Lived Tryst with Secularism

On 16 December 2021, Bangladesh achieved an important milestone as the country celebrated its 50 years of independence. The high point of the celebrations on the occasion was a public oath-taking ceremony in which hundreds of thousands of citizens joined Prime Minister Sheikh Hasina in taking an oath to build the country as a developed, prosperous, and non-communal Sonar Bangla (Golden Bengal) imbued with the ideology of Sheikh Mujibur Rahman. "We will build the country as a developed, prosperous Sonar Bangla with a non-communal spirit. May the Almighty help us," she said, concluding the oath.[35]

Hasina's decision to include "non-communal spirit" in the list of targets she set for the country drew attention in Bangladesh and beyond because of the country's chequered experience in dealing with religion. An independent Bangladesh under Mujib's Awami League, which led the country's freedom struggle, began its journey 50 years ago with a constitution that had four cornerstones – secularism, democracy, nationalism, and socialism.[36]

The decision to include "secularism" as one of the cornerstones by the founding fathers of a Muslim-majority country surprised many, but for Rahman it was the most obvious decision as millions of people, who responded to his call and joined the country's liberation struggle in 1971 did so irrespective of their religion. Those martyred in the struggle – estimates of lives lost in the war range between half a million to three million – belonged to all the major religious communities.[37] Hence an independent Bangladesh had to tread the path of "secularism."

The fledgling nation's tryst with secularism was short lived as Rahman was killed in a military coup on 15 August 1975 and the subsequent military rulers – beginning with Major General Ziaur Rahman – chose a different path. The process that Zia launched in 1977 by dropping "secularism" from the constitution by means of the eighth amendment to the constitution[38] was taken forward by another military ruler, Lt. Gen Hossein Mohammed Ershad, who made Islam the state religion in 1988.[39]

Against this backdrop of Bangladesh, which won independence riding on Bengali nationalism, Hasina's pledge to build a "non-communal" country captures her intent to adhere to the broad principles of the constitution that Mujib, her father, had envisioned for the country. Though "secularism" (*dharma niropekkho* in Bangla) and "non-communal" (*asampradayik* in Bangla) are often used interchangeably in Bangladesh, they do not mean the same. Secularism as a principle of state policy implies separation or neutrality of the state vis-à-vis religion. "Non-communal" on the other hand is, at best, a political statement of intent, whose parameters as state policy are not well defined.

Why did Hasina opt for "non-communal" instead of "secularism"? It was clearly a balancing act between the secular legacy of the liberation struggle carried over by the Awami League and the persisting influence wielded by Bangladesh's Islamist lobby, especially in the context of the global upsurge in radical Islam in the past few decades. Hasina had risked a confrontation with the Islamists in the past, riding on the other most potent sentiment in the country – Bengali nationalism. Back in 2009, at the beginning of her second term in office, Hasina asserted the secular tenets of Bengali nationhood, which the military rulers had wanted the citizens to forget. In 2010, Hasina set up a War Crimes Tribunal to try people accused of murder, torture, rape, and arson during the liberation war. Under Mujib, Bangladesh had begun war crimes trials in 1973 to punish those who had resisted the idea of secularism, but they were halted in 1975 after his assassination.[40]

As subsequent governments chose to ignore the repeated calls for justice from war heroes and families of those slain, Hasina made it a poll issue and pledged during her election campaign that if voted to power, she would ensure prosecution of war criminals. Latest reports in Bangladeshi media suggest that over the last 11 years, 100 persons – including 52 absconding convicts – were tried by the tribunals (a second tribunal was set up in 2012 to expedite the trials). Of them, 67 were sentenced to death, 26 got life sentences, five got 20 years, one person was sentenced for 90 years while only one was acquitted.[41]

There are, however, murmurs in Dhaka that the process of trials and executions of the accused have slowed down in recent years as the Hasina regime has realised that the issue has run its course. The government, however, attributes the apparent slowdown in the trials to the pandemic-induced restrictions. The country's law minister has even promised amendments to the existing acts to ensure trial of anti-liberation organisations like Jama'at-e Islami that supported the Pakistani army during the liberation war. The trials are likely to continue, but it has already become clear that Hasina wants to tread softly on the issue of secularism in a bid to avoid a possible Islamist backlash following the trials and execution of the war criminals.

14.6 Democracy Lost and Regained

After Mujib was overthrown and was killed with his entire family (except daughters Hasina and Rehana) in a coup d'etat, Radio Dhaka had hailed the overthrow of "an autocratic government."[42] The official broadcast from the Bangladesh capital added that the step was taken in the "greater interest of the country," seeking to delegitimise the Mujib regime. In the 16 years that followed, the country witnessed multiple coups and counter-coups as men in uniform grabbed the seat of power using military might. The continued bloodshed and violence resulted in the destruction of democratic institutions and the rehabilitation of the fundamentalist elements that were defeated in the historic liberation war, which was fought in defence of the verdict of one of the few free and fair elections that Pakistan had ever held.[43] However, Mujib's own BAKSAL experiment somewhat compromised his own credentials as a votary of democracy – not everyone takes his assurance that the experiment was going to be merely a temporary aberration. Both Zia and Ershad promised to "restore" democracy to Bangladesh but stopped short of allowing free and fair elections. Nevertheless, since Bangladesh was the result of a social revolution from below, as in Pakistan, its political class found it necessary to derive their respective claims to legitimacy in being representatives of the people – hence democracy continues to be the episodic discourse that is retained for the sake of political legitimacy.

Both Zia and Ershad used military might and Islamist ideology to remain in power. Yet, in search of political legitimacy, they conducted their own experiments by rolling out their respective political outfits and even conducting elections, which produced expected results – Bangladesh Nationalist Party sweeping the polls under the Zia regime while the Jatiya Party emerged victorious during Ershad's days in power. Zia also courted the Jama'at-e Islami and in a bid to rehabilitate that section of the Bangladeshi population who were disconcerted by the secularisation agenda of Mujib. Some of these were even part of the Islamist lobby in undivided Pakistan that had once provided the Razakars who stood with Pakistan during the war of independence.[44]

A believer in the free market economy, Zia de-nationalised industries and financial institutions and promoted private investments.[45] Even his detractors admit that he brought a semblance of discipline in the army. While Zia's contributions to Bangladesh's progress continue to be debated within the country, his commitment to democracy remained suspect in the eyes of the broader public, thereby denting his legitimacy.[46]

The tenure of Ershad, who seized power in 1982 in a bloodless military coup a few months after Zia was killed by a group of army officers, did witness some attempts to improve rural administration and creation of infrastructure, but the condition of Bangladesh worsened both in terms of law and order and corruption. Rising inequality and crony capitalism led to social unrest, with street protests beginning from the second year of his rule.[47]

In the early days of Ershad, the most prominent protests were against his education policy that proposed making English and Arabic mandatory in primary-level education and his decision to impose Martial Law, banning political activities. The demand for his ouster grew with each passing year, although the Jatiya Party won two controversial elections in 1986 and 1988. Finally, the united opposition of Awami League and BNP forced him to resign in December 1990.[48]

After Ershad stepped down, a transitional government was put in place, which revived the democratic institutions and elections – with candidates from over 100 parties – were held in February 1991. Khaleda Zia led BNP to victory in the free and participatory elections and became Bangladesh's first woman prime minister. In a few months, the country adopted a parliamentary system, ending 16 years of presidential rule under several military dictators.

Since 1991, Bangladesh's politics has been a tussle between Hasina and Khaleda Zia, who took turns to run the country till 2006. In January that year, a caretaker government, backed by the army, took charge with the mandate of conducting free and fair elections and handing over power to a legitimate government. Even as the country awaited the election under the caretaker government, reports of a plan emerged – Minus-Two formula according to Dhaka media – which raised questions even on the caretaker regime's legitimacy. The elections were held in 2008 and Hasina won with a thumping majority. She repeated the performance in two successive elections – first in 2013 and five years later in 2018. Hasina is now preparing for the next contest two years away.

However, both the two principal parties of Bangladesh have in their own ways undermined and weakened the strength of the institutions of democracy in the country. Whenever the BNP won the elections (as in 1991 and 2001), the Awami League refused to accept its defeat in good grace, claiming electoral manipulation, boycotting the parliament. Whenever the Awami League won (as in 1996, 2008, 2013, and 2018) the BNP reciprocated with identical accusations. The zero-sum approach to power of these two leading parties has vitiated Bangladeshi politics to such an extent that in 2004 a major attempt was made towards elimination of the entire Awami League leadership by means of a grenade attack at a rally addressed by Hasina, which she barely survived. As a result, ever since the 1990s, the politics of opposition has played out in Bangladesh outside the parliamentary arena on the streets of Bangladesh. Unless there is a change in the disposition of the various political forces, the future is unlikely to augur well for the health of the institutions of democratic government in Bangladesh.

14.7 The Road ahead for Bangladesh

Today Bangladesh is on track to graduate from the United Nations' Least Developed Countries (LDC) list in 2026 as it has fulfilled the eligibility criteria in terms of per capita income, human development, and economic and environmental vulnerability. Despite the slowdown in domestic economic activity, decline in exports of ready-made garments and drying up of remittances from abroad due to the pandemic, Bangladesh's real GDP growth is expected to increase to 6.6 per cent in 2022 and 7.1 per cent in the following year, as per the projections of the International Monetary Fund.[49]

Political stability under the Hasina regime has played a key role in transforming the economic trajectory of Bangladesh. From one of the poorest, war-ravaged nations at birth in 1971, Bangladesh reached lower middle-income status in 2015. The country, once described as an "international basket case," today enjoys the tag of a "development miracle" by economists because of achievements like steady decline in fertility rates, infant and child mortality rates, and success in ensuring gender parity in access to education.[50]

Not only did Hasina deliver steady economic performance in her 13 years at the helm since 2008; she has also played a vital role in keeping the fundamentalist forces at bay and cracking down on domestic terrorism.[51] These achievements have won her plaudits both at home and abroad and bolstered the regime's credibility.

However, Hasina's regime does face a number of questions. Foremost among them relate to the fairness of the last two general elections, especially the one held in December 2018. Opposition parties like the BNP have accused her of turning Bangladesh into a "single party state" by using the police and eroding the independence of the judiciary and the Election Commission.[52]

Many liberals in Bangladesh are upset with Hasina as they think that the country's new Digital Security Act is aimed at muzzling free speech.[53] The questions over human rights in Bangladesh recently got magnified after the US government, in December 2021, imposed sanctions on seven former and current high-level officials of Bangladesh's Rapid Action Battalion (RAB), accusing them of involvement in enforced disappearances and extrajudicial killings. Besides, there are also concerns about the security of minorities, especially Hindus, rise in corruption in the country, and her tactical deals with the radical Islamist Hefazat-e Islam.[54]

Needless to say, the opposition camp will create more noise around these questions in the run up to the next general elections. However, the BNP doesn't have much credibility on issues like corruption, minority rights, human rights violations, or the erosion of institutions, given the track record of BNP-led governments in 1991–1996 and 2001–2006. People still remember the heinous grenade attack on an Awami League rally on 21 August 2004, which was clearly aimed at annihilating the entire Awami League leadership, including Hasina, who was the main speaker at the programme. The Awami League, which was in opposition then, had accused the then BNP Prime Minister Khaleda Zia and her son Tarique Rahman of direct involvement in the attack that killed 24 people and injured more than 300.[55]

The convictions and incarceration of Khaleda Zia and her illness have created total disarray in the BNP-led opposition camp, which is why they are unlikely to put up a serious challenge to the ruling regime in the immediate future. As the country approaches the next election, Hasina's achievements on the economic front are likely to win her another term in power.

However, the crucial challenges of building a genuinely "secular" Bangladesh and restoring the autonomy of democratic institutions remain to be addressed and appear far more intricate today than they did five decades back. Despite the military's ostensible determination to remain confined to the barracks for nearly three decades, democratic institutions in Bangladesh suffer from a severe weakness largely on account of the zero-sum nature of political practice in the country. Both the principal political parties have in the past questioned the validity of democratic elections that they lost, thereby challenging the legitimacy of the civilian governments that have held power in Dhaka, occasionally resorting to militant opposition.

By itself, that may not have been the portent of any great danger, but in the backdrop of the changing social landscape it assumes greater significance. Even among the generation that had witnessed the *Muktijuddha*, the tension between being a state for the Bengali Muslims and an Islamic state of Bengal was quite palpable, with Mujib being the protagonist of the former and Zia ur-Rahman that of the latter. The state of Bangladesh had allowed both of these groups of people considerable stakes in the political establishment of the country. However, despite the rapid strides made by Bangladesh in overcoming economic backwardness in the last several decades, Bangladesh has not been able to generate nearly as much economic opportunities as it needs to. Hence a degree of disenchantment with the country's political establishment is palpable among the post-*Muktijuddha* generation. This disenchantment gains a definite slant because of the influence of those Bangladeshis who had gone to the oil-rich countries of the Persian Gulf (or even in the relatively more Islamised diaspora sub-culture in the United Kingdom) looking for economic opportunities, and subsequently returned with the distinct sense that Bangladeshi Muslim culture is not nearly Islamic enough – neither in their approach to piety nor in their sartorial preferences. Hence, a wave of Islamisation from the bottom up is discernible among the post-*Muktijuddha* generation. Prime Minister Hasina's growing association with the Hefazat-e Islam has to be seen as acknowledging this changing reality of Bangladesh society and leaves open the possibility that in the not-too-distant future, any democratic dispensation in Bangladesh would necessarily eschew the path of secularism and embrace Islamisation to remain representative of the people it rules over. By contrast, if the state were to confront this gradual Islamisation of the society, then the chances of Bangladesh being engulfed by social violence would be considerably higher – an outcome very much similar to Pakistan.

14.8 Conclusion

Pakistan always was multi-ethnic and polyglot, with far more numerous fault lines than the relatively homogenous population of Bangladesh. Hence, right from the very beginning, the nation of Pakistan was an artificial construct, built prima facie in the name of religion and a culture shaped by that religion. The attempt to homogenise in the name of religion the culturally heterogeneous population resulted in the break-up of the original Muslim "homeland" and the emergence of a homogenous Bangladesh alongside the (only marginally less) heterogeneous Pakistan.

For Pakistan, the break-up of the "homeland" betrayed the artificial nature of the idea and made the state resort to an even more determinedly instrumentalist approach to the Muslim identity, thereby giving respectability to a segment of the population who wanted the more essentialist approach to an Islamic identity instead. This tension between the instrumentalist and essentialist approaches to Islam in Pakistan makes it susceptible to precisely the kind of turmoil that characterises the country in the first quarter of the 21st century.

Bangladesh, too, is torn between the same dilemma of being Muslim or Islamic but appears to be headed for Islamisation from the bottom up unless successfully thwarted by those sections of the population who still consider themselves to be Bengali first and Muslim next. The difference is that while the Pakistani state comprises much harder, deeper, and stronger institutional complex, that of Bangladesh is comparatively weaker. Thus, the struggle for legitimacy between Islamists and votaries of the present dispensation is more delicately poised in Bangladesh than it appears to be in Pakistan. An era of major social violence seems to be upon South Asia, either way.

Notes

1 See, for instance, Stephane P. Cohen, *The Idea of Pakistan* (Washington, DC: Brookings Institution, 2004), 15–38; Christophe Jaffrelot, *The Pakistan Paradox: Instability and Resilience* [translated by Cynthia Schoch] (Oxford: Oxford University Press, 2015), 53–96.
2 Jaffrelot, *The Pakistan Paradox*, 98–126.
3 For an excellent study of this aspect, see Akbar S. Ahmed, *Religion and Politics in Muslim Society: Order and Conflict in Pakistan* (Cambridge: Cambridge University Press, 1983).
4 J.K. Ray, *Democracy and Nationalism on Trial: A Study of East Pakistan* (Simla: Indian Institute of Advanced Study, 1968), 75–76.
5 Jaffrelot, *The Pakistan Paradox*, 104–118.
6 Rasul Bakhsh Rais, *Imagining Pakistan: Modernism, State and the Politics of Islamic Revival* (New York and London: Lexington Books, 2017), 41–67.
7 Ibid., 17–27.
8 Ian Talbot, *Pakistan: A Modern History* (London: Hurst and Company, 1998), 141–147; Jaffrelot, *Pakistan Paradox*, 199–215.
9 Talbot, *Pakistan: A Modern History*, 185–214.
10 For the most coherent and substantive formulation of this thesis, see Ayesha Jalal, *The Sole Spokesman: Jinnah, the Muslim League and the Pakistan Demand* (Cambridge: Cambridge University Press, 1985).
11 See Ayesha Jalal, *Self and Sovereignty: Individual and Community in South Asian Islam Since 1850* (Oxford: Oxford University Press, 2001).
12 Ray, *Democracy and Nationalism on Trial*, 15–17.
13 Seyyed Vali Reza Nasr, *The Vanguard of the Islamic Revolution: The Jama'at-i Islami of Pakistan* (Berkeley: University of California Press, 1994), 30–44.
14 Seyyed Vali Reza Nasr, *Islamic Leviathan: Islam and the Making of State Power* (Oxford: Oxford University Press, 2001), 130–132.
15 Ali Riaz, *Bangladesh: A Political History Since Independence* (London and New York: I.B. Tauris, 2016), 38–75.
16 Ali Riaz, Kh. Ali ar-Razi, 'Who are the Islamists?' in Ali Riaz and C. Christine Fair (eds.), *Political Islam and Governance in Bangladesh* (London and New York: Routledge, 2011), 46–70.
17 David Lewis, *Bangladesh: Politics, Economy and Civil Society* (Cambridge: Cambridge University Press, 2011), 27.
18 Nasr, *Islamic Leviathan*, 98.
19 Ayesha Jalal, *The Struggle for Pakistan: A Muslim Homeland and Global Politics* (Cambridge, MA and London: Bellknap Press of Harvard University Press, 2014), 2.

20 Talbot, *Pakistan*, 218–220, 230–239; Jalal, *The Struggle for Pakistan*, 180–198.
21 Talbot, *Pakistan*, 222–228.
22 Ibid., 239–244.
23 Hasan Askari Rizvi, *the Military and Politics in Pakistan, 1947–86* (New Delhi: Konark, 1988), 22; Khalid Mahmood Arif, *Working with Zia: Pakistan's Power Politics 1977–88* (Karachi: Oxford University Press, 1995), 72–81.
24 Seyyed Vali Reza Nasr, 'Islamic Opposition to the Islamic State: The Jama`at-i Islami 1977–1988', *International Journal of Middle East Studies*, 25, no. 2 (May 1993): 268. Talbot, *Pakistan*, 245–262; Jalal, *The Struggle for Pakistan*, 209–215.
25 Pakistan's income from foreign aid rose sharply after the Soviet invasion of Afghanistan. During 1976–1979, foreign aid flowing into the country stood at around $900 million a year. During 1981–1985, it climbed up to around $1.3 billion a year. In 1981–1987, Pakistan received $3.2 billion in grants from the United States and was promised another $4.1 billion for the 1987–1993 period. In addition, Pakistan benefitted directly from aid to the Afghan fighters and refugees that in 1986–1989 reached $1.2 billion a year from American and Saudi sources alone. Nasr, *Islamic Leviathan*, 134.
26 C. Christine Fair, 'The Only Enemy Pakistan's Army Can Beat is its Own Democracy', *Foreign Policy* (August 2017). https://foreignpolicy.com/2017/08/09/the-only-enemy-pakistans-army-can-beat-is-its-own-democracy/ [accessed 3 March 2022].
27 Ayesha Siddiqa-Agha, *Pakistan's Arms' Procurement and Military Build-up 1979–99: In Search of a Policy* (New York: Palgrave Macmillan, 2001), 109–136.
28 Talbot, *Pakistan*, 270–283.
29 Nasr, *Islamic Leviathan*, 132; Mumtaz Ahmad, 'The Crescent and the Sword: Islam, the Military, and Political Legitimacy in Pakistan: 1977–1985', *Middle East Journal*, 50, no. 3 (Summer 1996): 372–386.
30 Kingshuk Chatterjee, 'Pakistan and Afghanistan: Of Instability and Umbilical Ties', in Kingshuk Chatterjee (ed.), *Pakistan and Afghanistan: The (In)Stability Factor in India's Neighbourhood* (New Delhi: KW Publishers, 2013), 42–45.
31 Ishtiaq Ahmed, *The Concept of an Islamic State in Pakistan: An Analysis of Ideological Controversies* (Lahore: Vanguard Books, 1991).
32 See for instance, Naved Butt, *Jamhuriyat masa'el ki jadh, khilafat masa'el ki hal* (Republic is the Root of the Problem, Caliphate is [its] Solution), [Peshawar: Hizb al-Tahrir, 2012].
33 Kingshuk Chatterjee, 'The Search for a New Discursive Space in the Muslim World', in Mathew Joseph C. (ed.), *Pakistan and the Muslim World* (New Delhi: KW Publishers, 2019), 39–42, 44, 48–49, 54–55.
34 All the opposition parties rallied behind the Islamists to oust Zulfiqar Ali Bhutto; Nawaz Sharif rallied the Islamists against Benazir Bhutto in 1996; Imran lent tacit support to Tehreek-e Labbaik Pakistan's demonstrations against Nawaz Sharif after the Panama papers scandal in 2017.
35 'We'll Continue to Move Ahead', *The Daily Star* (17 December 2021). https://www.thedailystar.net/news/bangladesh/news/well-continue-move-ahead-2919131
36 Ali Riaz, *State, Class and Military Rule: Political Economy of Martial Law in Bangladesh* (Dhaka: Nadi New Press, 1994), 116–163.
37 Willem van Schendel, *A History of Bangladesh* (Cambridge, Cambridge University Press, 2009), 173; Muntassir Mamoon, '25 March Keno Ganahatya Divas?' in Muntassir Mamoon and Chowdhury Shahed Kader (eds.), *Muktijuddha, Ganahatya O Bangabandhu*, (Khulna: 1971: Genocide-Torture Archive & Museum Trust, 2021), 83–93.
38 Riaz, *Bangladesh: Political History*, 72.
39 Ibid., 73.
40 Syedur Rahman, Craig Baxter, *Historical Dictionary of Bangladesh* (London: Rowman and Littlefield, 2010), 289.

41 '1971 War Crimes: Trials of Organisation Ever Elusive', *The Daily Star* (31 March 2021). https://www.thedailystar.net/backpage/news/1971-war-crimes-trials-organ isations-ever-elusive-2069217
42 Riaz, *Bangladesh: Political History*, 58.
43 See William B. Milam, *Bangladesh and Pakistan Flirting with Failure in South Asia* (London: Hurst and Company, 2009), 51–70, 95–113. For a brief account, see Riaz, 59–75.
44 Dina Mahnaz Siddiqi, 'Political Culture in Contemporary Bangladesh: Histories, ruptures and contradictions', in Fair Riaz (eds.), *Political Islam and Governance in Bangladesh* (Abingdon: Routledge, 2011), 19–20.
45 Stanley Kochanak, *Patron-Client Relationship and Business in Bangladesh* (New Delhi: Sage Publications, 1994), 93.
46 See, for instance, Milam, *Bangladesh and Pakistan*, 65–70.
47 Ibid., 95–105.
48 Ibid., 106–108.
49 'IMF Forecasts Bangladesh Economy to Grow 6.6% in FY 22', *Bloomberg* (19 December 2021). https://www.bloomberg.com/news/articles/2021-12-19/imf-forecasts-bang ladesh-economy-to-grow-6-6-next-fiscal-year#:~:text=Bangladesh's%20econom ic%20growth%20is%20expected,abates%20and%20policies%20remain%20ac commodative.
50 See, Azizur Rahman Khan, *The Economy of Bangladesh: A Quarter Century of Development* (New York: Palgrave Macmillan, 2015).
51 Zaydul Ahsan, Pavitra Banavar, 'Who are the Militants?' in Fair Riaz (eds.), *Political Islam and Governance*, 85–88.
52 M. Mizanur Rahman, 'Bangladesh Elections: Sheikh Hasina Wins, But at What Cost?', *South Asia@LSE Blog*. https://blogs.lse.ac.uk/southasia/2019/01/11/bangla desh-elections-sheikh-hasina-wins-but-at-what-cost/
53 'How is Bangladesh's Digital Security Act Muzzling Free Speech?', *DeutscheWelle* (3 March 2021). https://www.dw.com/en/how-is-bangladeshs-digital-security-act -muzzling-free-speech/a-56762799
54 Roshni Kapur, 'Hefazat-e-Islam and the Rise of Islamic Fundamentalism in Bangladesh', *East Asia Forum* (16 February 2022). https://www.eastasiaforum.org/2022/02/16/hefazat-e-islam-and-the-rise-of -islamic-fundamentalism-in-bangladesh/.
55 'August 21 Attack: "State-Backed Crime" Punished', *The Daily Star* (11 October 2018). https://www.thedailystar.net/august-21-carnage/21-august-grenade-attack -verdict-tarique-rahman-awarded-life-1645090.

Bibliography

'1971 War Crimes: Trials of Organisation Ever Elusive'. *The Daily Star* (31 March 2021). https://www.thedailystar.net/backpage/news/1971-war-crimes-trials-organisations -ever-elusive-2069217.

Ahmad, Mumtaz. 'The Crescent and the Sword: Islam, the Military, and Political Legitimacy in Pakistan: 1977–1985'. *Middle East Journal* 50, no. 3 (Summer 1996).

Ahmed, Ishtiaq. *The Concept of an Islamic State in Pakistan: An Analysis of Ideological Controversies*. Lahore: Vanguard Books, 1991.

Ahmed, S. Akbar. *Religion and Politics in Muslim Society: Order and Conflict in Pakistan*. Cambridge: Cambridge University Press, 1983.

Ahsan, Zaydul, and Pavitra Banavar. 'Who are the Militants?' In *Political Islam and Governance in Bangladesh*, edited by Ali Riaz and C. Christine Fair. London and New York: Routledge, 2011.

Arif Mahmood, Khalid. *Working With Zia: Pakistan's Power Politics 1977–88*. Karachi: Oxford University Press, 1995.

'August 21 Attack: "State-Backed Crime" Punished'. *The Daily Star* (11 October 2018). https://www.thedailystar.net/august-21-carnage/21-august-grenade-attack-verdict-tarique-rahman-awarded-life-1645090.

Bakhsh Rais, Rasul. *Imagining Pakistan: Modernism, State and the Politics of Islamic Revival*. New York and London: Lexington Books, 2017.

Butt, Naved. *Jamhuriyat masa'el ki jadh, khilafat masa'el ki hal (Republic is the Root of the Problem, Caliphate is [its] Solution)*. Peshawar: Hizb al-Tahrir, 2012.

Chatterjee, Kingshuk. 'Pakistan and Afghanistan: Of Instability and Umbilical Ties'. In *Pakistan and Afghanistan: The (In)Stability Factor in India's Neighbourhood*, edited by Kingshuk Chatterjee. New Delhi: KW Publishers, 2013.

Chatterjee, Kingshuk. 'The Search for a New Discursive Space in the Muslim World'. In *Pakistan and the Muslim World*, edited by Joseph C. Mathew. New Delhi: KW Publishers, 2019.

Cohen, P. Stephane. *The Idea of Pakistan*. Washington, DC: Brookings Institution, 2004.

Fair, C. Christine. 'The Only Enemy Pakistan's Army Can Beat is Its Own Democracy'. *Foreign Policy* (August 2017). https://foreignpolicy.com/2017/08/09/the-only-enemy-pakistans-army-can-beat-is-its-own-democracy/ (Accessed 3 March 2022).

'How is Bangladesh's Digital Security Act Muzzling Free Speech?'. *DeutscheWelle* (3 March 2021). https://www.dw.com/en/how-is-bangladeshs-digital-security-act-muzzling-free-speech/a-56762799.

'IMF Forecasts Bangladesh Economy to Grow 6.6% in FY 22'. *Bloomberg* (19 December 2021). https://www.bloomberg.com/news/articles/2021-12-19/imf-forecasts-bangladesh-economy-to-grow-6-6-next-fiscal-year#:~:text=Bangladesh's%20economic%20growth%20is%20expected,abates%20and%20policies%20remain%20accommodative.

Jaffrelot, Christophe. *The Pakistan Paradox: Instability and Resilience*. Translated by Cynthia Schoch. Oxford: Oxford University Press, 2015.

Jalal, Ayesha. *Self and Sovereignty: Individual and Community in South Asian Islam Since 1850*. Oxford: Oxford University Press, 2001.

Jalal, Ayesha. *The Sole Spokesman: Jinnah, the Muslim League and the Pakistan Demand*. Cambridge: Cambridge University Press, 1985.

Jalal, Ayesha. *The Struggle for Pakistan: A Muslim Homeland and Global Politics*. Cambridge, MA and London: Bellknap Press of Harvard University Press, 2014.

Kapur, Roshni. 'Hefazat-e-Islam and the Rise of Islamic Fundamentalism in Bangladesh'. *East Asia Forum* (16 February 2022). https://www.eastasiaforum.org/2022/02/16/hefazat-e-islam-and-the-rise-of-islamic-fundamentalism-in-bangladesh/.

Kochanak, Stanley. *Patron-Client Relationship and Business in Bangladesh*. New Delhi: Sage Publications, 1994.

Lewis, David. *Bangladesh: Politics, Economy and Civil Society*. Cambridge: Cambridge University Press, 2011.

Mamoon, Muntassir. '25 March Keno Ganahatya Divas?' In *Muktijuddha, Ganahatya O Bangabandhu*, edited by Muntassir Mamoon and Chowdhury Shahed Kader. Khulna: Genocide-Torture Archive & Museum Trust, 2021 [1971].

Rahman, M. Mizanur. 'Bangladesh Elections: Sheikh Hasina Wins, But at What Cost?'. *South Asia@LSE Blog*. https://blogs.lse.ac.uk/southasia/2019/01/11/bangladesh-elections-sheikh-hasina-wins-but-at-what-cost/.

Rahman, Syedur, and Craig Baxter. *Historical Dictionary of Bangladesh*. London: Rowman and Littlefield, 2010.

Rahman Khan, Azizur. *The Economy of Bangladesh: A Quarter Century of Development*. New York: Palgrave Macmillan, 2015.

Ray, J. K. *Democracy and Nationalism on Trial: A Study of East Pakistan*. Simla: Indian Institute of Advanced Study, 1968.

Riaz, Ali. *Bangladesh: A Political History Since Independence*. London and New York: I.B. Tauris, 2016.

Riaz, Ali. *State, Class and Military Rule: Political Economy of Martial Law in Bangladesh*. Dhaka: Nadi New Press, 1994.

Riaz, Ali, and Kh. Ali ar-Razi. 'Who Are the Islamists?' In *Political Islam and Governance in Bangladesh*, edited by Ali Riaz and C. Christine Fair. London and New York: Routledge, 2011.

Rizvi Askari, Hasan. *The Military and Politics in Pakistan, 1947–86*. New Delhi: Konark, 1988.

Schendel van, Willem. *A History of Bangladesh*. Cambridge: Cambridge University Press, 2009.

Seyyed, Nasr V. R. 'Islamic Opposition to the Islamic State: The Jama`at-i Islami 1977–1988'. *International Journal of Middle East Studies* 25, no. 2 (May 1993).

Seyyed, Nasr V. R. *Islamic Leviathan: Islam and the Making of State Power*. Oxford: Oxford University Press, 2001.

Seyyed, Nasr V. R. *The Vanguard of the Islamic Revolution: The Jama'at-i Islami of Pakistan*. Berkeley: University of California Press, 1994.

Siddiqa-Agha, Ayesha. *Pakistan's Arms' Procurement and Military Build-Up 1979–99: In Search of a Policy*. New York: Palgrave Macmillan, 2001.

Siddiqi Mahnaz, Dina. 'Political Culture in Contemporary Bangladesh: Histories, Ruptures and Contradictions'. In *Political Islam and Governance in Bangladesh*, edited by Ali Riaz and C. Christine Fair. Abingdon: Routledge, 2011.

Talbot, Ian. *Pakistan: A Modern History*. London: Hurst and Company, 1998.

'We'll Continue to Move Ahead'. *The Daily Star* (17 December 2021). https://www.thedailystar.net/news/bangladesh/news/well-continue-move-ahead-2919131.

William, Milam B. *Bangladesh and Pakistan Flirting With Failure in South Asia*. London: Hurst and Company, 2009.

15
INTERROGATING POWER AND LEGITIMACY IN THE INFORMATION AGE FROM AN INDIAN PERSPECTIVE

Pranay Kotasthane and Nitin Pai

15.1 Introduction

Even as the world has entered the Information Age, many of the formal structures and processes of international politics remain embedded in their Industrial Age origins. This chapter begins with conceptualising the ideas of power and legitimacy for the new Age. It then explores how nation states and other actors are employing them to promote their interests and how this might shape the politics of the coming decades. Finally, it discusses the relative strengths and weaknesses of liberal democracies and authoritarian states in the Information Age.

In any discussion on geopolitics today, the phrase *A Changing World Order* almost certainly finds a mention. The narrative arc of the phrase goes something like this: the liberal democratic world order led by the US is facing serious challenges not just from China but also a host of other state and non-state actors. As a result, the narrative predicts, international politics will change dramatically over the next couple of decades.

The discussion about alterations in power and legitimacy is ensconced in this larger conversation about the changing world order. This linkage is not new; every significant global reordering brings forth a fresh discussion on the distribution of power and the nature of just arrangements (legitimacy), as these are two fundamental ingredients of any world order.[1] Several chapters in this book contribute to this debate, primarily focusing on specific nation states as their unit of analysis. This chapter takes one step back and locates the changing meanings of power and legitimacy in the context of the Information Age.

The Information Age is defined as the period beginning in the last quarter of the 20th century marked by the increased production, transmission, consumption of, and reliance on information.[2] The impact of this Age on human minds, relationships, and communities is a primary area of research in many

DOI: 10.4324/9781003385233-15

fields of the arts and sciences today. While this Age began with the euphoria that the increased production, transmission, and consumption of information will make the world more peaceful by "connecting" people across geographic and sociological boundaries, recent assessments are far more sobering. Several studies have highlighted that certain forms of digital media take advantage of our cognitive vulnerabilities by creating urgency, encouraging constant seeking, recommending sensational content, and isolating us in bubbles.[3] Like other fields, the Information Age calls for a reassessment of the formal structures and processes of international politics, which are embedded in their Industrial Age origins. In fact, terms such as power and legitimacy, which underlie much of the international politics conversations, need to be reconceptualised in the context of the new Age.

This chapter will argue that the Information Age has a profound impact on the accumulation of power and generation of legitimacy in international affairs. We aim to drive home the point that assessments of changing world orders must consider these changes. Seen from the Information Age frame, several questions hit the core of this volume. Does the Information Age enable new ways of accumulating power? How do nation states gain legitimacy in an age where they are not the only actors setting narratives? Is the Information Age world order set to be dominated by authoritarian states prioritising control over all information? To answer these questions, the chapter is structured as follows. Section 15.2 looks at how the nature of accumulating power has changed in the Information Age. Section 15.3 analyses how gaining legitimacy has been transformed. Section 15.4 assesses the implications of these fundamental shifts and makes some broad recommendations for liberal democracies to confront the challenges thrown up by the new Age. Section 15.5 concludes the chapter.

15.2 Reconceptualising Power in the Information Age

The classic definition of power comes from Robert Dahl. Adopting a relational approach, Dahl argued that "A has power over B to the extent that he can get B to do something that B would not otherwise do."[4] In an international relations context, the notion of power occupies a central role. The distribution of power among various actors is a crucial determinant of any international order. However, there is no one way to calculate power. The variables, the methods, and even the definitions of power are an ongoing subject of contestation.

For this chapter, we use the Dahlian notion of power, meaning that if an entity can influence one's will over the others, irrespective of the other's will, it can be said to have power over the other. This definition is important because it emphasises the *cognitive aspects* of exercising power.

Conceptually, A can exercise power over B in three ways. First, by the direct use of force or the threat of use of force by direct or indirect means, A can get B to comply. A cyber-attack disabling another state's critical infrastructure falls in this category of exercising power. Second, A can exercise power over B at the decision-making level by changing B's desires, choice perceptions, and payoff calculations. Psychological warfare by a state A, which convinces another state B of A's superior power and hence the futility of conflict with A is an archetypical example. Finally, A can exercise power over B by changing B's preferences, morality, and understanding of reality. Successful interference by state A in a democratic state B's election process, for instance, can bring into question the concept of democracy, human agency, and reality itself.

The Information Age has impacted all three ways of exercising power in varying degrees. In the initial years, the focus and expectation were that the Information Age would significantly alter power dynamics in the first of the three ways by enabling new channels for disrupting another state's force-wielding capabilities. Ronfeldt and Arquilla termed this kind of show of power as a cyber-war.[5] Nation states were deploying and concerned about, new weapons of the Information Age that could directly attack critical infrastructure, debilitate military decision-making, or attack another country's information assets such as networks. The Stuxnet came to be hailed as the world's first digital weapon, and its deployment in derailing Iran's nuclear programme became a reference point of the power of cyberweapons. Over time though, the shine of such weapons has faded. While it is still true that cyberweapons can be used to attack another state's critical infrastructure, it is understood that this method of exercising power does not alter the global distribution of power significantly. At best, it has some effect on bilateral conflict dyads.

The big break from the past is about using power in the latter two ways, which focus on attacking the human mind rather than military or critical infrastructure. As far back as 1988, Susan Strange wrote that

> whoever is able to develop or acquire and to deny the access of others to a kind of knowledge respected and sought by others; and whoever can control the channels by which it is communicated to those given access to it, will exercise a very special kind of structural power.[6]

Hart and Kim argued that the Information Age makes the intangible sources of power more critical as "control over knowledge, beliefs and ideas is increasingly regarded as a complement to control over tangible resources such as military forces, raw materials, and economic productive capability."[7]

Even though these scholars foresaw the avenues that the Information Age presents for cognitive control, the on-ground deployment of these methods became common knowledge only in the 2010s. Russia's interference in the 2016 US Presidential elections showed how information weapons could achieve disproportional results by "hacking" minds rather than attacking critical or military infrastructure. That event also laid bare an asymmetry: even as liberal democracies were reaping the economic benefits of the Information Age, authoritarian regimes, concerned about sanitising the information that reaches their domestic audiences, had become better at deploying information power. Having gained expertise in deploying power on their domestic audiences, they were deploying them in the geopolitical arena.

Three crucial implications result from the deployment of information weapons to attack human minds at the global level. First, the path to accumulating power has changed. Route to gain power in international relations has become more accessible in the Information Age. Theorists of power might debate the weightage of specific constituents of national power. However, they all agree that the accumulation of economic power and military might is necessary to increase the power of nation states. Historians such as Paul Kennedy wrote about a spiral mode of accumulating national strength, where military power is used to acquire economic power and economic power, in turn, is used to produce more military power.[8] A corollary to these ideas is that gaining power was a process that took years, if not decades. Strength was built over time by first gaining economic strength and then converting it into military might. In the Industrial Age, gaining access to nuclear weapons also became an essential element of military power, a phenomenon that's still limited to a handful of countries. Information weapons, by contrast, are easier to attain. The route to gaining power is no longer sequential. Using information weapons, it is possible to influence an adversary's cognitive and decision-making systems directly.

Second, even though the monopoly over the use of force is likely to remain with states, the importance of violence to achieve geopolitical aims itself will decrease in the Information Age. Nation states that can directly attack the cognitive "layer" of competing states will have an asymmetric source of power. To be sure, this source of power cannot negate the military or economic power of the adversary altogether but has the potential to blunt the advantages that superior material resources allow.

Third, since information control is itself a weapon, entities other than nation states can wield this power. Twitter banning the account of a former US President illustrates how internet entities can exercise power in the Information Age. The monopoly over the legitimate use of force is not a precondition for exercising information power. Hence, many private internet entities become vital players in the geopolitical arena regardless of their intended goals or business models. The crackdown on internet companies in China should be seen in this context: private entities gaining significant information control are likely to pose an existential threat to the Chinese authoritarian party-state.

India has witnessed the playing out of Information Age politics over the past decade. Popular movements drawing hundreds of thousands of citizens protesting against corruption, sexual harassment, and unpopular legislation have been constructed with relatively low dependency on local leaders. Political entrepreneurs use social media as a key platform to rise within party hierarchies, create personal brands, and acquire electoral advantage. Political violence is sometimes employed towards the acquisition of narrative power. State authorities and political parties have engaged in a number of different strategies – from the commercial to the coercive – towards social media platforms in a bid to preserve their narrative dominance. Even so, private individuals and civil society groups have demonstrated that information power can be used to check state power. The preceding discussion on power suggests that more entities other than nation states will compete for power in the Information Age. The international order is likely to be a flux over the next decade due to the information dimension.

15.3 Reconceptualising Legitimacy in the Information Age

Even the most powerful nation states require another essential element to transform themselves into hegemons: an exercise of power that is deemed *legitimate* by other actors in the system. In other words, great power status is the quest for *authority* – an exercise of power that is not perceived as being coercion but as legitimate. Striking a balance between legitimacy and power between legitimacy and power is vital for any world-ordering project. Henry Kissinger writes that an exercise of power deemed illegitimate "will turn every disagreement into a test of strength; ambition will know no resting place; countries will be propelled into unsustainable tours de force of elusive calculations regarding the shifting configuration of power."[9] Others, such as Reus-Smit, have argued that legitimacy is one of the vital sources of power itself. While more resourceful actors can use material inducement to change other actors' behaviour, such an approach is costlier than "voluntary compliance legitimacy."[10]

Essentially, legitimacy requires conformity to a set of rules. Furthermore, because a single set of rules does not govern the international system, world leaders seek to gain legitimacy by projecting their own set of rules as superior to others and acting as credible upholders to these values.[11] The critical point is not whether such systems are fair objectively but that they are *perceived* as being fair. For instance, David C Kang writes that the tribute system in East Asia worked because many political units understood the prevalent institutions and norms as legitimate.[12] What therefore interests us is that gaining legitimacy, like power, is a cognitive act. It depends on the perceptions of another actor's promises, practices, and purposes. This is where the politics of the Information Age comes in.

Actors can easily use the weapons of the Information Age to delegitimise the narratives that old powers might have carefully constructed. Given that population-scale influence operations in a target country are now possible, delegitimising another state is a potent weapon in the Information Age in at least two ways. One, state failures set the agenda making any regime's story of its legitimacy less powerful. Martin Gurri, in his book *The Revolt of the Public*, discusses how gaining legitimacy is a significant challenge of the Information Age, particularly in open societies where problems such as "police brutality, economic mismanagement, foreign policy failures, botched responses to disasters … can no longer be concealed or explained away." Instead, he writes, such problems are

> seized on by the newly-empowered public, and placed front-and-center in open discussions … As the regime's story of legitimacy becomes less

and less persuasive, Homo informaticus adjusts his story of the world in opposition to that of the regime. He joins the ranks of similarly disaffected members of the public, who are hostile to the status quo, eager to pick fights with authority, and seek the means to broadcast their opinions and turn the tables on their rulers. The means of communication are of course provided by the information sphere.[13]

Two, in the Information Age, all local events are by default global. Local disturbances can be catapulted to the global information sphere using information weapons. In front of a crowded global information environment with global actors, states often find it difficult to adjust their stories of legitimacy. Facing a narrative loss, they respond, to their own detriment, by clamping down excessively on information flows.

The polarisation of public discourse in India in recent years has led to "echo chambers" that are persuaded of the rectitude of their own side's narratives (regardless of empirical facts) and dismissive of those of their perceived adversaries. Government policies, actions by law enforcement authorities, judicial decisions, and media coverage are primarily seen through partisan perspectives, undermining their legitimacy. As is to be expected, given they are cut of the same cloth as the broader citizenry, polarisation and partisanship have affected the language and actions of public officials themselves, strengthening the vicious cycle. In many ways, the Indian republic faces an internal challenge to its legitimacy from its own citizens who have divergent interpretations of the social contract and the purpose of the state. Thus, one of the defining features of the Information Age will be a decline in the legitimacy of nation states across the board. A crisis of authority, i.e. the exercise of perceived legitimate power, could well be the dominant narrative of this Age.

15.4 Implications of the Information Age on Future International Orders

This section discusses some implications of the changing dynamics of power and legitimacy in the Information Age. The central question to be addressed is how do information weapons tilt the balance of power, at the margin, between liberal democracies and authoritarian regimes? At the outset, it does appear that information control hands authoritarian regimes an asymmetric advantage. Having honed information weapons against their citizens, they are more likely to, and perhaps more adept at, deploying information power. From a legitimacy perspective, authoritarian regimes can discredit core narratives of liberal democracies while blocking reciprocal operations by censoring content accessed by their people. It is not surprising to see authoritarian regimes on the front foot in the information sphere, while liberal democracies appear to be confused.

However, reaching this conclusion ignores two significant effects that could play out over the long term. First, information censorship comes at an enormous opportunity cost. While censorship can perhaps be helpful for regime survival, it can also make information weapons unavailable for use against adversaries. For instance, it is estimated that the Great Firewall employs over 100,000 people to prevent the Chinese people from seeing what the party-state deems objectionable. As the list of objectionable content grows, information weapons and strategies will be locked in for domestic purposes. By contrast, liberal democracies are unburdened by the need to censor domestic content and can thus extract more value from the information weapons at their disposal.

Second, the absence of trusted sources of information for debunking propaganda outside the state apparatus makes authoritarian regimes susceptible to targeted information operations. Terming this as the Authoritarian Information Paradox, Rosenbach and Mansted contend that "even a small chink in the armor of authoritarian states' information control systems may have existential ramifications for those in power."[14] While authoritarian regimes might appear to have a head start on information power, liberal democracies have their strengths to fall back on.

In contrast to authoritarian setups, liberal democracies rely on social harmony and electoral politics as their information defence mechanisms. Instead of censorship, they rely on the political process to express popular will and on social capital to tide over mal-information campaigns by adversaries. Despite these long-term advantages, some liberal democracies might well be pulled towards adopting the same instruments as the authoritarian regimes in the information sphere due to the latter's short-term gains. Likely, many nation states will increasingly employ propaganda for offence and censorship for defence. There is a vigorous ongoing debate in India – in parliament and in the public sphere – on the nature of the balance between free speech and its legitimate restriction. An emerging aspect of this debate is the question of protecting citizens' rights from the information power of their own governments and corporations. The future of the world order in the Information Age might well be determined by the path liberal democracies choose: will they resist the tendency to copy the same means and tools deployed by authoritarian regimes, or will they strengthen their pluralistic characteristics?

15.5 Conclusion

We argued that the Information Age is likely to have changed the accumulation of power and legitimacy, two key variables underlying any international order. Information weapons have an asymmetric advantage in exercising power as they allow state and non-state actors to directly attack the adversary's cognitive layers of decision-making, morality, and reality itself. At the same time, states find it difficult to adjust their stories of authority in a contested, hyperglobal information environment, leading to an eventual loss of legitimacy in international affairs.

Information weapons appear to tilt the balance of power towards authoritarian regimes in the short term. However, over the long term, the opportunity costs of domestic censorship might constrain the use of these weapons for geopolitical purposes. Liberal democracies that strengthen social harmony are better placed over the long term to enhance their power and legitimacy in the information sphere. The question in India – as elsewhere in the world – is how long it will take and how much it would cost before this ancient wisdom is regained.

Notes

1. Henry Kissinger, *World Order* (New York: Penguin Press, 2014), 24.
2. 'What is Information Age?' *IGI Global*, https://www.igi-global.com/dictionary/information-age/14305
3. 'Social Media and the Brain: Why Is Persuasive Technology so Hard to Resist?', *Center for Humane Technology* (17 August 2021) https://www.humanetech.com/youth/social-media-and-the-brain#question-2
4. Robert A. Dahl, 'The Concept of Power', *Behavioral Science* 2 (1957): 201–215.
5. John Arquilla and David Ronfeldt, 'Cyberwar is Coming!', *Comparative Strategy* 12, no. 2 (Spring 1993): 141–165.
6. Susan Strange, *States and Markets* (London: Printer Publishers, 1988), 30.
7. Jeffrey A Hart and Sangbae Kim, 'Power in the Information Age', in Jose V. Ciprut (ed.), *Of Fears and Foes: International Relations in an Evolving Global Political Economy* (Westport, CT: Praeger, 2000).
8. Paul M. Kennedy, *The Rise and Fall of the Great Powers: Economic Change and Military Conflict from 1500 to 2000* (New York: Random House, 1987).
9. Henry Kissinger, *World Order* (New York: Penguin Press, 2014), 24.
10. Christian Reus-Smit, 'Power, Legitimacy, and Order', *The Chinese Journal of International Politics* (2014): 341–359.
11. Pranay Kotasthane, 'Ingredients of a World Order', *Pragati* (21 November 2017). https://www.thinkpragati.com/opinion/2694/ingredients-new-world-order/
12. David C. Kang, 'Authority and Legitimacy in International Relations: Evidence from Korean and Japanese Relations in Pre-Modern East Asia', *The Chinese Journal of International Politics* 5, no. 1 (Spring 2012): 55–71.
13. Martin Gurri, *The Revolt of the Public and the Crisis of Authority in the New Millennium* (California: Stripe Press, 2018).
14. Eric Rosenbach and Katherine Mansted, 'Can Democracy Survive in the Information Age?', *Belfer Center for Science and International Affairs, Harvard Kennedy School* (2018). https://www.belfercenter.org/publication/can-democracy-survive-information-age

Bibliography

Arquilla, John, and David Ronfeldt. 'Cyberwar is Coming!'. *Comparative Strategy* 12, no. 2 (Spring 1993): 141–165.

Dahl, Robert A. 'The Concept of Power'. *Behavioral Science* 2 (1957): 201–215.

Gurri, Martin. *The Revolt of the Public and the Crisis of Authority in the New Millennium*. California: Stripe Press, 2018.

Hart, Jeffrey A., and Sangbae Kim. 'Power in the Information Age'. In *Of Fears and Foes: International Relations in an Evolving Global Political Economy*, edited by Jose V. Ciprut. Westport, CT: Praeger, 2000.

Kang, David C. 'Authority and Legitimacy in International Relations: Evidence From Korean and Japanese Relations in Pre-Modern East Asia'. *The Chinese Journal of International Politics* 5, no. 1 (Spring 2012): 55–71. https://doi.org/10.1093/cjip/pos002.

Kennedy, Paul M. *The Rise and Fall of the Great Powers: Economic Change and Military Conflict From 1500 to 2000*. New York: Random House, 1987.

Kissinger, Henry. *World Order*. New York: Penguin Press, 2014.

Reus-Smit, Christian. 'Power, Legitimacy, and Order'. *The Chinese Journal of International Politics* (2014): 341–359.

Rosenbach, Eric, and Katherine Mansted. 'Can Democracy Survive in the Information Age?' *Belfer Center for Science and International Affairs, Harvard Kennedy School* (2018). https://www.belfercenter.org/publication/can-democracy-survive-information-age.

Strange, Susan. *States and Markets*. London: Printer Publishers, 1988.

16
LEGITIMACY, POLITICAL POWER, AND TIBETAN BUDDHISM

Jigme Yeshe Lama

16.1 Introduction

In terms of statehood and sovereignty, the 1600s or more precisely the 1640s was an interesting period. In 1648, the Treaty of Westphalia was signed, which led to the establishment of Westphalian sovereignty. Eventually, it became the foundation for the modern international system and the all-pervasive nation-states. Currently, all countries have adopted this framework. While the Westphalian system emerged in Europe, its seeds were pollinated in the imperial colonies. Even after independence and decolonisation, the postcolonial elites accepted and enforced the same system of the nation-states. The nation-states are taken for granted and have acquired an ahistorical status in the non-Western world, subsuming other sovereignties that existed in these places. For instance, in 1642, in a land surrounded by the highest mountains in the world, a unique form of statehood was established. Receiving support from Gushri Khan, the leader of the Qoshot Mongols, the Fifth Dalai Lama laid the foundation for the "Ganden Phodrang" government. This state derived its legitimacy from Tibetan Buddhism, in which the Dalai Lamas have played pivotal roles. It is termed "cho-si-sungdrel," an amalgamation of the religious and the political. The Ganden Phodrang government constructed its legitimacy around Tibetan Buddhist principles that influenced polities within a greater Tibetan Buddhist world.[1]

State sovereignty in these places was shaped around a different paradigm, one that was incomprehensible to the Westphalian framework. As a spiritual force Buddhism was established in Tibet in the 8th century AD during the Tibetan imperial age. Even after the empire disintegrated, Buddhism continued to develop, eventually becoming a dominant faith in much of Inner Asia and a potent political force as well.[2] As a matter of fact, Tibetan Buddhism assumed the shape it currently has in the immediate aftermath of the downfall of the Tibetan

DOI: 10.4324/9781003385233-16

empire. It became a source of legitimacy for political authority and a mode of interstate relations turning Tibet into the centre of the Tibetan Buddhist world. This world consisted of the polities on the Tibetan plateau, the Mongol polities of the Inner Asian steppe, and the polities on the southern slopes of the Himalayas. It influenced the political systems of the Mongol and Manchu imperial powers. As Matthew Kapstein has observed,

> post-imperial Tibet would come to substitute the spiritual potency of its Buddhist traditions for the political and military supremacy it formerly enjoyed, thereby ensuring a continuing Tibetan role in the affairs of China and Inner Asia down to modern times.[3]

16.2 Tibetan Buddhism and Mongol Power

The emergence of this unique political system can be traced to the 1240s, when in 1246, Kunga Gyaltsen, the hierarch of the Sakya school of Tibetan Buddhism, reached the Mongol court of Godan Khan. The Tibetan master was accompanied by his two young nephews (Pakpa Lodro Gyaltsen and Chana Dorje). Kunga Gyaltsen agreed in principle to act as the representative for Tibet.[4] Godan Khan and the Sakya masters laid the foundation for the priest-patron relationship or the "cho-yon" system, whereby numerous Mongol chieftains supported the various schools of Tibetan Buddhism. The four schools are Nyingma, Kagyu, Sakya, and Geluk. More importantly, the "cho-yon" system became an important mode of garnering legitimacy for the ruling elites in Tibet and Mongolia. For instance, Mongke Khan, the fourth Khagan emperor of the Mongol empire, chose to patronise the Drigung Kagyu, followers of the Kagyu lineage, while Kublai Khan supported the nephews of Kunga Gyaltsen. The ruling elites in both cases are seen to be exercising legitimacy through the priest-patron relationship. The Mongol ruling elites were enamoured by Tibetan Buddhism leading to their subjects becoming ardent followers of the religion, which has continued in the present.

Under the Mongols, Tibet was divided into 13 myriarchies that were administrative districts. Kublai Khan had bestowed authority over these districts to Pakpa Lodro Gyaltsen, one of the nephews of the Sakya Pandita.[5] He had full authority over the three historic provinces of Tibet and each of the 13 myriarchies was overseen by a myriarch. The administrator conducted a census of his area so that annual taxes could be calculated and paid to Sakya, following the Mongol system. In other areas, a suitable combination of lay and religious leaders was appointed and gradually military leaders were appointed in order to guard the borders.[6] The Tibetan state under the Sakyas derived its legitimacy from the principles of Tibetan Buddhism, which was the mode of communication between the Sakya lamas and their Mongol patrons. However, the Sakya hierarchs exercised considerable autonomy as it was not necessary to pay tribute to the Mongolians.[7]

Still, the Sakya rulers relied on the military strength of the Mongols, which was deployed to quell civil disturbances and suppress opponents. The Mongol army had marched into Tibet to suppress the Drigung Kagyu who were aided by the Oirat Mongols. The Sakya school legitimised their rule in Tibet through Mongol patronage. What is interesting is how the Sakya hierarchs obtained legitimacy from the Mongol rulers. This was done through the lamas bestowing secret Vajrayana initiations to the Mongol elites. The lama Pakpa Gyaltsen had conferred a number of initiations to Kublai Khan, for which the Khan offered all the three provinces of Tibet to his lama. The monk was also given the title of "Tisri," or the king's primary lama. During the initiation, Kublai Khan sat on a lower seat and while dealing with government affairs, both sat on thrones of equal height.[8] The "cho-yon" or priest-patron relationship became the primary linkage between the Tibetans and the Mongols and later the Manchus. It aided the Tibetan Buddhist hierarchs in acquiring legitimacy for their rule over Tibet and the larger Tibetan world. Tibetan Buddhism became the mode of gaining legitimacy in this part of the world.

It was the spiritual acumen and ritual prowess of the Tibetan lamas that provided them with authority and power in the Tibetan world. Spiritual legitimacy and cultural sovereignty were the defining features of the Tibetan Buddhist polity. A personification of this spiritual legitimacy that translated into the political is seen in the institution of the Dalai Lama. Mongolian power was involved in the rise of the Dalai Lamas and the Geluk school of Tibetan Buddhism. The title "Dalai Lama" is of Mongol in origin and was conferred upon the Third Dalai Lama, Sonam Gyatso by the leader of the Tumed Mongols, Altan Khan. The Mongol ruler was a devout Buddhist and, in 1577, had invited the Third Dalai Lama to visit Mongolia.[9] The Dalai Lama and his Geluk school received the patronage from the Mongols that bolstered the legitimacy of the Tibetan pontiff. Tibetan Buddhism turned into a binding agent for the Mongolian rulers. Even the Mongolian script was created by the Sakya Lama, Pakpa Gyaltsen. The Mongol rulers were converted to Buddhism that led to a major transformation in their community. For instance, the Third Dalai Lama converted Altan Khan who allowed the Dalai Lama to burn all the shamanic totems in his household.

The Khan ordered all his subjects to burn their totems and to renounce shamanism, or to face execution. Other Mongol princes followed suit. The Mongol princes banned blood sacrifices and active shamans were executed, while the Buddhist monks were given a high status.[10] However, some shamanic practices survived the mass conversion of the Mongols to Buddhism in the 16th century, but the nation as a whole took another path. The Mongol's loyalty to their princes, and the military structure of Mongol society made mass conversion possible.[11] Similar to the legitimising process initiated by the Sakya Lama, Pakpa, and Kublai Khan, the Third Dalai Lama gave tantric empowerments to Altan Khan and his subjects. Furthermore, Altan Khan was a direct descendant of Kublai Khan with whom Pakpa lama had established a priest-patron relationship in 1253, and the Third Dalai Lama made much of the symbolic parallels between him and Altan Khan.[12] Under their joint efforts, Mongolia's first monastery, Thegchen Chonkor was constructed. The Mongol devotees of the Third Dalai Lama commissioned the translation of Tibetan Buddhist texts into their language. Within five decades, nearly all Mongolians were Buddhists, while tens of thousands became monks. The majority of them became devout followers of the Geluk school, intensely loyal to the Dalai Lama.[13] The Third Dalai Lama also took every opportunity to establish relationships with other powerful figures in Central Asia, China and the easternmost part of the Tibetan lands, founding monasteries, formalising systems of patronage and gradually assuming a more political resonance as he negotiated peace among warring parties.[14]

The institution of the Dalai Lama along with Tibetan Buddhism spread to the far reaches of Central Asia, and as the religion spread, the Dalai Lamas gained tremendous influence as a pan-Asian spiritual and political leader, almost akin to a Buddhist pontiff. Lhasa was transformed into a new Buddhist Mecca that drew pilgrims from everywhere.[15] The legitimacy enjoyed by the Dalai Lama among the Mongols was also comprehended by the Ming dynasty in China, who wanted to use the Dalai Lama as a tool to help the rulers of China to keep the Mongols at bay.[16] Eventually, this idea became a major linkage in the political relationship between Mongolians, Tibetans, Chinese, and the Manchu.[17] The Dalai Lamas were however not the first reincarnation as the system of reincarnation started from the Third Karmapa, Rangjung Dorje in the 13th century. The Karmapas are an important religious figurehead in Tibetan Buddhism, with them assuming a central position in the Kagyu school. A major organising principle of Tibetan morality and cosmology is the system of reincarnation.[18] As an established tradition, reincarnation became a mode of gaining legitimacy for Buddhist hierarchs. It brought a sense of continuity, providing them with power and authority.

With Karmapa's reincarnation model proliferating, it eventually became a profoundly influential feature of Tibetan religion and society.[19] Furthermore, reincarnate figures like the Third Karmapa received acceptance from the Mongol court that increased his legitimacy.[20] Reincarnation can be termed as the unique feature legitimising Tibetan Buddhism, providing it with a mode of succession that continues till date. It provided a base for the growth of institutions and also the transfer of properties.[21] The possibilities of this model eventually led Tibetans to recognise an expanding group of people as the reincarnate heads of landowning institutions.[22] Politics is embedded in reincarnation as the reincarnate lama (tulku) exercised much respect and authority among the people with their monasteries extracting taxes from the local population. The final culmination of this system is seen with the reincarnation of the Dalai Lamas. A strong political motivation in the institution of the Dalai Lamas was seen in the reincarnation of the Fourth Dalai Lama named Yonten Gyatso, who coincidentally was the great grandson of Altan Khan, the Mongol patron of the Third Dalai Lama.

The Third Dalai Lama is seen to have used reincarnation to strengthen his political status. In his biography, he mentions how his visit to Mongolia was predestined by past karmic connections.[23] The political aspect of reincarnation becomes clearer as the Third Dalai Lama publicly proclaimed that he was a reincarnation of the Sakya Lama Pakpa and that Altan Khan was a reincarnation of Kublai Khan. This was used by the Mongol ruler as he wanted to become emperor, especially since the true descendant of the Great Khan happened to be another prince. The Dalai Lama, in turn, secured the military backing of Altan Khan. Hence, a degree of political machination is seen to be present in the relationship between both individuals.[24] This curious form of "reincarnate politics" reached its zenith with the Fifth Dalai Lama.

16.3 Buddhist Legitimacy and the Tibetan State

By the 16th century, Tibet became a site for the amalgamation of Buddhism and politics. As the historian, Samten Karmay writes that Tibet was in a state of religious, social, and political turmoil. Political power was shared among various factions supported by different religious schools who not only wished to propagate their teachings but also to establish their economic power and political influence.[25] In the aftermath of the downfall of the Mongols and the Sakya school, political power shifted to the Pakmodrupa hierarchs affiliated with the Kagyu school.[26] Tibet was effectively independent as it was free from military invasions from the Mongols or any other neighbours.[27] Led by the charismatic Jangchup Gyaltsen, the Pakmodrupa were earlier allies of the Il Khans of Persia and had rebelled against the Sakya hierarchs. For this insolence, Kublai Khan reduced the power and confiscated the lands of the Pakmodrupas. However, Jangchup Gyaltsen had reversed their fortunes and by 1350 he had taken the strategic forts of Central Tibet and had conquered Lhasa. In a final battle near Lhasa in 1353, Jangchup Gyaltsen emerged victorious. He reshaped Tibet, setting up a system of forts called dzongs and also replaced the Mongol legal code, with a system drawing on that of the old Tibetan empire.[28] Thus, Tibet was ruled by Tibetans. However, the Pakmodrupa dynasty collapsed due to internal divisions and the emergence of alternative centres of power that increased the autonomy of local hierarchs and princes until the kings of Tsang emerged as the most powerful in Central Tibet. They supported a number of schools of Tibetan Buddhism but established a strong affinity towards the Karma Kagyu school. Eventually, they were also defeated by the Qoshot Mongol leader Gushri Khan, who supported the Geluk school and its hierarch the Fifth Dalai Lama. This event led to the establishment of the Ganden Phodrang government in 1642, which became the centre of the Tibetan Buddhist civilisational world that endured, with only moderate change, down to the mid-20th century.[29]

The principal source of legitimacy to rule was through the institution of reincarnation. It led to the emergence of a governance based on the symbiosis of spiritual and political authority. It was understood that political authority was at the service of the spiritual authority and that spiritual masters should empower worldly rulers.[30] The relationship between the Fifth Dalai Lama and Gushri Khan is a good example. Under the "cho-yon" relationship, the victorious Mongol ruler gave Tibet as an offering to the Dalai Lama.[31] The Dalai Lama then assumed temporal rule over Tibet in addition to his spiritual rule, creating an enduring complementary religious and political governance system referred to as Ganden Phodrang.[32] The Fifth Dalai Lama increased his legitimacy through the vigorous expansion of Gelukpa monasteries across the plateau, shaping the Tibetan polity for centuries to come.[33] For instance, under directions from the Fifth Dalai Lama, the Hor Choje Ngawang Phuntsok, a high-ranking monk of the Geluk school established the 13 great monasteries in the Kham region of eastern Tibet.

The "cho-yon" system is one of the key modes of garnering legitimacy in the Tibetan Buddhist world. Under this, the patron would provide economic and in the case of the Mongols and Manchus even military power to the Tibetan Buddhist master and the Tibetan Buddhist faith. Within such a framework, rulers like Kublai Khan, Gushri Khan, and the Manchu emperors of Qing China were recognised as Dharma-kings or *chakravartins*. What is interesting is how many of these worldly rulers were recognised as incarnations of bodhisattvas, thus giving both parties in the priest-patron relationship the attributes of both worldly political authority and a sacred source of legitimacy.[34] Thus, Buddhist norms were in plenty in the political system prevalent in Tibet. While external attributes can be linked to the legitimacy present in the "cho-yon" tradition, a number of internal modes were present that boosted the legitimacy of the political elites in the Tibetan Buddhist world. These internal means were Buddhist in nature and included steps taken by the Fifth Dalai Lama and others. For instance, the Fifth Dalai Lama followed a universal approach towards the other schools in Tibetan Buddhism, which helped him gain wider acceptance. A degree of tolerance was adopted towards the other schools under his reign. Through such measures, the Fifth Dalai Lama enjoyed more legitimacy from the Tibetan people. Such a mode of exercising legitimacy continued till the Chinese takeover of Tibet in 1951. Even after the end of the rule of the Dalai Lamas, Tibetan Buddhist authority in the form of various residues has remained.

These residues have entered into an unsteady dialogue with modern nation-states. Although the Dalai Lama exercised considerable religious and political authority throughout the Tibetan[35] Buddhist world, polities outside Tibet did not come under the Dalai Lama's rule and were a part of other centres of authority. Thus, Himalayan polities were ruled by kings, chieftains, or lamas. While all subscribed to the religio-political principles of the Tibetan Buddhist world, they gave shape to them in ways that were often distinctive. What sustained the Tibetan Buddhist world as a whole were the common overarching religio-political concepts, principles, and constructs. Legitimacy was derived and exercised from the normative order of the Tibetan Buddhist world in these Himalayan states.

16.4 Tibetan Buddhist Legitimacy and the Himalayan States

Legitimacy obtained from Buddhist norms was the order of the day in a number of Himalayan states. Before the advent of the nation-states, the Himalayas had many independent states, principalities, and kingdoms. The kingdom of Ladakh, Mustang in western Nepal, Sikkim, and Bhutan are examples of Himalayan states, of which only Bhutan has retained its independence. The kingdoms of Ladakh and Sikkim were incorporated into India, while the remote kingdom of Mustang is under Nepal. Interestingly, the polities and societies as well as the forms of statecraft of these places were intimately tied to the Tibetan Buddhist world.[36] These polities were strongholds of non-Geluk schools and sub-schools of Tibetan Buddhism. Many of them were shaped around the same time as the establishment of the Ganden Phodrang government in Lhasa in 1642. For instance, the first ruler of Sikkim, Phuntsog Namgyal was enthroned by three monks (Lhatsun Namkha Jigme, Kathog Kuntu Zangpo, and Ngadak Phuntsog Rigzin) in 1642.[37] It was around 1625 that a reincarnate lama named Zhabdrung Rinpoche proclaimed the formation of a new state based on the "cho-si" principle. He appointed a regent, or "desi," in charge of civil affairs and an informal group of advisers. For the next 26 years, the Zhabdrung Rinpoche consolidated his position in the new state, Bhutan, holding off repeated threats and actual invasions from Tibet, including several launched by the Fifth Dalai Lama.[38]

The monk-ruler of Bhutan, Zhabdrung Nawang Namgyal sought legitimacy through Buddhism. He and his followers cultivated a spiritual persona who had mastery over Buddhist and the local protective deities, especially the raven-headed Mahakala, the wrathful aspect of Avalokiteshwara.[39] The importance of Buddhist deities continues in the modern period as understood through the display of the raven-headed Mahakala in the ceremonial headdress of the kings of Bhutan.[40] In Bhutan, the Drukpa Kagyu school is the dominant force, and it consolidated power through establishing branch monasteries in Western Bhutan and Ladakh and thus enlarged its political power. Beginning in the 13th century, tours by the order's hierarchs from Tibet were instrumental in bringing students from the leading families of Western Bhutan to the Drukpa Kagyu monastery of Ralung.[41] In the context of Sikkim, the Nyingmapa school of Tibetan Buddhism is dominant. Even the above-mentioned three lamas who presided over the coronation of the first Sikkimese king or Chogyal (Dharmaraja) belonged to the Nyingma school and hailed from Tibet. These lamas had sought refuge in Sikkim as the Gelukpas aided by the Mongol troops established their dominance.

The erstwhile kingdom of Sikkim also derived its legitimacy from Tibetan Buddhism. Governance was based on the religio-political theory of "cho-si-lugs-nyi," which centred on the idea that governance should include not just the secular but also the spiritual.[42] Religious influence shaped the political, which provided financial and other assistance to the religious. The state was obliged to actively preserve and promote Buddhism and thus the ruler was literally the "chogyal" or "dharma-raja." In Sikkim, one sees a clear-cut division between the political ruler and the religious order. However, the relationship between the temporal and spiritual spheres of social life, represented as a relationship of patronage, led to the formation and extraction of a unified religio-political concept known as the "*lugs-nyi.*" Under this, there is a complementarity present between the political and the religious worlds, bringing about certain guarantees and concessions to maintain the balance and stability of both social orders.[43] As the "chogyal," the former Sikkimese monarch sought legitimacy through maintaining a balance between the religious and the secular.

16.5 Conclusion

The dawn of the nation-state in Inner and South Asia brought about the eventual demise of other statehoods. Tibet, a bastion of a Buddhist political order, was invaded in 1950, by the People's Liberation Army (PLA) of the People's Republic of China (PRC). For nearly a decade, the communist Chinese attempted to co-exist with the traditional Tibetan state, headed by the Dalai Lama, a project that failed when the Tibetans from 1956 started rebelling against the Chinese. It culminated in a major uprising in 1959, which was brutally crushed by China. The Dalai Lama accompanied by thousands of Tibetans sought asylum in India, where he remains till date. Interestingly, the Dalai Lama established and headed a government in exile till 2011. The government in exile still exists but is headed by a non-religious figure. The current 14th Dalai Lama is seen to be enjoying much legitimacy even though he renounced his political authority. As a spiritual leader, he has sway over the global Tibetan Buddhist community and especially among communities in the Himalayas. Even in Tibet, where the Dalai Lama has been absent for the last six decades, he exercises tremendous legitimacy from the people. This is evident from the demands for his return made by Tibetans protesting inside Tibet. It is also understood from the commemoration of his birthday by Tibetans, which has evoked the ire of the Chinese authorities.

The Dalai Lama is the personification of legitimacy embedded in Tibetan Buddhism, a fact that is accepted by the modern Chinese state. Beijing acknowledges the hegemony of Tibetan Buddhism, especially by its proponents, and has followed a policy of co-option towards them. Their policies towards the previous and current Panchen Lamas (the second highest-ranking figurehead in Tibetan Buddhism) reflect the legitimacy present in these pre-modern Tibetan Buddhist institutions. This notion is further strengthened by the PRC, an atheist state attempting to control the reincarnation of Tibetan Buddhist lamas. Seen through the 2007 Rules on the Management of Reincarnation of Tibetan Living Buddhas,[44] which bans Tibetan Buddhist monks from reincarnating without permission, the Chinese state is trying to limit the legitimacy of the lamas especially the Dalai Lama. On the other hand, this policy reveals the legitimacy and authority enjoyed by Tibetan Buddhism. Furthermore, the sharp responses from Beijing towards world leaders receiving the Dalai Lama is an indication of the legitimacy enjoyed by the Tibetan religious leader. Tibetan Buddhism has legitimacy among the Himalayan communities in South Asia. This idea is strong in the context of Bhutan, the only democratic, mixed market economy in the world rooted constitutionally and culturally in Mahayana Buddhist principles and ethics.⁴⁵ Bhutanese governance is directed towards the goal of Gross National Happiness (GNH), which is of a distinctive Buddhist origin.⁴⁶

The presence of Buddhist norms in Bhutan's government is an example of legitimacy enjoyed by Tibetan Buddhism. Even in South Asian democracies like India, Tibetan Buddhist figureheads enjoy considerable legitimacy, with them contesting and winning elections. India has also used the legitimacy exercised by Tibetan Buddhist elites. For instance, during the 1990s, India appointed Bakula Rinpoche, a high-ranking reincarnate lama from Ladakh as the ambassador to Mongolia. He was involved in the revival of Buddhism in Mongolia. In 1975, Sikkim was incorporated into the Indian union. However, Buddhist principles enjoy legitimacy in this Indian state, with an Ecclesiastical department established by the state government. The Sikkim legislative assembly has a seat reserved for the Buddhist clergy. Tibetan Buddhism was a source of legitimacy for numerous polities in Asia. While it is no longer the case as all states have adopted a Westphalian model of statehood, the "residues" of Tibetan Buddhist legitimacy still endure.

Notes

1 Timothy Brook et al, *Sacred Mandates – Asian International Relations Since Chinggis Khan* (Chicago: The University of Chicago Press, 2018), xiv.
2 Ibid., 90.
3 Ibid.
4 Sam Van Schaik, *Tibet – A History* (Cornwall: Yale University Press, 2011), 77.
5 Tsepon Wangchuk Deden Shakabpa, *One Hundred Thousand Moons – An Advanced Political History of Tibet* (Netherlands: Brill, 2010), 218.
6 Ibid., 219.
7 Ibid.
8 Ibid., 218.
9 Thomas Laird, *The Story of Tibet: Conversations with the Dalai Lama* (Grove Press, 2007), 142.
10 Ibid., 143.
11 Ibid., 144.
12 Tsepon Wangchuk Deden Shakabpa, *One Hundred Thousand Moons – An Advanced Political History of Tibet* (Netherlands: Brill, 2010), 291.
13 Thomas Laird, *The Story of Tibet: Conversations with the Dalai Lama* (Grove Press, 2007), 144.
14 Tsepon Wangchuk Deden Shakabpa, *One Hundred Thousand Moons – An Advanced Political History of Tibet* (Netherlands: Brill, 2010), 291.
15 Thomas Laird, *The Story of Tibet: Conversations with the Dalai Lama* (Grove Press, 2007), 144.
16 Ibid.
17 Ibid., 145.
18 Ruth Gamble, *Reincarnation in Tibetan Buddhism: The Third Karmapa and the Invention of a Tradition* (New Delhi: Oxford University Press), 4.
19 Ibid., 3.
20 Ibid.
21 Ibid., 5.
22 Ibid.
23 Thomas Laird, *The Story of Tibet: Conversations with the Dalai Lama* (Grove Press, 2007), 145.

24 Ibid.
25 Samten Karmay, 'The Fifth Dalai Lama and his Reunification of Tibet', *Tibetan Buddhism in the West*.
26 Timothy Brook et al, *Sacred Mandates – Asian International Relations Since Chinggis Khan* (Chicago: The University of Chicago Press, 2018), 91.
27 Sam Van Schaik, *Tibet – A History* (Cornwall: Yale University Press, 2011), 111.
28 Ibid., 108.
29 Timothy Brook et al., *Sacred Mandates – Asian International Relations Since Chinggis Khan* (Chicago: The University of Chicago Press, 2018), 91.
30 Ibid., 91.
31 Ibid., 97.
32 Ibid.
33 Ibid.
34 Ibid.
35 Ibid., 100.
36 John A Ardussi, in edited Timothy Brook et al., *Sacred Mandates – Asian International Relations Since Chinggis Khan* (Chicago: The University of Chicago Press, 2018), 108.
37 Saul Mullard, *Opening the Hidden Land: State Formation and the Construction of Sikkimese History* (Gangtok: Rachna Publications, 2019), 45.
38 John A Ardussi, in edited Timothy Brook et al, *Sacred Mandates – Asian International Relations Since Chinggis Khan* (Chicago: The University of Chicago Press, 2018), 111.
39 Ibid.
40 Ibid., 111.
41 Ibid., 108.
42 Saul Mullard, *Opening the Hidden Land: State Formation and the Construction of Sikkimese History* (Gangtok: Rachna Publications, 2019), 24.
43 Ibid., 26.
44 'Beijing: Reincarnation of Dalai Lama Should Follow Chinese Law', *CGTN* (19 March 2019).
45 William Long, 'The Mouse that Roared: Bhutan's Buddhist Approach to Democracy and Development', *Journal of East-West Thought* (2015): 70.
46 Ibid., 77.

Bibliography

Ardussi, J. A., in edited Timothy Brook, Michael van Walt van Praag, and Miek Boltjes. *Sacred Mandates – Asian International Relations Since Chinggis Khan*. Chicago: The University of Chicago Press, 2018.

'Beijing: Reincarnation of Dalai Lama Should Follow Chinese Law'. *CGTN* (9 March 2019).

Brook, Timothy. 'Michael van Walt van Praag and Miek Boltjes'. In *Sacred Mandates – Asian International Relations Since Chinggis Khan*. Chicago: The University of Chicago Press, 2018.

Gamble, R. *Reincarnation in Tibetan Buddhism: The Third Karmapa and the Invention of a Tradition*. New Delhi: Oxford University Press, 2018.

Karmay, Samten G. 'The Fifth Dalai Lama and His Reunification of Tibet'. *Tibetan Buddhism in West*. https://info-buddhism.com/The_Great_5th-Dalai_Lama Ngagw ang_Lobzang_Gyatso_Samten_Karmay.html.

Laird, T. *The Story of Tibet: Conversations With the Dalai Lama*. New York: Grove Press, 2007.

Long, W. 'The Mouse That Roared: Bhutan's Buddhist Approach to Democracy and Development'. *Journal of East-West Thought* (2015).

Mullard, S. *Opening the Hidden Land – State Formation and the Construction of Sikkimese History*. Gangtok: Rachna Publications, 2019.
Schaik, S. V. *Tibet – A History*. New Haven, CT: Yale University Press, 2011.
Shakabpa, T.W.D. *One Hundred Thousand Moons – An Advanced Political History of Tibet*. Netherlands: Brill, 2010.

17
IN SEARCH OF LEGITIMACY
The ASEAN Way

Preeti Saran

> As a student of history, I believe that it is not common ideals but common fears that generally hold groups and nations together. The moment the common fear disappears, the brotherhood becomes an arena for dissension, conflict and even bloodshed.
>
> – S. Rajaratnam[1]

17.1 Introduction

When the Association of Southeast Asian Nations (ASEAN) was created in 1967, it was unimaginable that a region as diverse as Southeast Asia, with different governance systems, religions, languages, ethnicities, and different levels of development, would come together as a regional entity. Relations were fraught among all the original members of ASEAN – Indonesia, Malaysia, Philippines, Singapore, and Thailand. Malaysia and Singapore had recently separated, with racial tensions still very high between them. Indonesia had undergone an abortive Communist coup and just ended an undeclared war on Malaysia and Singapore – *Konfrontasi*. The Philippines had laid claim to a large part of East Malaysia (Sabah). National borders, established during the colonial period, were still uncertain, with overlapping claims on each other's land and maritime boundaries. The Indochina war brought the entire region into the frontline of the Cold War. With the withdrawal of the colonial powers, there was fear that a power vacuum would attract outsiders to step in for political gains, and a Communist takeover of the entire region was imminent. This fear compelled the founding members of ASEAN to set aside their differences and form the ASEAN regional association.

ASEAN has proved its sceptics wrong. It has delivered 55 years of peace to the region and improved the livelihoods of its people. It has expanded its membership to ten countries (Brunei, Cambodia, Indonesia, Laos, Malaysia, Myanmar, the Philippines, Singapore, Thailand, and Vietnam), including its erstwhile Cold War adversaries. ASEAN as a body did not judge or assess the legitimacy of governments when they were included in the regional grouping. It has managed critical regional issues, carefully navigating the geopolitical challenges of the times, to emerge as one of the most successful regional groupings in the developing world.

17.2 Challenges Ahead

The next decade will become much more difficult for ASEAN. The global order is changing. China's "not-so-peaceful" rise in Asia and the seeming retreat of the US have brought back fears of Cold War rivalries in the region. The contest between the US and China has sharpened after the COVID-19 pandemic, directly impacting Southeast Asia.

ASEAN, which advocates non-interference in each other's internal affairs, is increasingly being called upon to handle domestic problems within the "ASEAN family." This challenges ASEAN's internal cohesion and its consensus-based decision-making process. Developments in Myanmar, in particular, have consumed ASEAN's constant attention, often at the cost of its other priorities.

China's rise has drawn most ASEAN countries into China's orbit, causing domestic and regional discomfort. Chinese activities in the South China Sea (SCS) had seriously vitiated the atmospherics within ASEAN, especially since 2012 when the annual ASEAN Ministerial Meeting (AMM) failed to agree to a joint statement over the SCS issue. The SCS will become the litmus test for ASEAN's unity as the region gets sucked into US–China confrontation, posing the biggest existential threat to ASEAN. New groups without ASEAN's participation have come up in the region. ASEAN's legitimacy and "centrality" in regional affairs are being questioned. Questions have also arisen about whether ASEAN is equipped to respond to these emerging challenges. ASEAN's experience in dealing with its difficult past could provide answers to some of these questions.

17.3 The ASEAN Story: Diversity, Structure, and Legitimacy

The ASEAN story is a compelling one. From a war-torn region, it has transformed into an exemplary model of sustained economic growth, bringing peace and prosperity to the region. Today, the entire Southeast Asian region, with a combined GDP of $3 trillion and a total population of 667 million people, is one of the world's most promising regions.[2] The economic growth took place despite varying degrees of legitimacy deficits in the region.

ASEAN's evolution as a regional grouping has been a gradual process. It has moved step by step, slowly building trust among member states. Acceptance of differences has helped to reconcile vast gaps among member states. This includes the maritime and continental interests of its members and the economic gap between the more economically advanced countries and the Cambodia-Laos-Myanmar-Vietnam (CLMV) countries in Southeast Asia. Building consensus among ten diverse nations, with different domestic and foreign policy priorities was not easy, but there was a clear recognition among member states that regional cooperation was in their national interest. The guiding principles were flexibility, pragmatism, and inclusion. These laid the foundation of resolving conflicts through peaceful means, following consultations and consensus.

Since its establishment, ASEAN, as a regional organisation has created a strong institutional and legal framework. Some of the landmark institutional achievements, that built the ASEAN edifice, merit recapitulation. The Bangkok Declaration, which established ASEAN in 1967, was a short, simply worded document, and the aims and purposes included inter alia cooperation in economic, social, cultural, technical, educational, and other fields; promotion of regional peace and stability through abiding respect for justice; the rule of law; adherence to the principles of the United Nations Charter. It stated that the association would be open for participation by all States in the Southeast Asian region subscribing to its aims, principles, and purposes.[3] It proclaimed ASEAN as representing "the collective will of the nations of Southeast Asia to bind themselves together in friendship and cooperation and, through joint efforts and sacrifices, secure for their peoples and for posterity the blessings of peace, freedom and prosperity."[4] The Bangkok Declaration sought to establish ASEAN's legitimacy by bringing together countries with diverse political regimes under one tent. It took nearly a decade for ASEAN to meet at the Summit level in 1976. That was when the ASEAN Treaty of Amity and Cooperation (TAC) was adopted. The TAC is a seminal document that provided for the settlement of disputes by peaceful means, as well as the renunciation of threats or use of force. Subsequently, it required ASEAN's Dialogue Partners to also sign the TAC, before entering into any formal arrangement, signifying the importance of this Treaty in reinforcing the legitimacy of the ASEAN.

The declaration of the ASEAN Free Trade Area (FTA) in 1992 and the adoption of the Initiative for ASEAN Integration (IAI) in 2000 were important steps towards economic integration in the region. The IAI was launched to narrow the divide among ASEAN countries and to enhance ASEAN's competitiveness within the region. It laid down the measures and actions through which the more developed ASEAN member states, supported by ASEAN's Partners and international organisations, provided support and technical assistance to the CLMV countries. The purpose was to enhance their capacity in meeting regional commitments and obligations. ASEAN limited its engagement in its initial years to political and economic issues. The Eminent Persons Group (EPG) report in 2005 moved ASEAN towards a more ambitious agenda. It led to the adoption of the ASEAN Charter in 2007 which paved the way for the organisation to establish a strong legal and institutional framework. The most important institutional changes introduced in the Charter provided inter alia that:

- ASEAN leaders meet at Summit level twice a year;
- A Committee of Permanent Representatives (CPR) to ASEAN set up a permanent representation in Jakarta, where the ASEAN Secretariat was located;
- Non-member states and international organisations were allowed to appoint ambassadors;
- Three ASEAN Community Councils were set up, one each for three ASEAN Community pillars of the ASEAN Politico-Security Council (APSC), the ASEAN Economic Council (AEC), and the ASEAN Cultural Council (ACC);
- A single ASEAN Chairmanship was set up, such that a single Chair chaired all key ASEAN bodies;
- An ASEAN Human Rights body was set up;
- The ASEAN Secretary General (SG) was given an expanded role and mandate;
- The ASEAN Foundation was to report directly to the SG instead of to the Board of Trustees.[5]

The ASEAN Summits are the "supreme policy-making body of ASEAN." Frequent Summit meetings have helped to build mutual trust and confidence among the ASEAN leadership. Regular inter-governmental meetings, including two annual Summits, preceded by the ASEAN Foreign Ministers Meeting (AMM) and the Senior Officials Meeting (SOM), have created a strong matrix of ASEAN-led mechanisms, both for discussions within the regional grouping and for dealing with its external partners. These meetings have provided a suitable occasion for ASEAN to engage with its Dialogue Partners bilaterally as well in multilateral formats like the East Asia Summit (EAS) and the ASEAN Regional Forum (ARF). The annual ASEAN Summit meetings have thus become an enabler for wider regional and international interaction.

The ASEAN Community, which was launched in 2015, under its three pillars – the ASEAN Politico-Security Council (APSC), the ASEAN Economic Council (AEC), and the ASEAN Cultural Council (ACC) – have made a significant contribution in creating a strong sense of a regional identity. The ASEAN Secretariat in Jakarta functions as a coordinating Secretariat to help facilitate decision-making within and among ASEAN bodies. It is led by a Ministerial-rank Secretary General, who is "the Chief Administrative Officer of ASEAN." Six decades of ASEAN have built a strong bureaucracy of stakeholders at the government to government level that are committed to ASEAN's success. By creating obligations (such as IAI) among all member states, ensuring a wide network of engagements, and building stakeholder-oriented bureaucratic frameworks, ASEAN was able to reinforce its presence as an inclusive and legitimate body in the region.

17.4 The ASEAN Way: Legitimacy through Conflict Management

ASEAN's legitimacy was reinforced by its management of conflicts within its region. No two ASEAN countries have gone to war with each other since

ASEAN was established, although there have been instances of tense military stand-offs. In 2005, Indonesia and Malaysia carried out aggressive naval patrols around disputed islands of Sipadan and Ligitian, which were diffused with the support of other ASEAN members. In 2008, Cambodia and Thailand nearly went to war over the Preah Vihar temple issue but resolved it by accepting the International Court of Justice (ICJ) ruling, as did Malaysia and Singapore over Pedra Blanca/Batu Puteh and Middle Rocks dispute. Once again, ASEAN played a supportive role in the resolution of disputes. In 2014, Indonesia and the Philippines managed a delimitation agreement on their Exclusive Economic Zones, even though their discussions stretched over two decades. ASEAN has initiated discussions with Timor Leste for its membership in ASEAN, notwithstanding its bitter history of separation from Indonesia. Handling differences through consultations and peaceful resolution of disputes has become the quintessential "ASEAN way." It has delivered 55 years of peace to the Southeast Asian region.

17.4.1 Myanmar

Developments in Myanmar have put ASEAN under intense pressure. Time and again, ASEAN has been constrained to step in to deal with the internal problems in Myanmar. In 2003, ASEAN put its weight behind Myanmar's military government's Seven Point Roadmap for Democracy. In 2014, it supported Myanmar's Chairmanship of ASEAN, amidst international objections. There were expectations that this would encourage the military establishment in Myanmar towards democracy. So far, ASEAN has managed to present a unified position at international forums, including at the United Nations Security Council. This could change as differences have begun to emerge among ASEAN countries on their approach to the Myanmar issue.

ASEAN's refusal to allow Myanmar's General Min Aung Hlaing to attend the last ASEAN Summit in Brunei in October 2021 was an unprecedented step.[6] By questioning the legitimacy of the regime, for the first time, ASEAN opened itself to an intrusive role in the internal affairs of a member state. This has caused unease among those member states with similar vulnerabilities on democracy and human rights violations. On the other hand, larger democracies like Indonesia and Malaysia have been proponents of democracy and human rights in Myanmar. Cambodia's decision, as the next Chair of ASEAN, to engage with the military regime in Myanmar is expected to further divide opinion within ASEAN. There are limitations to the "ASEAN way" as was evident in 2012, when the ASEAN countries failed to take a unified position on the SCS. While the ASEAN Charter deals with broad aims and functioning of the organisation, it is not geared to deal with situations like the one in Myanmar. This could potentially cause fissures within ASEAN member states. Since the Myanmar issue has acquired an international dimension, there is interference from extra-regional powers. This dilutes ASEAN's role and its ability to manage its regional affairs. To retain its primacy, ASEAN will have to come up with innovative solutions that are acceptable to all and support ASEAN's internal cohesion.

17.4.2 South China Sea

Left to themselves, the SCS issue could be resolved peacefully, following the "ASEAN way" of consultations among the four ASEAN claimant states – Brunei, Malaysia, Philippines, and Vietnam. The issue has become difficult only because of China. The earliest attempts by ASEAN members to resolve their overlapping claims in SCS were undertaken with the objective of finding convergence. The aim was to transform the potential for conflict into areas of cooperation, without prejudice to the official position of the disputing parties. For the first time in 1992, the ASEAN member states formally spoke in one voice to emphasise the need to solve all sovereignty and jurisdiction issues by peaceful means, urging all parties to exercise restraint, calling for cooperation in certain fields, and applying the principles of TAC. This was possible because China was not party to this agreement. China's entry has muddied the waters of SCS discussions. Its historical claims with the "Nine Dash line" prevent a resolution. In 2002 ASEAN and China issued a Declaration on the Conduct of Parties (DOC), which contained a specific reference to the 1982 United Nations Convention on the Law of the Sea (UNCLOS).[7] In spite of this, China has violated its international commitments, as also confirmed by the decision of the Permanent Court of Arbitration (PCA) in 2016.[8] The PCA decision has given greater legitimacy to the ASEAN's approach to resolving the issue. Despite these developments, China has undertaken the construction of artificial islands and military installations in the disputed territories of SCS. The need to exercise restraint, as stipulated in the DOC, is not reflected in Chinese actions. There is a considerable gap in its rhetoric in the diplomatic process and the developments on the ground. Two decades after the DOC, the SCS issue has become even more intractable.

Meanwhile, China has used force and belligerence to intimidate the smaller claimant states. China has also subverted the process by inciting non-claimant ASEAN states like Cambodia, Laos, and Myanmar to create a wedge within ASEAN, jeopardising years of a painstakingly achieved consensus and exposing weaknesses within ASEAN. According to Marty Natalegawa, former Foreign Minister of Indonesia, ASEAN's failure to issue a Ministerial statement in 2012, because of disagreements over the SCS issue, was "the lowest point in ASEAN's history."[9] China's influence over Cambodia, the then ASEAN Chair, stalled the process completely. A few years later, it was the Philippines' turn to succumb to China's pressure. In 2016, President Duterte overturned his country's long-held position and decided not to pursue the PCA decision that was in favour of the Philippines. Such moves by individual countries have complicated matters within ASEAN. It is expected that China will continue to play divisive politics among the ASEAN countries. It will enmesh ASEAN into an endless cycle of discussions over the COC, coerce the weaker states into submission, and break

ASEAN consensus. Its aim is clear – to change facts on the ground and negotiate directly with the claimant states from a position of strength. Unless the ASEAN countries take determined steps to stay united, the SCS will become ASEAN's biggest challenge.

17.5 Extra-regional Cooperation and Legitimacy

The emergence of an economically vibrant Southeast Asia has enabled a confident ASEAN to create a global network of alliances, dialogue partners, and diplomatic missions. ASEAN has adapted to make itself relevant to the extra-regional powers. In a way, it has become a facilitator of regional multilateral diplomacy that no other organisation can replicate. Over the years, ASEAN has established Dialogue Partner relationships with Australia, Canada, China, India, Japan, New Zealand, the Republic of Korea (ROK), Russia, the United Kingdom, the US, the European Union (EU), and the United Nations. ASEAN has also interacted with additional sectoral and development partners, Special Observers and Guests, that are invited during the annual ASEAN meetings. As a result, ASEAN has created several ASEAN-led mechanisms like the ASEAN Regional Forum (ARF), the East Asia Summit (EAS), the Asia-Europe Meeting (ASEM), the ASEAN Maritime Forum, the ASEAN Defence Ministers Meeting (ADMM) Plus, the ASEAN Plus One bilateral meeting with its Dialogue Partners, and the ASEAN Plus Three meeting with China-Japan-ROK. By hosting these meetings, ASEAN has been able to attract healthy competition amongst its development partners, which has worked to ASEAN's advantage.

Since its first meeting in 2005, the EAS with the ten ASEAN members and eight extra-regional partners (Australia, China, Japan, ROK, India, New Zealand, Russia, and the US) has emerged as a premier leaders-led forum for holding a strategic dialogue on regional and global issues. It meets annually during the ASEAN Summit. The bigger countries have a vested interest in keeping ASEAN relevant as they have a common interest in ASEAN's survival and success, despite divergences of interests. Similarly, the ARF, with 27 members, including the ten ASEAN countries, has provided an opportunity for discussions at the Ministerial level, on issues in the wider region. These meetings have become an important platform for countries like the US, China, Russia, and even North and South Korea to interact in a neutral environment. ASEAN has also developed partnerships with several other regional groups like the Gulf Cooperation Council (GCC), the South Asian Association for Regional Cooperation (SAARC), the Shanghai Cooperation Organisation (SCO), and Mercosur, to name some. The ASEM, as a forum for discussions among countries from Asia and Europe, gives primacy to the central role played by ASEAN and the EU, respectively, reinforcing ASEAN's importance in such discussions. Through its engagement with other regional and global institutions, Summit meetings, EAS forums, and a wide array of other partnerships, ASEAN has become a hub of discussions on regional economic, political, and security issues.

Consequently, many regional powers often purposely refer to the legitimacy of ASEAN centrality in the regional architecture.

17.6 US–China Rivalry and Implications for ASEAN Legitimacy

In its initial years, ASEAN was perceived to be pro-American. Goodwill for the US has endured in the regional group, even after the inclusion of several countries from the Communist bloc, because of a significant improvement in relations between the US and its former adversaries like Vietnam. The US continues to be viewed positively as a destination for educational and employment opportunities. While trade and investment relations with the US remain robust, China has overtaken the US in its economic engagement with the region. In 2000, the total US trade with ASEAN was $135 billion, more than three times China's trade of $40 billion. By 2020, China's trade of $685 billion was almost double that of the US trade of $362 billion.[10] China's relations with the ASEAN countries are strong and growing. Southeast Asian countries have been beneficiaries of China's Belt Road Initiative (BRI). China has built high-speed railways in Indonesia, Laos, Malaysia, and Thailand.[11] In spite of its distrust of China, Vietnam has allowed several infrastructure projects including power projects and the metro system of Hanoi to be built by China. China is the largest trading partner for most ASEAN countries, with strong supply chain linkages. ASEAN's economic integration with China is expected to become stronger with the Regional Cooperation for Economic Partnership (RCEP). China was also the main source of COVID vaccines and medicines during the COVID-19 pandemic. Yet, relations between China and several ASEAN states are complicated and face challenges. Increasingly, ASEAN countries are being asked to take sides in the US-China rivalry, much to their discomfort. ASEAN has tried to balance its relations between US and China, by engaging with other regional powers, including its other Dialogue Partners-Australia, Japan, India, Russia, ROK, and New Zealand.

ASEAN's external environment is becoming complex and multifaceted. US-China rivalry has aggravated the geopolitics in the region. Chinese aggression in the Taiwan Strait, the East Sea, and the SCS has affected ASEAN. Further, developments in the Korean Peninsula, a deepening divide between Russia and the West, and a growing closeness of Russia and China have brought back fears of the old Cold War rivalries. China's gravitational pull has affected the ability of individual ASEAN member countries from taking independent decisions in their foreign policy and in the ASEAN framework. At some stage ASEAN and its members would have to determine whether they wish to be part of a Chinese-led region or seek a more independent path. Their decision will have a long-term impact on whether ASEAN will be perceived as a legitimate and premier organisation in the region.

17.7 Going Forward

Going forward, ASEAN needs a cohesive strategy to deal with its emerging challenges. It is imperative that ASEAN countries stay united and resist all attempts to break this unity. "United we stand, divided we fall" should be ASEAN's motto. A flexible, pragmatic, and inclusive approach helped ASEAN become a strong, cohesive regional grouping. That culture is deeply engrained in its decision-making process. The same approach will help ASEAN deal with its present predicament.

Regional cooperation has contributed to regional prosperity in Southeast Asia and strengthened ASEAN's legitimacy. Despite the negative impact of the COVID-19 pandemic, most Southeast Asian economies have remained resilient. The ASEAN region is expected to grow at an average rate of 5%, increasing the number of middle class in the region to several million. Apart from its known strengths in the manufacturing sector, ASEAN's digital economy was valued at around $170 billion in 2020. By 2030, it could reach $1 trillion. This explosion of the region's digital economy will generate new webs of interdependence, strengthening the regional ecosystem.

A vibrant ASEAN can become an important partner for trade and investment, especially at a time when there is a growing sentiment to "decouple" from China. In this context, ASEAN should review the existing trade arrangements with its non-RCEP trading partners. For example, the ASEAN-India Free Trade Agreement has been pending review and should be undertaken expeditiously, given that India will be the third largest economy and the second largest consumer market by 2030.[12] India is also expected to recover from the COVID pandemic, to become one of the fastest-growing economies. Similarly, ASEAN should look beyond the RCEP partners to enhance its economic cooperation with the US, EU, and Latin America. Diversification of trade will help the ASEAN countries to reduce their economic dependence upon China. It will deter the Chinese propensity to use trade as an economic weapon for coercion on geopolitical issues.

The entire Asian region is moving from a bipolar world to a multipolar order. Other powers are coming together to establish new arrangements. These include the four-nation group of Quad, with Australia, India, Japan, and the US, and the Trilateral Security Dialogue of Australia, the United Kingdom, and the US (AUKUS).[13] Although these arrangements have been established outside the existing ASEAN-led mechanisms, their focus is on the Indo-Pacific region. Quad has acknowledged ASEAN's centrality and endorsed the ASEAN Outlook for the Indo-Pacific (AOIP).[14] Groupings like Quad should be viewed as an opportunity by the ASEAN countries. Enhanced partnerships with countries like Australia, India, France, Japan, and Russia, with strong historical linkages to the Southeast region, can also help to create a multipolar Asia. Their presence will support a rules-based international order in the SCS that upholds freedom of navigation and respects the territorial integrity and sovereignty of all countries and the "ASEAN way" of peaceful resolution of disputes.

To remain a cohesive and legitimate force, it is important that ASEAN countries manage their internal, bilateral, and intra-regional matters without undue interference from external players. The Myanmar issue is one such instance, where ASEAN should retain its primacy and find a solution from within. It is incumbent upon the larger countries of ASEAN to provide that leadership role. Their support will prevent the smaller countries in the regional group from succumbing to the divisive influences of other countries. Regional partners that have upheld ASEAN's internal cohesion can help support ASEAN's unity. India is one such country, with strong historical, civilisational, and cultural ties to the entire ASEAN region. India is supportive of ASEAN's unity and centrality in the regional architecture. As the largest democratic country in the neighbourhood, it has supported ASEAN's Five-Point consensus on Myanmar.[15] India has no negative historical baggage in the region. Support from countries like India contributes to ASEAN's internal cohesion.

ASEAN has built a strong institutional and legal framework. This has facilitated important decisions being taken on a wide range of issues for regional cooperation. ASEAN would be much more effective if it improved its internal monitoring system for the implementation of its decisions. ASEAN has also established a strong sense of an ASEAN community around its three pillars of cooperation, namely politico-security, economic, and culture. So far, the ASEAN community has remained largely focused on political and economic issues. The time has come for ASEAN to strengthen its third pillar. It should enlarge the scope of its activities beyond the governments to the people of the region. This would entail a greater participation of the academic community, civil society, media, cultural personalities, and the general public from the region. Including the people of the region as direct stakeholders in the success of the organisation will help ASEAN to remain relevant.

17.8 Conclusion

Six decades back, internal divisions and fears of external threats had galvanised Southeast Asian countries to come together as a strong regional group. A unified ASEAN helped to bring peace and prosperity to the region. The success of ASEAN and the wide acceptance of "the ASEAN way" have ensured that the organisation has not only been one of the most effective regional groupings but one whose legitimacy has been accepted not merely by its own members but by outside powers as well. The Southeast Asian region now faces new challenges that threaten ASEAN's unity and question its relevance in the regional architecture. ASEAN needs a united strategy to meet these emerging challenges. Lessons learnt from its past successes should help ASEAN reinvent itself and deal with its upcoming challenges.

Notes

1. S Rajaratnam, 'ASEAN: The Way Ahead', *The ASEAN Secretariat Jakarta* (1 September 1992).
2. The ASEAN Secretariat, 'ASEAN Key Figures 2021', *ASEAN Community Relations Division Jakarta* (December 2021). https://asean.org/book/asean-key-figures-2021/
3. The ASEAN Secretariat, 'The ASEAN Declaration (Bangkok Declaration) – 8 August 1967', *ASEAN Community Relations Division Jakarta* (2020). https://agreement.asean.org/media/download/20140117154159.pdf
4. The ASEAN Secretariat, 'The Founding of ASEAN' (2020). https://asean.org/about-asean/the-founding-of-asean/
5. The ASEAN Secretariat, 'ASEAN Charter in 2007', *ASEAN Public Affairs Office Jakarta* (January 2008).
6. Ain Bandial, 'ASEAN Excludes Myanmar Junta Leader from Summit in Rare Move', *Reuters* (17 October 2021). https://www.reuters.com/world/asia-pacific/asean-chair-brunei-confirms-junta-leader-not-invited-summit-2021-10-16/
7. 'Declaration on the Conduct of Parties in the South China Sea', *ASEAN* (4 November 2002). https://asean.org/declaration-on-the-conduct-of-parties-in-the-south-china-sea-2/
8. 'The South China Sea Arbitration (The Republic of Philippines v. The People's Republic of China)', *Permanent Court Of Arbitration* (12 July 2016). https://pca-cpa.org/en/cases/7/
9. Marty Natalegawa, *Does ASEAN Matter? A View from Within* (Singapore: ISEAS – Yusof Ishak Institute, 2018).
10. 'Association of Southeast Asian Nations (ASEAN)', *USTR* (2021). https://ustr.gov/countries-regions/southeast-asia-pacific/association-southeast-asian-nations-asean
11. Agatha Kratz and Dragan Pavlićević, 'Chinese High-Speed Rail in Southeast Asia', *CSIS* (18 September 2017) ; also see Yang Han and Prime Sarmiento, 'Benefits from China's Partnership with ASEAN seen Spreading Far and Wide', *China Daily* (23 November 2021). http://global.chinadaily.com.cn/a/202111/23/WS619c1ee0a310cdd39bc76d2b.html
12. 'Modi Calls for Early Review of Free Trade Agreement', *Business Line* (12 November 2020). available at https://www.thehindubusinessline.com/news/world/modi-calls-for-early-review-of-free-trade-agreement/article33086211.ece
13. 'Joint Leaders Statement on AUKUS', *White House* (15 September 2021). https://www.whitehouse.gov/briefing-room/statements-releases/2021/09/15/joint-leaders-statement-on-aukus/
14. 'ASEAN Outlook on the Indo-Pacific', *ASEAN* (23 June 2019). https://asean.org/speechandstatement/asean-outlook-on-the-indo-pacific/
15. "Chairman's Statement on the ASEAN Leaders' Meeting", *ASEAN Secretariat Jakarta*, 24 April 2021, https://asean.org/wp-content/uploads/Chairmans-Statement-on-ALM-Five-Point-Consensus-24-April-2021-FINAL-a-1.pdf

Bibliography

Acharya, Amitav. *ASEAN and Regionals Order: Revisiting Security Community in Southeast Asia*. London: Routledge, 2021.

Alagappa, Muthiah (ed.). *Political Legitimacy in Southeast Asia: The Quest for Moral Authority*. Stanford: Stanford University Press, 1995.

Competing Visions of International Order in the South China Sea. Brussels: International Crisis Group, 2021.

Connelly, Aaron. 'Why ASEAN's Rebuke of Myanmar's Top General Matters'. *IISS* (21 October 2021). https://www.iiss.org/blogs/analysis/2021/10/why-aseans-rebuke-of-myanmars-top-general-matters/

Hu, Le. 'Examining ASEAN's Effectiveness in Managing South China Sea Disputes'. *The Pacific Review* (2021).

Narine, Shaun. 'State Sovereignty, Political Legitimacy and Regional Institutionalism in the Asia-Pacific'. *The Pacific Review* 17, no. 3 (2004): 423–450.

Natalegawa, Marty. *Does ASEAN Matter? A View From Within*. Singapore: ISEAS – Yusof Ishak Institute, 2018.

Poole, Avery. 'The World is Outraged: Legitimacy in the Making of the ASEAN Human Rights Body'. *Contemporary Southeast Asia* 37, no. 3 (2015): 355–380.

Roberts, Christopher. *ASEAN's Myanmar Crisis: Challenges to the Pursuit of a Security Community*. Singapore: Institute of Southeast Asian Studies, 2010.

White, Lynn. *Legitimacy: Ambiguities of Political Success or Failure in East and Southeast Asia*. Princeton, NJ: Princeton University, 2005.

Yang, Alan H. 'The South China Sea Arbitration and Its Implications for ASEAN Centrality'. In *Asian Yearbook of International Law, Volume 21*, edited by Seokwoo Lee, Hee Eun Lee, and Lowell Bautista. Leiden: Brill, 2015.

INDEX

abandonment 72
Abbasid 153–55
Abduh, Mohammed 155
abortion 93
abstention 46
Abu Dhabi 167
academic 8, 57, 166, 218
acclamation 153
accommodate 32, 162, 172, 175, 176
accountability 8, 9, 54, 55, 138, 145, 147, 163; by governments 9; for human rights violations 139, 140; of individuals 55; of leaders 145; of rulers 147
acrimony 24
activism 53, 67, 159, 163; on human rights 53
Adib-Moghaddam Arshin 161
adversary 192, 195
Afghan assets 46
Afghan government 33
Afghanistan 24, 42, 45, 46, 64, 66, 67, 164, 175–77; and Iraq 64, 66, 67; and Kashmir 176, 177; Mujahideen 175
Africa 14, 15, 43, 44, 52, 60, 131, 141–48, 155, 156, 158, 164; Africa charter 142; Africa charter on democracy 142; South Africa 149

African 12, 15, 41, 43, 44, 47, 55, 131, 141–48; African-American 65; countries 15, 144; intellectuals 145
African Union (AU) 44, 142, 148; AU's Peace and Security Council (PSC) 143
Africans 131, 141, 144, 145, 148
aggression 7, 161, 216
aggressive 7, 57, 69, 120, 213
agitation 53, 159–61, 164, 165
Ahmadinejad, Mahmoud 161
Alaouite 158
al-Ashari 155
Alaska 65
al-Assad, Bashar 168
al-Assad, Hafez 162
Alawi 168
al-Awwa, Mohammed Salem 163
al-Baghdadi, Abu Bakr 164
al-Banna, Hassan 162
Albavision 135
al-Bishri. Tariq 163
Alfaro, Ricardo 51
Algeria 156, 165, 171
Al-Hogra 165
Ali 153
Ali Bhutto, Zulfiqar 175, 185
al-Momineen, Amir 158
Al Nahda 155, 156

222 Index

Al-Qaeda 23, 64, 66, 155, 156, 164, 166, 167
Al-Saud 156, 157, 167; Abdulaziz 156, 157
Amazon 138
ambassador 44, 212
America 12, 53, 60, 64–66, 68–70, 90, 106, 131–36, 138, 217; America First 64, 66
American 2, 6, 40–42, 53, 57, 63–66, 68–72, 105, 124, 125, 131–33, 135–38, 145, 148, 161, 175, 177; democracy 69, 71; hegemony 72; ideals 128, 130; institutions 128, 130; leadership 70, 124; military 53, 175; president 2, 64; regimes 133, 135, 137; society 65, 68, 72
Amin, Idi 56
anarchical 31, 32, 119
Anderson, Benedict 28
Anglo-American 105
Angola 144
annexation of Crimea 93, 94
Anno, Tadashi 16, 118
Arab 16, 43, 152, 155, 156, 158, 159, 162–65, 167–70; intellectuals 155, 163; republics 158, 163; republics as "populist-corporatist regimes 158; spring 164, 165, 168–70; state 156, 158, 165, 169, 170; world 156, 163, 164, 168, 170
Arabia 156, 157, 163–68, 171
Arabian 156
Arabian Peninsula 156
Arquilla, John 191
asampradayik 178
ASEAN 16, 113, 132, 210–18; centrality 216, 220; charter 211, 213, 219; community 212, 218, 219; countries 210–18; human rights 212, 220; leaders 212, 219; member 211, 213, 214, 216; secretariat 212, 219; summit 212, 213, 215; way 209, 212–14, 218
ASEAN Outlook for the Indo-Pacific (AOIP) 217
ASEAN Politico-Security Council (APSC) 212
ASEM 215
Asia 3, 14, 15, 28, 29, 44, 53, 67, 69, 79, 80, 92, 106, 131, 145, 147, 152, 153, 159, 162, 167, 193, 198, 199, 201, 205, 209–12, 217; and Europe 215; and North Africa 155, 156, 158, 164; Pacific region 48, 71
Asian 2–4, 10, 15, 30, 41, 45, 60, 65, 92, 123, 131, 147, 152, 158, 159, 166, 199, 209–11, 213, 215–18; democracies 147, 206; international relations 206, 207; Islam 184, 187; region 30, 210, 211, 213, 217, 218; values 123
assassination 133, 177, 179
assassinations 57, 58, 133
asymmetric 13, 192, 194, 195
asymmetry 112, 191
Atlantic 70, 80, 82, 92
Australia 56, 64, 67, 80, 147, 215, 217
Austria 76, 80, 82
authoritarian 6, 11, 26, 29, 39, 71, 88, 94, 95, 107, 122, 124, 125, 127, 147, 160, 163–68, 189–92, 194, 195; government 72, 122; order 163, 164; party-state 192; regimes 26, 29, 168, 191, 194, 195; state capitalism 107; states 107, 125, 189, 190, 195
authoritarianism 9, 10, 71, 86–88, 144, 148, 152
autocracies 15, 91
autocracy 9, 26, 86, 87, 131, 132, 167
autocrat 86, 91, 138
autocratic 8, 87, 88, 137, 144, 160, 179
Avalokiteshwara 204
Awami League 174, 178–82
Ayatollah 160
Ayesha 153
Ayubi, Nazih 152, 157, 158, 165
Azzam, Abdullah 163

Bachelet, Michelle 136
Bahrain 156, 167, 168
Bakr, Abu 153, 164
BAKSAL 180
Baloch 172
Baltic 92
Baltics 75
Bangkok 211
Bangla 178
Bangladesh 56, 171–74, 178–84
Bangladesh National Party (BNP) 174, 180–82
Bangladeshi 179–81, 183; media 179; Muslim culture 183
Basque 57
Batu Puteh 213
bayat 153
Ba'athism 158
Beijing 10, 46, 48, 147, 205
Belarus 44, 92
Belgium 136
Belt and Road Initiative (BRI) 113, 116, 137, 216; BRI 113–15, 216
Bengal 178, 183

Index **223**

Bengali 172–74, 178, 179, 183; culture 173; Muslims 183; nationalism 178, 179; values 174
Benin 148
Bentham, Jeremy 21
Berdal, Mats 15, 16, 38
Berlin 24
Bhatia, Rajiv 16, 141
Bhojwani, Deepak 15, 16, 131
Bhutan 204, 205
Bhutto 175, 176
Bible 142
bida 155
Biden, Joseph R. 63, 64, 69–71, 73, 142, 144, 149, 150
Bill and Melinda Gates Foundation 46
bin-Laden, Osama 58
bipolar 217
bipolarity 32
Blair, Tony 75
blasphemy 176, 177
blockade of Qatar 166
Bo Xilai 103
bodhisattvas 203
Bolivar, Simon 17, 19, 132, 140
Bolsheviks 24, 94
Bolsonaro 13, 133, 134
book ban 28
Boric, Gabriel 137
bourgeois 22, 47; morality 47
Boutros-Ghali, Boutros 41
Brazil 13, 15, 43, 131, 133, 135, 137, 138
Brazil's 13, 134
Breton, Thierry 81
Bretton Woods 2, 40
Brexit 77
Britain 105, 156, 157
British 40, 44, 57, 146, 156, 157, 172; "mandate" 157; colony 146; government 44; Indian establishment 172; Indian military 172; US coalition 160
Brookings 46
Brotherhood 162, 163, 167, 168; administration 167
Brunei 209, 213, 214
Brussels 75, 77, 81
Buddhas 205
Buddhism 198–206; and politics 202; in Mongolia 206
Buddhism's 111
Buddhist 198–206; authority 203; clergy 206; deities 204; legitimacy 202, 203, 206; polity 200; world 198, 199, 203, 204

Buhari, Muhammadu 144
Bukele, Nayib 134
Bull, Hedley 31
bureaucracies 100
bureaucracy 91, 99, 101–4, 172, 173, 175, 212
bureaucratic 103, 136, 212
Burhan, Abdel Fattah 143
Burleigh, Peter 15, 16, 63
Bush, George 57

caliph 154, 155, 164
caliphate 119, 153–55
caliphs 153, 154, 159, 162
Cambodia-Laos-Myanmar-Vietnam (CLMV) 211
Canada 28, 56, 215
Canadian 56
Canadian-led 42, 43
capitalism 13, 28, 87, 88, 102, 107, 109, 115, 120, 180; and populist 87; and socialism 109, 115
capitalist 99, 125
Carnegie 88, 89, 144
Casablanca 165
Castro, Fidel 132, 136
Castro, Xiomara 135
Catholic 132
censorship 88, 135, 194–96
centralisation 6, 173
centrifugalism 173
Chad 143, 144
Chahir, Aziz 166
chakravartins 203
Chang, Ha-Joon 23
charismatic 13, 22, 91, 103, 137, 202
Chatterjee, Kingshuk 16, 171
Chavez, Hugo 132, 136, 138
Chile 80, 133, 136, 137
China 4, 7, 10, 14, 16, 26, 27, 29, 30, 32, 40, 43–48, 56, 59, 63, 67, 70, 71, 78–80, 83, 90, 92, 99, 100, 102–8, 110, 111, 113–16, 119, 124, 125, 133, 137, 144, 147, 189, 192, 199, 201, 203, 205, 210, 214–17; and Inner Asia 199; diplomacy 113; India, 30, 40, 80, 215; the Islamic caliphate 119; Japan 32, 215; New Zealand 215; Pakistan 49, 113; the pandemic-related lockdown 26; Russia 10, 90, 92, 98, 144, 215; Vietnam 216
Chinese 4, 7, 10, 16, 21, 24, 26, 42, 43, 48, 70, 71, 99–101, 103, 106, 109–11, 113, 116, 122, 125, 147, 192, 195, 201, 203, 205, 210, 214, 216, 217;

administrative 108; aggression 216; and western 111; authoritarian party-state 192; characteristics 48, 112; communist party 7, 24, 116; law 207; philosophy 111; political history 101; political theory 99, 106; traditional culture 111; vaccines 26; worldview 113
Chipko movement 25
Chogyal 204, 205
Chongqing 103
cho-yon 199, 200, 202, 203
Christianity 76
Christians 96, 164
church 55, 87, 93, 132, 162
citizen 90
citizenship 12
Clarin, Grupo 135
clergy 159–61
cleric 156, 160, 161
clerical 159–61
Clinton, Bill 56
Clinton, Hillary 29
coalition 65, 67, 160
coalitions 71, 134
Cold War 2, 25, 30, 40, 47, 56, 74, 92, 93, 133, 145, 163, 209; end of the Cold War, 24, 38, 39, 41, 42, 45, 48, 53, 87, 120, 122, 124, 125; post-Cold War, 42, 45, 124; rivalries 210, 216
Collective Security Treaty Organization (CSTO) 92
colonial 2, 16, 47, 119–21, 131, 141, 145, 147, 155–57, 163, 172, 173; domination 119, 156; empires 16; era 131, 173; frontiers 145; racial discrimination 119; subjugation 141, 155
colonialism 15, 142, 145
colonies 2, 40, 156, 198
colonisation 131, 139
Comisión Internacional contra la Impunidad en Guatemala (CICIG) 134
Commander of the Faithful 143
Committee of Permanent Representatives (CPR) 212
Commonwealth of Independent States (CIS) 92
communism 47, 95, 163
communist 24, 25, 47, 87, 93, 99, 102, 132, 205, 209, 216; bloc 216; countries 25; coup 209; doctrine 93; manifesto 47; state 99; states 24; takeover 209
confederation 45
confederations 128
Confucian 101, 111
Confucius 99–101

Congo 43, 47, 144
Constantinople 93
constitution 52, 64, 89, 92, 116, 133–35, 142, 143, 146, 159–61, 164, 165, 173, 175, 178
constitutionalism 142, 163
constitutionally 158, 205
Constitutive Act of the African Union (AU) 142, 144
constitutional 4, 57, 75, 134, 160, 165, 168
corporate 25, 102–7
corporations 24, 25, 104, 105, 195
Coomaraswamy, Radhika 16, 51
corporatism 158
corporatist populism 158
Correa, Rafael 133, 136
Costa Rica 133, 136, 137
coups 142–44, 179
covenant 52, 157, 167; on civil and political 52; on economic and social 52
creole 131
Crimea 77, 88, 93, 94, 125
Croatian 55
crusades 6
Cuba 132, 134, 136, 137
Cuban 47, 132
culture 1, 4, 7–9, 13, 47, 72, 94, 108–11, 113, 116, 121, 122, 130, 135, 146, 159, 160, 172–74, 183, 217, 218; of democracy 9; of harmony 111; of nepotism 135; plurality 7; and strategic 47; theory 128, 130; wars 13; and western 111
cyber 35, 112
cyber-attack 93, 190
cyberspace 114
cyber-war 191
cyberwarfare 30
Cyrus 160
Czechoslovakia 92

Dahl, Robert 20, 190
Dalai Lama 198, 200–205
dawla 154
Déby, Mahamat Idriss 143
decentralised 111, 112, 164
decision-making 136, 147, 191, 192, 195, 212; process 24, 25, 31, 210, 217; systems 192
decolonisation 12, 52, 120, 121, 141, 198
demagoguery 137
demagogues 136
democracies 8–11, 14–16, 22, 23, 28, 29, 39, 67, 118, 120, 123, 125, 127, 128, 137, 144, 146, 147, 189–91,

195; and authoritarian 189, 194; and authoritarians 71; like India 206; like Indonesia 213
democracy 2, 6, 8–11, 17, 20, 23, 27, 63, 66, 69, 71, 87, 89, 90, 107, 111, 120, 122–25, 133, 135–38, 142–48, 161, 162, 164, 172, 174, 175, 178–81, 191; accountability 145; and authoritarianism 86, 148; and capitalism 107; and constitutionalism 142; and freedom 110, 113; and human rights 13, 213; and liberty 6; market economy 120; nationalism 178, 184, 188
democratic 4, 7–11, 13, 23, 28, 31, 43, 70–72, 74–76, 86, 106, 120, 126, 132, 133, 137, 138, 146, 165, 167, 177, 180–83, 205, 218; countries 26, 71; elections 175, 183; governance 107, 144, 148; government 2, 32, 181; institutions 16, 75, 144, 180, 182; legitimacy 74, 75; order 41, 160, 168; process 139, 140; renewal 145, 149, 150; republic 43, 92, 144; societies 1, 72, 122, 127, 144; state 173, 191; states 26, 124, 145; values 32, 71, 145; world 5, 15, 65, 189
democratisation 122, 124, 125
democratising 24, 124
democrats 47
Deng Xiaoping 102
Denmark 91
despotic 91, 138, 142
despotism 121
Devermont, Judd 143, 149, 150
Dhaka 179, 181, 183
dharma 178
Dharma-kings 203
dharma niropekkho 178
Dharmaraja 204
Diamond, Larry 28
Diaz, Porfirio 133
dictators 91, 181
dictatorship 8, 87, 133, 136, 165, 176
digital 6, 11, 13, 16, 26–29, 32, 80, 81, 182, 190, 191, 217; digital economy 217; digital security 182
diplomatic 4, 31, 42, 46, 67, 75, 144, 214, 215; missions 215; practice 117
disarmament 124
Djilo, Félicité 143, 149, 150
doctrine 56, 72, 93, 132, 133, 154, 157; of Islam 157; of liberation theology 132
doctrines of collateral damage and military necessity 58
Dominican Republic 137

Donetsk 94
Dorje, Chana 199, 201
Dorje, Rang Jung 201
Duterte, Rodrigo 214
dynastic 100, 101, 153, 154, 162, 167
dynasty 99–102, 104, 154, 158–60, 201, 202; in China 201; in Iran 160
dzongs 202

East Asia 1, 12, 14, 15, 20, 28, 30, 32, 38, 44, 48, 67, 69, 71, 106, 156, 172–74, 177, 193, 209, 212, 215, 216
East Asia Summit (EAS) 212, 215
East European 97
East Malaysia (Sabah) 209
East Pakistan 172–74, 177, 184, 188
East Sea 216
East Timor 1
Easton, David 22
eco-friendly 113
Ecologically 112
Economic Community of West African States (ECOWAS) 143, 146
Ecuador 132, 133, 136
Egypt 144, 155, 156, 162–68; Sudan 156; Uganda 144; Yemen 164
Egyptian 155, 163
Egypt's 158
Eleanor Roosevelt 51
elections 8–11, 15, 28, 29, 63, 68–70, 87–91, 133, 134, 146, 158–61, 163–65, 175, 176, 180–83, 191, 206; for congress 70; in democracies 29; and governance 142, 144; in Honduras 139, 140; Islamic law 163; in Russia 96; and voting 63
electoral 1, 8, 9, 11, 29, 64, 68, 86, 91, 134, 135, 175, 181, 192, 195; authoritarianism 86; autocracy 9; democracy 9; legitimacy 1; mandates 91; manipulation 181; politics 195; tribunal 134
electorate 8, 9
electorates 9, 75, 76
El Salvador 132, 134, 137
enlightenment 47, 121, 145
Eritrea 44
Erixon, Fredrik 16, 74
Ershad, Hossein Mohammed 178, 180
Ethiopia 35, 144
ethnic 31, 58, 94, 125, 138, 172
ethnically 159, 173
Eurasia 87
Eurasian 92
euro 75, 76, 79

Euro-American modernity 107
Eurocentric 120
Europe 13–15, 28, 30, 45, 53, 67, 69, 74–83, 92, 119, 120, 131, 133, 137, 145, 164, 198, 215
European 2, 6, 16, 30, 40, 47, 53, 74–83, 90, 92, 119–21, 132, 134, 139, 141, 147, 215; civilisation 119; colonial 121; colonialists 141; commission 77, 84, 85; council 84, 85; countries 14, 52, 79; economy 80; firms 78; investment 78, 84, 85; leaders 74, 83; and normative 117; nations 78, 82; nation-state 150, 151; parliament 80, 81, 84, 85; powers 6, 67, 141; project 76, 77; and the US 67, 133
Evans, Gareth 56
European Union 16, 30, 74-77, 82, 90, 92, 132, 134, 215
Eurozone 74–76
Extremism 112

Fabricius, Peter 144, 149, 150
faith 23, 40, 45, 57, 125, 153, 159, 163, 164, 172, 198, 203
Faithful 158
FATA 177
federal 69, 75, 83, 87, 88, 90, 92, 136, 156, 172, 173; election 90; government 136; institutions 75, 83; legislature 173; republic 92; revenues 88
federalist 76
Federation 92
Fein, Julius George Stephen 15, 16, 86
Fei Xiaotong 113, 117
feminists 91
feudal 102
finance 113, 135
finances 12, 45
financial 1, 8, 64, 65, 76, 80, 106, 133, 136, 175, 177, 204; crises 106; crisis 23, 25, 46, 75; inducements 1; institutions 25, 180; sanctions 15, 67, 82; support 69, 75
Fish, Steven 72, 87
foreign 30, 56, 63–69, 79, 87, 93, 111, 120, 122, 133, 146, 147, 167, 185, 187, 193, 211, 212, 214, 216; assistance 122; bases 67; experts 146; governments 63; influence 88, 160; intervention 133; observers 63; policy concept 92, 96; talent 79
formalisation of the economy 138
four confidences 113
fragmentation 4, 15, 174; into successor states, 4; of the global order 15

France 28, 43, 76, 80, 156, 217; Germany 76; Russia 217; Japan 28
fraternity 10
free and fair elections 10, 180, 181
freedom 8, 9, 12, 21, 28, 66, 69, 110, 113, 121, 122, 132, 145, 158, 164, 165, 167, 178, 211, 217; and autonomy 122; and dignity 119, 128; and equality 127, 162; of expression 9; and justice 162; from torture 54, 57; of navigation 217
free market 180
free press 8, 69
free speech 182, 195
free trade 80, 211, 217, 219
French 8, 132, 148, 158; government 81; president 77, 81, 131; revolution 8; revolutions 132
Friedman, Thomas L 28
Fry, Timothy 86
Frye 89
Fuerzas Armadas Revolucionarias de Colombia (FARC) 132, 133
Fujimori, Alberto 134
Fukuyama, Francis 47, 71
fundamentalism 126
fundamentalist 180, 182

Gaddafi 168
Ganden Phodrang 198, 202–4
Gandhi 1
Gaulle, Charles de 131
Gaza 58
Geluk 199–203
Gelukpa 203
Gelukpas 204
gender 12, 28, 76, 121, 182; mixed-gender 166; parity 182; and sexuality 76
General Agreement on Tariffs and Trade (GATT) 40
General Assembly 2, 9, 40, 42–44, 51, 113, 136
Geneva 54, 114
genocide 31, 41, 43, 52, 55, 56, 60; and Srebrenica 43; in Rwanda 60
geo-economic 15
geopolitical 5, 14, 15, 29, 76, 77, 89, 92, 192, 210, 217
geopolitics 141, 145, 189, 216
German 81, 92
Germany 10, 24, 67, 75, 76, 78, 82, 160
Ghana 142, 148
global 3, 4, 14, 19, 24–27, 29, 31, 34–36, 41–44, 48, 59, 61–63, 75–80, 83–85, 106, 107, 109, 110, 112–17, 119, 122,

124, 131, 139–41, 150, 157, 159, 163, 170, 177, 179, 184, 187, 189, 191, 192, 194, 196, 205, 215, 219; balance of power 32, 125, 127; climate 13, 105; commons 112; economic system 107; economy 26, 74, 77, 82, 138; governance 105, 110, 112–14; inequality: 34, 36; order 5, 15, 17, 32, 98, 129, 167, 210
Global Community of Shared Future (GCSF) 109, 113, 116; GCSF 109–16
globalisation 4, 6, 12–16, 20, 26, 27, 115, 121, 125, 147; culture 121; and new technologies 20; under stress 6
globalism 116
God 21, 153, 154, 160, 161
Gopaldas, Ronek 144
governor 111, 135
Greece 75
green 84, 85, 104, 107, 112, 113, 161; movement 161; technology 104
Gross Domestic Product (GDP) 13, 78, 79, 141, 181, 210
Guantanamo 57
Guatemala 134, 135
Gulf 42, 156, 157, 161, 165–68, 183, 215
Gulf Cooperation Council (GCC) 168, 215
Gulf monarchies 157, 165, 166
Gulf Sheikhdoms 156, 157
Gulf War 42
Gurri, Martin 193, 196
Guterres, Antonio 27
Gyaltsen 199, 200, 202
Gyatso 200, 201, 207

Habermas, Jürgen 23
Hadith 153, 154, 162
Hadood 176
Hama 162
Hamdok, Abdalla 143
Hamilton Moment 83
Hammarskjold, Dag 45
Han 101, 103, 116
Hanafi 154
Hanbal, Ibn 155
Hanbali 154
Handy, Paul-Simon 143, 149, 150
Hannay, David 44
Hanoi 216
harmonious family 109
harmonisation of interests 5
harmonise the principles of Islam 162
harmony 16, 29, 32, 111, 112, 115, 116, 141, 146, 195, 196

Harshe, Rajen 141
Hart, Jeffrey A 191, 196
Hasina, Sheikh 178, 179, 181, 182
Hefazat-e-Islam 182,
hegemon 7, 125
hegemonic 3, 7, 39, 86, 152, 168; electoral authoritarianism 86; legitimacy 98
hegemons 193
hegemony 7, 22, 75, 205; crisis 33; of Tibetan Buddhism 205; of the US 75; and western concepts 38
he-he 111
Hernandez, Juan Orlando 135
Hidden Imam 161
Hidden Imam 161, 207, 208
Himalayan 203–5; states 203, 204
Himalayas 199, 203, 205
Hindus 21, 182
Hispanic 65
Hlaing, Min Aung 213
Hobbes, Thomas 21
holocaust 51, 54
homosexuality 93
homosexuals 91
Honduras 135
Hong Kong 109, 115
hot pursuit 58, 156
Houthi 168
Houthis 168
humanitarian 30, 31, 42, 54–58, 60, 147; intervention 42, 55–57; law 54, 55, 57, 58
humanitarianism 111
humility 128
Hussein, Saddam 42, 158, 161
Hutu 55

idealism 158
ideological 8, 47, 92, 113, 132, 133, 136, 137, 144, 161–63, 166, 167; confrontations 133; contention 136; controversies 185, 186
ideologically 137
ideologies 90, 93, 115, 122, 126, 131, 132
ideologues 12, 132
ideology 87, 89, 93, 105, 120, 122, 137, 152, 156, 158, 163, 178, 180; Ba'athism 158; of economics 105; of economics and statecraft 105; of resistance 163; of Sheikh Mujibur Rahman 178; wahhabiyya 156
illegitimacy 53, 146
illegitimate 24, 142, 144, 193; non-state actor 24
illiberal 81, 87

Imagined Communities 28
imperial 2, 4, 94, 99, 105, 156, 198, 199; bureaucracy 101, 102, 104; China 104, 108, 119
imperialist 120, 145, 156
imperialistic 57
imperial powers 2, 199
imperial system 102, 105
independence 2, 40, 69, 71, 92, 93, 131, 145, 147, 154, 160, 174, 178, 180, 182, 198, 204; and decolonisation 198; of election administrators 69; from foreign influence 160; of the judiciary 182; from Russian influence 92
independent 11, 82, 93, 95, 109, 110, 114, 116, 131, 135, 154, 159, 176, 178, 202, 216; Bangladesh 178; journalists 88; judiciary 8, 9, 68, 69; media 88, 90; states 92, 204
India 9, 11, 15, 25, 28, 30, 32, 40, 42, 43, 56, 67, 80, 92, 147, 148, 156, 172, 175, 192, 194, 195, 204–6, 215–18; and Russia 217; and Brazil 43; and Pakistan 92; and South Africa 15; and Zimbabwe 42
Indian 1, 44, 148, 171–74, 189, 194; and foreign affairs 169; perspective 189; republic 194; subcontinent 171, 172, 174; values 148
Indochina 209
Indonesia 11, 40, 147, 209, 213, 214, 216; Myanmar 209; Singapore 209
Indo-Pacific 217
industrial 2, 77, 80–82, 102, 112, 159; age 189, 190, 192; industrial revolution 4.0 112; industrial world 2
industrialised 25
inequalities 10, 14, 22
inequality 8, 11, 12, 16, 21, 63, 65, 68, 88, 102–7, 136–38, 180; in American society 65; in China 102; and corruption 105; and crony capitalism 180; and cultural 63; and legitimacy 11; of opportunity 136; and powerlessness 8; and redistribution 18, 19; and social divisions 12
inequities 27
inequity 143
information age 189–95
Information and Communication Technologies (ICT) 28, 29
information communication technologies 16
infrastructural 100

infrastructure 11, 100–102, 106, 107, 115, 147, 177, 180, 190, 191; projects 104, 216
Institutional Revolutionary Party (PRI) 136
institutionalised 160, 163
insurgency 134
institution 16, 26, 40, 82, 86, 155, 175, 200–202
institutional 2, 6, 22, 45, 94, 101, 131, 133, 135–38, 145, 172, 173, 177, 184, 211, 218; change 74, 82; legitimacy 47, 135
insurrection 131, 132
International Court of Justice (ICJ) 213
International Criminal Court (ICC) 55, 60
internationalisation 80
internationalism 42, 116
internationalists 2, 48
internationalist values 42, 44
internet 28, 29, 80, 112, 115, 143, 192
intervention 25, 31, 42–44, 55–57, 133, 168; in Libya 31; in Somalia 56
interventionist 57
Iran 29, 159–62, 167, 168, 171; and Venezuela 29; Kingdom of Saudi 171; under authoritarian 160; Iraq 161; Islamic identity 160; Shia Islam 159
Iranian 160–62, 168
Iraq 41, 42, 59, 64, 66, 67, 156, 158, 160, 161, 164, 165; and Lebanon 165; and Syria 164
Irish 48
Islam 152–55, 157–64, 166, 167, 171–79, 182, 183; and governance 184, 186, 188; in Pakistan 176, 184; political Islam 176, 177; radical Islamist 182; Shia Islam 159; and the sovereignty 160; Sunni Islam 154, 158
Islamabad 177
Islamic 23, 119, 153–55, 159–64, 166, 167, 169–77, 183–88
Islamic Hegira calendar 160
Islamic Revolution Guard Corps (IRGC) 161
Islamic State (ISIS) 23, 164
Islamisation 162, 171, 174, 176, 183; of political order 162; of the society 183
Islamist 165, 174, 176–80, 182; discourse 177; justice 165; lobby 177–80
Islamist Justice and Development Party 165
Islamists 164, 173, 177, 179

Ismail, Shah 159
isolationism 66, 72
Israel 35, 160
Israelis 57
Istanbul 167
Italian 40, 156
Italy 75, 78, 82

Jaish-e Muhammad 177
Jakarta 212
Jama'at-e Islami 174, 179, 180
Jami'at-e 'Ulema 174
Japan 15, 26, 28, 32, 64, 67, 71, 78, 147, 215–17; and Australia 64; and China 78; and India 32; and Russia 217; and Taiwan 71
Japanese 118, 148
Jeddah 163
Jewish 57
Jigme, Lhatsun Namkha 204
jihad 164, 176
Jilin 26
Johnson, Boris 13
Jordan 156, 157, 166, 169
Jose Vasconcelos of Mexico 132
judicial 53, 134, 165, 194; killings 53; reform 165
judiciary 8, 9, 11, 68, 69, 134, 135, 158, 159, 172, 182; and the election commission 182; and the electoral tribunal 134
juntas 53
jurisprudence 153, 154
jurists 154
jus ad bellum/jus in bello 30
justice 7, 16, 22, 57, 59, 60, 110, 112, 113, 119, 127, 136, 145, 148, 162, 165, 179, 211, 213; and development 165; and sovereignty 119

Kagyu 199–202, 204
Kamrava, Mehran 158, 165
Kang, David C 193, 196
Kapstein, Matthew 199
Karaganov, Sergey 92, 93
Karma 111, 202
Karmapa 201
karmic 201
Karroubi, Mehdi 161
Kashmir 176, 177
Kazakhstan 92
Keiko 134
Keynesian approach 25
Khadija 153

Khadr, Omar 57
Khagan emperor 199
Khalifat 153
Khalifat Rasul Allah 153, 184, 187
Kham 203
Khan, Altan 200–202
Khan, Godan 199
Khan, Gushri 198, 202, 203
Khan, Imran 177, 178
Khan, Kublai 199, 200, 202, 203
Khan, Mongke 199
Khans of Persia 202
Khashoggi, Jamal 167
Khomeini 160, 161
Khrushchev, Nikita 47
khud-mukhtari 177
Khyber-Pakthunkhwah 177
Kim,Sangbae 191
king 99, 157, 165, 204; of the poor 165; or Chogyal 204
Kirill 93
Kissinger, Henry 5, 193
Kofi, Annan 43, 56
Komitet Gosudarstvennoy Bezopasnosti (KGB) 86
Konfrontasi 209
Koran 154, 162
Koranic 154
Korea 4, 5, 15, 26, 28, 44, 53, 106, 215; North Korea 5, 44, 106; South Korea 4, 15, 26, 34, 53, 215
Korean 216
Kosovo 17, 19, 43
Kotasthane, Pranay 16, 189
Kremlin 90, 94
Kremlin's 89
KTI 18, 19
Kurds 42
Kuwait 41, 156
Kymlicka 122, 129, 130
Kyrgyzstan 92

Ladakh 204
Lahore 177, 185, 186
lama 16, 198, 200–206
Lama, Yeshe 198
Laos 209, 214, 216
Laruelle, Marlene 87
Latino 65
laws 39, 59, 100, 132, 142; blasphemy laws 177; and constitutions 142; labour laws 137
League of Nations 39, 41
Least Developed Countries (LDC) 181

Lebanon 156, 165
left-wing 132–34, 137; governments 133; guerrillas 134; political movements 132
Leninism 120
Leninist 120
Levada Center 89, 90, 97
Leyen, Ursula von der 77, 81
LGBTQ 27
Lhasa 201, 202, 204
liberal 24, 39, 42, 44, 47, 48, 87, 107, 118–25; backsliding 10; democracy 8, 10, 122–25; democratic 1, 5, 7, 32, 122, 124, 127, 189; democracies 16, 22, 118, 120, 125, 127, 128, 189–91, 194–96; international order 72, 106, 118–20, 124, 127, 128
liberalisation 80, 88, 107, 125
liberalism 10, 16, 118–28; Overreach of Liberalism 118, 119, 121; universalistic liberalism 126
liberals 47, 93, 121–23, 127, 182
liberation 145, 174, 178–80, 205; technology 28, 35, 36; theology 132, 139, 140
libertarian 12, 46
liberties 8, 22, 57, 126
liberty 6, 10, 22, 89, 120, 122–24
Libya 31, 43, 44, 57, 156, 164, 168
Ligitian 213
Lisbon 79
Locke, John 21
London School of Economics 23
lone-wolves 164
Lubanga, Thomas 55, 60
Luhansk 94
Lula da Silva 137

Maastricht Treaty 75
Machiavelli 3
Machiavellian 54
Madinah 155
Maduro regime 134
Magna Carta 136
Mahakala 204
Mahayana Buddhist principles 205
Mahdi 161
Majd, Kamal Abdul 163
majorities 64
majority 1, 11, 12, 40, 42, 44, 46, 47, 87, 89, 92, 93, 125, 134, 138, 165, 168, 181, 201
Malawi 149
Malaysia 49, 209, 213, 214, 216
Maliki 154, 158
Manchu 199, 201, 203
Manchus 200, 203
Mandela 1
Maoist 99, 103, 134
Mao Zedong 3, 48, 102, 103
Mapuche 136
Mariategui of Peru 132
Marrakesh 165
Marti 132
Marx 99
Marxism 111, 116, 120
Marxists 22, 47, 160
maslaha 154, 155
Matolino, Bernard 142, 147
Maulana Fazl ur-Rahman 177
Maulana Maududi 174
Mencius 100
Mercosur 80, 215
meritocracy 16, 101, 104, 108
meritocratic 10, 100, 107; meritocratic bureaucracy 99, 103
Merkel, Angela 77, 81
Messiah 161
Mexican 132
Mexico 11, 15, 132, 133, 135, 136, 139
Milanovic, Branko 26
Military-bureaucratic centralisation 173
military-industrial complex 175
minorities 4, 122, 126, 182
minority 1, 65, 72, 91, 123, 126, 134, 182
missionaries 142
modern 2, 6, 12, 24, 45, 48, 59, 64, 75, 107, 111, 118, 119, 123, 128, 132, 144, 147, 167, 198, 199, 203–5; Africa 147; democracies 8; international institutions 24; international order 4, 119; nation-states 203; technology 8, 148
modernisation 80, 111, 158
modernism 172, 184, 187
Modi, Narendra 148
mohajir 172, 175
Mohammed bin Salman Al Saud (MBS) 166
Mohammed's 153, 161
Mongol 155, 199–202, 204
Mongolia 199–201
Mongolia's 201
Mongolian 200
Mongols 198–203
monks 200, 201, 204, 205
Monroe Doctrine 133, 139
moral 6, 22, 91, 99, 124, 146, 152, 154, 157, 219; philosophy 22; relativism 1, 120

Morales, Evo 132, 133, 135, 136
Morales, Jimmy 135
morality 47, 91, 126, 191, 195, 201
Moroccan 165
Morocco 156–58, 165
Moscow 77, 82, 88, 93
Mossadeq, Mohammed 160
Mousavi, Hossein 161
Moyn, Samuel 55
Mubarak, Hosni 162
Mujahideen 175, 176
Mujib 178–80, 183
Muktijuddha 174, 183, 185, 187
multilateralism 12, 38, 39, 41, 42, 45
multipolar 137, 217
multipolarity 32, 74
Musharraf, Pervez 177
Muslim 57, 76, 155, 161–63, 171–74, 176, 187; brotherhood 162, 167; community 153, 159; culture 172, 173, 183; homeland 183; league 173, 178
Muslims 21, 153, 154, 162, 164, 171–74, 176, 177, 183
Mustang 204
Mutijuddha 174
Myanmar 29, 209, 210, 213, 214, 218, 220
myriarch 199
myriarchies 199

Najaf 160
Najd, Mohammed bin Saud 157
Namgyal, Phuntsog 204
narcotics 135, 136, 138
Nasser, Gamal Abdel 158, 162
Natalegawa, Marty 214
nation 5–8, 71, 109, 110, 124, 143, 158, 173–75, 183, 189–95, 200; of pakistan 183; states 189–95
national 7, 8, 11, 25, 28, 47, 51–53, 58, 59, 68, 69, 71, 89, 111, 112, 124–26, 132, 142, 147, 156, 158–61, 165, 168, 173–75, 192; assembly 158, 161, 164; borders 14, 125, 161, 209; defence 124; interest 2, 30, 82, 133, 167, 211; interests 30, 31, 114, 152; security 3, 15, 88, 129, 175
national self-determination 2
nationalism 12, 16, 44, 76, 88, 106, 158, 163, 166, 178, 179; and expansionism 16; and pan-Islamism 166; and secularism 163; socialism 163
nationalist 77, 87, 160, 180
nationalistic 113
nationalists 40, 57

nation-state 55, 56, 145, 147, 205; nation-states 15, 16, 24, 52, 56, 57, 121, 125, 131, 132, 135, 198, 203
Nazi 51
Neo-colonial 147
neo-colonialism 141
neoliberal 12, 104, 105, 159
Nepal 204
Netanyahu, Benjamin 29
Netherlands 1
neutrality 118, 122, 179
New Partnership for Africa's Development (NEPAD) 145
NGOs 24, 25
Nicaragua 132, 134, 135, 136, 137
Nicholas II 94
Niger 143
Nigeria 144
Nigerian 144, 145
nihilism 12
Nizam-e Mustafa 177
Nkrumah, Kwame 142
Non-Aligned 42, 47
non-alignment 163
North Atlantic Treaty Organization (NATO) 42, 44, 64, 67, 69, 82, 92, 124
Northeast Asia 15
North-South divide 40
nuclear 1, 6, 74, 191; conflict 74; weapons 15, 83, 192
Nye, Joseph 4
Nyingma 199, 204
Nyingmapa school of Tibetan Buddhism 204

Odebrecht Case 138
oligarchical 138
Olympics 10
Oman 156
Omayyads 153, 154
Orban, Victor 77
Organisation for Economic Co-operation and Development (OECD) 40, 136
Organisation of American States (OAS) 137
Organisation of the Islamic Conference 163
Ortega, Daniel 132, 135, 136
orthodox church 87, 93
Osaghae, Eghosa.E 145
Osama Bin Laden 58
Ostpolitik 76, 82
Othman 153
Ottoman 155, 156, 159
O'Brien, Connor Cruise 48

Index

Pacific 48, 71, 80, 138
Pahlavi, Reza Shah 160
Pai, Nitin 16, 189
Pakistan 29, 92, 113, 171–78, 180, 183; and Afghanistan; and Bangladesh 171, 172; and ASEAN 113; the break-up of the "homeland" 183
Pakmodrupa 202
Palestine 156
Palestinian 163
Pan-Africanism 142
Panama 51, 137
Panchen Lamas 205
Pancho Villa 132
pandemic 3, 8, 12–16, 25–27, 32, 44, 46, 68, 71, 82, 83, 89, 133, 134, 137, 181, 210; Covid 16, 216, 217; export bans 83; geopolitical competition 14; lockdown 26; Southeast Asia 14; sovereign states 27
Pandora Papers 137
papacy 28
paradigm 9, 87, 132, 198
Paraguay's 133
parliament 80, 81, 90, 134, 135, 148, 181, 195
parliamentary 88, 89, 134, 135, 165, 176, 181; democracy 162, 172, 174; elections 89; majority 134; oversight 134
parliaments 134, 136, 163
party-state 147, 192, 195
paternalistic societies 131
Pathans 172
Patriarch 93
Patriarchate of Constantinople 93
Patriot Act 57
patriotic 88, 93, 124
patriotism 5, 12, 124
Paul, Kennedy 192
peace 6, 7, 16, 41, 43, 44, 75, 89, 110, 111, 113–15, 119, 142, 148, 161, 201, 209–11, 213; and legitimacy 20, 30; preventive diplomacy 17, 18; and prosperity 9, 210, 218; research 150, 151; security 54, 143; and stability 82, 211; and war 38, 50
peace-building 42, 43
peaceful 31, 83, 111, 118, 122, 136, 163, 164, 190, 211, 213, 214, 218
Peacekeeping Operations (PKOs) 146
Pedra Blanca 213
People's Liberation Army (PLA) 205
Permanent Court of Arbitration (PCA) 214
Peronism 136

Persepolis 160
Persia 202
Persian 156, 159–61, 183
Persian Gulf 156, 161, 183
Peru 132–34, 138
Peruvians 134
Peskov, Dmitry 94
Peugeot 81
Pew Research Center 11
Philippines 60, 209, 210, 213, 214
Phuntsok, Hor Choje Ngawang 203
Pinera, Sebastian 137
Pines, Yuri 108
Pinochet, Augusto 133, 136
pluralism 9, 12
pluralist 32, 47, 48
pluralistic 9, 161, 162, 195
Poland 76, 77, 92
Popper, Karl 3
populism 8, 10, 12, 137, 158
populist 10, 75, 87, 106; autocracy 87; corporatist regimes 158; leaders 12, 13, 15, 137, 138; nationalism 169
Portugal 131
post-colonial 132, 137, 141, 142
postcolonial elites 198
power politics 2, 12, 47, 121
Preah Vihar temple 213
Preamble 31, 39
presidential 29, 68, 87, 89, 92, 143, 176, 181, 191; election 63, 70, 134, 135
priest-patron relationship 199, 200, 203
proletariat 13
prophet 21, 153–55, 157, 158
Prophet Mohammed 153, 155
protectionism 12, 81, 84, 85
protectionist 81
Protestantism 28
proto-state 164
Puett, Michael 16, 99
Pulipaka, Sanjay 15, 16, 20
Punjab 175
Punjabi 172, 173
Purohit, Devadeep 16, 171
Putin, Vladimir 5, 10, 86–94
Putinism 94
putsch 143

qadis 154
Qadisiyya 159
Qajar dynasty 159
Qatar 156, 166
Qin 100, 101
Qing 203
qiyas 154, 155

Qoshot Mongol 198
Quad 67, 217
Qutb, Sayyid 163

Rabat 163, 165
racial 52, 65, 68, 119, 125, 126, 138, 209
racism 28, 126
rahbar 161
Rahman, Sheikh Mujibur 174, 178
Rahman, Tarique 182
railways 216
Ralung 204
Rapid Action Battalion (RAB) 182
Rawls, John 22, 91
Razakars 174, 180
realism 47
realist 3
realistic 9, 30, 39, 41, 79, 106
realpolitik 15, 45
referendum 76, 136
reform 2, 32, 45, 46, 74, 83, 118, 120, 134, 156, 160, 161, 164–68, 177; EU institutions 83; and repression 169, 170; of the UNSC 46
refugees 44, 75, 76
Rehana 179
reincarnate 201, 202, 204
reincarnation 201, 202, 205
relativism 1, 120
Renaissance 155
Renault 81, 84, 85
ren lei ming yun gong tong ti 109
representation 8, 23, 45, 89, 173, 212
representative 51, 69, 173, 183, 199; democracy 8, 138, 139
repression 89, 94, 132, 162
repressive 88, 146
republic 43, 46, 92, 99, 102, 115, 137, 144, 159, 161, 175, 194, 205, 215; of Iran 160, 171
republican 68, 70, 132, 158; ideals 132; state order 158
republics 156, 158, 163, 165
resistance 119, 135, 152, 153, 163
responsibilities 4, 5, 31, 109, 110, 113, 115, 116, 133, 154
responsibility to protect 31, 42, 49, 50, 54, 56
restitution 93
restoration 93, 111, 115
revolution 8, 11, 22, 24, 91, 102, 103, 112, 116, 132, 156, 160, 161, 163, 167, 180; in Egypt 156; in Iran 160, 167
revolutionaries 133, 158
Rida, Rashid 155

right 2, 10, 12, 22, 25, 30, 40, 48, 53, 54, 57, 77, 81, 82, 120, 136, 137, 141, 145, 160; divine right 21; to govern 3, 168; to life 21, 124; might is right 145; political rights 9, 52, 59; to rule 90, 96, 97
right-wing 57, 120, 137
Rigzin, Ngadak Phuntsog 204
Rinpoche 204
Roman Empire 77
Romania 92
Romanov Empire 24
Romanovs 94
Rome 55
Ronfeldt, David 191
Roosevelt, Eleanor 51
Rosenbach, Eric 195
Rousseau, Jean-Jacques 21
Roy, M. N 132
Ruble 88
Rumsfeld, Donald 57
Russia 10, 15, 29, 44, 67, 71, 77, 82, 83, 86–94, 113, 124, 144, 215–17; and China 43, 56, 59, 125, 133, 137, 216; and Eurasia 87; Fascist 87, 95, 97; invaded Ukraine on 94; traditionalist values 77; and the West 216; under Yeltsin 91
Russian 42, 86–94, 125, 137; domestic legitimacy 87; federation 92; foreign policy 92; invasion of Crimea 125; invasion of Ukraine 15, 16, 30, 44; political system 86, 94
Rutherford, Bruce 163
Rwanda 54–56, 144
Rwandan genocide 41, 43, 56

Sadat, Anwar 162
Safavid dynasty 159
Sahwa 164
Sakya 199, 200, 202
Sakya lamas 198–201, 203–205
Saljuk Turks 154
Samten, Karmay 202
sanctions 15, 24, 67, 80, 82, 182
Sandinistas 132
Sandino, Augusto 132
Saran, Preeti 16, 209
Saudi Arabia 156, 157, 163–68, 171
Schatzberg, Michael G 146, 149, 151
Schengen agreement 76
Schnabel, Simone 147
secessionist 2
sectarian 168
secularisation 180

234 Index

secularism 162, 163, 178, 179, 183
securitisation 166
sedition 12
self-determination 2, 9, 40, 120, 121
self-sufficiency 81
Senkaku Islands 30
Serb 55
servicification 80
Shafai 154
Shah, Mohammed Reza 160, 184, 185
shamanic 200
Shanghai 26, 92, 215
Shanghai Cooperation Organisation (SCO) 215
Sharia 154, 155, 160–63
Sheikhdoms 156, 157
Shenzhen 26
Shia 159, 161, 164, 168
Shiism 155, 159
Shining Path 132, 134
shura 153, 155, 162, 163
si ge zi xin 113
Sikkim 204
Sikkimese 204, 205
Silva, Lula da 137
Sindhris 172
Singapore 15, 209, 210, 213
Sino-centric world order 46, 47
Sipadan 213
siyasa shariyya 154
Slovenia 81
socialism 12, 109, 112, 115, 158, 163, 178
socialist 48, 131
sociological 190
solidarist 44, 48
solidarity 12, 16, 41, 44, 176
Somalia 56
Songhai 148
South Asian Association for Regional Cooperation (SAARC) 215
South China Sea (SCS) 210, 213–17
Southeast Asia 14, 28, 80, 209–11, 215, 217
Southeast Asian 209–11, 213, 216–18
sovereign 125, 156, 173; authority 21, 119; sovereign states 2, 4, 23, 24, 26, 27, 29–33, 39, 119–21
sovereignty 7, 15, 24, 31, 39, 40, 43, 48, 51–53, 56, 59, 81, 87, 111, 114, 119–21, 160, 163, 198, 200, 214, 218; in Europe 81; and jurisdiction issues 214; and non-interference 59; popular sovereignty 175, 177; of the states 24, 31; and territorial integrity 15

Soviet 87, 163, 175; Union 24, 39, 47, 86, 92, 93, 95
Spain 57, 131
Spanish 134
Spengler, Oswald 72
Srebrenica 41, 43
Sri Lankan 52
Srinivasan, Krishnan 1
Stalin 93
statehood 198
statesmanship 6
steppe region 101, 199
Stoner, Kathryn 87
Strange, Susan 191
strategic autonomy 74, 77–82, 84, 85
structure of international politics 32
structure of world politics 128
Stuxnet 191
subcontinent 171–74
sub-Saharan Africa 146
subversive 177
subvert 132
subverted 138, 153, 214
Sudan 43, 45, 60, 143, 144, 156, 165, 168
Suez 156
sultanate 156
sultanism 167, 169, 170
sultans 159, 167
Sunni 154, 155, 158, 159, 164
superstate 75, 83, 84
surveillance 29, 57, 58, 104, 107, 157
Swat valley 177
Sweden 79, 82
Syria 44, 57, 75, 93, 156, 162–64, 168
Syrian 162

taboo 51, 52
Taiwan 24, 71, 137, 216
Tajikistan 92
Taliban 5, 24, 46
Tangiers 165
tantric 200
Tanzania 56
Taoism 111
Taseer, Salman 177
Taylor, A. J. P 3, 130
technocratic 23, 88
technological 6, 10, 28, 57, 58, 78, 81, 104; development 13, 79; disruption 10; sovereignty 81
technologies 3, 16, 20, 31, 79, 81, 107, 157; digital technologies 13, 28, 29, 32; of warfare 58

Index 235

technology 8, 14, 16, 27, 28, 30, 58, 68, 74, 77, 79, 80, 82, 104, 107, 124, 143, 147, 148, 155, 166
Tehreek-e Insaaf 177, 178
Tehreek-e Labbaik 178
Tehreek-e Taliban 177, 178
tenets 157, 162, 167, 179
terror 51, 57, 58, 125
terrorism 2, 46, 57, 182
terrorist 24, 58
Thailand 209, 210, 213, 216
Thegchen Chonkor 201
theocracy 162
Tian 111
Tianjin 26
tianxia 111
Tibet 198–200, 202–5
Tibetan 198–205
Timor Leste 213
Tisri 200
Tobruk 168
tolerance 203
traditions 10, 14, 23, 65, 66, 101, 111, 116, 122, 128, 148, 153, 160, 199
Transatlantic 74, 82
transitions 23, 170
Treaty of Versailles 51
Treaty of Westphalia 198
tribal 16, 118, 123, 126, 127, 142, 153
tribalism 118, 126, 128, 162
tributary system 48
tribute 193, 199
Trilateral Security Dialogue 217
Tripoli 168
troika 47
Trump, Donald J 12, 13, 46, 57, 59, 63, 68–70
Trumpian 166
Trump-like 70
Tsang 202
Tsar 94
Tsars 87, 93
Tsinghua University 103
tulku 201
Tunisia 156, 164, 168
Turk 159
Turkey 29, 42, 164, 167, 171
Turkish 42
Turkmenistan 92
Tutu, Desmond 142
Tutus 55
tyrannical 152, 154
tyranny 72, 120, 153, 161, 163

Ufa 113
Uganda 56, 144
Ugandan 148
Ukraine 10, 15, 16, 30, 44, 45, 67, 71, 74, 77, 82, 83, 92–94, 161; airlines civilian aircraft 161; conflict 15; invasion 10; and Russia 67
Ukrainian 94
ulama 161, 162
ul-Haq, Zia 175
Umma Arabiya Wahda, Dhaath Risala Khalida 158
UN charter 31, 39, 40, 51, 111
unemployment 159, 165
UN General Assembly 9, 113, 117
UN human rights 51–54, 135
UNICEF 44
unilateral 15, 56, 66, 123
unilaterally 57, 64, 173
unipolar 7
unipolarity 32
United Arab Emirates (UAE) 165, 167, 168
United Kingdom (UK) 74, 76 75, 90, 183, 215, 217
United Nations (UN) 7, 9, 15, 16, 24, 25, 27, 32, 38–48, 51–54, 56–58, 111, 113, 114, 116, 135, 136, 148; legitimacy 31, 39, 43, 44, 47; peacekeeping 42, 49, 56
United Nations Conference on Trade and Development (UNCTAD) 40
United Nations Convention on the Law of the Sea (UNCLOS) 214
United Nations High Commissioner for Refugees (UNHCR) 44
United Nations Operation in the Congo (ONUC) 47
United States 4, 24, 39–41, 43, 45, 46, 54, 56–59, 63, 66, 72, 74, 75, 78, 79, 82, 83, 90, 104–107, 116, 131
Urquhart, Brian 35, 38
US 6, 7, 12, 14, 15, 24, 28, 29, 53, 54, 57, 63–71, 74–75, 81, 104–6, 114, 120, 125, 133, 135, 137, 138, 142, 145, 157, 164, 182, 189, 191, 192, 215, 217; adversaries 67, 69; and its allies 125; assault on al-Qaeda 164; and China 210, 216; domestic politics 64, 70; and Europe 137; and European 67; foreign policy 64; military 67, 124; and the USSR 145; the West 114
USA 1, 6, 11–14, 16, 90
USSR 39, 124, 145, 175
Utilitarian 22, 30, 32
Uzbekistan 92

vaccine 14, 27, 46, 143
vaccines 13, 26, 27, 83, 216
Vajrayana 200
V-Dem 9, 10
veil of ignorance 22
veil of sovereignty 52, 53
Velasquez case 53
Venezuela 29, 132, 134–38
veto 31, 39, 55; vetoes 40, 42, 56; vetoing 43
Victor, Jonah 146, 150, 151
Vienna Declaration 122
vilayet-e-faqih 160
Virgin Mary 55
vote 1, 5, 11, 42, 43, 63, 69, 161
voting 9, 15, 46, 63, 163

wage 26
Wahda, Hurriya, Ishtarakia 158
Wahhab, Sheikh Mohammed ibn Abdul 156, 167
Wahhabi 164, 167
Wahhabiyya 156, 157, 167
Waltz, Kenneth 3
Walzer, Michael 30
Wang Yiwei 15, 16, 109
warfare 13, 30, 58, 59, 119, 120, 125, 191
Warsaw Pact 92
Washington 77
weapon 16, 88, 191–93, 217
weaponisation of social media 30
weapons 15, 21, 56, 59, 83, 191–96; for geopolitical purposes 196; of the information age 191, 193
Weber, Max 22, 91
West 2, 3, 8, 10, 16, 23, 38, 44, 46, 47, 57, 60, 70, 72, 87, 90, 94, 99, 124, 125, 141, 147, 159, 162, 204; anti-vax 46; civilisation 111, 119; democracies 14, 39; and democratic societies 72; liberal democracies 125; liberal democracy 8; liberal thinking 124; nations 8, 152, 163; powers 31, 39, 40, 42, 43, 45, 67, 131, 155–57, 160, 162, 163, 168; traditions 111, 116; values 45, 111, 120, 123
Westminster 172
Westphalian 7, 111, 119, 198, 206
Wilson, Woodrow 2, 120
win-win 110
wisdom 11, 48, 66
World War I, 30, 120, 156, 157
World War II, 6, 12, 38, 40, 51, 60, 76, 89, 93, 107, 156, 160
worldview 7, 92, 111, 113, 116, 121, 149, 150
Wuhan 27

xenophobic 8, 88
Xi Jinping 48, 102–4, 108, 109, 114
Xiongnu Empire 101
Xunzi 111

Yeltsin, Boris 86, 87, 91
Yemen 156, 164, 166, 168
Yugoslavia 55

Zaidi 168
zakat 176
Zangpo, Kathog Kuntu 204
Zapata 132
Zardari, Asif Ali 177
Zayed, Sheikh Mohammed bin 167
Zelaya, Manuel 135
Zhabdrung 204
Zhou 99, 100
Zia, Khaleda 180–82
Zia ul-haq 175
Ziaur 174, 178
Zia ur-rahman 183
Zimbabwe 42, 144, 148

Printed in the United States
by Baker & Taylor Publisher Services